INTERNATIONAL LAW:
MODERN FEMINIST APPROACHES

Feminist scholars and activists have turned their attention to international law with apparently dramatic results. The impact of feminist engagement is felt in diverse areas, from human rights to environmental law. But what do these successes signal for the future? How open is international law to feminist enquiry? What does it mean to do feminist theory in international law? What lessons have we learned from engaging with international law, and what directions do we still need to explore?

International Law: Modern Feminist Approaches brings together feminist scholars from Australia, Canada, Serbia and Montenegro, Sweden, the United States and the United Kingdom. Drawing on diverse theoretical approaches, the chapters explore feminist engagements with various areas of international law, from human rights, trade and development, and gender mainstreaming, to humanitarian intervention and environmental law.

ACKNOWLEDGEMENTS

This book benefited from the enthusiasm and support of many people. We would like to thank Sally Sheldon, Anne Bottomley and Richard Hart in particular. We are also grateful to Davina Cooper and Philip Alston for their advice, and to Mary Robinson for agreeing to write the foreword.

International Law: Modern Feminist Approaches

Edited by

Doris Buss
Department of Law, Carleton University
and
Ambreena Manji
Law Department, University of Keele

·H A R T·
PUBLISHING

OXFORD AND PORTLAND, OREGON
2005

Published in North America (US and Canada) by
Hart Publishing
c/o International Specialized Book Services
5804 NE Hassalo Street
Portland, Oregon
97213–3644
USA

Hart Publishing is a specialist legal publisher based in Oxford, England. To order
further copies of this book or to request a list of other publications please write to:

Hart Publishing, Salters Boatyard, Folly Bridge, Abingdon Rd, Oxford, OX1 4LB
Telephone: +44 (0)1865 245533 Fax: +44 (0) 1865 794882
email: mail@hartpub.co.uk
WEBSITE: http//:www.hartpub.co.uk

British Library Cataloguing in Publication Data
Data Available

ISBN 1–84113–427–9 (paperback)

Typeset by Datamatics Technologies Ltd, India
Printed and bound in Great Britain by
Biddles Ltd, Kings Lynn, Norfolk

FOREWORD

Mary Robinson

Executive Director of Realizing Rights: The Ethical Globalization Initiative,
former United Nations High Commissioner for Human Rights,
and President of Ireland

When international law became the subject of sustained feminist scholarly scrutiny and activism over a decade ago, it opened up new thinking, new language and new priorities. It became clear that international human rights law had suffered from the absence of women's voices. Within a field of international law constituted as objective and neutral, women's rights were often dismissed as either too partial or too domestic to come within the ambit of international law. Without the inclusion of women, and an understanding of their social, economic and political experiences, human rights were hampered in their claims to universal significance. What place could there be for an international protection of the right to life, for example, that did not address the alarming incidences of maternal mortality among the world's women? And, how seriously was state-sponsored violence condemned if widespread and often fatal violence against women, both in the public and private spheres, excited little comment from international human rights institutions and actors?

As a result of the hard work and dedication of many feminist scholars and activists we now have in place a healthier international human rights regime, one that is prepared to rethink its human rights mandate more fully to comprehend and address the human rights of all. This is an important achievement, and one that should not be overlooked.

The essays in this book invite us to consider the question of what comes next for international law, human rights and feminism. Their focus is on what Hilary Charlesworth, Christine Chinkin and Shelley Wright describe in their essay as 'both the increased attention to the language of feminism and the limited progress women have made.' Each of the essays presented here is alert to this tension in both scholarship and activism. By reflecting on the limits of feminist engagement with international law, the authors acknowledge that the task is not simply to offer feminist analyses of the field but fundamentally to challenge its constitution and boundaries.

This volume of essays comes at a very important time. The challenges facing international law and human rights, as well as the institutional integrity of the United Nations are pressing. The opportunity for reflection on feminist futures offered by this volume should be one that is taken up by everyone. We are at a point where the international community, its institutions, priorities, processes, and self-definition, are being renegotiated. For those committed to human rights and a more inclusive and effective United Nations, a number of developments raise questions.

Formal state and institutional support for the idea and language of human rights is overwhelming. What impact will this professed support for human rights have on international law's ability to make lasting and meaningful change in people's lives? Can we close the gap, even partially, between the professed support for human rights and its open and flagrant violation by many nation-states? And what of the United Nations and proposed reform of bodies such as the Commission on Human Rights? Can they continue to attract international credibility while the gap between commitment and aspiration remains so wide?

The area of women's rights in particular raises a number of questions. How can the current international consensus on the human rights of women be translated into meaningful change? As the essays in this collection highlight, we may very well be entering into a new era of human rights and international law where the formal 'successes' of feminist and other activists pose unexpected challenges to future change.

These complex questions need to be raised and pursued if we are going to ensure that a future international community places at its centre the needs and lived realities of all people.

International lawyers, activists and policy-workers are sometimes accused of doing nothing more than talking while the lived reality of women and men throughout the globe remains a daily struggle against profound inequalities. Talking should never be used to avoid acting. Equally, we need to be wary of the allure of action without thought.

The essays contained here provide timely explorations of the most important questions facing feminist international lawyers today. I warmly welcome this book and hope it will reach a wide audience.

CONTENTS

Acknowledgements   ii
Foreword   v
Notes on Contributors   ix

1 **Introduction**   1
   Doris Buss and Ambreena Manji

2 **Feminist Approaches to International Law: Reflections from**   17
   Another Century
   Christine Chinkin, Shelley Wright and Hilary Charlesworth

3 **International Human Rights and Feminisms: When Discourses**   47
   Keep Meeting
   Karen Engle

4 **Feminism Here and Feminism There: Law, Theory and Choice**   67
   Thérèse Murphy

5 ***Austerlitz*** **and International Law: A Feminist Reading**   87
   at the Boundaries
   Doris Buss

6 **Disconcerting 'Masculinities': Reinventing the Gendered Subject(s)** 105
   of International Human Rights Law
   Dianne Otto

7 **The 'Unforgiven' Sources of International Law:**   131
   Nation-Building, Violence and Gender in the West(ern)
   Ruth Buchanan and Rebecca Johnson

8 **'The Beautyful Ones' of Law and Development**   159
   Ambreena Manji

9 **Feminist Perspectives in International Economic Law**   173
   Fiona Beveridge

10 Transcending the Conquest of Nature and Women: 203
    A Feminist Perspective on International Environmental Law
    Annie Rochette

11 The United Nations and Gender Mainstreaming: 237
    Limits and Possibilities
    Sari Kouvo

12 Women's Rights and the Organization of African Unity   253
    and African Union: The Protocol on the Rights of
    Women in Africa
    Rachel Murray

13 Sexual Violence, International Law and Restorative Justice   273
    Vesna Nikolic-Ristanovic

Index   295

NOTES ON CONTRIBUTORS

Fiona Beveridge is Reader in Law at the University of Liverpool and Convenor of the Feminist Legal Research Unit at Liverpool Law School. She teaches international economic law, foreign investment and European Union law, and has written on foreign investment and gender mainstreaming. She is co-editor of and contributor (with Nott and Steven) to *Making Women Count: Integrating Gender into Law and Policy-Making* (2000), and (with Shaw) of *Feminist Legal Studies* Special Issue on *Mainstreaming Gender in European Public Policy* (2002). She is currently working on a project on the decade of mainstreaming 1995–2005.

Ruth Buchanan is Associate Professor of Law at the University of British Columbia. She researches in the areas of globalisation and law, international economic institutions, social and legal theory, and the sociology of law. She is the author of 'Global Civil Society and Cosmopolitan Legality at the WTO: Perpetual Peace or Perpetual Process?' (2003) *Leiden Journal of International Law*, and (with S Pahuja) 'Collaboration, Cosmopolitanism, Complicity' (2002) *Nordic Journal of International Law*.

Doris Buss is Assistant Professor of Law, Carleton University, Ottawa. She teaches and researches in the areas of international human rights law, globalisation, feminist theory, social movements, and international criminal law. Her recent publications include 'Finding the Homosexual in Women's Rights: The Christian Right in International Politics' (2004) *International Feminist Journal of Politics*, and (with Didi Herman) *Globalizing Family Values: The Christian Right in International Politics* (2003).

Hilary Charlesworth is Professor of International Law in the Faculty of Law and Professor in the Regulatory Institutions Network in the Research School of Social Sciences at the Australian National University. She teaches and researches in the area of international and human rights law, and is the author (with Christine Chinkin) of *The Boundaries of International Law: A Feminist Analysis* (2000).

Christine Chinkin is currently Professor of International Law at the London School of Economics and Political Science, and an Overseas Affiliated Faculty Member, School of Law, University of Michigan. Her primary teaching and research interests are in public international law and dispute resolution. She is the author of *Third Parties in International Law* (1993), and *Halsbury's Laws of Australia, Foreign Relations Law* (1993; second edition 2001); and co-author of *Dispute Resolution in Australia* (1992; 2nd edition 2002) and *The Boundaries of International Law; A Feminist Analysis*, (2000). She is now working with Hilary Charlesworth on a *Feminist Analysis of International Dispute Resolution*, funded by a John D and Catherine T MacArthur Foundation Research and Writing Award.

Karen Engle is WH Francis Junior Professor in Law at the University of Texas School of Law, and teaches international law, international human rights and employment discrimination. She is co-editor (with Dan Danielsen) of *After Identity: A Reader in Law and Politics* (1992) and has published extensively in the human rights and international law field. Her most recent international law articles include 'The Construction of Good Aliens and Good Citizens: Legitimizing the War on Terrorism' (2004) *Colorado Law Review* and 'From Skepticism to Embrace: Human Rights and the American Anthropological Association from 1947–1999' (2001) *Human Rights Quarterly*.

Rebecca Johnson is an Associate Professsor of Law at the University of Victoria, Canada. Her teaching interests are in the areas of constitutional law, criminal law, feminist advocacy, social/legal theory, and law-and-film. Her research interests involve issues of intersectionality, and particularly the discourses and practices of power operating at the intersection of law and culture. Her current research projects concern nursing mothers and the saloon as a site of citizenship, and the relationships between reason, passion and the law in judicial dissent. She is the author of *Taxing Choices: The Intersection of Class, Gender, Parenthood and the Law* (2002).

Sari Kouvo is a researcher and lecturer at the Department of Law, School of Economics and Commercial Law at the University of Göteborg, Sweden, and is currently the rule of law, human rights and gender adviser at the European Union Social Representative's office in Kabul, Afghanistan. Dr Kouvo teaches and researches in the areas of gender and law, human rights, international law, and social movements, and is the author of *Making Just Rights? Mainstreaming Women's Human Rights and a Gender Perspective* (2004).

Ambreena Manji is a Reader in Law at the University of Keele, UK. In 2005 she is a Senior Fellow at the Faculty of Law University of Melbourne. Her research is in the area of law and development, particularly the politics of land reform in Africa, the role of international financial institutions and women's land rights. She has also published work on legal pluralism, African legal history, law and African literature, and is the author of *Towards a Sociology of Land Reform in Africa* (2005, forthcoming). She is a member of the editorial board of *Social and Legal Studies: An International Journal*.

Thérèse Murphy is Professor of Law & Critical Theory at the University of Nottingham, UK. Her recent work includes *Civil Liberties Law: The Human Rights Act Era* (2001) (with Noel Whitty and Stephen Livingstone), as well as several essays in the Cavendish 'Feminist Perspectives on Law' series. Her current research examines iconic concepts in health care law.

Rachel Murray is a Reader in Law at the University of Bristol, where she teaches international law and human rights-related subjects. She has taught previously at Birkbeck College, University of London, and Queen's University Belfast, where she was the Assistant Director of the Human Rights Centre. Her publications include *The African Commission on Human and Peoples' Rights and International Law* (2000) and as co-editor (with Professor Evans), *The African*

Charter on Human and Peoples' Rights: The System in Practice. 1986–2000 (2002). She is currently finalising a Nuffield-funded evaluation of the Northern Ireland Human Rights Commission, co-authored with the late Professor Stephen Livingstone, Queen's University Belfast.

Vesna Nikolic-Ristanovic is a criminology professor at Belgrade University, Serbia. She is also president of the Victimology Society of Serbia, editor in chief of the journal *Temida* and corresponding editor of *Feminist Review*. She has published widely on women and war, violence against women and women's crimes, as well as on truth and reconciliation in Serbia, and is the author of *Social Change, Gender, and Violence: Post-Communist and War Affected Societies* (2002).

Dianne Otto is Associate Professor of Law, Melbourne University, where she teaches in the areas of human rights, international law and criminal law. Her research interests include utilising feminist, postcolonial and queer theory to reveal the voices and interests that are marginalised or silenced by mainstream international legal discourse. She has published extensively in the international human rights field. Her recent publications include 'Securing the "Gender Legitimacy" of the UN Security Council: Prising gender from its historical moorings' in Charlesworth and Coicaud (eds), *Faultlines of International Legitimacy* (2004); 'Addressing Homelessness: Does Australia's Indirect Implementation of Human Rights Comply with its International Obligations?' in Stone, Campbell and Goldsworthy (eds), *Protecting Human Rights: Instruments and Institutions* (2003).

Annie Rochette is Assistant Professor of Law, University of British Columbia, where she teaches and researches in the areas of international and domestic environmental law, feminist and eco-feminist approaches to international law, legal research, and issues in pedagogy and legal education. She holds a Certificate for Teaching and Learning in Higher Education, and is the President of the Canadian Association of Law Teachers.

Shelley Wright is currently the Northern Director of the Akitsiraq Law School based in Iqaluit Nunavut, and an Adjunct Professor of the University of Victoria, Faculty of Law. Her interests are International Law, Human Rights, Intellectual Property, Indigenous Rights and Legal Theory, and she is the author of *International Human Rights, Decolonisation and Globalisation: Becoming Human* (2001).

1

Introduction

DORIS BUSS AND AMBREENA MANJI

Since the early 1990s and the publication of Hilary Charlesworth, Christine Chinkin and Shelley Wright's 'Feminist Approaches to International Law',[1] feminist scholarship on international law has developed and expanded to the point where it appears to be an 'accepted' part of the legal academy. Room is made for feminists to sit on panels at the main international law conferences, feminist articles appear (infrequently) in mainstream international law journals, and topics of particular concern to feminist legal scholars—violence against women, for example—occasionally make it into international legal textbooks.[2]

In scholarly terms, the 1990s witnessed an impressive publication of feminist research and writing in the international law field. The American Society of International Law published Dorinda Dallmeyer's edited collection of essays, *Reconceiving Reality: Women and International Law,* in 1993,[3] conference panels were dedicated to feminist analyses of international law topics,[4] and the decade ended with the publication of Charlesworth and Chinkin's landmark text, *The Boundaries of International Law.*[5] Although primarily focused on public international law,[6] this scholarly production also explored the breadth of the international legal field: the use of force and collective security,[7] state sovereignty and non-interference,[8] self-determination,[9] humanitarian

---

[1] H Charlesworth, C Chinkin, and S Wright, 'Feminist Approaches to International Law' (1991) 85 *American Journal of International Law* 613.

[2] HJ Steiner and P Alston, *International Human Rights in Context, 2nd edn* (Oxford, Oxford University Press, 2000).

[3] Washington, DC, American Society of International Law, 1993.

[4] See, eg, 'Sources of International Law: Entrenching the Gender Bias', *Contemporary International Law Issues: Opportunities at a Time of Momentus Change: Proceedings of the Second Joint Conference Held in The Hague, The Netherlands, July 22–24, 1993* (Dordrecht, Martinus Nijhoff Publishers, 1994).

[5] (Manchester, Manchester University Press, 2000).

[6] But see, S Wright, 'Women and the Global Economic Order: A Feminist Perspective' (1995) 10 *American University Journal of International Law and Policy* 861; A Orford, 'Locating the International: Military and Monetary Interventions after the Cold War' (1997) 38 *Harvard International Law Journal* 443; K Engle, 'Views from the Margins: A Response to David Kennedy' (1994) 1 *Utah Law Review* 105.

[7] A Orford, 'The Politics of Collective Security' (1996) 17(2) *Michigan Journal of International Law* 373; Orford, *ibid.*

[8] K Knop, 'Re/Statements: Feminism and State Sovereignty in International Law' (1993) 3 *Transnational Law & Contemporary Problems* 293; K Walker, 'An Exploration of Article 2(7) of the United Nations Charter as an Embodiment in International Law' (1994) 26 *International Law and Politics* 173.

[9] C Chinkin and S Wright, 'The Hunger Trap: Women, Food and Self-Determination' (1993) 14 *Michigan Journal of International Law* 262; K Knop, *Diversity and Self-Determination in International Law* (Cambridge, Cambridge University Press, 2001).

law,[10] nationality,[11] and a sustained analysis of international human rights law.[12] More recent scholarship reveals an extensive feminist engagement with the new institutions of international criminal law[13] as well as international economic law.[14]

The central concern of much of the scholarship in the 1990s was why international law was not doing more to address the inequality and oppression of women. As Karen Engle notes in her chapter for this volume, this scholarship focused on the structural bias of international law, the ways in which the discipline's doctrinal manoeuvres position women's inequality as outside international law's remit. If international law was structurally biased, then the task was not for women to be included within a slightly reformed international law. A more fundamental restructuring process was required, one that would 'lead to the creation of international regimes that focus on structural abuse and the revision of our notions of state responsibility'.[15]

The scope and depth of existing feminist literature indicates a sustained effort to engage with, and even rewrite, the disciplinary categories of international law. But while feminist scholars took on the discipline of international law, there is little to suggest that the other practitioners of international law were prepared to

---

[10] J Gardam, 'The Law of Armed Conflict: a Gendered Perspective' in D Dallmeyer (ed), *Reconceiving Reality: Women and International Law* (Washington DC, American Society of International Law, 1993).

[11] K Knop and C Chinkin, 'Remembering Chrystal MacMillan: Women's Equality and Nationality in International Law' (2001) 22 *Michigan Journal of International Law* 523; LC Stratton, 'The Right to Have Rights: Gender Discrimination in Nationality Laws' (1992) 77 *Minnesota Law Review* 195.

[12] See, eg R Copelon, 'Recognizing the Egregious in the Everyday: Domestic Violence as Torture,' (1994) 25 *Columbia Human Rights Law Review* 291; C Romany, 'Women as *Aliens*: A Feminist Critique of the Public/Private Distinction in International Human Rights Law' (1993) 6 *Harvard Human Rights Journal* 87; K Engle, 'International Human Rights and Feminism: When Discourses Meet' (1992) 13 *Michigan Journal of International Law* 317; C MacKinnon, 'On Torture: A Feminist Perspective on Human Rights' in KE Mahoney and P Mahoney (eds), *Human Rights in the Twenty-First Century: A Global Challenge* (Martinus Nijhoff, Dordrecht, 1993); H Charlesworth, 'What are "Women's International Human Rights"?' in R Cook (ed), *Human Rights of Women: National and International Perspectives* (University of Pennsylvania, Philadelphia, 1994); U O'Hare, 'Realizing Human Rights for Women' (1999) 21 *Human Rights Quarterly* 364; D Otto, 'A Post-Beijing Reflection on the Limits and Potential of Human Rights Discourse for Women' in K Askin and D Koenig (eds), *Women and International Human Rights Law* (Ardsley, NY, Transnational Publishers, 1999); D. Otto, 'Holding Up Half the Sky, but for Whose Benefit? A Critical Analysis of the Fourth World Conference on Women' (1996) 6 *Australian Feminist Law Journal* 7; S Wright, *International Human Rights, Decolonisation and Globalisation: Becoming Human* (London, Routledge, 2001).

[13] See, eg, KD Askin, 'Prosecuting wartime rape and other gender related crimes under international law: Extraordinary Advances, Enduring Obstacles' (2003) 21 *Berkeley Journal of International Law* 288; D Buss, 'Women at the Borders: Rape and Nationalism in International Law' (1998) 6(2) *Feminist Legal Studies* 171-203; R Copelon, 'Integrating Crimes Against Women into International Criminal Law' (2000) 46 *McGill Law Journal* 217; N LaViolette, 'Commanding Rape: Sexual Violence, Command Responsibility, and the Prosecution of Superiors by the International Criminal Tribunal for the Former Yugoslavia and Rwanda' (1998) *The Canadian Yearbook of International Law 1998* 93; J Mertus, 'The Impact of International Trials for Wartime Rape on Women's Agency' (2004) 6 *International Feminist Journal of Politics* 110.

[14] See, eg, S Pahuja, 'Trading Spaces: Locating Sites for Challenge within International Trade Law' (2000) 14 *Australian Feminist Law Journal* 38–54.

[15] Charlesworth and Chinkin, above n 5, at 644.

engage with feminists. Hilary Charlesworth, in a 1996 article,[16] describes how the responses to feminist analysis of international law were divided into two camps: those who decried the unfair assault on a discipline that could do good for women; and those from the more critical camp who merely offered whispered words of encouragement. Christine Sylvester identifies similar trends in the international relations field, describing critical scholars as merely tipping their hats in the direction of feminist theory.[17] In their chapter in this volume, Chinkin, Wright and Charlesworth describe responses to feminist international legal scholarship as ranging from 'support' to 'a mass of passively resistant inertia'.[18] We might conclude that the international legal academy and its political brethren seem prepared to include feminist scholars within the discipline, provided the discipline's foundational assumptions and modes of operation are left unaltered. That is, international lawyers may not change *what* they do or *how* they do it, but they now seem willing to tolerate feminists at their side *as* they do it.

Feminist engagement with international law, however, has never been confined solely to the academy. Indeed, some of feminism's more high-profile 'successes' have occurred at the conferences, meetings, institutions and courts that develop and implement international law and policy. From the vantage point of 2004, a number of feminist campaigns to secure greater international attention to women's oppression—and the conditions that sustain that oppression—are particularly worthy of note. A list of such celebrated successes might include the 1994 Cairo Conference on Population and Development,[19] with its prioritisation of women's autonomy and health; the 1995 Beijing Conference on Women,[20] with its recognition of women's sexual and reproductive rights; the strengthening of the Committee that oversees the 'Women's Convention,'[21] that for many years shivered in the cold of its exclusion from the mainstream of human rights; the negotiation of the protocol to the Women's Convention to allow individual complaints;[22] the recognition of the need for gender analyses and 'gender mainstreaming' throughout the UN;[23] the drafting of the Declaration on the Elimination of Violence Against Women[24] and the inter-

---

[16] 'Cries and Whispers: Responses to Feminist Scholarship in International Law' (1996) 65 *Nordic Journal of International Law* 561.

[17] C Sylvester, *Feminist International Relations: An Unfinished Journey* (Cambridge, Cambridge University Press, 2002), at 264.

[18] 'Feminist Approaches to International Law: Reflections from Another Century', this volume.

[19] *Report of the International Conference on Population and Development, Cairo 5–13 September 1994, Annex, Programme of Action of the International Conference on Population and Development*, A/CONF.171/13, 18 October 1994.

[20] *Beijing Declaration and Platform for Action, Fourth World Conference on Women, Beijing, China, 4–15 September 1995*. UN Doc DPI/1766/Wom (1996).

[21] *The Convention on the Elimination of all Forms of Discrimination Against Women, 1979*, UN Doc A/34/46 (1979).

[22] *Optional Protocol to the Convention on the Elimination of Discrimination Against Women, 1999*, UN Doc A/54/49 (Vol I) (2000).

[23] See Kouvo, this volume. For a discussion of gender mainstreaming in international economic law, see Beveridge, this volume. There is a growing body of literature analysing gender mainstreaming in different areas of the UN apparatus. On peacekeeping and related activities, see S Whitworth, *Men, Militarism and UN Peacekeeping: A Gendered Analysis* (Boulder, CO, Lynne Rienner, 2004);

[24] *Declaration on the Elimination of Violence Against Women, 1993* A/RES 48/104 (1994).

national recognition of violence against women as a serious human rights issue; the prosecution of rape as a war crime at the ad hoc tribunals in Rwanda and Yugoslavia;[25] the inclusion of gender analyses and women's human rights frameworks within multiple international agreements;[26] the increased participation of feminist and women's NGOs at all levels of UN activity; and the increased representation of women in senior positions at the UN.[27]

Although it is possible—and necessary—to question the impact of these changes on women's lives, collectively they signal a sustained feminist presence in the international realm, and one that has challenged the depiction of international law as concerned exclusively with a narrow range of matters related to affairs between states. They also suggest a shift in the scholarly project of 'asking the woman question'. Karen Knop, in her introduction to a recent collection of essays on women's human rights,[28] traces a number of shifts in the literature that suggest women's human rights may be emerging as a distinct disciplinary field, with all the problems and prospects that constituting a discrete area of study brings.

Is there a similar shift in the literature on feminist approaches to international law? The chapters in this volume by Karen Engle, and by Christine Chinkin, Shelley Wright and Hilary Charlesworth, provide a map of feminist engagement with international law. Karen Engle develops a periodisation of feminist scholarship on international human rights, exploring the questions that motivated feminist research and the problems that animated feminist analyses throughout the 1990s. These changed over time from demands for inclusion to more fundamental problematising of the very structures of human rights law. Chinkin, Wright and Charlesworth similarly reflect on feminist engagement with international law, locating their analysis in the context of 'seismic shifts' in scholarship and on the geo-political, institutional and educational planes of international law.

Both these chapters highlight different problems, conflicts and challenges that face feminist engagement with 'the international' and with law. For Engle, the most pressing question is how feminism confronts the two 'elephants in the room'. First, the 'feminist' question: what constitutes 'feminist' international law and are we doing it now? And, second, the issue of diversity and imperialism: whether and how Western feminists can avoid speaking of and for the ubiquitous Third World Woman. One of the key questions underpinning Chinkin, Wright and Charlesworth's analysis is what comes after the apparent feminist successes in including gender, however partially and problematically, in the practice and study of international law?

---

[25] See, eg, *Prosecutor v Dragoljub Kunarac, Radomir Kovac and Zoran Vukovic,* Judgment, IT-96-23-T & IT-96-23/1-T (22 February 2001; last accessed 5 October 2004), and Copelon, above n 13.

[26] See, for eg, *Declaration of Commitments on HIV/AIDS, UN General Assembly Special Session on HIV/AIDS, 25–27 June 2001,* http://www.unaids.org/EN/events/un+special+session+on+hiv_aids/declaration+of+commitment+on+hiv_aids.asp (last accessed 10 October 2004).

[27] For a discussion of the recent statistics on the UN and the representation of women, see Chinkin, Wright and Charlesworth, this volume.

[28] *Gender and Human Rights* (Oxford, Oxford University Press, 2004).

This brings us to the motivation behind the present volume of essays. The idea of this project arose out of a sense that feminist legal scholarship in the international law field had unfolded in a piecemeal, ad hoc and dispersed manner. It is clear that feminist international scholars are as productive today as they were in the 1990s, but is there a field or area of study that we could call 'feminist international legal scholarship'? With Charlesworth, Chinkin and Wright's landmark paper 'Feminist Approaches to International Law' over a decade old, what were feminists doing, thinking, writing about now? And, to take up the question asked recently by an international law colleague, do feminists have anything more to say about international law? Could it be, as this colleague suggested, that everything that feminists have to say has been said, and that the various doctrines of international law have been comprehensively canvassed for their gendered character?

This volume is oriented around these questions. The chapters included here reflect feminist work on different aspects of international law. Our self-imposed task has not been to offer a definitive account of feminism and international law, even if this were possible. Rather, the objectives of this volume are more limited: to offer a snap-shot of current feminist thinking on some of the doctrinal, applied and theoretical aspects of both international law and feminist engagement with 'the international'. And, more importantly, through this snap-shot, to complicate understandings of both feminist analyses and international law.

The chapters in this volume have in common a concern with reading, negotiating and troubling boundaries. One of the principal boundaries under scrutiny here is the disciplinary one: what do we define as international law? How might a feminist analysis of law and 'the international' offer a more transgressive account of international law and its impact? How might we tell a different story of international law, one that recognises its constitutive relationship with the theory and practice of other fields and systems not traditionally seen as part of international law: development, economic and environment law, criminology and victimology, pedagogy, imperialism and colonialism? How might we ourselves cross disciplinary boundaries to read and view international law through literature and film?

The chapters in this volume are unabashedly interdisciplinary. But we urge caution in seeing this as purely an exercise in interdisciplinarity for its own sake. To do so risks overlooking the more essential critique offered by these chapters of the very idea of boundary. Many of the authors in this volume question, subvert and challenge the orthodoxy of disciplinary boundaries that mark inside and outside. In doing so, they disrupt the received wisdom of what is and is not international law, and what counts, or does not count, as feminist theory.[29]

The chapters in this volume are organised around the twin objectives of mapping what it means to bring feminist perspectives to international law, and reflecting on what it means for feminists to include 'the international' in their

---

[29] The idea of what 'counts' as feminist theory is taken from T Murphy, Book Review: 'KD Askin and DM Koenig, eds. *Women and International Human Rights*, Vols I, II, III' (2002) 2 *Human Rights Law Review* 167.

theory and practice. We view the chapters contained here as part of an ongoing conversation about the possible impact of feminist engagement with 'the international'. What constitutes a feminist theory of international law? What are the implications for feminists of the ostensible successes of feminist scholarship and practice in international law? What concepts, strategies and questions might need to be reassessed by feminists in coming years?

The chapters in this collection are all reflective, scholarly accounts of three aspects of feminist international legal scholarship suggested in the volume's title: the range, direction and implications of *feminist approaches* to international law; the constitution, definition and possibilities of *international law*; and the place of the *modern* in changing global circumstances.

Feminist Approaches

So far, we have referred to feminist analyses of international law as though there is agreement as to what constitutes such a project. As Denise Réaume has noted, 'efforts to systematize [feminist scholarship] sit uneasily with the simultaneous trumpeting of the diversity within feminist thought'.[30] Referring to 'feminist approaches to international law' might imply a shared intellectual project, and one that takes place within the international legal academy. Neither of these assumptions holds true. Indeed, we thought it important to bring the essays presented here together precisely because of the diversity of feminist engagement with international law which is, furthermore, increasingly conducted by scholars who may not explicitly locate themselves within the international law field.

And yet there is an emerging terrain of feminist international legal scholarship, the broad contours of which are evident in the following essays. Certainly, feminist scholars of international law may be still only stretching their theoretical legs, and conversations about the questions we need to ask and the tools we need to employ are only just beginning.[31] Further, there are differences in the theoretical perspectives that feminist international scholars bring to their work, from poststructural and post-modern preferences,[32] to more materialist analyses.[33] But

---

[30] 'What's Distinctive about Feminist Analysis of Law?: A Conceptual Analysis of Women's Exclusion from Law,' (1996) 2 *Legal Theory* 265, at 269.

[31] See, eg, A Orford, 'Feminism, Imperialism and the Mission of International Law' (2002) 71 *Nordic Journal of International Law* 275; H Charlesworth, 'Feminist Methods in International Law' (1999) 93 *American Journal of International Law* 379; K Engle, 'After the Collapse of the Public/Private Distinction: Strategizing Women's Rights' in DG Dallmeyer (ed), *Reconceiving Reality: Women and International Law* (Washington, DC, American Society of International Law, 1993); D Buss, 'Going Global: Feminist Theory, International Law and the Public/Private Divide' in SB Boyd (ed), *Challenging the Public/Private Divide: Feminism, Law, and Public Policy* (Toronto, University of Toronto Press, 1997).

[32] D Otto, 'Rethinking the "Universality" of Human Rights' (1997) 29 *Columbia Human Rights Law Review* 1; and A Orford, *Reading Humanitarian Intervention: Human Rights and the Use of Force in International Law* (Cambridge, Cambridge University Press, 2003).

[33] See Rochette, this volume; S Wright, above n 6.

these differences and emerging conversations foretell analytical richness rather than ideological divisions.

Chapters 2 and 3 in this volume, by Chinkin, Wright and Charlesworth, and by Engle, provide the important historical context for the remaining chapters. Substantively, Chinkin, Wright and Charlesworth place the ostensible gains of feminist activism, together with the seismic shifts of the end of the cold war and the events of September 11, 2001 at the centre of their analysis. Presaging some of the themes developed in subsequent chapters in this volume, these three authors note the advances in the substance and procedures of international human rights, the mainstreaming of gender in international institutions, the 'troubling triumphalism' of human rights, and the complexity of doing and teaching feminism and law as something *other* than a subject of curiosity. Engle's chapter orders the feminist literature on women's rights according to the methods and objectives employed primarily in the 1990s in feminist approaches to international law.

These two chapters raise, in different ways, a key theme pursued throughout this volume: the emergence of an identifiable field of feminist international law and politics in which feminists have achieved ostensible successes of varying significance. For Engle, the emergence of a field of scholarship on international law can be detected in the debates that unfolded in the 1990s, in which feminist scholars began to consider *what* they were trying to achieve and the means by which they would do so. While this chapter is exclusively focused on American scholarship, its analysis could also pertain to the literature by Australian, Canadian and British feminists. In painting a picture of two elephants at the heart of this emerging field—the meaning of *feminist* theory and the difficulties and inevitabilities of the Exotic Other Female—Engle's analysis suggests that at the very moment of its birth, feminist international law was bedeviled by the complexity and uncertainty of its politics.

Chinkin, Wright and Charlesworth also outline the many apparent successes of feminist activism in international law and human rights. While each of these successes is important, the authors highlight a more troubling development: the instrumental connection between human rights discourse and neo-liberalism.[34] What implications does this connection have for feminist activism in international human rights? Do we, the authors ask, 'bring human rights and democracy, for example, to Iraq, even while we recognise that this will provide the desired environment for economic reconstruction of the country in line with neo-liberal policies with all their inherent disregard for human security, especially gendered security?'[35] Having achieved inclusion within mainstream human rights, the authors note, feminists are now faced with the difficulties of a human rights discourse itself side-lined by the war on terror and the over-arching concern of 'security'. 'Just as women have sought to become "insiders" in human rights discourse, human rights

---

[34] 'Feminist Approaches to International Law: Reflections from Another Century', this volume.
[35] *Ibid.*

has become an "outsider" discourse.'[36] Have feminists finally been invited to the party, only to find everyone else has already left?

We see, in these two chapters, a distinct shift in the types of questions posed and methods employed by feminist international lawyers. Engle's chapter demonstrates that feminist scholarship in the 1990s is best characterised as 'asking the woman question'. Feminists began to ask, perhaps with Susan Marks's 'faux naiveté',[37] where were the women in international law, and how might international law be made to work better for women? In her study of democracy and international law, Susan Marks argues that posing the question of why 'more is not being done to realize the ideals of freedom, justice and equality' is itself a critical method. For Marks, '*asking the question* is not the casual and innocent act' it appears.[38] The same might be said of feminist challenges to international law. In asking 'where are the women', or questioning 'why more was not being done', Karen Engle argues, feminists were calling attention to the gender bias in the very structures of international law. And drawing on Marks, we would argue that they were taking international law at its word, demanding that more be done to achieve the humanitarian ideals of 'freedom, justice and equality'. But what happens when international law and its institutions appear to respond to the 'woman question' by formally including women *within* international law, and agreeing to initiatives designed to address 'the ideal of freedom, justice and equality' for women?

For a number of the authors in this volume, such as Fiona Beveridge, Vesna Nikolic-Ristanovic, Sari Kouvo, and Rachel Murray, this is the problem at the heart of their analyses. Each of these authors explores different subject areas to consider the implications of this 'accommodation of gender'[39] in international institutions. The chapters by Nikolic-Ristanovic and Kouvo address what are often seen as two of the key successes of feminist international politics: the criminal prosecution of wartime rape and gender mainstreaming. Nikolic-Ristanovic's chapter, 'Sexual Violence, International Law and Restorative Justice', considers the effectiveness and consequences of international prosecution of sexual violence against women through the legal apparatus of the war crimes tribunals for the Former Yugoslavia and Rwanda. She is concerned by the inherent limitations of the criminal trial as a forum for hearing and healing women. Carefully dismantling the arguments often made in favour of international criminal prosecution—that it provides a neutral forum to hear grievance, validates the stories of victims, establishes historical record, and contributes to the restoration of peace—Nikolic Ristanovic considers how alternative mechanisms, such as truth and reconciliation processes, may work alongside the legalism of criminal trials more effectively to address wartime violence against women.

---

[36] *Ibid.*

[37] *The Riddle of all Constitutions: International Law, Democracy and the Critique of Ideology* (Oxford, Oxford University Press, 2000), at 5.

[38] *Ibid.*

[39] Fiona Beveridge, 'Feminist Perspectives on International Economic Law', this volume.

Kouvo's focus is on the mainstreaming of gender at the United Nations. The formal agreements and statements on gender mainstreaming, with their detailed provisions and institution-wide design, stand in sharp contrast to the difficult reality of actually mainstreaming gender. How is it possible to translate the complex ideas encapsulated in the term 'gender' into a policy applied across a large bureaucratic institution by various actors, with different, and possibily conflicting, understandings of what 'gender' means? Is it possible to mainstream gender without losing an understanding of gender as a complex social ordering process, not simply reducible to 'male' or 'female'? Kouvo's analysis does not offer heartening news on the prospects for gender mainstreaming at the UN, and her chapter raises questions about the difficulties facing feminists in trying to mobilise and institutionalise gender politics.

Annie Rochette and Fiona Beveridge turn their sights to the possibilities and limits of feminist engagement with two fields often overlooked in feminist accounts of international law: environmental law and international economic law respectively. Beveridge sets out to explore the 'potential foundations for feminist critiques of international economic law'.[40] Feminist analyses of this area will need to confront what Beveridge identifies as the complete absence of a gender agenda at the World Trade Organisation. Like Kouvo, Beveridge highlights the political and practical difficulties facing any project to achieve gender equality within existing institutional structures such as the WTO and World Bank, to say nothing of harnessing them for the benefit of women. And, like Kouvo, Beveridge provides a rich account of the structural limitations of institutional reform. There is, for Beveridge, a larger difficulty with the international trade system. Not only has the WTO 'shown no commitment to gender mainstreaming and no systematic effort ...to consider the differential impact of the WTO trade rules', but the 'core values' of the WTO maybe themselves at odds with feminist objectives. With its adherence to a 'dichotomy between market and state', and its insistence on distinguishing between the state and market on one hand and social interests on the other, will gender mainstreaming enable feminists to draw any more attention to the social costs of trade law?

In her chapter, Annie Rochette provides a detailed and nuanced overview of the emergence of 'women, environment and development' as a field of political activity, focusing on its effect on international environmental law and policy. Rochette's chapter is premised on a detailed reading of the various international environmental agreements and frameworks that recognise, to a limited degree, women's relationship with the environment. Rochette subjects these documents to detailed analysis and argues that such recognition is no more than a nod in the direction of feminist lobbying on the environment. It does little to address the underlying structural and institutional commitments through which environmental degradation is sustained and women's inequality ensured. Where Beveridge and Kouvo focus on gender mainstreaming, Rochette's chapter highlights

---

[40] *Ibid.*

another aspect of institutional reform directed at women: inclusion within decision-making bodies. Whereas Chinkin, Wright and Charlesworth note in their
chapter that efforts have been made, some more successful than others, to increase
the representation and participation of women at different international law-
making bodies, Rochette's chapter provides a substantive, critical analysis of
efforts to include women in environmental decision-making. She argues that this
is premised on a limited equality model and 'does little to address the structural
barriers to women's equal participation in decision-making or the obstacles to
environmental protection'.[41]

Rochette's chapter highlights clearly another theme visible throughout the
chapters in this volume. This is the question of how international law, and the
many institutional and instrumental reforms aimed at women, serve to bring
into being variations on Carol Smart's 'woman of legal discourse'.[42] For
Rochette international environmental agreements can be read as creating an
archetypal woman of international environmental law who is from the Third
World, a 'victim of environmental degradation and an environmental user and
manager, who, if given equal access to decision-making, will empower herself
and save the environment'.[43]

In her chapter, Dianne Otto explicitly takes up Smart's analysis of the construction of female subject positions in law to consider the gendered subjectivities
that have emerged in international human rights over the long period of feminist
engagement at the United Nations. Otto's chapter is, at the outset, an important
and insightful mapping of the 'genealogy of the female subjects constituted by ...
international discourse on human rights'.[44] This chapter, like Engle's, provides an
important history and careful reading of feminist engagement at the international
level. As Otto reminds us, 'without historical memory, participants in a liberation
movement are deprived of knowledge about the longevity and complexities of
their struggle. They may also believe that they are only at the beginning, when
their struggle may have advanced to a point where reinvention is necessary.'[45]

Otto also raises the issue of 'reinvention', centering her analysis on debates
about feminist strategy in international human rights: do feminists seek inclusion
of women *within* the meaning of the universal human rights bearing subject, with
the risk that the gendered aspects of human rights violations are erased? Or do
feminists highlight the gendered nature of human rights, and seek recognition of
women's specificity, thus complicating the 'universal' of human rights? This chapter demonstrates that both strategies are compelling, for different reasons, and
both are ultimately limited. In her genealogy of women's activism on international
human rights, Otto traces how the familiar gender tropes—of women as mother,

---

[41] 'Transcending the Conquest of Nature and Women: A Feminist Perspective on International
Environmental Law', this volume.
[42] 'The Woman of Legal Discourse' (1992) 1 *Social & Legal Studies* 29.
[43] Above n 41.
[44] 'Disconcerting "Masculinities": Reinventing the Subject of International Human Rights', this volume.
[45] *Ibid.*

wife and victim—serve to inscribe gender stereotypes into an understanding of human rights, thus ultimately 'restaging the masculinity of the universal subject of human rights law'.[46]

For Otto, '[t]he international struggle for the full inclusion of women in the paradigm of universal human rights has reached a point where it needs reinvention'. Her source of hope for this reinvention lies in the possibilities offered by gender hybridity. That is, the recognition of gender as fluid, variable and multiple may provide a means for moving away from the overarching trope of sex/gender through which masculine and feminine subjects are reinscribed along established binary lines. 'Understanding gender-identity as the hybrid result of choices and desires, as a cultural perception rather then something innate, offers the most complete vision of equality between women and men that has yet to be imagined'. A risky project, certainly, for as Otto notes, hybridity carries with it the danger of erasing the very female subject it seeks to complicate. And even if she is not erased, can hybridity, with all the intangibility it suggests, dislodge the universal subject of international human right law with its constitutive masculinity? In her darker moments, the author wonders aloud if 'women's full inclusion in the universal register may indeed be an impossibility'.[47]

Given the inroads made by feminist activism at the international level, it is perhaps unsurprising that many of the chapters in this volume consider the consequences and implications stemming from these ostensible feminist gains. Neither should it alarm us that many of the chapters, including Otto's, touch on darker questions about the limitations and possibilities of feminist transformation of 'the international'. But, as Otto concludes in her chapter 'it is still too soon to … [reject] the project of universal human rights as an irredeemably masculinist endeavour.' For her, reconsidering feminist strategy has led to a new possibility for feminist inroads in international human rights, 'destabilising and particularising the masculine universal'.[48]

The stock-taking exercise that characterises the essays in this volume returns us to the question: is there such a thing as a coherent feminist international legal scholarship about which we can speak? Our discussion so far suggests that there is a very current and urgent feminist international law literature, clearly linked to feminist political projects and brimming with a range of theoretical and analytical concerns. While the chapters in this volume are to varying degrees engaged in a process of self-reflection about feminist political engagement with 'the international', we may well ask if we have gone far enough in our critique and whether there are self-imposed limits on what we are doing?

This is the question that underpins Thérèse Murphy's chapter, 'Feminism Here and Feminism There: Law, Theory and Choice'. Murphy confronts head-on the question of *why* feminist perspectives on international law. *Why* are feminists engaging with international law, and what does this tell us about feminism in particular?

---

[46] *Ibid.*
[47] *Ibid.*
[48] *Ibid.*

Murphy's chapter raises the possibility that some western feminists might be *attracted* to the international realm because it seems easier, more like first or second wave feminism, than the project of feminism that remains at the domestic level. The 'allure of the international', as Murphy labels it, is compelling and problematic. Might it be the case, she asks, that in pursuing feminist work there (internationally) rather than here (domestically, in the west), feminists might be trying 'to recreate the glory days of feminism'?[49]

Murphy continues in her chapter to consider the relationship between feminism here and feminism there by looking at the tendency for feminist international legal scholars to see themselves not as theorists, but merely as 'borrowers' of concepts developed in domestic feminist legal theory. Can concepts be 'borrowed' in this way? What might be lost in the process of translation? Like Otto and Kouvo, Murphy is concerned by the term 'gender' and feminist efforts to bring a gender politics to the international realm. Where Kouvo is worried about the depoliticisation of gender through mainstreaming, and Otto highlights the intransigence of gendered subjectivities, Murphy offers an additional perspective. Having 'borrowed' feminist insights developed in the domestic context about the radical potential of gender, does the emergence of a 'self-contained'[50] field of feminist legal scholarship work against on-going reflection on concepts borrowed? That is, do 'the practices of feminist legal internationalism … function to constrain both feminist legal internationalism itself and feminism in general'?[51] Have feminists been reflective enough about the differences that the 'international' poses for feminist understandings of, for example, gender as an ordering system?

Rachel Murray's chapter, 'Women's Rights and the Organization of African Unity and African Union: The Protocol on the Rights of Women in Africa', also considers the problems that arise when translating feminist concepts and strategies from one context to another. Murray draws our attention to the often-overlooked African Charter and Commission on Human and People's Rights, and the newly established African Union. She provides a comprehensive account of the status of women's rights within these organisations, focusing on the recent adoption of the additional Protocol on the Rights of Women in Africa. In this chapter, Murray asks a variant of Karen Engle's 'feminist question'. For Murray, the issue is not whether the Protocol is feminist in nature, but why it is that African feminist non-governmental organisations (NGOs) regarded it as necessary to lobby for this Protocol? The author begins with a sceptical analysis of the legal possibilities offered by this instrument, and considers how its adoption may be shaped more by the influence of external human rights developments than legal effectiveness. Murray's analysis raises questions about the impact of the 'women's rights as human rights' campaign. Is it the case that one of the overlooked consequences of feminist human rights activism is the formalisation of women's rights instruments? That is, have women's rights instruments become de rigueur; such an accepted and anticipated part of institution-building that we assume rather than interrogate their necessity? And if these instruments

---

[49] 'Feminism Here and Feminism There: Law, Theory and Choice', this volume.
[50] Knop, above n 28.
[51] 'Feminism Here and Feminism There: Law, Theory and Choice', this volume.

are simply de rigueur, lacking in clear objectives and likely to be limited in their impact, we need to consider, particular with Otto's analysis in mind, what other, less desirable discursive roles such instruments might play.

International Law

The chapters in this volume share in common a concern with law's constitutive and legitimating functions. Each in their own way explores the implications of Anne Orford's warning about 'the ways in which feminist legal theory is invited to participate in the project of constituting women and the international community'.[52] For some authors, particularly Ruth Buchanan, Rebecca Johnson, Doris Buss and Ambreena Manji, Orford's warning raises acute questions about international law, and its role in what David Kennedy describes as 'keeping a terribly unjust international order up and running, even as it seeks with great passion to be a voice for humanitarian reform, even as it renews itself constantly to be more effective'.[53] Sharing a concern with international law's origins, alert to the increasing invocation of the 'rule of law' in contexts such as humanitarian intervention, and straining at international law's disciplinary boundaries, the chapters by Buchanan and Johnson, Buss, and Manji interrogate the international law with which feminists engage.

Buchanan and Johnson's chapter takes us to the frontiers of law through a (mis)reading[54] of Clint Eastwood's film *Unforgiven*. For these two authors, that film, and the genre of the western more generally, provides 'a mythic location, the frontier, in which the anxieties about law's foundations, nation building, and sexual and racial differences, can be played out'. The western, like international law, yields insights into the stories we tell about 'the operation of modern law'. Both the 'west' of the western genre and international law are defined by the 'inescapable link between the founding violence of frontier justice and the (American) ideal of the rule of law'. And, for both, the mythical accounts of justice and law are 'intertwined' with 'the narrative of the masculinised hero rescuing the feminised victim'.[55]

The frontier is an apt location for thinking about and tracing the arenas of international law's constitution. It is at the frontier where the myths of law's founding are most evident. The rule of law, in dominant accounts of the frontier—including the

---

[52] 'Feminism, Imperialism and the Mission of International Law' (2002) 71 *Nordic Journal of International Law* 275, at 276.

[53] 'When Renewal Repeats: Thinking Against the Box' in W Brown and J Halley (eds), *Left Legalism/Left Critique* (Duke University Press, Durham, 2002), 373 at 384.

[54] 'The "Unforgiven" Sources of International Law: Nation-Building, Violence and Gender in the West(ern)', this volume.

[55] *Ibid.* See also, A Orford, 'Muscular Humanitarianism: Reading the Narratives of the New Interventionism' (1999) 10 *European Journal of International Law* 679.

frontier that is the international — is the antidote to ruthless violence; the end to
the chaos of lawlessness. Buchanan and Johnson's compelling reading of *Unforgiven*
shows us that in its very imposition, the rule of law is itself an act of violence. The
originary act of law's founding, however, becomes obscured through the (re)writing
of law's origins and the maintenance of boundaries 'between male and female,
inside and outside, law and violence, civilization and savagery'.[56]

The inscription of international law's boundaries is at the heart of the chapters
by Buss and Manji. For Buss, the disciplinary account of the 'international' of
international law is a structuring process through 'which particular relationships,
subjects, and interests are sited, positioned and prioritised. The definition of the
international governs what we see as international law, how we see its impact, and
who we see as law's subject.'[57] The drawing of boundaries, she argues, is part of
the process through which in/out, proper/improper, male/female are regulated. In
her chapter, Buss offers a partial reading of WG Sebald's *Austerlitz*, arguing that
his discussion of the Antwerp citadel offers an account of the architecture of
European violence, with implications for understanding violence and the architecture of international law.

Buss's analysis focuses on boundaries, in this case the disciplinary boundaries
of international law, to highlight what she sees as a 'central tension in feminist theoretical accounts of the international: the question of inside and outside'.
Boundaries are part of the architecture of exclusion, but may also be a productive
place of trouble. Through a careful reading of feminist accounts of the public/private
divides in international law, particularly in the context of violence against women,
Buss argues against an analysis focused on shifting boundaries or inclusion within
boundaries. If the drawing of boundaries is itself an act of power through which
we come to know 'the international', and boundaries stand as material structures
of oppression, the redrawing of boundaries may offer little more than a reinscrip-
tion of existing structuring processes.

Like Buss, as well as Buchanan and Johnson, Manji bases her chapter on an
account of international law through a reading of a fictional text, Ayi Kwei
Armah's novel, *The Beautyful Ones Are Not Yet Born*.[58] Manji employs Armah's
novel, written in the heady period of Ghanaian decolonisation, both to explore
the history of 'law and development' as a field of study and to question its rebirth
in the contemporary era.[59] Manji harnesses Armah's suggestive treatment of ideas
of birth and rebirth to critique the possibilities of law and development in an era
of neo-liberalism. 'What are the prospects' she asks 'for contemporary law and
development, dragged from the womb this time not by the Cold War but by economic globalisation?'

Illustrating her chapter with evidence from the African experience of land
reform since the early 1990s, Manji is sceptical of law and development's apparent

[56] 'The "Unforgiven"', this volume.
[57] '*Austerlitz* and International Law: A Feminist Reading at the Boundaries', this volume.
[58] (Nairobi, East African Educational Publishers, 1968).
[59] '"The Beautyful Ones" of Law and Development', this volume.

'turn to law', noting a transmogrification from 'concern with the economic growth of the developmental state' to the 'promotion of good governance and the rule of law'. Her task in this chapter is to consider the possibilities offered by *The Beautyful Ones* in reconceiving 'the political' at the heart of law and development.

Each of these three chapters—by Buchanan and Johnson, Buss, and Manji—shares a scepticism about and reluctance to place feminist faith in the law. If, as these authors argue, we need to exercise more scepticism about what we call international law, where we find it, and what we displace with it, then what implications does this have for feminist engagements with international law? These chapters reveal uncertainties about the possibilities for feminist transformations of the international. But they also suggest concurrence with Otto's view that it is premature to conclude that prospects are bleak for feminist international politics. For, as Buchanan and Johnson remind us, 'narratives only cohere or sustain themselves through endless repetition. And with repetition comes the possibility of writing things differently.'

This volume of essays can be read as an ongoing conversation about the current state of feminist engagement with international law and the possibilities 'of writing things differently'. But in this hopeful moment, the authors in this collection urge a careful consideration of feminist's dalliance with international law. Could it be that we have allowed ourselves to be seduced by a 'new age' international law, sympathetic to the 'plight' of women, eager to listen to our stories and complaints, there with a knowing smile and a reassuring affirmation of women's suffering? When international law agrees to meet us part way, did we ask, part way to where? To paraphrase Engle, which women and men do we want to benefit from our activism? And how prepared are we—Western and elite third world women—to challenge the material bases of women's oppression?

The Modern

The chapters in this volume are neither modernist in outlook, nor modernist in theoretical orientation. So why is it that we have named this volume 'modern feminist approaches'? As editors, we decided to hold onto the idea of the modern in this volume for a number of reasons. International law is, in many ways, a modernist discipline. It sees itself earnestly endeavouring to perform an essentially humanitarian function,[60] fundamentally imbricated in the ultimate modernist mission: the bringing of civilization. Its self-definition is inherently entwined with

---

[60] On this point, see generally, Kennedy, above n 53.

the great modernist projects of institution building, global economic development, and the eradication of violence and chaos through the imposition of law.

In this volume, we place international law's claims to a humanitarian, progressive, modernist orientation at the heart of our analysis. We do so in order critically
to interrogate international law's own account of itself. Through the analyses
offered in these chapters, we challenge law's claim to ahistoricity and despatiality.
Our chapters draw on feminist theory and politics to locate international law;[61] to
highlight its spatial and temporal frames, to explore its originary myths, to uncover
its nexus to the political, economic, and social worlds it strives to keep at a distance. By placing international law's categories at the centre of our analysis, we
reveal their normative purchase, and the importance of law as 'one realm in which
the rearguard action of shoring up' the categories of chaos/order, female/male,
national/international is made possible.[62]

The modern of international law is also deeply implicated in the myths it narrates about the origins and role of law. Several of the chapters in this volume
perform a 'reading' of international law, highlighting the importance of law's narratives; the stories we tell about international law and its civilising mission. The
process of narration is an important mechanism through which we define and
reinscribe the 'international' and its gendered and raced character. But reinscrip-
tion is an ongoing, fluid and uncertain process. For Chinkin, Wright and
Charlesworth, the events of September 11, 2001 disrupted the 'modern story of
international law'. Its renegotiation in the context of the 'war on terror' and the
hegemony of 'security', served to alter, but also to reinscribe, gender relations.
Similarly, for Buchanan and Johnson the continual rewriting of law's narratives
may be a productive place of intervention, offering the possibility of rewriting the
gendered and racial scripts of law's originary myths.[63]

Finally, holding onto 'the modern' may also help us retain a sense of productive anger: over human rights abuses, economic inequality, wars fought for hubris
and economics. It is a refusal of resignation. Perhaps this productive anger can be
marshalled to compel us to confront what Chinkin, Wright and Charlesworth call
'the here and now'; the complex arenas of international law, the small spaces
where we find law, the places where we 'recapture a sense of hope and energy'.[64]

---

[61] See Orford, 'Locating the International', above n 6.
[62] Buchanan and Johnson, this volume.
[63] *Ibid.*
[64] Chinkin, Wright and Charlesworth, this volume.

2

Feminist Approaches to International Law: Reflections from Another Century

CHRISTINE CHINKIN,* SHELLEY WRIGHT,**
HILARY CHARLESWORTH***

Introduction

The ideas that led to our article 'Feminist Approaches to International Law'[1] were first aired at the annual meeting of international lawyers organised by Professor Don Greig at the Australian National University in Canberra in 1989. During a late-night dinner several months previously we had discussed our separate interests in feminist legal theory and the difficulties in applying feminist thought to international law. A conference paper, we thought, would test and refine our fuzzy ideas. We expected that our paper proposal would be rejected as too off-beat and provocative, so we were surprised, and rather daunted, when Professor Greig accepted it without hesitation. We began writing the paper with no sense of where we would end up, and would regularly share bouts of long-distance panic by phone. We wondered constantly whether we would ever manage to pull it all together. In the end, facing a room full of our curious colleagues, Shelley began with a general overview of feminist legal theory; Christine followed with a discussion of legal instruments and the gender imbalance within international organisations; and Hilary ended with a discussion of the international right to development as an example of how the gendered nature of international law serves to disempower and marginalise women.

The reaction to our paper was mixed. Several people were enthusiastic, while many of the audience looked discomfited and embarrassed (perhaps on our behalf!). One senior figure in the Australian international law community said in the discussion following the paper that the ideas were quite unrealistic as they

---

* Professor of Law, London School of Economics.
** Professor of Law and Northern Director, Akitsiraq Law School.
*** Professor of Law, Australian National University.
[1] H Charlesworth, C Chinkin, and S Wright, 'Feminist Approaches to International Law' (1991) 85 *American Journal of International Law* 613.

would mean enlarging the scope of international law and depriving our discipline of its distinctive character. Some of our colleagues advised us to get back to 'real world' international law for the sake of our careers. Another type of reaction was interest in the paper as an intriguing academic sideshow. Afterwards we found that we began to be asked to appear at symposia and on panels to present what were seen as controversial and contentious feminist ideas, but that the ideas were rarely taken up or engaged with. As the three of us became more closely associated with 'feminist approaches to international law' our colleagues were sometimes rather disconcerted if we spoke on international law issues *without* taking an explicitly feminist approach. It seemed, then, we had created a splash without waves.

Over the years feminist work in international law has attracted both strongly negative responses and support from unexpected sources, but most of all a mass of passively resistant inertia. Looking back, however, we can see that the impact of the article for us was as much personal and emotional as it was intellectual or academic. The article gave us a focused identity in our discipline and brought us into contact with a wonderful group of people. We ourselves have sometimes disagreed vigorously about the directions of our work. More than 10 years later we still struggle with what feminist approaches might mean, but have retained close ties of friendship.

At the end of the 1980s, when we first began to speculate whether feminist legal theory could be applied to the field of international law, Ronald Reagan was still President of the United States, the first Gulf War between Iraq and Iran was raging, the crushing of a Chinese democracy movement in Tiananmen Square had not yet happened, East Timor had experienced nearly 15 years of oppression under the grip of occupation by Indonesia with 10 more years to come, Nelson Mandela was a political prisoner on Robben Island while South African apartheid doggedly survived, Slobodan Milosevic had just been elected President of a still-intact Yugoslavia, the Berlin Wall was still standing and the Union of Soviet Socialist Republics was a communist empire stretching from the Baltic to the Pacific.

Despite many years of work by women's organisations both internationally and nationally, women were still facing inequality, discrimination and violence on a global scale. The UN Convention on the Elimination of All Forms of Discrimination Against Women (CEDAW)[2] had been in force for less than a decade. The UN General Assembly Declaration on the Elimination of Violence Against Women[3] had yet to be drafted. The concept that women's rights were human rights was not accepted, even rhetorically. Although the United Nations and other international organisations were formally committed to sex equality, real equality between women and men was not a serious political issue.

While the fall of communist regimes in Eastern Europe, including the Soviet Union, from 1989 onwards introduced democratic reforms and human rights to

---

[2] Convention on the Elimination of All Forms of Discrimination Against Women, 18 December 1979, 1249 UNTS 13 (in force 3 September 1981).
[3] GA Res 48/103, 20 December 1993.

most of Europe, the social and economic benefits that had existed under socialist regimes disappeared. Women in Eastern Europe found themselves without adequate child care or workplace family support; without controls on the price of housing; without rights protecting them from a rapid rise in unemployment, increases in the cost of education, a massive increase in the sex industry and intense wars in many parts of ex-Yugoslavia and the old Soviet Republics that still cause havoc today. Abortion and reproductive rights came under threat, while political rights and economic development were often captured by individual and corporate entities inimical to social justice. The divisions between rich and poor increased, with women often shouldering the burdens of keeping families and communities functioning.

The attacks against the United States on 11 September 2001 seem to have caused yet another deep shift in global politics. While the 1990s represented an era of increasing freedoms and 'globalisation', the post-11 September world is fixated on the 'war on terror', with intense levels of conflict between the United States, the United Kingdom and its allies against so-called 'Islamic fundamentalism', terrorists and all those who are 'not with us, but against us'. Since we first began exploring feminist approaches to international law, US President Ronald Reagan's 'Evil Empire' has been replaced by President George W Bush's 'Axis of Evil'. The villains may be different, but the rhetoric is largely similar. One change is the identification of the enemy in the war on terror with repressive treatment of women and the development of the notion of a war for women's rights. Thus the war in Afghanistan after 11 September was justified in part as a liberation of women from the strictures of the Taliban regime. This justification was much harder to sustain in the context of the invasion of Iraq in 2003, although it appeared as a strand in the argument that Iraq had to be invaded to achieve democratic governance. The problematic nature of the idea of a war for women is underlined by the aftermath of the Afghanistan and Iraq conflicts: in both cases, daily security for women has been reduced and women remain largely excluded from the public, political realm.

This chapter reflects on developments in some areas of international law since 1991: both the increased attention to the language of feminism and the limited progress women have made.

Representing Women

A consistent feminist concern in international law has been to redress the virtual exclusion of women from the most prestigious international positions and the need for new thinking on how to reform the regime to ensure that it better accommodates women's concerns and voices.[4] To what extent has this goal been

---

[4] D Dallmeyer (ed), *Reconceiving Reality: Women and International Law* (Washington, ASIL, Studies in Transnational Legal Policy, No 25, 1993).

reached? Have women been able to participate more in influential policy and decision-making bodies? The Committee on the Elimination of Discrimination Against Women has noted that '[t]here are few opportunities for women and men, on equal terms, to represent Governments at the international level and to participate in the work of international organizations. This is frequently the result of an absence of objective criteria and processes for appointment and promotion to relevant positions and official delegations.'[5] This conclusion can be evidenced by women's representation in international courts and tribunals.[6]

In September 2002, only 26 of 173 judicial positions in 12 international courts and tribunals were held by women—some 14–15%.[7] Six of these institutions have explicit human rights jurisdiction:[8] the European and American Courts of Human Rights, the ad hoc International Criminal Tribunals and two that had not yet come into existence, the International Criminal Court (ICC) and the African Court of Human Rights. Ten out of the 26 women judges were members of the European Court of Human Rights, but there were no women judges on the American Court of Human Rights. There was one woman judge on the International War Crimes Tribunal for the Former Yugoslavia (ICTY) and three on the International War Crimes Tribunal for Rwanda (ICTR). By mid-2003 the statistics looked better because of the success in securing the election of women as judges on the ICC. After a complex process requiring 33 ballots over 4 days, 7 women judges were elected to the bench of 18 and were sworn in at The Hague on 11 March 2003. The success of the intense lobbying by women's groups both at Rome and then at the meetings of the Assembly of States Parties, shows that it is possible to gain provisions for equitable gender representation within the constitutive instrument of an international court[9] and also to insist upon voting procedures to ensure that the commitment is met.

Women holding seven out of 18 positions as judges is not, however, equality— the standard of international human rights law—although it does reach the 30–35% range which the Committee on the Elimination of Discrimination Against Women has argued may constitute the 'critical mass' needed to influence the style, substance and process of any body.[10] Other questions remain. Why is the

---

[5] Committee on the Elimination of Discrimination against Women, General Recommendation No 23, Political and Public life, sixteenth session, 13 January 1997, para 38.

[6] For discussion of women's participation in other international bodies see H Charlesworth and C Chinkin *The Boundaries of International Law: a Feminist Analysis* (Manchester, Manchester University Press, 2000), ch 6.

[7] J Linehan, *Women and Public International Litigation 2002*, background paper for the Project on International Courts and Tribunals, available at <http://www.pict-pcti.org/publications/PICT_articles/Women1.pdf.>, last accessed 24 September 2004.

[8] In other international courts important human rights matters may well be raised, perhaps especially in the International Court of Justice and the European Court of Justice.

[9] The Protocol on the Establishment of an African Court on Human and Peoples' Rights 1998, Article 12(2) requires due consideration to be given 'to adequate gender representation in the nomination process.' For further discussion of the African Court on Human and People's Rights, see R Murray, this volume.

[10] Committee on the Elimination of Discrimination against Women, General Recommendation No 23, Political and Public Life, sixteenth session, 31 January 1997, para 16.

concept of 'equity' preferred to equality? Why are there no women on other international judicial bodies such as the International Tribunal on the Law of the Sea or the WTO Appellate Body? Why do states not nominate women for such positions? Why is there still only one woman on the International Court of Justice? Why is equitable geographic distribution so much more important than that based on gender? Is serious thought being given to rethinking the gender divide in international institutions, or to adapting workplace practices and assumptions in ways that might make them more accommodating to women?

The greater number of women judges on the European Court of Human Rights and the ICC perhaps suggests that women are more acceptable in bodies dealing with 'soft' issues such as human rights or international crimes, where gendered crimes are explicitly included within the tribunal's jurisdiction, than in those that adjudicate 'hard' areas of international law such as trade and the law of the sea. This view is reinforced by the increased number of women thematic special rapporteurs and experts mandated by the Commission on Human Rights. On the other hand it is challenged by the current lack of any women members on the American Court of Human Rights. Even within human rights there appears to be further differentiation: women remain significantly under-represented on all the treaty bodies,[11] except the Committee on the Elimination of Discrimination against Women[12] and the Committee on the Rights of the Child.[13]

Women's Human Rights

Throughout the 1990s significant advances were made in the institutions, substance and procedures of international human rights law as it is applied to women. Women's NGOs have worked for many years for the recognition and application of women's human rights through various international institutions, political, diplomatic and judicial. At the Vienna Conference on Human Rights in 1993, it was affirmed that the 'human rights of women and of the girl-child are an inalienable, integral and indivisible part of universal human rights';[14] and at the 1994 Conference on Population and Development in Cairo, women's reproductive rights were guaranteed.[15] The central place of CEDAW—the United Nations'

---

[11] In 2003, the Committee on the Elimination of Racial Discrimination had one woman member and 17 men; the Committee against Torture had one woman member and 10 men; the Human Rights Committee had two women members and 16 men; the Committee on Economic, Social and Cultural Rights had one women member and 10 men.

[12] In 2003, 21 out of 23 members were women.

[13] In 2003, 11 out of 18 members were women.

[14] UN World Conference on Human Rights, Vienna Declaration and Programme of Action, 25 June 1993, UN Doc A/Conf. 157/23, 1993 (hereinafter Vienna), paras 1, 18. This was reaffirmed at the Fourth World Conference on Women, Declaration and Platform for Action, Beijing, UN Doc A/Conf. 177/20, 1995 (hereinafter Beijing), para 213.

[15] Report of the International Conference on Population and Development, Cairo, UN Doc A/Conf 171/13, 1994.

'landmark treaty in the struggle for women's rights'[16]—was affirmed[17] and emphasis was placed on enhancing its enforcement mechanisms.[18] This objective was achieved through the adoption of the Optional Protocol in 1999, which establishes an individual complaints mechanism of violations of the Convention and empowers the Committee to commence an inquiry procedure where there is reliable information of 'grave or systematic violations'.[19]

Despite the importance of CEDAW in defining discrimination against women and highlighting those areas in public and private life where discrimination is most marked, its equality paradigm meant that it did not address violence against women.[20] Throughout the 1990s there was growing acceptance through diverse arenas that gender specific violence against women both constitutes a direct violation of women's human rights and contributes to their inability to enjoy the full range of civil, political, economic, social and cultural rights.[21] The obligation upon states to investigate, eliminate and punish such violence, whether committed by state officials or by non-state actors, was reiterated through the adoption by consensus of the General Assembly Declaration on the Elimination of Violence against Women,[22] the acceptance by over 30 states in the Americas of a convention for the elimination of violence against women,[23] and the appointment of a special rapporteur with the mandate to examine the causes and consequences of violence against women.[24] The regional human rights courts have analysed sexual abuse as violating human rights within the terms of their respective conventions; for example, rape as amounting to torture contrary to Article 3 of the European Convention for the Protection of Human Rights and Fundamental Freedoms[25] and Article 5 of the Inter-American Convention on Human Rights.[26]

---

[16] *The United Nations and the Advancement of Women, 1945–1995* (United Nations Blue Books Series, Volume VI) (New York, United Nations), para 12.

[17] Vienna, II, para 39; Beijing, Platform for Action, para 230.

[18] The Vienna Conference called for '[n]ew procedures ... to strengthen implementation of the commitment to women's equality' (Vienna, II, para 40); and at Beijing among the action to be taken by governments was to '[s]upport the process initiated by the Commission on the Status of Women with a view to elaborating a draft optional protocol to the [CEDAW] that could enter into force as soon as possible on a right of petition procedure, ...' (Beijing, Platform for Action, para 230 (k)).

[19] Optional Protocol to the Convention on the Elimination of All Forms of Discrimination Against Women, GA Res 54/4, annex, 54 UN GAOR Supp (No 49) at 5, UN Doc A/54/49 (Vol I) (2000), in force 22 December 2000.

[20] H Charlesworth and C Chinkin, 'Violence Against Women: A Global Issue' in J Stubbs (ed), *Women, Male Violence and the Law* (Sydney, Federation Press, 1994), 13.

[21] Committee on the Elimination of Discrimination against Women, General Recommendation No 19, Violence against Women, 29 January 1992.

[22] General Assembly Declaration on the Elimination of Violence against Women, GA Res 48/103, 20 December 1993.

[23] American Convention on the Prevention, Punishment and Eradication of Violence against Women, Belem do Para, 1994. Reprinted in (1994) 33 *International Legal Materials* 1535.

[24] Commission on Human Rights Res 1994/45; UN Doc ESCOR 1994, Supp No 4, 11 March 1994.

[25] Eg *Aydin v Turkey* (Case 57/1996/676/866) (1998) 3 *Butterworths Human Rights Cases* 300.

[26] Eg *Mejia Egocheaga v Peru* (Case 10.970; Report 5/96, 1996) (1997) 1 *Butterworths Human Rights Cases* 229.

The incidence of targeted violence against women in armed conflict, and its manifestations through war crimes against protected persons, crimes against humanity and genocide, also led to the inclusion of sexual crimes against women within the jurisdiction of the ICTY and ICTR,[27] and the Rome Statute for the International Criminal Court.[28] The provisions of the Statutes of the ad hoc tribunals have been developed by the tribunals' jurisprudence analysing the conditions under which forms of sexual violence have been considered as war crimes;[29] as 'cruel treatment'[30] and 'outrages on personal dignity'[31] constituting breaches of the Geneva Convention common Article 3; as a violation of the laws and customs of war; as a crime against humanity; as constituting torture[32] and enslavement;[33] and as genocide.[34] These developments make gender-related crimes a striking example of the move from impunity to accountability under international criminal law that took place throughout the 1990s. Indeed, the ICTY Appeal Chamber has asserted that:

> The general question of bringing justice to the perpetrators of crimes such as rape, was one of the reasons that the Security Council established the Tribunal.[35]

In the area of human rights, then, considerable rhetorical progress has been made in recognising women's rights, largely through the energies of women's NGOs. Beneath this apparent progress lie a number of different trends that pull in opposite directions and which make uncertain the direction for future strategic action. Triumphalism about human rights pervaded the 1990s, at least in the West.[36] There was an assumption that human rights was a dominant discourse to be carried into the twenty-first century as an antidote to darker discourses,

---

[27] The Statute of the International Criminal Tribunal for Former Yugoslavia, SC Res 827, 25 May 1993, Article 2 does not explicitly include sexual crimes within grave breaches of the Geneva Conventions, but Article 5(g) lists rape as a crime against humanity; Statute of the International Criminal Tribunal for Rwanda, SC Res 955, 8 November 1994, Article 3(g) lists rape as a crime against humanity, and Article 4(e) includes rape as a violation of Geneva Conventions, common Article 3. For further discussion of the ICTY and its prosecution of sexual crimes, see V Nikolic-Ristanovic, this volume.

[28] Rome Statute for the International Criminal Court, 1998, UN Doc A/Conf 183/C1/L76, Articles 7(1)(g) (rape and other forms of sexual violence as a crime against humanity); 8(2)(b)(xxii) (sexual violence as contrary to the laws and customs of war); 8(2)(e)(vi) (sexual violence contrary to laws and customs applicable to non-international conflict).

[29] *Prosecutor v Anto Furundzija*, IT–95–17/1–A, 21 July 2000, para 210 (hereinafter *Furundzija*, appeal).

[30] *Prosecutor v Dusko Tadic*, IT–94–17, 7 May 1997, paras 724–6; *Prosecutor v Zejnil Delalic Zdravko Mucic aka 'Pavo', Hazim Delic Esad Landzo aka 'Zenga'* (hereinafter *Celebici*), IT–96–21, 16 November 1998, para 1066; *Prosecutor v Tihomir Blaskic* IT–95–14, 3 March 2000, paras 692, 695, 700.

[31] *Prosecutor v Dragoljub Kunarac, Radomir Kovac and Zoran Vukovic*, 22 February 2001, IT–96–23 and IT–96–23/1 'Foca', (hereinafter *Kunarac*), para 436.

[32] *Celebici*, paras 475, 495; *Furundzija*, appeal, para 114.

[33] *Kunarac*, paras 515–43.

[34] *Prosecutor v Jean-Paul Akayesu*, ICTR–96–4, 2 September 1998, especially paras 507–9, 731; *Prosecutor v Kayishema*, ICTR–95–1, 21 May 1999, especially paras 95, 114–118, 299, 446, 532.

[35] *Furundzija*, appeal, para 201.

[36] The expression 'West' is problematic, not least because of its continued cold war associations and its failure to distinguish between Eastern and Central Europe. An alternative might be 'North' as contrasted with the 'South'. This too is not geographically accurate as it excludes Australia and New Zealand.

such as those of nationalism, extremism, militarism and fundamentalism. As Michael Ignatieff put it:

> We are scarcely aware of the extent to which our moral imagination has been transformed since 1945 by the growth of a language and practice of moral universalism, expressed above all in a shared human rights culture.[37]

The political endorsement of this commitment, expressed through the trilogy of values—democratisation, human rights and the rule of law—formed the ideological dividing line between the liberal democracies of Western Europe and the socialist states of the East. After the fall of the Berlin Wall these principles were reaffirmed as the basis for the social and political framework for the economic restructuring of Eastern Europe.[38] Indeed, it has been argued that:

> Respect for fundamental human rights is now accepted as a central element in the construction of a democratic and united Europe and as a critical component of the EU image as a space of civility and modernity.[39]

This may be contrasted with other spaces that are perceived as 'uncivilised' because the darker discourses of tribalism, nationalism, extremism and religious fundamentalism seem to prevail. These dark places are regularly portrayed as areas where conflict, savagery and bloodshed are the rule, with little or no acknowledgement of the link between this darkness and our sense of enlightenment. The West has taken different approaches in deciding how it should deal with such 'other' places. One view is that the distinction between liberal and non-liberal states should be accepted, coupled with the rejection of the concept of universally applicable international law.[40] At its most extreme, this view sees international law as applying only as between the liberal states in their dealings *inter se*, leaving non-liberal states beyond the periphery.[41] Another tactic is that of confrontation and contestation, or, its fraternal twin, that of 'saving' such states to bring them the benefits of civilisation. The collapse or abuse of governmental

---

[37] M Ignatieff, *The Warrior's Honour: Ethnic War and the Modern Conscience* (London, Chatto & Windus, 1998), 8.

[38] Eg Charter of Paris for a New Europe, 19–21 November 1990, Principle 1, Human Rights, Democracy and the Rule of Law; the Prague Document on Further Development of the Institutions and Structures of the CSCE, in (1992) 31 *International Legal Materials* 976; the Copenhagen Document Conference on Human Dimension, 5 June–29 July 1990, I(1), (2) and (3), and the Summit meetings of the OSCE.

[39] J Bhabha, 'Citizenship and Post-national Rights in Europe' (1999) 1 *International Social Science Journal* 11, at 22.

[40] A-M Slaughter, 'International Law in a World of Liberal States' (1995) 6 *European Journal of International Law* 503.

[41] Eg Slaughter argues that only liberal states operate within a 'zone of law' and that liberal courts should impose a badge of 'alienage' on laws of non-liberal states: A-M Slaughter, 'Law Among Liberal States: Liberal Internationalism and the Act of State Doctrine' (1992) 92 *Columbia Law Review* 1907. For critique of this approach see J Alvarez, 'Do Liberal States Behave Better? A Critique of Slaughter's Liberal Theory' (2001) 12 *European Journal of International Law* 183.

institutions, allowing gross violations of human rights, has become the hallmark of states that are labelled as 'failed' or 'rogue'. Such states (for example, Somalia, Haiti, Bosnia-Herzegovina, Serbia and Montenegro, Sierra Leone, Afghanistan, Iraq) have been made subject to international (Western) intervention, apparently to restore to these nations the hallmarks of civilisation.[42] As part of this mission, international accountability has been demanded for gross human rights violations committed by the 'uncivilised', through assertions of universal jurisdiction and the establishment of the first international criminal tribunals since the end of World War II. In their institutional reinvention of themselves through the establishment of the African Union, African states have sought to come in from the periphery by committing themselves to these same values.[43]

Human rights triumphalism has been the backdrop for many advances in the acceptance of women's human rights. The liberal model of equality and assertions of the rule of law and democracy have offered women a greater opportunity to acquire guarantees protecting their human dignity as opposed to the denial of their rights associated with nationalist ideologies[44] and religious extremisms,[45] both of which have had especially vicious consequences for women. It has seemed obvious that women should embrace the human rights social movement and to seek to ensure its benefits for themselves. Accordingly, women have campaigned for these values, and on the whole have been remarkably successful in drawing attention to questions of gender within the human rights legal framework. We can now say 'that we have moved forward because now we are present in the discourse of the powerful and a "gender perspective" figures in almost all their projects.'[46]

There are many tensions, however, both about the appropriateness of the framework itself and about the place of human rights law in contemporary international law and relations. We must be cautious about overstating the advances that have been achieved. The guarantee of women's human rights goes well beyond adopting a new instrument, adding a new institution, ensuring the inclusion of women in the composition of decision- or policy-making committees, or

---

[42] Even in the midst of this civilising process there have been dark moments when other imperatives have deterred assistance: the failure to intervene to prevent genocide in Rwanda, or to ensure the safety of those sheltering within the internationally established safe havens in Bosnia-Herzegovina are two such examples.

[43] The Preamble to the Constitutive Act of the African Union, Lome, Togo, 11 July 2000 asserts African states to be 'DETERMINED to promote and protect human and peoples' rights, consolidate democratic institutions and culture, and to ensure good governance and the rule of law'; Article 4(m) reiterates these same principles.

[44] For different perspectives on the impact of nationalist ideologies on women, see the various articles in V Moghadam (ed), *Gender and National Identity* (London, Zed Books, 1994); J Jaquette and S Wolchik (eds), *Women and Democracy in Latin America and Eastern Europe* (Johns Hopkins University Press, 1998); S Ramet (ed), *Gender Politics in the Western Balkans* (University Park, Pennsylvania State University Press, 1999).

[45] C Howland (ed), *Religious Fundamentalisms and the Human Rights of Women* (New York, Palgrave, 1999).

[46] A Facio, *Globalization and Feminism* (2003) WHRnet Perspective, available at <http://www.whrnet.org/docs/perspective-facio-0302.html>.

extending the jurisdiction of an institution such as the inclusion of crimes against women in the international criminal tribunals. It requires challenging the structural inequalities and power imbalances that make continued violations inevitable. For example, in the context of international criminal law—an area of much acclaimed success—it is relatively easy to add crimes against women into the ambit of international criminal law.

The Women's International War Crimes Tribunal

While women's NGOs have sought—with considerable success—to advance women's human rights through the formal institutions and instruments of international law, they recognise that mainstream international institutions may be inimical to their claims. They have accordingly created their own spaces within local and international arenas, for example through initiatives such as the Women's International War Crimes Tribunal.[47] This Peoples' Tribunal was conceived of and organised by women's NGOs across Asia. It was established to determine the criminal liability of leading high-ranking Japanese military and political officials, and the separate responsibility of Japan for the rapes and sexual slavery committed against so-called comfort women across the Asia Pacific region in the 1930s and 1940s.[48] Oral and documentary evidence was given before a bench of 'judges' of the brutal and relentless treatment women had received at the hands of the Japanese military in the comfort stations. A full judgment providing factual and legal analysis was issued at The Hague on 4 December 2001.[49]

The Tribunal was the response to an overwhelming sense among surviving comfort women and their supporters that international human rights and criminal law had failed to address war-time sexual violence. The International Military Tribunal for the Far East had not adequately considered rape and sexual enslavement, and had not brought charges arising out of the detention of an estimated 200,000 women for sexual services. The negotiators of the Peace Agreements concluded between the allies and Japan in the 1950s had also failed to include a provision for recompense, apology or even acknowledgment that the sexual violence had occurred. As the survivors grew older, the situation of comfort women was eventually brought before the new UN human rights institutions, but with no positive outcome. Cases in national courts were dismissed, often summarily.

---

[47] C Chinkin, 'Women's International Tribunal on Japanese Military Sexual Slavery' (2001) 95 *American Journal of International Law* 335.

[48] See further G Hicks, *The Comfort Women* (St Leonards, NSW, Allen & Unwin, 1995); International Commission of Jurists, *Comfort Women An Unfinished Ordeal* (Report of a Mission, ISBN 92 9037 086—6).

[49] Women's International War Crimes Tribunal for the Trial of Japan's Military Sexual Slavery, *The Prosecutors and the Peoples of the Asia Pacific Region v Emperor Hirohito et al; The Prosecutors and the Peoples of the Asia Pacific Region v the Government of Japan*, Case No PT–2000–1–T, 4 December 2001.

Impetus for the Tribunal came from women's groups, who argued that international human rights law must be understood as an instrument of global civil society. The idea was that when states fail to exercise their obligations to ensure justice, civil society can legitimately step in. Where traditional, state-based forms of international law-making and application fail those marginalised by the law—in this case women from Japan's colonial possessions and women subject to military occupation—other processes and methodologies for redress must be sought. The Tribunal used the legitimacy bestowed by legal argument and analysis and the symbolism of courtroom proceedings, although its authority was only moral.

The case of the comfort women illustrates a major concern of those promoting women's international human rights: avoiding essentialising women and recognising the diversity in the situations and priorities of women around the world.[50] The comfort women were subjected to sexual slavery because they were women, because of their race, because of their status as colonised or defeated peoples,[51] and because they were poor. Women's various identities intersect, and diverse forms of discrimination and prejudice interlock and affect each other. Previously sceptical bodies, such as the Committee on the Elimination of Racial Discrimination, have now identified and recognised the importance of intersectional analysis.[52] At the institutional level, intersectionality has to some extent become enmeshed with the principle of mainstreaming, both gender and human rights, within the institutions of the United Nations.[53] Gender mainstreaming is a practical tool for the enhancement of women's human rights through

> the process of assessing the implications for women and men of any planned action, including legislation [that might be required by the agreement] policies or programmes in any area and at all levels. It is a strategy for making women's concerns as well as men's concerns and experiences an integral dimension in the design, implementation, monitoring, and evaluation of policies and programmes in all political, economic and social spheres so that women and men benefit equally and inequality is not perpetuated.[54]

But practical application still too often rests on the willingness and commitment of individuals to give it effect. In reality gender mainstreaming has a tendency to

---

[50] C Mohanty, 'Under Western Eyes: Feminist Scholarship and Colonial Discourses' (1998) 30 *Feminist Review* 61; M Lugones and E Spelman, 'Have we got a theory for you! Feminist Theory, Cultural Imperialism and the Demand for "The Woman's Voice"' (1983) 6 *Women's Studies International Forum* 573.

[51] The majority of the comfort women were Korean, Korea then being a colony of Japan. While there were some Japanese comfort women, many were from the southern island of Okinawa, which was not seen as Japan 'proper', and others were perceived as prostitutes.

[52] Committee on the Elimination of Racial Discrimination, General Recommendation No 25, Gender Related Dimensions of Racial Discrimination, 20 March 2000; see also UN Office of the High Commissioner for Human Rights, Gender Dimensions of Racial Discrimination (2001).

[53] A Gallagher, 'Ending the Marginalisation. Strategies for Incorporating Women into the United Nations' Human Rights System' (1997) 19 *Human Rights Quarterly* 283.

[54] C Chinkin, *Gender Mainstreaming in Legal and Constitutional Affairs* (London, Commonwealth Secretariat, 2001), 12.

become an additional task bestowed upon an already overburdened person (frequently a woman) who 'shows an interest in gender'. Unless the responsibility is specifically allocated and effective monitoring mechanisms are put in place, mainstreaming can justify inaction or omitting any form of discrimination from the institutional agenda. And certain forms of diversity are still resisted even at the formal level: for example, the refusal to include persecution on the grounds of sexual identity as a crime against humanity in the Statute of the International Criminal Court.

The feminist challenge remains to ensure that human rights principles and standards do not create stories of victimhood that both dehumanise and disempower the people they are designed to benefit. For example, the inclusion of charges of sexual violence against women does not challenge the structures and assumptions that continue to make sexual violence part of conflict (especially conflict associated with ethnic cleansing), nor provide any basis for stopping its recurrence.[55] International criminal law and human rights regimes tend to present women as victims of wrongs rather than as transformative agents. Women continue to be excluded from formal processes for societal change, for example peace agreements and programmes for post-conflict reconstruction.[56] The continuing and widespread gross violations of women's human rights indicate that legal norms do not inevitably alter behaviour.[57] There are many obstacles to the internalisation of these norms.[58] What is needed is the development of a human rights culture within the particular contexts of diverse societies, and of a mindset that rejects the different forms of adverse treatment meted out to women worldwide.

The Effects of Globalisation

Is triumphalism about the benefits of human rights itself misplaced? Human rights discourse can be seen as merely an instrumental part of the neo-liberal requirements supporting the promotion of economic investment, the free flow of capital and foreign investment in a globalised economy.[59] Indeed these objectives may be seen

---

[55] C Chinkin, 'Feminist Reflections on International Criminal Law' in A Zimmermann (ed), *International Criminal Law and the Current Development of Public International Law* (Berlin, Duncker and Humblot, 2002) 125; R Dixon, 'Rape as a Crime in International Humanitarian Law: Where to from Here?' (2002) 13 *European Journal of International Law* 697.

[56] SC Res 1325, 31 October 2000, recognises the important role women play in conflict resolution and peace-building, and 'calls upon all actors involved when negotiating and implementing peace agreements to adopt a gender perspective'. The Resolution has not ensured the inclusion of women in all such processes: *Women, Peace and Security*, Study submitted by the Secretary-General pursuant to SC Res 1325, 31 October (2000), paras 166, 179.

[57] *The World's Women 1995: Trends and Statistics* (New York, United Nations, 1995).

[58] R Cook (ed) *Human Rights of Women: National and International Perspectives* (Philadelphia, Pennsylvania University Press, 1995); K Askin and D Koenig (eds), *Women and International Human Rights Law* (Ardsley, Transnational Press, 1999).

[59] This is perhaps most explicit in the context of post-conflict reconstruction; see C Chinkin and K Paradine, 'Vision and Reality: Democracy and Citizenship of Women in the Dayton Peace Accords' (2001) 26 *Yale Journal of International Law* 103.

as a fourth component of the human rights, democracy and rule of law mantra. Thus precisely as Western women have been arguing the benefits of the values of human rights and the rule of law as the framework for women's empowerment, the adverse effects of globalisation and neo-liberalism on such empowerment have become evident.

Globalisation has affected gender relations in complex and contradictory ways.[60] The centralisation of power within the sovereign state that has been fragmented by globalisation was not predicated upon, nor necessarily supportive of, equality between women and men. The power structures of the Westphalian state were organised around patriarchal assumptions that accorded men monopoly over power, authority and wealth. Central to this was the public/private dichotomy with its subordination of women within the family.[61] Emphasis upon the normative impact of the public/private divide has been legitimately criticised for universalising a Western model of social ordering.[62] While recognising the fluidity of any demarcation between public and private spheres, divisions between productive and un(re)productive work and presenting women's work as lacking economic value,[63] combined with the primary responsibilities of women within the family, have impeded their advancement across many, if not all, societies. The opening up of new spaces by the apparent weakening of the nation state held open the possibility of undermining the traditional gender hierarchies and devising new bases for gender relations.

This vision of new spaces for women's empowerment has, however, run up against the ways in which the non-democratic forces of 'globalisation from above'— corporate enterprises, markets and movements of capital[64]—have weakened the effective decision- and policy-making power of the state, notably in economic and labour policies. The human rights movement looks to governments to fulfil their international obligations by asserting their authority against non-state actors. But governments are unwilling to assert the human rights of their workers where to do so would discourage investment, and corporate actors remain largely unregulated by international law.[65] Consequences such as social exclusion, unemployment or low-paid employment, and weakening of trade union organisation, all have gendered dimensions. Women are favoured as a passive, compliant, temporary workforce that will accept low wages without demanding labour and human rights. The traditional

---

[60] C Chinkin, 'Gender and International Society Law and Policy' in R Thakur and E Newman (eds), *New Millennium New Perspectives: The United Nations, Security and Governance* (Tokyo, United Nations University, Millennium Series, 2000), 242.

[61] On the public/private dichotomy see M Thornton (ed), *Public and Private Feminist Legal Debates* (Melbourne, Oxford University Press, 1995). For an overview of the public/private in feminist international legal scholarship, see D Buss, this volume.

[62] Eg, J Alexander and C Mohanty (eds), *Feminist Genealogies, Colonial Legacies, Democratic Futures* (London, Routledge, 1997).

[63] M Waring, *Counting for Nothing: What Men Value and What Women are Worth* (Wellington, Allen & Unwin, 1998).

[64] R Krut, *Globalisation and Civil Society: NGO Influence in International Decision-Making* (Geneva, United Nations Research Institute for Social Development, 1997).

[65] S Ratner, 'Corporations and Human Rights: A Theory of Legal Responsibility' (2001) 111 *Yale Law Journal* 443.

sexual division of labour (the location of women in employment regarded as inherently suitable for them, for example the caring professions) has been furthered through the addition of new locations and forms of work (services industry, tourism, work in free trade and export process zones).[66] What remains constant is the low economic value accorded to work performed primarily by women, often migrants, frequently in conditions of exploitation, poor and unsafe working conditions, no job security and violations of human rights.

The impact of economic reconstruction through privatisation and structural adjustment programmes upon the enjoyment of human rights, particularly economic and social rights, has attracted the attention of the United Nations human rights bodies.[67] This too has a gendered impact and has contributed to the feminisation of poverty.

> Globalization may have dire consequences for human rights generally and women's human rights particularly, in terms of eroding civil, political, economic, social and cultural rights in the name of development and macro-level economic restructuring and stability. In the countries of the South, structural adjustment programmes have led to increased impoverishment, particularly amongst women, displacement and internal strife resulting from the political instabilities caused by devaluing national currencies, increasing debt and dependence on foreign direct investment.[68]

Great numbers of women migrate across international borders. Social exclusion, loss of previously accepted benefits (for example, affordable childcare and maternity leave) and personal insecurity are aggravated by dislocation and unemployment. The greater mobility of persons facilitated by ease of communications, including some more open borders, has contributed to the phenomenon of women's poverty and lack of security. Migrant women are typically located as temporary workers in the unregulated, informal labour market of most countries, 'working as domestic, industrial or agricultural labour or in the service sector'.[69] Such work, viewed as 'women's work', is low paid and unregulated, leaving women at the mercy of their employers and the state's willingness to allow them to stay and continue to work. 'Many women who migrate for promised jobs in domestic service, catering or entertainment find themselves tricked into prostitution.'[70] Migrant

---

[66] Preliminary Report submitted by the Special Rapporteur on Violence against Women, its Causes and Consequences, Ms Radhika Coomaraswamy, UN Doc E/CN4/1995/42, para 55.

[67] Effects of Structural Adjustment Policies on the Full Enjoyment of Human Rights, report by the independent expert, Mr Fantu Cheru, submitted in accordance with Commission Decisions 1998/102 and 1997/103, UN Doc E/CN4/1999/50, 24 February 1999.

[68] Report of the Special Rapporteur on Violence Against Women, its Causes and Consequences, Ms Radhika Coomaraswamy, on trafficking in women, migration and violence against women submitted in accordance with Commission on Human Rights Resolution 1997/44, UN Doc E/CN4/2000/68, 29 February 2000, para 59.

[69] 'Human Rights of Migrants, Report of the Special Rapporteur, Ms Gabriela Rodríguez Pizarro, submitted pursuant to Commission on Human Rights Resolution 1999/44, UN Doc E/CN4/2000/82, 6 January 2000.

[70] Report of the Secretary-General on Violence Against Women Migrant Workers, UN Doc E/CN4/2000/76, 9 December 1999, para 11.

workers in positions of powerlessness and dependency are 'exposed to acute risks of physical or psychological violence', and often to deception and theft of their economic gains. Impoverished women are also especially vulnerable to being tricked or coerced into being trafficked, to being subjected to sexual violence, and to exploitation.[71]

Economic liberalisation has encouraged organised transnational enterprises based on the sex trade, prostitution and pornography in persons and goods (including trade on the internet). Free trade imperatives of the market have inhibited restrictions upon sale of pornography and erotica that reinforce and work alongside the market in persons. International efforts to combat trafficking have led to new conventions,[72] but there remain tremendous problems in stemming this lucrative business.

Despite the potential for such abuses, the consequences of globalisation have not been exclusively detrimental for women. There have also been benefits. For example, global pursuit of profit has enhanced paid employment opportunities for women. While the conditions of work may be exploitative, paid employment has nevertheless facilitated a degree of economic independence for many women and lessened their subordination within the family, for example by freeing them from early marriage or pregnancy. This in turn provides the public space for women to assert their own agency and generates the self-esteem that comes from such independence. Families (especially children) also benefit from women's earnings.

Of course, the choices women may have are restricted by nation state barriers, including restrictive and hostile immigration laws and a reluctance to recognise the human rights of migrant workers.[73] One of the most insidious aspects of neoliberal ideology has been the construction of ideas about the market and free movement of capital as natural and inevitable. Thus, at the 1995 Beijing Women's Conference no alternative voice was offered in opposition to the benefits of market policies: the goal was to ensure women's participation in and access to the dominant structures of the market, not to question their underlying assumptions or even to consider alternative models.[74] The structural violence against women

---

[71] Report of the Special Rapporteur on Violence Against Women, its Causes and Consequences, Ms Radhika Coomaraswamy, Report on the Mission to Poland on the Issue of Trafficking and the Forced Prostitution of Women (24 May–1 June 1996), UN Doc E/CN4/1997/Add 1, 1996.

[72] Protocol to Prevent, Suppress and Punish Trafficking in Persons, especially Women and Children, supplementing the United Nations Convention against Transnational Organised Crime, 2000.

[73] The International Convention on the Protection of the Rights of All Migrant Workers and Members of Their Families, GA Res 45/158, annex, GAOR (Supp No 49A) at 262, UN Doc A 45/49 (1990), did not come into force until 1 July 2003. In 2005 it has only 31 states parties. The human rights of trafficked persons are highlighted in Office of the United Nations High Commissioner for Human Rights, Recommended Principles and Guidelines on Human Rights and Human Trafficking, UN Doc E/2002/68/Add1, 20 May 2002, available at <http://www.unhchr.ch/huridocda/huridoca.nsf/ (Symbol)/E.2002.68.Add.1.En?Opendocument.>, last accessed 24 September 2004.

[74] D Otto, 'Holding up Half the Sky, but for Whose Benefit? A Critical Analysis of the Fourth World Conference on Women' (1996) 6 *Australian Feminist Law Journal* 7.

associated with these economic policies was not addressed.[75] Another adverse consequence is that it has distorted priorities, for example pursuit of global profits rather than gender equality or human rights. In Alda Facio's terms, this has deprived us of our Utopia, our vision of an ideal future. We have been caught in a vice. She writes:

> Working on Democracy, on fundamental freedoms and Human Rights in general has been a strategy for the feminist movement, particularly during the last decade. Yet globalization has denigrated these values, which even Capitalism supposedly considered fundamental ... Why should we settle for bringing proposals inside this system, like political participation quotas or domestic violence penalties, instead of imagining and fighting for a real democracy? How do we defend 'freedom of speech' if it has become freedom for big business to manipulate the truth at their will?[76]

The War on Terror

On 11 September 2001, massive acts of terror against the United States caused immense suffering and trauma. The governmental response was the declaration of a 'war on terror', a campaign that has become synonymous with international virtue. The war on terror has so completely dominated the global stage, it is easy to forget other crises. Sudan is descending into famine and disintegration; the Democratic Republic of the Congo remains mired in chaos and violence; HIV/AIDS is destroying a whole generation of workers and caregivers from South Africa to China; and women's capacity to support themselves and their families in many parts of the world is deteriorating. Moreover, international legal rules that might temper the violence of reprisal and 'homeland security' are reinterpreted to further the war on terror.[77] International law looks increasingly fragile against agendas of terror and war, whether perpetrated by marginalised young Islamic men, or by aging Cold Warriors contemptuous of international laws governing the use of force.[78]

The war on terror has undermined attention to human rights in national and international policy-making.[79] The struggle seems to have flattened all identities into a stark horizontal dichotomy between terrorists and non-terrorists. Those labelled as terrorists or suspected terrorists have lost their claims to be prisoners

---

[75] Y Lee, 'Violence against Women: Reflections on the Past and Strategies for the Future — An NGO Perspective' (1997) 19 *Adelaide Law Review* 45, terms this 'indirect violence'.

[76] F Alda, 'Globalization and Feminism', WHRnet Perspective, available at <http://www.whrnet.org/docs/perspective-facio-0302.html.>, last accessed 24 September 2004.

[77] Eg, the doctrine of 'pre-emptive self-defence': see 'The National Security Strategy of the United States of America' (17 September 2002), the White House, at <http://www.whitehouse.gov/nsc/nss.html.>, last accessed 24 September 2004.

[78] H Charlesworth and C Chinkin, 'Sex, Gender, and September 11' (2002) 96 *American Journal of International Law* 600; S Wright, 'The Horizon of Becoming: Culture, Gender and History after September 11' (2002) 71 *Nordic Journal of International Law* 215 at 223–4.

[79] See Amnesty International Report 2004, POL 10/004/2004 (26 May 2004) in which the deterioration of human rights around the world directly related to terrorism and the war against terrorism is documented: available at <http://web.amnesty.org/report2004/index-eng.>, last accessed 24 September 2004.

of war or protected civilians under the Geneva Conventions;[80] children protected under the UN Convention on the Rights of the Child;[81] legal or illegal immigrants, asylum seekers or nationals of particular states; or even individuals entitled to basic civil and political, economic and social human rights.[82] It had been assumed by most international lawyers that these laws continued to have permanent, progressive effect. Where legal identities are eliminated and replaced by one ill-defined label—'terrorist'—the 'other' becomes depersonalised, rampant, alien and barbaric, diversity becomes a threat and gender or other identities simply vanish as organising categories. Human rights has become an 'outsider' discourse, especially in national security decision-making and within those very states that present human rights and freedoms as part of their civilising mission.[83]

What are the ramifications of the events of 11 September 2001 for women, international law and gender? The gendered images associated with terrorism are rarely analysed.[84] The war on terror has both increased women's vulnerability and decreased attention to long-term systemic violence and discrimination. Twentieth-century developments in international law on the use of force have been undercut by the revival of the idea that there are 'civilised' and 'uncivilised' *subjects* of international law, for example 'US/us' versus 'the axis of evil'. Women have sometimes been paraded as the *objects* of the conduct of 'uncivilised' states, such as Afghanistan, justifying at least in part punitive action by the 'civilised'. The situation of some women in Afghanistan has improved since the overthrow of the Taliban regime, but many women remain subject to deeply repressive practices. Those using the rhetoric of women's rights to justify their actions rarely consider the views of women themselves, particularly those women who are not members of urban literate elites. The attention to women's rights also tends to be partial and limited. For example, the US has taken the opportunity to back away from women's rights domestically[85] and has attempted to do so internationally.[86]

---

[80] See in particular Geneva Conventions III (relative to the Treatment of Prisoners of War) and IV (relative to the Protection of Civilian Persons in Time of War) and Protocol I additional to the Geneva Conventions of 7 December 1949 (8 June 1977). See the UN High Commissioner for Human Rights website at <http://www.unhchr.ch/html/intlinst.htm>, last accessed 24 September 2004, for links to the full texts of these Conventions.

[81] 20 November 1989: see UNHCHR website above n 80. 'Children younger than 16 are being held as "enemy combatants"...'. O Burkeman, 'Children held at Guantanamo Bay', *The Guardian*, 24 April 2003.

[82] Lawyers Committee for Human Rights 2002, 'A Year of Loss, Reexamining Civil Liberties since September 11', available at <http://www.lchr.org/pubs/descriptions/loss_report.pdf>; Lawyers Committee for Human Rights 2003, 'Imbalance of Powers: How Changes to US Law and Security Since 9/11 Erode Human Rights and Civil Liberties', available at <http://www.lchr.org/us_law/ loss/imbalance/powers.pdf.>.

[83] Eg, see *Boudellaa v Bosnia and Herzegovina and the Federation of Bosnia and Herzegovina* (2003) 13 *Butterworths Human Rights Cases* 297.

[84] See, however, R Morgan, *The Demon Lover On the Sexuality of Terrorism* (London, Mandarin, 1989).

[85] Eg, with respect to abortion rights, see R Cook and B Dickens, 'Human Rights Dynamics of Abortion Law Reform' (2003) 25 *Human Rights Quarterly* 1, 7.

[86] At the Second Preparatory Committee Meeting for the Fifth Asian and Pacific Population Conference, 29–31 October 2002, the Bush administration refused to reaffirm its commitment to the Cairo Programme of Action, stating that its position was not negotiable. At the Conference itself

One example of sidelined human rights issues is the position of women whose male relatives have been detained as suspected terrorists or unlawful combatants. This issue is generally ignored in discussions of the war on terror. For such women their relatives have effectively disappeared for an unspecified period of time, leaving them with an uncertain future, perhaps in a state that does not wish to be seen as offering succour to those accused of terrorist sympathies. Two cases in Canada illustrate this problem. First, the wife and mother of suspected Al-Qaeda operatives, Maha El Samnah, returned to Canada from Pakistan in April 2004 to obtain medical treatment for her 14 year old son. He had been severely wounded in a shoot-out with Pakistani troops during a raid in which his father, a suspected leader within Al-Qaeda, was killed. Another son had been detained as a terrorist and two sons were allegedly part of Osama bin Laden's training camps. The entire family was vilified when they returned to Canada. The Canadian government had been extremely reluctant to grant them travel documents despite their Canadian citizenship.[87] Second, Maher Arar, a Canadian citizen, was detained by authorities in the US and deported to Syria on suspicion of being connected to terrorists. After a year in detention and interrogation (including alleged torture) he returned to Canada, where a public inquiry into the role of Canadian security forces in his arrest and deportation is now under way. His wife, Monia Mazigh, fought for his release and for this public inquiry into his detention. She ran in the 2004 Canadian federal election on a platform supporting the protection of human rights for all Canadian citizens, including those suspected of terrorist affiliations.[88]

What feminist approaches to international law could be useful? One observation is that civilians are the primary targets of terrorist acts, including the destruction of the World Trade Center in New York. Whether directly involved in murdering or injuring people, or whether forcing people to live in a pervasive atmosphere of fear and increased state security, terrorists aim at creating chaos and fear. Terrorists do not distinguish between military and non-military targets —indeed their 'success' depends on ignoring this distinction to the maximum effect in disrupting ordinary people's lives and putting state security mechanisms on continual high alert. Responses to terrorism tend to increase this heightened sense of fear and violence through bombings, displacement of refugees, increases in reprisals, urban warfare and police or military actions against alleged 'terrorists'. Continual security alerts are signs of the success of terrorism, not its defeat. Women are frequently the direct and indirect victims of such attacks. The

---

(December 2002) the US proposals were rejected; 'Population Conference Rejects US Abortion and Condom Use Policies', AP 17 December 2002, available at <http://www.foxnews.com/story/0,2933,73259,00.html.>

[87] See 'Khadr Mother, Brother Arrive in Canada', CBC News, 9 April 2004, at <http://www.cbc.ca/stories/2004/04/09/canada/khadr_20040409>, last accessed 24 September 2004. See also C Freeze, 'Khadr Matriarch returning to Canada', *Toronto Globe and Mail*, 9 April 2004, at <http:// www.globeandmail.com/servlet/story/RTGAM.20040409.wkhadr0409/BNStory/Front/>, last accessed 24 September 2004.

[88] See <http://www.cbc.ca/news/background/arar/.>, last accessed 24 September 2004.

increased level of fear in societies has had a profound effect on the lives of women, men and children, whether they are working in potentially targeted markets or buildings, commuting on public transport, or generally trying to live their lives on a personal and community level.

A second observation is to emphasise that the increased attention on terrorism by international organisations, nation states and private individuals means that other kinds of violence and gender discrimination have been sidelined. Family violence or workplace harassment and discrimination are subsumed to what are seen as more pressing agendas. The structural and systemic causes of gender discrimination become entangled with the politics and legal debates over anti-terrorism.[89]

Where are the voices of women in the contemporary international debate over war and peace, human rights and freedom? The perspectives of women are usually found within the details of daily life hidden within war, political battles, and anti-terrorism activities. International law has typically prioritised this dominant vision within legal regimes governing the use of force, sovereignty, the state, international trade, even humanitarian law and human rights. For women the story of modern terrorism is complex. The perpetrators of public violence are almost always male and the war they instigate is gendered as masculine.[90] Part of the revulsion expressed over violations of human rights by American soldiers at the Abu Ghraib Prison in Baghdad stems from the sight of young American women apparently engaged in despicable acts of humiliation and inhumane treatment of Iraqi male prisoners.[91] The shock registered by commentators at the use of children and women, especially girls and young mothers, as suicide bombers in the Middle East and during the hostage-taking in a Moscow theatre in 2003, is an echo of this underlying sense that terrorism and war are, or should be, adult male occupations. The voices of women political leaders in this debate—Madeleine Albright, Condoleeza Rice, Hanan Ashrawi, Gloria Arroyo, Megawati Sukarnoputri, Clare Short—are few and far between. They have been co-opted by militaristic agendas, vilified or silenced.

A possible feminist response to international law in the war on terror is to refocus our attention onto specific issues women believe to be important. We need to pay more attention to the needs of women and men struggling with their own particular problems, the solutions to which might be applied to global frameworks and the reform of international law. This means rejecting the seduction of false alarms of terrorism and false sentimentality on the virtues or vices of warfare. It means reframing the debate over global security, human rights and international law from the ground up. This has the advantage of countering sometimes inflammatory rhetoric with the reality of human work, education,

---

[89] See S Wright, 'The Horizon of Becoming: Culture, Gender and History after September 11', above n 78; H Charlesworth and C Chinkin, 'Sex, Gender, and September 11', above n 78.

[90] S Wright, *International Human Rights, Decolonisation and Globalisation: Becoming Human* (London, Routledge, 2001), 76–83, 160–186.

[91] Photos can be seen by following the links at the CBS News website — <http://www.cbsnews.com/stories/2004/04/27/60II/main614063.shtml.>, last accessed 24 September 2004.

health, community and development on a smaller and more manageable level. In this more focused work there is the ability to recapture a sense of hope and energy.

Akitsiraq—the Place of Judgment and Learning

We end our reflections on feminism in international law with Shelley's most recent experiences. She has temporarily left the traditional academic world to work at the local level as the Northern Director of the Akitsiraq Law School. Just one week before the attacks on the World Trade Center and the Pentagon, a unique opportunity in indigenous self-determination through legal education opened up just south of the Arctic Circle in Iqaluit, Nunavut.[92] This is the Akitsiraq Law School— a four-year law degree program offering Inuit students an opportunity to obtain a Bachelor of Law degree while remaining in or near their home communities in the North. Of the original 15 entrants, 11 remained as of July 2004—10 women and one man. They range in age from their mid-20s to over 40 years. The oldest is a single mother with five children. Almost all the others have families. All are Inuit or have been raised as Inuit in Nunavut or (in the case of one student) Greenland. The students, once they have completed their studies, will have taken a full complement of law subjects similar to their southern counterparts in the rest of Canada. The University of Victoria based in British Columbia will grant the law degree. In addition to subjects such as Criminal Law, Torts, Contracts, Property Law and Constitutional Law, the Akitsiraq students also take courses specifically geared towards their Northern experience, whether through Advanced Criminal Law, a Workshop on the Nunavut Land Claims Agreement, Aboriginal Law or Inuit Traditional Law. This last course is offered by the Akitsiraq 'Elder-in-Residence', Mr Lucien Ukaliannuk, who also teaches compulsory courses in Inuktitut (the Inuit language). Inuit Traditional Law is itself taught in Inuktitut as a series of seminar credit courses towards their LLB degree.[93]

The need for tertiary professional education in the North had been recognised for at least 10 years prior to this. There are only a handful of Inuit law graduates, or university graduates more generally, partly because of the enormous distances, expense and cultural dislocation for Inuit in 'going South' to receive a higher education.[94] The only Inuk lawyer currently in Nunavut is the Premier of

[92] Nunavut is the newest territory in Canada, covering about 20% of Canada's land mass, adjacent sea and permanent ice shelf. It covers the Arctic Archipelago from Hudson's Bay north to the islands next to Greenland. The Law School is located at Nunavut Arctic College in Iqaluit, the capital of Nunavut, on Baffin Island. Nunavut has a population of just under 30,000, 85% of which is Inuit.

[93] The word *Inuit* means 'people' in Inuktitut, the language of the majority of people in Nunavut. Inuit live mostly north of the tree line throughout the Arctic region (Canada, Greenland, eastern Siberia and Alaska). *Inuk* is the singular form of Inuit meaning 'person'. There are no grammatical distinctions based on gender in Inuktitut.

[94] K Gallagher-Mackay, 'Affirmative Action and Aboriginal Government: The Case of Legal Education in Nunavut' (1999) 14 *Canadian Journal of Law and Society/Revue Canadienne Droit et Société* 21.

the Territory, Paul Okalik. He obtained his degree after much difficulty and sacrifice from the University of Ottawa. As one of the Akitsiraq students, Sandra Inutiq, commented soon after starting her law studies:

> The assimilation practices of the past are gone. This is going to set a precedent for other fields of study. Conservative lawyers would say, no, you can't have a law program outside a university. But we argued that we have a right to be educated, and we have these connections to our community and families. Finally, it's happening.[95]

The name 'Akitsiraq' comes from a sacred secret place near Cape Dorset on the southern end of Baffin Island, where the 'Inuit Great Council' decided the most difficult cases in accordance with traditional Inuit justice.[96] These meetings of traditional justice continued until as recently as 1924.[97] The word *akitsiraq* itself means in Inuktitut 'to strike out disharmony/wrongdoing; to render justice'.[98] The administration of justice in Inuit society was normally done on a much less formal basis through meetings of the whole community and/or by elders (both male and female) confronting the wrongdoer and the victim. 'Justice' had to include an admission of wrong by the person most responsible for the disruption or harm, followed by counselling and forgiveness (thus, the right to silence in modern criminal trials seems alien and dysfunctional to Inuit). Once this process was completed it was considered inappropriate to raise the matter again.[99] Repeat offenders would be dealt with more severely up to and including banishment or death, depending on the level of harm they were causing to the group and the unlikelihood of their changing their bad ways. The aim was not retribution, deterrence or even rehabilitation, but rather social harmony for the benefit of the group's survival.

Although there was significant separation in the roles that women and men played, there was no sex discrimination as we understand it in modern industrialised countries. This is a difficult concept for Western feminists to grasp, particularly when learning that arranged marriages (usually by parents when children were babies) and child marriages, polygamy, 'custom' adoption (sometimes forcible), some levels of violence and even rape not involving physical harm were accepted as part of Inuit culture before the introduction of Christianity and Western law (and still are to some extent).[100] But for both students and teachers

---

[95] As quoted in W Johnson, 'Condemned and Redeemed — the New World of Inuit Law' (1 September 2001) *Toronto Globe and Mail*, <http://www.globeandmail.com.>, last accessed 24 September 2004.

[96] S Wright, 'The Akitsiraq Law School: A Unique Approach to Indigenous Legal Education' (2002) 5.19 *Indigenous Law Bulletin* 14.

[97] N Hellendy (with Ipeelee, Manning, Saila and Saila), 'The Last Traditional Inuit Trial on Southwest Baffin Island in the Canadian Arctic', Background Paper No 2 for 'Places of Power and Objects of Veneration in the Canadian Arctic', World Archeological Congress III, Ottawa, 1994.

[98] 'Akitsiraqvik: The Naming of the Akitsiraq Law School' *Akitsiraq News* (Nunavut), Summer 2001, 9. See also T Grant, 'An Arctic Law School Tailored to Native Needs' (29 January 2002) *Christian Science Monitor*, <http://www.csmonitor.com/2002/0129/pl14s01-lehl.htm.>

[99] L Ukaliannuk, oral lecture given in Inuit Traditional Law, Fall Semester, 2004.

[100] See Aupilaarjuk, Tulimaaq, Joamie, Imaruttuq, and Nutaraaluk, as edited by Ossten, Laugrand and Rasing, *Interviewing Inuit Elders: Volume 2 — Perspectives on Traditional Law* (Nunavut Arctic College, Iqaluit, 1999).

at the Akitsiraq Law School, suspending existing preconceptions of what 'feminism' is, what 'Western' or *qallunat*[101] law is, and what Inuit knowledge or *Inuit Qaujimijatuqangit*[102] might be are essential.

The predominance of women in Akitsiraq has been frequently noted and is the source of much speculation. There were well over 100 applicants for the 15 original places offered in the Law School. A few of these were men. It seems that not many Inuit men have the necessary skills that were felt to be a prerequisite for admission into the program. Selection was based on a combination of educational experience and accomplishment (but did not require a tertiary degree, or even completion of high school in some cases), previous work experience, 'life' experience, a written entrance test and (for those short-listed) an oral interview. References were also required. Inuktitut language skills were tested, as the Law School from the beginning has insisted that all students take Inuktitut in order to achieve at least functional competence in the language before graduating. The majority of students are in fact already fluent. These students take 'Advanced Inuktitut', looking at legal terminology issues from both a traditional and a modern perspective, including translation between English and Inuktitut. Some students struggle with English as the dominant medium of instruction where Inuktitut is their first language. Women applicants to the program generally tended to have better linguistic skills, better education and more varied work experience, often coming from senior positions as teachers or public servants. Several gave up high-paying jobs to 'go back to school'.

There are a number of theories as to why Inuit women tend to do better both in educational and work experience.[103] Some of the students currently in the program speculate that women traditionally performed a wider variety of tasks than men, including sewing, childcare and providing food, light and warmth. Men's skills revolved around hunting. The principal sources of food, light, heat, shelter and survival generally in traditional Inuit society are meat (including seal, caribou, walrus, musk ox, polar bear, whale, ptarmigan, water fowl, fish, shellfish and birds' eggs), skins, fur, antler, bone, ivory and oil—with other material provided by women gathering berries, moss and other plant material during the summer and fall (July to October) which was, and still is, used as medicine, food, sod for insulation and cotton wicks for oil lamps. Survival meant that men traditionally hunted 'on the land' (which includes the sea ice and water), while women did

---

[101] The Inuktitut term for all foreigners or non-Inuit. It roughly translates as 'big eyebrows or big stomach'.

[102] A difficult term to pronounce or translate. It is usually shortened to 'IQ'. It means basically 'knowledge Inuit elders have always known'.

[103] G Massa, 'La femme inuite: hier, aujourd'hui et demain' (2004) 3 *Le Toit Du Monde: Actualiés Circumpolaires* 26. See also an examination of the phenomenon of girls raised as boys in traditional Inuit society in H Stewart, 'KIPIJUITUQ in Netsilik Society: Changing Patterns of Gender and Patterns of Changing Gender' in L Frink, R Shepard, and GA Reinhardt (eds), *Many Faces of Gender: Roles and Relationships Through Time in Indigenous Northern Communities* (Calgary, University of Calgary Press, 2002), 13. 'One of the Akitsiraq students from Clyde River on Baffin Island was raised as a boy until she was 8 or 9 years old.'

everything else. This greater diversity in traditional roles for women meant it was perhaps easier for them to adapt to modern education and paid employment. In addition, as Aaju Peter (one of the students and herself the mother of five children) has insisted, whatever else is going on women have to get up and feed their children. This creates a greater sense of responsibility on the part of women.

Men in Inuit society have had great difficulties adjusting to a life that no longer centres on their traditional role of hunting. The transition to modern life has been within the lifetime of most elders, ie since the beginning of the Cold War. Many can still remember what it was like to live in skin tents or *qammaaq* during the summer and fall, and snow houses or *igluvigait* in the winter heated by oil lamps called *qulliiq*. The only form of transport, aside from walking, was by dog sled or *qamutik*. Shamanism was an active religion practised by male and female *angakkuuq*, or shamans. Women carried their babies in the hoods of their parkas, or *amautiiq*, and the art of sewing skin and fur clothing was central to their role in ensuring the survival of the group. Since the influx of Christian missionaries, the Royal Canadian Mounted Police (RCMP) and Canadian government institutions, particularly after 1950, Inuit were increasingly encouraged to move off the land and into small settlements established along the coastline of the Arctic Archipelago from Hudson's Bay to Ellesmere Island. Many Inuit were forcibly transplanted from one area to another, resulting in massive hardship and, in many cases, starvation.[104] The RCMP regularly shot Inuit dogs essential to the men's role as hunters, destroying the principal mode of transportation during winter (eight to nine months of the year) before the advent of the snowmobile. The shooting of dogs is still remembered with great pain and bitterness in Nunavut.

The increase in government regulation and resettlement was and is directly related to Canadian concerns about sovereignty in the North—a matter that is still in dispute.[105] Incursions by American and Soviet submarines occurred well into the 1980s and perhaps beyond. Intense negotiations over the implementation of a Missile Defence Shield largely over the Arctic is now ongoing between Canada and the United States with Inuit people, through their local political leaders in Nunavut and other northern governments, demanding a 'seat at the table'. Denmark is currently disputing sovereignty over a small island between Ellesmere Island and Greenland.[106] Nunavut itself was created in 1999 as a means of recognising Canadian control and jurisdiction over the North, and also as a means of recognising the

---

[104] FJ Tester and P Kulchyski, *Tammarniit (Mistakes); Inuit Relocation in the Eastern Arctic 1939 to 1963* (Vancouver, University of British Columbia Press, 1994). See also the very moving film by a former student of (and current Inuit Cultural Facilitator to) the Law School, Elisapee Karetak — *Kikkik E1-472* (Inuit Broadcasting Corporation, 2003). For more information contact <http://www. info@inuitbroadcasting.ca.>, last accessed 24 September 2004.

[105] S Grant, *Arctic Justice: On Trial for Murder* (Montreal, McGill-Queen's University Press, 2002).

[106] See K Harper, 'Hans Island Rightfully belongs to Greenland, Denmark' (9 April 2004) *Nunatsiaq News,* at <http://www.nunatsiaq.com/opinionEditorial/opinions.html.>, last accessed 24 September 2004.

surrender of sovereignty by Inuit over their land (*Nunavut* means 'our land' in Inuktitut).[107] Inuit, however, still dispute the extent of this surrender and Canada's rights of sovereignty over the Arctic. A significant circumpolar movement of indigenous peoples, primarily through the Inuit Circumpolar Conference, maintains a strong presence at both international and regional fora.

Prior to 1950 the Inuit were mainly a nomadic people, moving over vast territories and distances in search of game. Their routes followed known trails, trapping lines, places known to have good fishing or good berries, or where caribou, seal, walrus or even whales congregated at particular times of the year. There were rules carefully governing the relationship between different groups. Although violence of course occurred within and among Inuit communities, inter-group warfare seems to have been rare (although Inuit and other indigenous groups such as Cree, Dene or other 'Indians' were often in dispute over territory and game).[108] The drive to push Inuit into coastal hamlets meant the creation of national governmental control over a newly 'settled' population. Throughout much of the twentieth century all Inuit were issued little round 'dogtags' by the Canadian government with numbers on them (such as E1-472, the number of a former Akitsiraq student Elisapee Karetak's mother Kikkik—Elisapee Karetak herself has an old tag with her number on it). These tags and numbers were used to keep records, including police and social welfare records, until the 1970s, when Inuit had mostly adopted Christian first names and were recorded as part of the Canadian census. Families were forced into the wage economy or into the social welfare system. Their children were put into white-run schools, frequently mission schools or residential schools on the coast of Hudson's Bay or down south. The primary purpose of this activity was to affirm Canadian sovereignty over the Arctic by surveying and patrolling defined territorial boundaries (that would have been impossible without Inuit guides and maps), and by establishing settled communities with 'permanent' populations susceptible to governmental control, primarily through the RCMP.[109] Canada's assertion of sovereignty against other Arctic claimants (primarily Denmark, Norway, the US and Russia) still depends on this relocation and governance of Inuit.

But this movement of Inuit into coastal settlements also resulted in massive dislocation, including famine, with continuing severe social, medical and cultural problems. Nunavut has very high rates of mental illness, health problems (such as chronic respiratory infections in children), alcoholism and other substance abuse, child neglect and child abuse (often committed in local white-run schools

---

[107] Nunavut Land Claims Agreement between the Inuit and the Government of Canada (May 1993), Article 2.7.

[108] See H Brody, *The Other Side of Eden: Hunters, Farmers and the Shaping of the World* (Vancouver, Douglas & McIntyre, 2000).

[109] Convention on the Rights and Duties of States or 'Montevideo Convention' (26 December 1933) defines the criteria for statehood in Article 1 as 'a person of international law [possessing] the following qualifications: (a) a permanent population; (b) a defined territory; (c) government; and (d) capacity to enter into relations with other states.'

or residential schools in the South and carried on through second and third generations by formerly abused parents), domestic violence and suicide (estimated at around eight times the national average).[110] Inuit men are disproportionately represented in Canadian prisons—another possible reason for the difficulties they have moving into higher education or professional jobs. Since Shelley's arrival in January 2003, she has been struck by the numbers of deaths all over Nunavut through suicide, accidents, murders, and premature deaths through illness and lack of adequate medical treatment. Almost every death has been of an individual who is known and loved by someone connected to Akitsiraq. Nunavut is a very small community spread over a vast territory. No loss or death ever occurs without causing deep grief and mourning to the whole territory. Women meanwhile have continued trying to hold together their fractured communities and families in the face of massive displacement and ongoing problems.

The students in the Akitsiraq Law School Program bring this history with them into the classroom.[111] While studying law they have continued to shoulder responsibilities for childcare (almost all are mothers, several are single mothers) and responsibilities to extended families. Some have faced severe domestic violence and marital breakdown as a result of the pressures of law school impacting on their private lives, often as a result of longstanding issues of abuse and disadvantage. The cultural dislocation of learning a difficult professional discipline in (for many) a foreign language has compounded the level of stress. Euro-Canadian law itself contributed extensively to the colonisation and dislocation of Inuit in the North, something the students are very well aware of and frequently point out to their instructors. The interplay of Canadian law and international law around the issue of sovereignty has not been adequately examined from the point of view of women's and human rights. But, as Susan Enuaraq (another of our students) has said when asked how she deals with these issues: 'I choose not to be a victim.'

Reflecting the strength and adaptability of Inuit women from a traditional background, these students continue to work and learn, including winning prizes and scholarships, judicial clerkships (one, Madeleine Redfern, has accepted a clerkship with the Supreme Court of Canada starting September 2005) and offers to attend prestigious conferences both in Canada and overseas. Their influence on the development of Canadian law is already becoming apparent. On a recent trip to Ottawa they met with Justice Louise Arbour, then of the Canadian Supreme Court (more recently the UN High Commissioner for Human Rights), and asked why Aboriginal judges were not on the Court and why there were no northern

---

[110] Between April 1999, when Nunavut became a territory, and October 2003 there were more than 115 suicides in Nunavut, mostly of young men. This is out of a population of less than 30,000. See J Caines, 'Vivre! Interventions pour la prévention du suicide au Nunavut' (2004) 3 *Le Toit Du Monde: Actualités Circumpolaires* 33.

[111] See in particular the wonderful and challenging work by N Wachowich, in collaboration with Apphia A K Katsak, and S P Katsak, *Saqijuq: Stories from the Lives of Three Inuit Women* (Montreal McGill-Queen's University Press, and Kingston, 1999). The youngest of the three collaborators, Sandra, is now married with two children and living in Iqaluit, where she is enrolled in the Akitsiraq Law School as Sandra Omik.

judges. In May 2004 the class met with Mr Rodolfo Stavenhagen, the UN Special Rapporteur on the Human Rights of Indigenous Peoples, in Iqaluit. He got a succinct description of the problems of education policies in the North and the lack of good instruction for Inuit children in Inuktitut, as well as other concerns. In a meeting with the federal Minister of Justice in Ottawa students raised Aboriginal and northern representation on the Supreme Court and other issues. The Minister is on record as being 'inspired' by Akitsiraq actively to consider an Aboriginal for one of the two current vacancies on the Court.[112]

The teaching of skills to Inuit women is part of the larger project of indigenous self-determination in the circumpolar region. The lessons learned in Nunavut and the Akitsiraq Law School can serve as models for indigenous development elsewhere. The Law School has had to rethink traditional ideas of legal education not only to accommodate a different culture, but also to support the needs of female students with childcare and other 'women's' responsibilities. In practical terms this means limiting classroom hours to children's school hours, assisting with day care and babysitting, providing substantial income-support through sponsorship and bursaries, engaging in intensive one-on-one counselling as well as group 'healing' and conflict resolution, providing emergency support, being sensitive to cultural and psychological issues around domestic violence and marital problems, and ensuring that children and spouses are included in Law School activities.

But the learning is anything but one-sided. The southern instructors and non-Inuit administrative staff have also gained an amazing experience in the value of Inuit culture and the perspectives of Inuit women. Although many of the problems appear to be issues of victimhood, in fact what is being learned on all sides is the meaning of 'grassroots' problem-solving for everyone. The Law School does not have precedents to draw on—this is both a source of intense anxiety (at times) but also gives a wonderful opportunity for creativity. Many of the students have been actively involved in the establishment of the Law School and in their own education through serving on the Akitsiraq Law School Society Board of Directors both before and after the students actually started classes, representing student issues in the community, helping to develop workshops and classes on issues of specific interest to Inuit, and even drafting course outlines and reading materials for Inuit Traditional Law (in both Inuktitut and English). There are four permanent staff members in the North—the Northern Director (Shelley), a Program Administrator (Symatuk Itorcheak, an Inuk woman who is a former student in the Program), Mr Ukaliannuk (the Elder-in-Residence) and an Inuit Cultural Facilitator (Elisapee Karetak). The Akitsiraq Law School is in fact a pioneering experiment in indigenous legal education, especially for women, as well as offering (arguably) the best legal education available in Canada. The women and one man who are on their way to graduation will be future leaders in Nunavut, in Canada and internationally. The preponderance of women is itself

---

[112] C Schmitz, 'Consider Aboriginal Judge for Top Court: Cotler', *Ottawa Citizen* (24 January 2004), A3.

rewriting the rules on legal education and law reform both in the Arctic region and internationally.

How does the story of Akitsiraq form part of a feminist account of international law? International law is not only about the Great Events of war, terrorism, international trade and diplomacy, but also about the details of everyday life. The Akitsiraq Law School is training a small contingent of women—and one man— whose influence is being felt not only in Nunavut, but also in Canada and throughout the circumpolar region. It is about how war and terrorism may be the real side issue, although a bitterly painful and destructive one. Even in the heat of security alerts and fear of terrorism, women are working all over the world to change the world they live in.

Training indigenous lawyers, especially women, means that international law is no longer impermeable to the power of those traditionally seen as on the margins (and in the Arctic, literally on the margins!) of world events. Canada's presence in the Arctic depends on Inuit cooperation, as is acknowledged in the Nunavut Land Claims Agreement out of which Nunavut was created. Canadian sovereignty in the Arctic is also historically an outgrowth of the need for surveillance and defence against nuclear attack represented by the 'DEWline' (Distant Early Warning) system built by the American and Canadian military in the early 1950s (how interesting that use of the word 'distant'). Iqaluit is the capital of Nunavut partly because, as Frobisher Bay, it was the principal air base for northern operations in the Eastern Arctic during the Cold War. The debate over 'star wars' defence continues to bring the Arctic, Nunavut and its people into the centre of geopolitical concerns and international law. The story of Nunavut is a curious mixture of Cold War politics, post-Cold War security concerns, Arctic sovereignty, indigenous self-determination, human rights and the stubborn exercise of those rights within a legal framework (buttressed by international legal recognition). Akitsiraq represents the possible 'indigenising' and feminisation of law and power in the Canadian Arctic by training women who can insist, in the language of the most powerful as well as in their own language, that their concerns are not marginal.[113] Nunavut itself is a creation of Inuit, Canadian and international law structuring sovereignty and self-determination in the Arctic. The creation of the Akitsiraq Law School shows that this structure of sovereignty and rights must be about *Inuit* agendas, and that these agendas must be responsive to the demands of women and their needs.

Conclusion

Our work on feminism in international law has been concerned with questions about the location of women in its structures and investigating the role that

---

[113] See LT Smith, *Decolonizing Methodologies: Research and Indigenous Peoples* (London, Zed Books, 1999) for a description of 'indigenising' education from a Maori perspective.

gender plays in its formation. Because of the significant scholarly literature in this area over the last 15 years, some feminist ideas have now been absorbed into the rhetoric of international law and its institutions. In many areas, however, progress has been limited. Feminist issues have been either corralled in the margins, or rendered so bland that they have no transformative bite. The use of feminist ideas in international law moreover is beset by tensions and contradictions. Some questions include: Do we respond to the marginalising of international law in the twenty-first century by mobilising and insisting on its application to all global activities and to all nations and peoples? Is a focus on double standards of powerful countries with respect to international law useful? Of what value is a challenge to the neo-liberal basis of international law? How do we conceptualise the critical project in international law by exposing its gendered (and other) biases and hierarchies, while nevertheless seeking its widest possible application and enforcement?

The acceptance of international law by centres of power at the beginning of the twenty-first century is ambivalent. Challenging this law with feminist questions may contribute to this fragility. Martti Koskenniemi has criticised the feminist project of reconceiving international law for this reason. 'We can reconceive international law every now and then, but not all the time' he has argued.

> Our immediate fears and hopes do not necessarily match to produce the good society … At some point, we need distance from those fears and hopes—if not objective distance, then at least a partial, consensual, formal distance. That the law makes this distance possible (if always only for a moment) is not a defect of law, but its most immediate benefit.[114]

Our argument is, however, that international law does not provide even a momentary distance from subjectivity. It is intertwined with a sexed and gendered subjectivity, and reinforces a system of male power. Until international law focuses on *all* people and peoples, not just the powerful few, it will always be subject to geopolitical agendas inimical to genuine security—such as security in food, fresh water, a clean and stable environment, economic development that is sustainable, trade that is fair, and adequate safeguards protecting the rights of migrants, prisoners-of-war, children, as well as vulnerable women and men. Smaller non-state entities, such as Nunavut, may provide a model for self-determination and nation-building much more promising than what is currently going on in Iraq.

Conventions, declarations, standard-setting, UN resolutions, challenges before international courts and tribunals are not enough to protect and enhance the international standing and rights of women. But they are important as a framework for both theorising difference and putting that difference into practice in a way that empowers women, men and children. The Women's International

---

[114] M Koskenniemi, Book review of D Dallmeyer (ed), *Reconceiving Reality: Women and International Law* (above n 4) (1995) 89 *American Journal of International Law* 227, 230.

Tribunal on Japanese Military Sexual Slavery is an example of voicing the failure of law to recognise and compensate women who have been subjected to gross violations of their human rights. Woman have highlighted the barriers within international law to the protection of women's rights to fair work practices and sustainable development. The fact that one woman, Monia Mazigh, could use her experiences as the wife of a man wrongfully deported for alleged terrorist connections to launch a political career suggests that the outcomes of the war on terror may not be utterly negative for women. The Akitsiraq Law School is another story of empowerment of women who come from one of the most oppressed and marginalised groups in the world—a status shared by Inuit and indigenous peoples globally. Feminist explorations in international law require critique, theorising, law reform, legal challenges, advocacy, education and grass-roots work. Above all, they depend on hope and activism. As Sheila Watt-Cloutier, President of the Inuit Circumpolar Conference, has said:

> Even the UN recognises the Arctic as the barometer for global climate change. We Inuit are the mercury in that barometer. We have survived for thousands of years without destroying any animals or our environment. By protecting *our* way of life, we are saving the world.[115]

---

[115] This is a close paraphrase of part of a speech made by Ms Watt-Cloutier at a gathering hosted by the Walter and Duncan Gordon Foundation for political, legal, educational and financial leaders in Iqaluit, Nunavut (14 June 2004).

3

International Human Rights and Feminisms: When Discourses Keep Meeting

KAREN ENGLE*

Introduction

In 1992, I analysed what seemed to be an emerging literature of feminist critiques of international human rights law.[1] I began the project in 1989, at which point I had searched law reviews, books, and some non-legal literature, and discovered about a dozen sizeable academic pieces attempting to theorise 'women's human rights'. Nearly all had been written in the 1980s. In those days, women's rights advocates largely saw themselves as engaged in a common mission to include women's rights within the protection of international human rights norms. The aim of my project was in part to uncover the different assumptions about both gender and human rights that underpinned these various projects, and to suggest some underlying tensions between the various approaches.

This essay revisits that project, with a focus on the literature that has emerged since 1992. Three developments have occurred in the past decade that I would never have predicted. First, articles theorising gender and human rights have proliferated at such an astonishing rate that even the thought of counting them in any accurate way would seem to be a pointless, and likely impossible, task.[2] Second,

* WH Francis, Jr Professor in Law, University of Texas. This piece was originally presented as a lecture at a conference on 'Structural Bias' organised by the European Law Research Center at Harvard Law School. It has since benefited from the feedback of many people and groups. I am particularly grateful to Antony Anghie, Doris Buss, David Kennedy, Duncan Kennedy, Ranjana Khanna, Karen Knop, Mitchel Lasser, Ambreena Manji, Gretchen Ritter and Mary Westby, as well as to audiences at the law schools at the University of Cincinnati, Columbia, Duke and the University of Pittsburgh, and at the Van Leer Institute in Jerusalem for their thoughtful comments on early drafts. I am also appreciative of the research assistance of Chad Derum and Benjamin Putnam.

[1] K Engle, 'International Human Rights and Feminism: Where Discourses Meet' (1992) 13 *Michigan Journal of International Law* 517.

[2] The explosion has not been limited to theoretical or academic literature. Karen Knop points out that Rebecca Cook's working bibliography on women's human rights grew from 142 publications, 10 cases, and a list of 15 sources of information in 1989 to a website that, in 2003, included 700 articles, over 766

gender has become mainstreamed; references to women are commonly found in many articles on human rights, and gender issues have become increasingly institutionalised within international organisations. Third, accounts of structural bias based on gender—which dominated the scene in the late 1980s—have largely disappeared in critical discussions of human rights law. These three developments stand in paradoxical relationship to one another. How could discussion of gender be ubiquitous, on one hand, and structural accounts of gender bias have disappeared on the other?

This essay attempts to study this paradox by mapping the history of feminist critiques of human rights law that have emerged over the past 15 years. Taking full advantage of hindsight, I set forth a narrative of the rise and fall of the feminist critique of structural bias in international law. Part of the explanation for this fall, and resulting paradox, I argue, lies with the emergence and development of what I label third world feminist approaches to human rights. Third world feminist approaches to international human rights law study both the mainstream international human rights regime and its feminist critics, often pointing to their failure to address the needs of third world women. The form of their approach that is crucial to my narrative attacks structural bias feminism for its near-exclusive focus on the male/female divide which, they argue, obscures economic, social and cultural differences between first and third world women.

In mapping this history, I identify and describe three stages in the development of feminist critiques of human rights law—liberal inclusion, structural bias and third world. These stages overlap, of course, and elements of each can be found in the others. I do not mean to suggest that these stages represent a developmental progression in the sense of becoming more mature or politically astute over time. Rather, I hope to emphasise the changing nature of the approaches toward women and human rights over the years, in which subsequent stages have tended to react to the ones that preceded them.

In exploring these stages, I focus primarily on legal scholarship and exclusively on scholarship that is available in English. Thus, I do not claim a complete analysis of 'global feminist' activism. That story begins long before 1985, going back at least to the World Conference on Women in 1975 in Mexico and likely much earlier.[3] Activism and legal scholarship often overlap in the literature I explore, however, and I would contend that the stages I identify here are not unique to legal scholarship. The legal literature also overlaps with, is influenced by and in some cases precedes a great deal of literature among non-legal feminists. To the extent that non-legal feminists address human rights law specifically,

---

legal documents and 346 website links. K Knop, 'Introduction' in K Knop (ed), *Gender and Human Rights* (New York, Oxford University Press, 2004) at 1 (citing R Cook, 'The International Right to Nondiscrimination on the Basis of Sex: A Bibliography' (1989) 14 *Yale Journal of International Law* 161; women's rights resources, at (http://www.law-lib.utoronto.ca/diana/index.htm.) last accessed 17 Sept 04.

[3] See, for example, D Otto (this volume) on the influence of women's activism on the drafting of the Universal Declaration of Human Rights, and K Knop, on the impact of feminist activism on self-determination in the post-WWI period: 'Of the Male Persuasion: The Power of Liberal Internationalism for Women' (1999) *Proceedings of the American Society of International Law* 177.

I sometimes discuss their work. But I do not in any way claim to do justice to the influence that feminist and postcolonial theorists have had on the legal literature in general.

I have divided the past two decades into three crude time periods. The period 1985–90 was one of liberal inclusion. The task of feminist scholarship in international law during this period was to add women to human rights protections guaranteed under international law. The second period, 1987–95, was primarily filled with critiques of human rights law that argued that it was structurally biased against women. Implicit in these analyses was a critique of liberal feminism because, for structural bias critics, simple inclusion of women into human rights law was impossible. Rather, they saw international law and institutions as structured to permit, even require, women's subordination. Third world feminist approaches make up the third period, which began around 1992 and has dominated since 1995. These critiques often implicitly or explicitly critique the failure of the previous stages for their exclusion or false representation of third world women. The work during this third period corresponds roughly with the rise of 'TWAIL', or 'Third World Approaches to International Law'.[4] Although I refer to the work of individual scholars throughout this essay and often identify individuals with particular positions, the stages refer to the approaches taken toward women's human rights rather than to scholars themselves. Indeed, many scholars have done work in more than one of the stages, and some even offer more than one approach within a single piece.

Before telling the story of feminist critiques of international human rights, I want to move ahead to the end of my tale. Looking back at these stages, how has each one fared? In many ways, it would seem that liberal inclusion has succeeded. There are increasing numbers of women involved in both the academic and practical pursuits of international human rights law, and women's rights have become a part of the mainstream human rights and humanitarian law agenda.[5] Structural bias critiques, on the other hand, are relatively scarce and their impact is less obvious. They succeeded in bringing many issues into public awareness—such as trafficking, female genital mutilation and war-time rape—and organised the discussions about gender around these issues. Indeed, the success of structural bias feminism in defining the women's rights agenda for some time also at some level engendered its demise. Structural bias feminists largely seemed unwilling or unable to respond to the attacks by other feminists, particularly by third world feminists, who argued that the male/female divide might not be the best means by

---

[4] I use the term 'third world' advisedly. For an explication of TWAIL, see A Anghie and BS Chimni, 'Third World Approaches to International Law and Individual Responsibility in Internal Conflict' in S Ratner and A Slaughter (eds), *The Methods of International Law* (Washington, DC, American Society of International Law, 2004). For one recent collection of such works, see A Anghie et al (eds), *The Third World and International Order: Law, Politics and Globalization* (Leiden, M Nijhoff, 2003).

[5] For a detailed critical discussion of the extent to which women's rights have been integrated into, or mainstreamed by, international institutions, see S Kouvo, *Making Just Rights? Mainstreaming Women's Human Rights and a Gender Perspective* (Uppsala, Iustus, 2004), at 200–98.

which to understand international law, and that women's bodies might not constitute the locus of women's oppression. Third world feminist critiques have succeeded in challenging strategies that exclusively focus on gender bias, primarily through asserting arguments about cultural difference. The critiques, however, seem to have become trapped in the age-old debate about the universal and the particular debate that was revived by an attention to culture. In the end, (former) structural bias critics and third world feminist critics seemed to have reached a compromise, and have championed a new slogan—culturally sensitive universalism. I will argue that this compromise fails to attend to the most radical potential of third world feminist critiques, which is their refusal to separate the cultural from the economic. Taken seriously, such critiques require attention to the gendered and cultural dimensions of the global distribution of wealth, and to the economic dimensions of politics and policies about gender and culture.

While much of this essay is about the extent to which structural bias feminism has been undermined, there is one area in which it has retained its success—in the overt inclusion of rape and other sexual violence against women in international criminal law. Although some of the work I discuss below addresses the issue of rape as a violation of international criminal law, I do not explore in depth the relatively large body of literature that has developed in this area. The reports of rapes in Bosnia in the early 1990s, in particular, captivated the attention of feminists in the United States and Europe.[6] When the United Nations established the International Criminal Tribunals for Rwanda and for the former Yugoslavia, feminists of all stripes successfully lobbied for rules of evidence and prosecutions that would ensure individual responsibility for sexual violence against women as crimes of war, crimes against humanity and, at least in the case of Rwanda, genocide.[7]

In many ways, this success could be attributed to structural bias feminism, as the rules of evidence and some of the jurisprudence about consent rely upon a strong understanding of male over female domination that would make a consent defence meaningless.[8] At the same time, questions about the relationship between nationalism and feminism split structural bias feminists early on over the question of whether rape should be treated as genocide.[9] This body of literature

---

[6] For an early collection of articles about rape in Bosnia, see A Stiglmayer (ed), *Mass Rape: The War Against Women in Bosnia-Herzegovina* (Lincoln, University of Nebraska, 1994).

[7] See KD Askin, *War Crimes Against Women: Prosecution in International War Crimes Tribunals* (The Hague, Kluwer, 1997); PV Sellers, 'Individual(s') Liability for Collective Sexual Violence' in *Gender and Human Rights*, above n 2, at 153.

[8] For a discussion of the development of the rule of evidence regarding consent, see PV Sellers, above n 7, at 159–60.

[9] Some feminists distinguished the rapes from 'everyday rape', arguing that the rapes were a tool for the systematic extermination of Bosnian Muslims. They were not simply rapes; they were a means by which genocide was being committed. Catharine MacKinnon, for example, seemed to turn from her long-held approach to rape that made difficult even a distinction between everyday heterosexual sex and rape to one that saw the rape of Bosnian Muslim women as special. At one point, she argued, '[t]hese rapes are to everyday rape what the Holocaust was to everyday anti-Semitism'. C MacKinnon, 'Rape, Genocide, and Women's Human Rights' in *Mass Rape*, above n 6, at 186–7. Others questioned

is thus clearly connected to the themes and debates explored in this chapter.[10] For reasons of length, however, I have chosen to set aside the topic of rape and humanitarian law.

The following discussion is just one of many narratives that could be told of the history of women's human rights discourse and the challenges that have been aimed at the reliance of structural bias feminism on a male/female dichotomy. It does not, for example, account for the pro-sex or queer critiques that have surfaced in law and feminist theory, if not so much in discussions of women's human rights. These critiques have influenced my approach to the treatment of rape as a war crime, but they can also be found in discussions about prostitution and trafficking. They have not, I believe, been as successful as third world feminist critiques at altering the terms of the discourse, in part because they tend to challenge feminist positions that are often, if uneasily, aligned with projects of the Christian right.[11]

Liberal Inclusion: 1985–1990

During this era, liberal inclusionists argued that women should *and could* be included in international human rights and humanitarian law. Women were as much subjects of international law as were men and thus, if properly applied, international legal doctrine could assimilate women's concerns.

the focus on genocide, pointing out that, unfortunately, the rape of women in war time, even in such large numbers, was nothing new. Rhonda Copelon, for example, argued that 'to emphasize as unparalleled [which many had done] the horror of genocidal rape is factually dubious and risks rendering rape invisible once again'. R Copelon, 'Resurfacing Gender: Reconceptualizing Crimes Against Women in Time of War' in *Mass Rape*, above n 6, at 198.

[10] Much of this debate occurred among structural bias feminists, and I have seen little third world feminist critique of the work, even though nationalism and assumptions about Islam played such a dominant role in the debate. Curiously, debates about whether rape was genocidal tended to focus on Bosnia, not on Rwanda, where rape was found to be a part of genocide. See *Prosecutor v Jean-Paul Akayesu*, Case No ICTR–96–4–T (International Criminal Tribunal for Rwanda, 1998). I am currently engaged in a separate analysis of the debate, tracing it from 1993 through the jurisprudence of the International Criminal Tribunal for the former Yugoslavia. My preliminary conclusion is that the success of structural bias, or radical feminism, has—if unwittingly—denied women sexual and political agency and, paradoxically, turned them into the same 'women and children' who were always subjects of war-time protection. Moreover, it has perpetuated an essentialised understanding of ethnic identity.

[11] For a discussion of the influence that the Christian Right has had on Bush administration support of international initiatives opposing sex trafficking among other issues, see E Bumiller, 'Evangelicals Sway White House On Human Rights Issues Abroad' (Oct 26, 2003) *New York Times*, at A1. Doris Buss has written about the international power of the Christian Right on issues that are far from aligned with radical feminism. See D Buss, 'Gods, Guns, and Globalization: Religious Radicalism and International Political Economy' (2004) 13 *The International Political Economy Yearbook*; D Buss, 'Finding the Homosexual in Women's Rights: The Christian Right in International Politics' (2004) *International Feminist Journal of Politics* 259.

Much of the scholarship during this era argued for doctrinal inclusion and institutional expansion.[12] Liberal inclusionists argued that women were, in principle, protected from rape in armed conflict by humanitarian law of war, protected from domestic violence and clitoridectomy by international human rights law, and guaranteed economic and social rights such as the right to health. For each of these proponents of inclusion, the necessary international legal doctrine existed to assimilate women into existing international human rights law and insitutions. If the doctrine was not being used to protect women's rights, it was due to a lack of enforcement, not a lack of law.

Some liberal inclusionists focused on enforcement. Much work was spent analysing international institutions to see why mainstream institutions failed to address women's issues. While some argued that increasing the number of women in these organisations might lead to greater attention to women's needs, others aimed to have the institutions recognise that, because international legal doctrine covered women, the mandates of the institutions must follow suit. The institutions, then, should address women's issues, and, it was thought, they could do so without major structural change. The right people or right attention within the institutions would necessarily lead to consideration of the human rights concerns of women.

Structural Bias Critique: 1987–1995

For structural bias critics, simple inclusion of women into international law was impossible. International law was seen as male and therefore structurally biased against women. Implicit in the structural bias approach, then, was a critique of liberal inclusion. The structure of international law prevented women's assimilation; the regime must be changed to accommodate women.

Structural bias feminists addressed many of the same issues as liberal inclusion feminists. They too were concerned about the laws of war, domestic violence and clitoridectomy. To the extent that international legal doctrine offered protection to women in these areas, it did so for the wrong reasons or with the wrong emphasis. Hilary Charlesworth argued, for example, that even though rape during armed conflict clearly violated international law, international law was concerned about women's honour (and therefore about the men who were harmed by the attack on this honour) or about genocide, not about women—*qua women*—as subjects of international law.[13] Most structural bias critics agreed with liberal inclusionists that international legal institutions failed to address women's

---

[12] It would include the work of those I identifed as doctrinalists and institutionalists in 1992. See K Engle, above n 1, at 521.

[13] H Charlesworth, 'Feminist Methods in International Law' (1999) 93 *American Journal of International Law* 379, 386–87.

issues. For structural bias critics, however, some major reordering of international legal doctrine and institutions would be required to accommodate women. As Dorothy Thomas put it: 'The fundamental challenge for the movement for women's human rights is that it not become a reformist project; its recipe should not read, "Add women and stir," but "Add women and alter."'[14]

This critique dominated feminist discourse on international law from the late 1980s to the mid-1990s, but some examples had already emerged by the early 1980s. The early pieces primarily criticised human rights doctrine and the structure of international human rights institutions for being inattentive to women's issues. The most systematic example of the structural bias critique of international law in general, not just of human rights, is the 1991 article by Hilary Charlesworth, Christine Chinkin and Shelly Wright, which was the first feminist piece published in the *American Journal of International Law*.[15]

Structural bias critics identified a series of dichotomies in public international law that perpetuated the inability of international human rights law to attend to women. The most commonly discussed dichotomy was the public/private distinction. For some critics, the distinction actually existed; international law only applied to the public sphere. Torture, for example, might well lie outside international law to the extent that it involved private individuals. And while state *action* might bring torture within the scope of human rights law, state *inaction* with regard to violence against women was likely to leave women outside international law's scope. Thus, a radical reordering of the international legal order was called for. In particular, human rights law needed to apply to non-state actors.

Other critics of the public/private distinction tended not to see that distinction as embedded in the doctrine of international law. Rather, the public/private distinction was more a problem of ideology than of doctrine. These critics argued that the public/private distinction was broken down in international law all the time (the prohibition on slavery was commonly given as an example of international law's intervention in the private realm), but not when doing so would offer protection to women. The bias was considered structural, but not as intransigent as the first view suggested.[16]

Regardless how they viewed it, that structural bias critics centered much of their analyses around the public/private distinction forms an important part of my narrative of the rise and fall of structural bias feminist critiques of international law. By focusing on women's 'private' lives, structural bias feminists treated the

---

[14] DQ Thomas, 'Conclusion' in J Peters and A Wolper (eds), *Women's Rights, Human Rights* (New York, Routledge, 1995), at 358.

[15] H Charlesworth, C Chinkin, and S Wright, 'Feminist Approaches to International Law' (1991) 85 *American Journal of International Law* 613.

[16] For a detailed analysis of public/private discussions in the early 1990s, see K Engle, 'After the Collapse of the Public/Private Distinction: Strategizing Women's Rights' in DG Dallmeyer (ed), *Reconceiving Reality: Women and International Law* (Washington DC, American Society of International Law, 1993), at 143. See also D Sullivan, 'The Public/Private Distinction in International Human Rights Law' in *Women's Rights, Human Rights*, above n 14, at 126.

private as the locus of women's oppression. Women were more directly oppressed by their families than by their governments, although governmental inaction facilitated the perpetuation of that oppression. Thus, culture was seen as responsible for the bulk of women's problems. It is therefore not surprising that structural bias feminists tended to focus on female genital mutilation, domestic violence, and even food taboos that kept women undernourished.[17]

The public/private distinction might be the most discussed example of structural gender bias in international law, but the literature is filled with a number of others. International law's priority of the state over civil society[18] and of civil and political rights over economic and social rights,[19] for example, were also seen both to represent and constitute structural bias against women.[20]

Elephants in the Room: 1980–1995

For liberal inclusionists and structural bias critics, two questions loomed large. They created constant, if mostly unrecognised, challenges to both critiques. First, what is feminist about women's human rights advocacy? And second, how would the advocates' arguments be read by women in other cultures, particularly those for whose benefit such work is ostensibly undertaken?

The Feminist Question

If rarely specifically articulated, the question whether the analysis of either the liberal inclusion or structural bias critics is unique to issues of gender plagues and affects much of the critiques offered by both approaches. Liberal inclusionists and structural bias critics have responded to the 'feminist question' in different ways.

---

[17] For but a few examples, see C Bunch, 'Transforming Human Rights from a Feminist Perspective' in *Women's Rights, Human Rights*, above n 14, at 11 (discussing widespread violence against women); J Mertus, 'State Discriminatory Family Law and Customary Abuses' in *Women's Rights, Human Rights*, above n 14, at 135, 137, 140 (discussing the role of global family law in perpetuating domestic abuse); N Toubia, 'Female Genital Mutilation' in *Women's Rights, Human Rights*, above n 14, at 224 (discussing causes and effects of female genital mutilation); R Cook, 'International Human Rights and Women's Reproductive Health' in *Women's Rights, Human Rights*, above n 14, at 256, 260 (same); CM Cerna and JC Wallace, 'Women and Culture' in KD Askin and DM Koenig (eds), *Women and International Human Rights Law I* (Ardsley N Y, Transnational Publishers, 1999) at 623, 633 (discussing food taboos that result in malnutrition of women and girls).

[18] See, eg, K Knop, 'Re/Statements: Feminism and State Sovereignty in International Law' (1993) 3 *Transnational Law and Contemporary Problems* 293.

[19] See, eg, B Stark, 'The "Other" Half of the International Bill of Rights' in *Reconceiving Reality*, above n 16 at 19; Sullivan, above n 16, at 126–27.

[20] Hilary Charlesworth offers an even more extensive list of dichotomies: 'objective/subjective, legal/political, logic/emotion, order/anarchy, mind/body, culture/nature, action/passivity, public/private, protector/protected, independence/dependence'. H Charlesworth, above n 13, at 382.

The liberal inclusionist focus on women seems to define the analysis as feminist, although some liberal inclusionists might not even embrace that term. They are essentially liberal feminists. They do not focus much on the ways women are excluded from human rights, precisely because they want to bring women into the mainstream without any substantial modification. Indeed, liberal inclusionists argue that women *are* already included, even if their presence is sometimes overlooked by attendant institutions.

There is more at stake in the feminist title, however, for the structural bias critics. Their critiques center around an understanding of international law as male or as reflecting male bias. Thus, its 'maleness' must distinguish it from other biases that have been identified and challenged in international law.

Hilary Charlesworth has acknowledged the importance of the feminist question when considering how her feminist analysis differs from other international legal theory methods. Acknowledging that methods 'from positivism to critical legal studies' might usefully be drawn upon by feminists,[21] she insists that her method is distinct:

> [U]nlike these other methods, my account of feminism asserts the importance of gender as an issue in international law: it argues that ideas about 'femininity' and 'masculinity' are incorporated into international legal rules and structures, silencing women's voices and reinforcing the globally observed domination of women by men.[22]

In their early piece, Charlesworth, Chinkin and Wright specifically consider the relationship between feminist and third world approaches to international law. Although they contend that there are many analogies between the two approaches, they conclude that '[t]hus far, however, the "different voice" of developing nations in international law has shown little concern for feminist perspectives.'[23]

At least some structural bias critics, then, see their work as feminist because it focuses on gender hierarchy. While a few have acknowledged that other critiques of international law might share some of the same concerns and lead to some of the same conclusions as feminist critiques,[24] structural bias feminists aim to analyse international law for its deployment of literal and metaphorical distinctions between male and female.

Some of the writing during the structural bias period responds to the feminist question somewhat differently, with a method that I call structural bias instrumentalism. This set of approaches does not necessarily see the male/female divide as central to the structure of international law, but searches for methods

---

[21] *Ibid*, at 392.

[22] *Ibid*.

[23] H Charlesworth, C Chinkin and S Wright, above n 15, at 618.

[24] See, eg, E Stamatopoulou, 'Women's Rights and the United Nations' in *Women's Rights, Human Rights*, above n 14, at 36, 39 ('The Third World critique of international law and insistence on diversity may well have prepared the philosophical ground for feminist critiques.').

and critiques of international law that would improve distributional consequences for women. Structural bias instrumentalism comes in three forms. The first uses progressive but non-feminist critiques of international law to assist women. The second suggests using feminist critiques to assist other disadvantaged groups. The third flips the structural bias argument by suggesting ways that women might take advantage of structural bias.

Karen Knop best represents the first group. In her call for the need to decentralise the state in international law, for example, she has suggested that feminists learn from the efforts of indigenous rights advocates in this area.[25] In other work, she has argued that 'liberal self-determination' might provide critical power for women.[26] Celina Romany has taken a similar approach by arguing that decentering the state, paying more attention to economic and social rights, and developing third generation rights (like the right to development) are all likely to have positive, if unintended, consequences for women.[27]

Anne Orford provides an example of the second approach. In her work on globalisation, Orford identifies ways in which the fight against economic exploitation might draw on feminist critiques. Orford argues that feminist insights can assist in rescripting globalism so as to avoid a sense of it as inevitable and intransigent. She also notes that the organisational techniques of feminist activists provide a useful set of tools for resisting globalisation.[28]

I would characterise some of my own early work, as well as the work of Lama Abu-Odeh, as falling under the third approach. Acknowledging that structural biases exist, this approach argues for ways to subvert the biases. I have argued, for example, that feminists might be wary of an all-out rejection of the public/private distinction and might instead imagine ways that the private could be liberating for women.[29] In a similar vein, Abu-Odeh has shown how the veil, even while representing formal inequality between men and women, might offer women the possibility of some private space and of decreasing harassment.[30] Sometimes this approach challenges the equation of male with one side of the dichotomy and

---

[25] See K Knop, above n 18.

[26] See K Knop, above n 2.

[27] C Romany, 'Women as Aliens: A Feminist Critique of the Public/Private Distinction in International Human Rights Law' (1993) 6 *Harvard Human Rights Journal* 87. But see H Charlesworth, 'Human Rights as Men's Rights' in *Women's Rights, Human Rights*, above n 14, at 109 (arguing that third generation rights, such as the right to development, are contrary to women's interests because 'the right to development ... is both defined and implemented internationally to support male economic dominance'); RE Howard, 'Women's Rights and the Right to Development' in *Women's Rights, Human Rights*, above n 14, at 303 ('Women's rights, like civil and political rights, are in danger of subordination to the development ideology, whose very absorption of all other rights implies their irrelevance.').

[28] A Orford, 'Contesting Globalization: A Feminist Perspective on the Future of Human Rights' (1998) 8 *Transnational Law and Contemporary Problems* 171, reprinted in BH Weston and SP Marks (eds), *The Future of International Human Rights* (Ardsley NY, Transnational Publishers, 1999) at 157.

[29] See K Engle, above n 16.

[30] See L Abu-Odeh, 'Post-Colonial Feminism and the Veil: Considering the Differences' (1992) 26 *New England Law Review* 1527.

female with the other. Even if the dichotomy has been coded in that way, this method suggests flipping the dichotomy to see how the male side might be useful for women (and perhaps vice versa).

The approaches that I have grouped under the label of structural bias instrumentalism, much like liberal inclusionism, are not particularly concerned about the feminist question. While women might be the primary subjects of analysis (at least in the first and third incarnations), structural bias instrumentalism is willing to use whatever tools seem available. Its advocates feel comfortable borrowing from poststructuralism, postcolonialism, even liberalism, to achieve their ends.

The Culture Question

The second elephant in the room that, if unconsciously, affected much of the feminist critique of international law is that of the 'exotic other female'.[31] I have used this term elsewhere to refer to an imagined woman—generally from the third world—who is seen to defend and promote practices that liberal and structural bias critics view as violations of women's human rights. I have discussed the exotic other female in the debates over clitoridectomy and have placed her in the third world, but she could just as easily be a woman in the first world who has had or supported breast augmentation surgery, or a defender of 'family values' who is reluctant to permit any state intervention in the family.[32] The exotic other female is thus a construct of a woman who participates, if unwittingly, in her own and in other women's oppression. Liberal inclusionism and structural bias feminism have responded in significantly different ways to this imagined other.

Liberal inclusionism aims to convince the exotic other female. Those who take this approach understand that a number of different doctrinal strategies could be used to pursue the protection of women's human rights. As a result, they aim to pick the strategy that will be least offensive and prove most convincing to their imagined other. With regard to clitoridectomy, for example, some have argued for the use of the right to health over the right to bodily integrity because they believe that third world women will be most sympathetic to the former.[33]

The structural bias critique, on the other hand, tends to attribute false consciousness to its constructed other. Sometimes it does so overtly, but generally the argument is subtle, at least in women's human rights scholarship. As suggested earlier, structural bias approaches do not ignore third world women. Rather, women from outside the West tend to be the objects of their study. Structural bias

---

[31] See K Engle, 'Female Subjects of Public International Law: Human Rights and the Exotic Other Female' (1992) 26 *New England Law Review* 1509.

[32] Cf A Dworkin, *Right Wing Women* (New York, Perigee, 1993).

[33] For a discussion and critique of examples of this right to health argument, see K Engle, above n 31, at 1514–15.

feminists locate women's oppression in the private sphere, and non-Western women are thought to be particularly vulnerable due to the oppressive cultures they are seen to inhabit.

If liberal inclusionists seek to convince the women whom they largely aim to protect that they are indeed oppressed, structural bias feminists often see little reason to engage such women at all. By relying on a male/female dichotomy, the structural bias critique avoids the need to attend to differences among women. Thus, this approach often conflates first and third world women's interests and suggests that the agendas of both groups (and all within each group) are similar.

To be fair, over time, particularly since the emergence of third world feminist critiques, those who approach international law through the lens of structural gender bias have begun to acknowledge the existence of other female voices. As Charlesworth specifically states, 'certainly no monolithic "women's point of view" can be assumed'.[34] Such acknowledgements, however, sit awkwardly aside and in tension with an ongoing insistence on structural bias. Charlesworth, for example, states on the same page as her disavowal of a monolithic voice that 'patriarchy and the devaluing of women, although manifest differently within different societies, are almost universal'.[35]

If first and third world women are thought to share some universal oppression, first and third world *feminists* are imagined to share a common goal under the structural bias approach. Charlesworth, Chinkin and Wright, for example, insist that, despite women's cultural and historical differences, 'feminists from all worlds share a central concern: their domination by men'.[36] They continue:

> [T]he constant theme in both western and Third World feminism is the challenge to structures that permit male domination, although the form of the challenge and the male structures may differ from society to society. An international feminist perspective on international law will have as its goal the rethinking and revision of those structures and principles which exclude women's voices.

By focusing only on feminism here, Charlesworth, Chinkin and Wright avoid confronting non-feminists in the first or third world who might disagree with their aim. Yet they also assume that all feminists, be they from the first or third world, share the same strategies and goals, which happen to coincide with those of structural bias feminism. Hence, the assumption of structural bias feminism is that the exotic other female will benefit from the work of structural bias feminists, whether she realises it or not.

---

[34] H Charlesworth, above n 27, at 103.
[35] *Ibid.*
[36] H Charlesworth, C Chinkin and S Wright, above n 15, at 621.

Third World Feminist Critiques: Since 1992

The feminist methodology and culture elephants set the stage for what I term third world feminist critiques of international law. The elephants were, I contend, in the room from the moment feminists began to articulate critiques of human rights law. By suggesting that other critical methods might be similar to feminist methodology (and equally helpful to women) and that the male/female divide might not be the defining bias in international law, the elephants undermined two crucial assumptions of structural bias feminism. It is therefore not surprising that the third world critiques began in the early 1990s, around the same time that a coherent theory of structural bias was being articulated.

The third world feminist critiques have largely come in two forms. The first attacks international law, either for its exclusion of or structural bias against third world women. The second, on which I will focus, challenges structural bias feminism for its failure to attend to third world women. These approaches are related, of course, and their form is often determined by their intended audience. I refer to these critiques as feminist, although, as we shall see, the critics themselves often struggle with the question of whether and in what ways they are feminist. Even if some would deny the appropriateness of applying the feminist label to their work, I use it here to highlight the extent to which the approaches focus on third world, or at least non-Western, women as the subject of their analysis.

Critiques of International Law

There are two types of third world feminist critiques of international law and institutions. They mirror the feminist critiques of international law we have already seen—liberal inclusion and structural bias. The liberal inclusion position argues that international law and institutions have ignored the concerns of third world women and should assimilate them, while the structural bias position suggests that international (and sometimes municipal) law is so structurally biased against third world women that it would need to be significantly restructured to accommodate them.

The liberal inclusion form of the third world feminist critique is structurally indistinguishable from early feminist doctrinal inclusion arguments. Those who deploy the third world feminist liberal inclusion approach focus on third world, or non-Western, women rather than claiming to attend to all women. Still, they aim to interpret and deploy existing law to achieve their strategic aims.[37] In contrast, the structural bias form of the third world feminist critique suggests that

[37] For examples of this type of work, see AK Wing, 'Rape, Ethnicity and Culture: Spirit Injury from Bosnia to Black America' (1993) 25 *Columbia Human Rights Law Review* 1; AK Wing, 'Critical Race Feminism and the International Human Rights of Women in Bosnia, Palestine, and South Africa: Issues for Latcrit Theory' (1997) 28 *University of Miami Inter-American Law Review* 337.

international law will need to change significantly to accommodate third world women. Ruth Gana, for example, argues that the right to development, because of its group focus, is incapable of attending to women in the third world.[38] The argument that international law is structurally biased against third world women often tends to be regionally and ethnographically specific. Indeed, the critique of international law, to the extent that it is articulated, is often of its failure to change local practices. Celestine Nyamu, for example, has shown how governmental invocation of international legal deference to culture often combines with formal (colonial) legal structures to disadvantage Kenyan women in the area of property rights.[39]

This structural bias approach also appears in critiques of globalisation. Kerry Rittich and Anne Orford, for example, have each demonstrated how international legal processes that facilitate globalisation have a negative impact on women in the third world.[40] In this volume, Ambreena Manji shows how structural adjustment programmes of international financial institutions that encourage private property regimes depend up and perpetuate a conception of women's labour in the third world as 'free, flexible and willing'.[41] For Manji, 'plans to enable and encourage the use of land as collateral are built on the backs of women'.[42]

Critiques of Structural Bias Feminism

Third world feminist critiques of international law implicitly challenge liberal and structural bias feminism by suggesting that the effects of international law on women must be examined in light of class, culture and race. Third world feminist approaches to structural bias feminism make these critiques explicit. Again, there is both a liberal inclusion and a structural bias form of the critique.

The liberal inclusion form argues that structural bias feminists fail to include third world women in their analysis. The position tends to assume that third world women *could be* assimilated to the structural bias critique without disrupting the analysis; they would simply need to be included. This approach is, in

---

[38] RL Gana, 'Which "Self"? Race and Gender in the Right to Self-Determination as a Prerequisite to the Right to Development' (1995) 14 *Wisconsin International Law Journal* 133.

[39] See C Nyamu, 'How Should Human Rights and Development Respond to Cultural Legitimisation of Gender Hierarchy in Developing Countries?' (2000) 41 *Harvard International Law Journal* 381. Others do not make the explicit connection to international law, but instead centre on the structural bias in the municipal law of particular countries. See, eg, K Muli, 'Help Me Balance the Load: Gender Discrimination in Kenya' in *Women's Rights, Human Rights*, above n 14, at 78 (providing a brief overview of systemic gender bias in Kenya); A Mirhosseini, 'After the Revolution: Violations of Women's Human Rights in Iran' in *Women's Rights, Human Rights*, above n 14, at 72 (providing a detailed portrait of the difficulties facing women in Iran, including marriage, domestic abuse, and property distribution).

[40] See, eg, K Rittich, *Recharacterizing Restructuring: Law, Distribution and Gender in Market Reform* (Leiden, M Nijhoff, 2003); A Orford, above n 28.

[41] See A Manji (this volume).

[42] *Ibid.*

effect, what structural bias feminists respond to when they acknowledge that there is no essential woman's voice. As with liberal inclusion, this approach has in many ways succeeded. It is responsible for the near-obligatory references to the existence of non-Western women as subjects, not just objects, of international law.

The structural bias form of the third world feminist critique refuses the gesture to add third world women and stir. In effect, it suggests that attending to third world women would require a radical restructuring of the structural bias critique. A number of third world feminist critiques have been aimed at structural bias feminism in this regard, but I will focus on three here. First, through an overt (re)assertion of the distinction between the first and third worlds, those who approach structural bias feminism from this third world feminist perspective often argue that Western feminism has misrepresented women through its near exclusive focus on culture. Second, they suggest that this focus displaces those issues that have the greatest importance to women in the third world. Third, they argue that first world feminists are complicit in the perpetuation of colonial or neocolonial agendas. The first two critiques, I believe, are largely responsible for the paradox regarding the disappearance of structural bias feminist approaches I described at the beginning of the essay. The third has not been as successful. As we shall see, they are related.

Critiques of Western Representations of Women and Focus on Culture

Third world feminist approaches have challenged the representations about non-Western women they argue are made by both liberal inclusionist and structural bias approaches to women's human rights. In particular, they critique the conflation of the interests of women in the first and third worlds, and argue for the need to attend to cultural differences. Aihwa Ong asserts, for example, that 'North-South conflict erupts when liberal feminists disregard alternative political moralities that shape the ways women in other societies make moral judgments about their interests and goals in life, and use other cultural criteria about what it means to be female and human.' [43] Much of the early work that I would consider to comprise third world feminist approaches calls attention to cultural differences the authors believe are ignored by liberal and structural bias feminists, as well as to the failure of first world feminists to see similar types of oppression in their own cultures.[44]

---

[43] A Ong, 'Strategic Sisterhood or Sisters in Solidarity? Questions of Communitarianism in Asia' (1996) 4 *Indiana Journal of Global Legal Studies* 107, 113.

[44] See, eg K Engle, above n 31; I Gunning, 'Arrogant Perception, World-Travelling and Multicultural Feminism: The Case of Female Genital Surgeries' (1991–92) 23 *Columbia Human Rights Law Review* 189; V Nesiah, 'Toward a Feminist Internationality: A Critique of US Feminist Legal Scholarship' (1993) 16 *Harvard Women's Law Journal* 189; H Lewis, 'Between "Irua" and "Female Genital Mutilation"' (1995) 8 *Harvard Human Rights Journal* 1, 32.

Third world feminist critiques have also challenged the extent to which structural bias feminism denies women's agency in its representation of women as victims. Paula Johnson and Leslye Obiora have noted that feminist critiques 'tend to conflate the specificities and meanings of women's experiences and to perpetuate the dubious portrayal of women as mere epiphenomena or passive objects of male transactions'.[45] Of course, that critique could be and has been aimed at first world feminists for their representations of first world women, but third world feminist critics see its effect as particularly problematic in the context of third world women. As Vasuki Nesiah explains, 'a discourse about the experience of oppression often participates in the imperially charged agenda of defining "Third World" women as victims of oppression.'[46] If white men had, during colonial times, sought to 'sav[e] brown women from brown men',[47] third world feminist critics often charge white women with attempting to do the same.

In addition to questioning first world feminist understandings of culture, third world feminist critics also challenge the structural bias focus on culture as the principal site of women's oppression. As Obiora puts it: 'The truth of the matter is that, despite popular feminist discourses, culture may not be the dispositive influence on the responses of women.'[48] For many third world critics, the focus on culture or on 'private' sphere rights detracts from issues and concerns of greater importance to women in the third world. As Obiora explains, '[c]ampaigns for sexual rights and freedoms [have been] disparaged as the trite obsession of privileged Western feminists by some [third world] feminists who preferred to emphasize economic concerns.'[49] Even when Western feminists attempt to address economic issues, such as the rights of female workers in the third world, third world critics argue that they sometimes miss the source of the problems by analysing them through the structural bias lens. Ong notes, for example, that it is not only 'local patriarchal norms' that are responsible for mistreatment of female workers, and that if Western feminists really want to address the problems of women's inequalities, they will need 'to confront not only cultural practices in Third World countries, but also metropolitan capitalist enterprises that are driven by profits to seek cheap female labor in the South.'[50]

---

[45] P Johnson and LA Obiora, 'How Does the Universal Declaration of Human Rights Protect African Women' (1999) 26 *Syracuse Journal of International Law and Commerce* 195, 207. See also R Kapur, 'The Tragedy of Victimization Rhetoric: Resurrecting the "Native" Subject in International/Post-colonial Feminist Legal Politics' (2002) 15 *Harvard Human Rights Journal* 1.

[46] V Nesiah, above n 44, at 197.

[47] This term was coined by Gayatri Spivak. See GC Spivak, 'Can the Subaltern Speak?' in C Nelson and L Grossberg (eds), *Marxism and the Interpretation of Culture* (Urbana-Champaign, University of Illinois, 1988) at 271, 296.

[48] LA Obiora, 'Feminism, Globalization, and Culture: After Beijing' (1997) 4 *Indiana Journal of Global Legal Studies* 355, 385. See also *ibid*, at 370–71 (agreeing with the 'poignant objections raised against solipsistic researchers who zero in on clitoridectomy as the sole point of reference and definition for women's oppression in Africa and the Middle East').

[49] *Ibid*, at 363.

[50] A Ong, above n 43, at 126.

Culturally Sensitive Universalism

At a basic level, the critiques of Western feminist representation of and focus on culture have succeeded. They have resulted in a compromise that I call 'culturally sensitive universalism'. Indeed, this compromise has proved so successful that it has made its way into official documents. The Beijing Declaration, which emerged from the 1995 World Conference on Women in Beijing, states that while 'the significance of national and regional particularities and various historical, cultural and religious backgrounds must be borne in mind, it is the duty of States, regardless of their political, economic and cultural systems, to promote and protect all human rights and fundamental freedoms.'[51] The Beijing Declaration simply repeated language that had already been settled on in the Vienna Declaration,[52] a document emerging from the World Conference on Human Rights in 1993 at which the question of culture dominated.[53]

The compromise of culturally sensitive universalism, of which the Beijing Declaration is merely an expression, has had significant impact on the development of feminist approaches to international law. I believe it is crucial to understanding the near disappearance of structural bias feminism on one hand and the rise in discussion of women's human rights on the other. At one level, 'culturally sensitive universalm' signals a success for the third world feminist assertions of cultural difference. For Obiora, it represents a 'contradictory turn' for the discourse of women's rights instruments. It is in contrast, she argues, to language in other documents on women's rights that specifically disavows the significance of cultural difference for women's rights. Obiora accepts the compromise, noting that '[g]iven the centrality of culture as a framework for existence, the legitimacy of the international human rights regime is necessarily enhanced by culturally sensitive approaches'.[54] If culturally sensitive approaches are the norm, structural bias feminism is incapable of responding. To the extent that structural bias critiques continue to emerge, they tend to be tempered (and threatened) by acknowledgements that not all women in all parts of the world are the same, or at least by disclaimers that situate the authors in the first world.[55]

At another level, culturally sensitive universalism has raised as many questions as it seems to have settled. Dianne Otto argued shortly after Beijing that the compromise merely deferred the debate between relativism and universalism: '[That] the overall

---

[51] *Women from Beijing, a Platform for Action and a Clear Mandate for Women's Progress*, UN Doc DP1/1749/Wom.–95–30876 (1995) ch 1, para 9.

[52] See *Vienna Declaration and Programme of Action*, A/CONF 157/23 (1993), para 5.

[53] For discussion, critique of and reaction to this compromise in the context of the Vienna Declaration, see K Engle, 'Culture and Human Rights: The Asian Values Debate in Context' (2000) 32 *New York University Journal of International Law and Politics* 291, 320–24.

[54] LA Obiora, above n 48, at 377.

[55] Obiora observes the dwindling of feminist approaches that focus on the male/female dichotomy as well, noting that 'women are becoming less enthralled with the once-orthodox myth of "global sisterhood" and more attuned to the pervasiveness of profound differences in their lives'. LA Obiora, above n 48, at 368.

outcome can be read as supporting either the universalist or relativist position reflects the paralysis of the debate and leaves the issue firmly on the international human rights agenda for another day.[56] Rather than having deferred the debate, I would contend that it has restructured it. Since 1995, a plethora of articles have been written that aim to find a middle way between universalism and relativism.[57] Most reach a conclusion consistent with cultural sensitivity.

There is a tendency at times to see the assertion of cultural difference as having emanated from third world feminist critiques, or at the very least from multiculturalists with whom some feminists have allied.[58] Pinning the move to culture on third world or multiculturalist feminist critiques, however, misses an important piece of the history of the debates. Structural bias and liberal inclusion feminists, not third world feminists, are largely responsible for the discussion of culture. The structural bias critics, in particular, are the ones who first located culture as the locus of women's oppression by pointing to the ways that international law sanctioned women's oppression in the private sphere. The private sphere is the problem in their analysis. If international law could be restructured or reimagined so as to enter women's 'private' lives, according to structural bias feminism, women could become full participants in society. In this sense, it is important to remember that structural bias feminists have not overlooked or excluded third world women; they have sought to save them.

Moreover, although much of the third world feminist critique is aimed at the assumptions about culture embodied in structural bias and sometimes liberal inclusion arguments, third world feminists in fact rarely defend any particular culture. Indeed, third world critics are generally loath to accept a static understanding of culture, and often deconstruct popular or state articulations or propagation of

---

[56] D Otto, 'Rethinking the "Universality" of Human Rights Law' (1997) 29 *Columbia Human Rights Law Review* 1, 11.

[57] See, eg, B Stark, 'Bottom Line Feminist Theory: The Dream of a Common Language' (2000) 23 *Harvard Women's Law Journal* 227; S Desai, 'Hearing Afghan Women's Voices: Feminist Theory's Re-Conceptualization of Women's Human Rights' (1999) 16 *Arizona Journal of International and Comparative Law* 805; E Brems, 'Enemies or Allies? Feminism and Cultural Relativism as Dissident Voices in Human Rights Discourse' (1997) 19 *Human Rights Quarterly* 136; B Cossman, 'Turning the Gaze Back on Itself: Comparative Law, Feminist Legal Studies, and the Postcolonial Project' (1997) 2 *Utah Law Review* 525; A Garay, 'Women, Cultural Relativism, and International Human Rights: A Question of Mutual Exclusivity or Balance?' (1996) 12 *International Insights* 19; TE Higgins, 'Anti-Essentialism, Relativism, and Human Rights' (1996) 19 *Harvard Women's Law Journal* 89; SK Hom, 'Commentary: Re-Positioning Human Rights Discourse on "Asian" Perspectives' (1996) 3 *Buffalo Journal of International Law* 209; C Romany, 'Black Women and Gender Equality in a New South Africa: Human Rights Law and the Intersection of Race and Gender' (1996) 21 *Brooklyn Journal of International Law*, 857; H Stacey, 'Legal Discourse and the Feminist Political Economy: Moving Beyond Sameness/Difference' (1996) 6 *Australian Feminist Law Journal* 115; J Oloka-Onyango and S Tamale, '"The Personal is Political," or Why Women's Rights are Indeed Human Rights: An African Perspective on International Feminism' (1995) 17 *Human Rights Quarterly* 691; N Kim, 'Toward a Feminist Theory of Human Rights: Straddling the Fence Between Western Imperialism and Uncritical Absolutism' (1993) 25 *Columbia Human Rights Law Review* 49.

[58] See, eg, SM Okin, 'Is Multiculturalism Bad for Women?' in SM Okin, et al, *Is Multiculturalism Bad for Women?* (Princeton, Princeton University Press, 1999) at 9.

culture in an attempt to find room for women to challenge dominant understandings of their culture. As Vasuki Nesiah has recently argued, 'the invocation of
particular cultures, is not a descriptive but a constitutive effort—a project aligned
with and contesting other projects, a projection of the very notion of culture.'[59]
Thus, arguments about culture are often about more than what they might at first
seem, and in this sense are largely untouched by the compromise around culturally
sensitive universalism.

Culture, Class or Colonialism?

I would argue that the most damaging critique of structural bias feminism posed
by third world feminist approaches is contained, sometimes implicitly but often
explicitly, within the cultural representation and priorities arguments. In their
most critical forms, both arguments attack massive inequalities in wealth between
the first and third worlds, and suggest that first world feminists are implicated in
these inequalities. That first world feminists focus on culture, rather than poverty,
as the locus of women's oppression, for example, misses the role played by economics in the construction of women's identities and concerns in both the first
and third world. More significantly, because of a history of colonialism and
economic and political exploitation, when first world feminists make their primary aim to save brown women from the cultural oppression imposed by brown
men, they are deeply implicated in the plight of the third world.

First world feminist critiques, in this telling, are not clearly distinguishable
from the imperial or neocolonial politics of the first world in general. As Ong
notes, '[W]estern feminists, whether academic or activist, are often seen as working in collaboration with the imperialist hegemonies of Northern countries. For
instance, Northern feminists at the Beijing Conference represented themselves as
enlightened and liberated subjects with the answers to the problems of women in
non-Western cultures.'[60] Obiora puts it even more strongly:

> Western feminist scholarship cannot avoid the challenge of examining its inscription
> in particular relations of structural dominance and struggle, its role in the discur-
> sive colonization of the material complexities and historical heterogeneity of the
> lives of Third World women, as well as its complicity in value systems that exacerbate
> and sustain harsh realities in dependent political economies.[61]

If the first world benefits from and perhaps even depends upon the exploitation
of the third world, first world feminists are also beneficiaries. As Anne Orford
explains: 'Those who celebrate the age of globalization "actively forget" the extent
to which access to the bodies, labour and resources of people in states subject to

---

[59] V Nesiah, 'The Ground Beneath Her Feet: TWAIL Feminisms' in *The Third World and International
Order*, above n 4, at 133, 139.
[60] A Ong, above n 43, at 113.
[61] LA Obiora, above n 48, at 372–73.

monetary intervention is the condition of the prosperous lifestyles of international lawyers and their audiences in industrialized liberal democracies.'[62] Questioning the alliance of feminism and internationalism, Orford admonishes feminist internationalists to 'consider whether, and when, our work contributes to the erasure of the "actual price-in-exploitation" of globalization'.[63]

In this reading, culturally sensitive universalism would seem to serve less as a compromise then as a displacement. Both first world and third world feminists can use culturally sensitive universalism to avoid some of the deeper implications of this third world feminist critique. Feminists in neither group are forced to address how committed they are in fact to a radical redistribution of wealth.

Conclusion: Back to the Future?

My narrative might suggest that the assertion of economics is threatening to undermine arguments about gender as well as culture. The compromise of culturally sensitive universalism would seem bound to unravel under the pressure of arguments against a global distribution of capital that perpetuates the distinction between the first and thirds worlds. Yet, it would be a mistake to see the economic and cultural realms as separate. Borrowing from the work of Judith Butler and of some contemporary feminist economists, Vasuki Nesiah puts it nicely: '[T]he putative distinction between the economic and the cultural is itself another moment in the production of each—a denial of the culture of the economy and the economics of culture.'[64] Attention to the ways that culture and economics are mutually constitutive, I believe, would also threaten to undermine the compromise around culturally sensitive universalism. By refusing an analysis that focuses on *either* gender/culture *or* economics, however, it might, paradoxically, challenge the compromise in a way that brings gender back to the fore.

---

[62] A Orford, 'Feminism, Imperialism and the Mission of International Law' (2002) 71 *Nordic Journal of International Law* 275, 290.

[63] *Ibid*, at 291 (citing GC Spivak, *In Other Worlds* (New York, Routledge, 1988) at 167).

[64] V Nesiah, above n 59, at 141 (citing J Butler, 'Merely Cultural' (1998) *New Left Review* 33).

4

Feminism Here and Feminism There: Law, Theory and Choice

THÉRÈSE MURPHY[*]

Introduction

This essay is about choice. As such, it is about an issue that has strong and long-standing associations with both feminism and femininity. In popular culture, for example, women with choices—about what to wear, eat or pack, or how to park the car—almost always seem unable to choose. Interestingly, popular characterisations of *feminist* engagements with choice rarely highlight indecisiveness. Indeed, according to these accounts, the issue of choice is rigidly straightforward for a feminist: women ought to have the right to choose what to do with their bodies and, as regards abortion, dogged attachment to a pro-choice position is the only option.

This essay will have none of the sure and total judgement popularly associated with a feminist stance on choice. That, however, may be no bad thing. When one puts the popular account aside, two important points become clear: first, feminism has no monopoly on being 'for choice' and, second, being 'for choice' is no guarantee of feminist outcomes. These points are well illustrated by *Webster v Reproductive Health Services*,[1] wherein the US Supreme Court upheld the constitutionality of a law prohibiting the use of public facilities and publicly-employed staff in abortions. The Supreme Court did not see itself as limiting choice; instead its reasoning was that, in curtailing public funds, the state was leaving pregnant women 'with the same choices as if the state had chosen not to operate any hospitals at all'.[2]

---

[*] Thanks to Doris Buss and Ambreena Manji for their comments on earlier versions, and to my colleague Robert Cryer for a whistlestop tour of trends in international law theory.

[1] 492 US 490 (1989).

[2] *Ibid.* A further illustration of the complexity of being 'for choice' is that in the US (and elsewhere) the voices of women who have terminated one or more pregnancies are oddly uniform: it would seem that, today, in speaking of the decision to abort one *must* declare oneself saddened by the 'choice': see T Murphy, 'Health Confidentiality in the Age of Talk' in S Sheldon and M Thomson (eds), *Feminist Perspectives on Health Care Law* (London, Cavendish, 1998), 155–72, 164. See also M Poovey, 'The Abortion Question and the Death of Man' in J Butler and JW Scott (eds), *Feminists Theorize the Political* (New York and London, Routledge, 1992), 239–56.

So, following Elspeth Probyn, my starting point in this essay is that, as a feminist, being 'for choice' doesn't take one very far.[3] As Probyn explains, it is better—far better—to focus on being 'by choice'.[4] The key difference between the two—between being by choice and being for choice—is that the former pulls away from abstract principle and plunges one into practices of choosing. The latter, by contrast, has a desperately misleading aura of finality which submerges important and ongoing questions. Putting that another way, the 'challenge that being by choice offers' is that:

> It acknowledges that choice is always situational, that it is never a mere abstract issue that can be deadened and arranged on one side of a moral line. …[B]eing by choice returns us to an ethics wherein we ask alongside our actions, our words, our choices, what is implicated here? And this question is couched not in moral and transcendental terms but in very concrete ways. … In simple terms, being by choice focuses us on practices not principles, practices that take their meaning in relations with others.[5]

With this in mind, I shall use this essay to look into one instance of choice within feminism. Specifically, I am interested in the following question: what is implicated when a feminist—in particular, a feminist legal scholar—selects an international orientation over a domestic one, or vice versa?[6]

A Flawed Question

I am well aware that this question rests on a contrived distinction. The boundaries between the domestic and the international—whether, for example, between law 'here' and law 'there',[7] or between feminism 'here' and feminism 'there'—are contingent ones. That is to say, although such boundaries have real effects, they nevertheless remain open to variation across time and place. Indeed, the possibility of variation could be said to underpin cosmopolitan, or pluralist, approaches to law and legal institutions; these approaches urge us to engage imaginatively with law and lawyering in a world that is both 'of' and 'beyond' nation states.[8] Further evidence of the contingency of the boundaries between

---

[3] E Probyn, 'Perverts By Choice: Towards an Ethics of Choosing' in D Elam and R Wiegman (eds), *Feminism Beside Itself* (New York and London, Routledge, 1995), 261–81, 262–63.

[4] *Ibid*, 264.

[5] *Ibid*, 276.

[6] This essay focuses on domestic and international legal feminism. Although beyond the remit of this essay, there is also of course scope for analysis of the relationships between domestic and/or international legal feminism and other embodiments of legal feminism, eg, supranational legal feminism (I am thinking in particular of feminism that is focused on the EU legal order) or foreign legal feminism.

[7] This terminology is taken from K Knop, 'Here and There: International Law in Domestic Courts' (1999) 32 *New York University Journal of International Law and Politics* 511.

[8] See generally D Held and A McGrew (eds), *Global Transformations Reader*, 2nd edn (Oxford, Blackwell, 2003).

the domestic and the international can be found in their thriving interdependencies: consider, for example, the way in which the interpretative practices of domestic courts and legislatures sustain and generate international law,[9] or the fact that domestic human rights abuses prompt and focus the work of both international and domestic legal feminists.

The problem of contrived distinction is not, however, the only difficulty bedevilling my question. As a result, some further explanations are in order. First, I do not mean to suggest that there is a one-time-only, last-a-lifetime choice between the domestic and the international, or that this is the only relevant choice.[10] Secondly, I appreciate that, for a range of reasons, there may not always be a choice. Finally, I accept that there are strong reasons to adopt a general scepticism towards 'either/or' choices. The dangers of thinking in an 'either/or' way become clear if one looks at Anglo-American feminism's recent history; the dangers are also made clear by even the most basic understanding of critical theory or the crudest pragmatic instinct. Thus recent disputes within Anglo-American academic feminism can be held up as a caution against artificial and ghettoising distinctions between 'types' of feminists.[11] Critical theory, as Wendy Brown has pointed out, strikes a broader note of caution about distinctions: it teaches that 'identity is created through borders and oppositions. That the outside constructs the inside and then hides this work of fabrication in an entity that appears to give birth to itself'.[12] And, lastly, pragmatism suggests that by adopting a 'polarized either/or view of the tension between national and cosmopolitan consciousness' we may overlook 'the originality of our political circumstances ... an originality that makes both poles problematic'.[13]

Given all of the above, one might well ask: why opt for such a problematic question? My answer is simple: I have chosen this question because I think that it can facilitate a deeper understanding of the challenges that feminism faces at this particular time. In short, I believe, first, that there is currently a dynamic of 'here' and 'there' in academic legal feminism (in the courses we teach, in what we write about and whom we choose to reference, in where we aim to publish our writing and in how we picture our audiences) and, second, that there is something to be learnt from understanding more about this dynamic.

---

[9] See especially K Knop, above n 7.

[10] See, eg, C Smart, 'A History of Ambivalence and Conflict in the Discursive Construction of the "Child Victim" of Sexual Abuse' (1999) 8 *Social and Legal Studies* 391, 391 ('There have been moments when I felt that theoretical work was the most important, because of the limits of contemporary analysis or because I felt that my historical or empirical work had given rise to ways of thinking which called for expression in a transferable medium — and theory is always more widely read than empirical or historical work. But at other times I have found the focus on theory to be rather sterile and unrewarding and at such times I have found that empirical work poses new challenges and forces me to think in new ways. ... Empirical work, in my experience, always changes how one understands the social world.').

[11] Which is not to say that feminism should suspend internal critique or avoid judgement.

[12] W Brown, 'At the Edge' (2002) 30 *Political Theory* 556, 556.

[13] R Falk, 'Revisioning Cosmopolitanism' in M Nussbaum (ed), *For the Love of Country: Debating the Limits of Patriotism* (Boston, Beacon Press, 1996), 53.

In order to pursue these hunches, a series of questions demands consideration. As I see it, obvious contenders include the following: How do domestic and international legal feminisms relate to one another? What do they imagine themselves to be and to be for—both individually and in relationship to one another? In addition, in what ways are they being imagined by others, and how have they responded to such accounts? In what follows, I shall not answer all of these questions; indeed, I won't even broach some of them. Moreover, I shall have nothing to say about feminist activism versus feminist theorising as a potential further layer in the dynamic of 'here' and 'there'. Rather, focusing on Anglo-American feminist legal scholarship, I intend first to suggest reasons for what I see as the burgeoning allure of the international. Thereafter, I shall nominate two trends in scholarship—one in international legal feminism, the other in domestic legal feminism—in order to support my argument that we need to be more attentive to the choices that we make.

One final preliminary point is in order. It concerns the repeated use of the term 'Anglo-American' in this essay. I appreciate that this is an unsatisfactory descriptor. In using it, I do not intend to suggest any deep 'in-steppedness' or commonality between Unitedstatesean (legal) feminism and British (legal) feminism.[14] Nor do I want to submerge discussion of whether contemporary trends, such as US unilateralism, are generating new differences and/or commonalities between Unitedstatesean feminism and the other feminisms that have traditionally been included in the category 'Anglo-American'. I use the term only because I have been unable to devise a better shorthand way to capture what appear to be some common influences and trends in Unitedstatesean and British legal feminist scholarship.

A Case of the Emperor's New Clothes?

It seems to me that at present, at least in some countries, it is easier to be a feminist internationalist than a domestic feminist. For starters, the domestic feminism with which I am familiar—the Anglo-American legal academic variety—has been tough going in recent years. Speaking bluntly, there were times when it was miserable. I know that I am not alone in feeling like this: Janet Halley, for example, has observed that, in the US, women complain to her that 'academic feminism has lost its zing'.[15] Here I can only hint at the reasons for the trouble.[16] First, in popular culture, there were (and continue to be) mixed messages; most notably, deepening

---

[14] In this essay, 'Anglo' stands for British rather than a broader category including, eg, Australian and Canadian as well as British.

[15] J Halley, 'Take a Break from Feminism?' in K Knop (ed), *Gender and Human Rights* (Oxford, OUP, 2004), 57–82, 65. For an earlier version of this essay and responses thereto, see B Cossman et al, 'Gender, Sexuality and Power: Is Feminist Theory Enough?' (2003) 12 *Columbia Journal of Gender and Law* 601.

[16] See further J Halley, *ibid*.

concern about a range of inequalities[17] alongside shrill insistence that our societies are beyond or 'post' feminism.[18] Secondly, feminism started to get 'a seat at the table'; in other words, feminists became policy-makers, or found themselves or their ideas being included by policy-makers. Progress was uneven, both in terms of the take-up of feminist arguments and in terms of whether allegedly 'feminist-friendly' rules and policies actually furthered feminist ends.[19] For present purposes, however, the more important point is that many feminists were ill-prepared for this apparent transition from outsider to insider, with the result that the experience was as unnerving as it was energising. Meanwhile, in academic feminism, progress and anti-progress narratives on the question of essentialism proved almost all-consuming. There was also, I think, a sense that other critical theories acquired an edge over feminism; queer theory certainly seemed enviably urbane to me as I struggled with sage, but challenging, feminist counsel which advised that the critique of essentialism within feminism ought to be understood 'as an acknowledgement of the dangerousness of something one cannot not use'.[20]

Of late, things seem to have settled a little in Anglo-American academic feminism. Internal critique goes on (which is good), but producing it, and consuming it, seem less mind-wrecking than before. Later in this essay, I shall return to contemporary Anglo-American feminism: for now, my point is simply that against the above backdrop, feminist internationalism cannot but seem hospitable terrain. Indeed, it could be that the apparent lull in hostilities in Anglo-American academic feminism is in part attributable to a reorientation (flight?) towards the international (or the cosmopolitan, or the foreign) or, in any event, towards topics with an undeniably international element (for example, human rights) by significant numbers of domestic feminists.

For me, one of the current attractions of feminist internationalism is that it seems to render the question 'who and what is feminism for?' a great deal less fraught. As I shall explain in the following paragraphs, feminist internationalism achieves this in several different ways. First, the themes of international law—described by Ruth Buchanan and Sundhya Pahuja as peace, human rights and equality between nations[21]—are endearingly grand; all the more so if one has felt encircled by the

---

[17] This expanding recognition of inequalities has generated questions within academic feminism about the pros and cons of focusing on gender difference alone: see, eg, A Phillips, 'Feminism and the Politics of Difference, Or, Where Have All the Women Gone?' in S James and S Palmer (eds), *Visible Women: Essays on Feminist Legal Theory and Political Philosophy* (Oxford, Hart, 2002), 11–28.

[18] See, eg, the surveys discussed by N Walter, *The New Feminism* (London, Virago, 1999).

[19] See, eg, W Brown, *States of Injury: Power and Freedom in Late Modernity* (Princeton NJ, Princeton UP, 1995), 52–76 (highlighting problems with the emphasis on injury in rights claims by feminists); J Young, *The Exclusive Society* (London, Sage, 2000) 138 (identifying feminist arguments as one of the seeds of zero tolerance policing).

[20] G Spivak with E Rooney, '"In a Word": Interview' (1989) 1 *Differences* 124, reprinted in L Nicholson (ed), *The Second Wave: A Reader in Feminist Theory* (London, Routledge, 1997), 356, 359. I also found little solace in Spivak's argument that critique 'should not be seen as being critical in the colloquial, Anglo-American sense of being adversely inclined but as a critique in the robust European philosophical sense' (*ibid*).

[21] R Buchanan and S Pahuja, 'Collaboration, Cosmopolitanism and Complicity' (2002) 71 *Nordic Journal of International Law* 297, 298.

almost-obsessive discussion of experience, identity and subjectivity within recent Anglo-American academic feminism. And the allure of the international increases when one realises that feminist legal internationalists continue to speak, albeit cautiously and not without criticism,[22] in terms of issues that 'cross cultural, religious or class boundaries': Shelley Wright has nominated violence as one such cross-cutting issue, and noted that '[i]nequality of opportunity, including entrenched poverty, is another'.[23] In large part, the appeal of these issues is that they keep one focused on structural discrimination in a way that discussion of experience, identity and subjectivity does not. Finally, the international further enhances its standing via a series of winning credentials: as David Kennedy observes, international law 'has been associated with pacificism, with critique of the American empire, with the progressive movement, with the left, with law as an instrument of social change, as well as with an insistently pluralist and cosmopolitan attitude towards the national political and legal culture'.[24]

I accept that for some domestic feminist academics all of the above will seem akin to 'seeing the big picture'[25] and will therefore be unacceptably close to a modernist outlook. It is also possible to pour cold water on the allure of the international by emphasising the ugly and longstanding counterparts to international law's grand themes and winning credentials. As Gerry Simpson points out, '[e]xclusion, civilization, culture and difference are as deeply embedded in the system as universality, legality and equality'. Or, to put that another way, 'inter-state hierarchy or anti-pluralism has a long pedigree in international law'.[26] Moreover, a further legitimate complaint against the international would be that, until recently, international legal scholarship was to a large extent bewitched by the question of whether international law is truly law.[27]

I suspect, however, that these criticisms are rebuttable. There are, for example, clear indications that it is possible to follow an internationalist path without dishonouring the ideals of critical theory. Consider, first, the energy and persistence of critical international legal scholarship such as New Approaches to International Law. More specifically, consider the resonance between favoured concepts in critical theory and aspects of international practice. One obvious example is the internationalists' practice of holding conferences 'in counterpoint':[28] in other words, conferences that appear to aspire to the critical theoretical ideal of

---

[22] See, eg, R Kapur, 'The Tragedy of Victimization Rhetoric: Resurrecting the "Native" Subject in International/Post-colonial Feminist Legal Rhetoric' (2002) 15 *Harvard Human Rights Law Journal* 1.

[23] S Wright, 'The Horizon of Becoming: Culture, Gender and History after September 11' (2002) 71 *Nordic Journal of International Law* 215, 219.

[24] D Kennedy, 'When Renewal Repeats: Thinking Against the Box' (2000) 32 *New York University Journal of International Law and Politics* 335, 470.

[25] *Ibid.*

[26] G Simpson, 'Two Liberalisms' (2001) 12 *European Journal of International Law* 537, 571.

[27] As noted, eg, by T Franck, *Fairness in International Law and Institutions* (Cambridge, CUP, 1995).

[28] For the idea of counterpoint, see W Brown, 'Gender in Counterpoint' (2003) 4 *Feminist Theory* 365 and also W Brown, above n 12, 568 ('Counterpoint involves, first, the complicating of a single or dominant theme through the addition of contrasting themes or forces... Second, counterpoint sets off or articulates a thematic by means of contrast or juxtaposition').

distinct but interrelated, or cognate, spaces. One such event was the 1995 UN Fourth World Conference on Women in Beijing, which had a widely-reported non-governmental counterpart in nearby Huairou.[29] More generally, it can be noted that the gamut of ideas concerning location, multi-positionality and migration, which is so dominant in contemporary critical theory, appears tailor-made for use by internationalists.[30] Indeed, the burgeoning internationalist interest in what is sometimes described as 'actually existing cosmopolitanism'— that is, the acknowledgement that refugees and migrant workers, for example, are as much cosmopolites as the elite of the world's global cities[31]—could be said to give an important grounding to these critical ideas. In so doing, it reduces the risk that the ideas will unravel into an unthinking enthusiasm for 'nomadic consciousness', thereby eliding power and neglecting what Seyla Benhabib describes as the 'enormous difference between having no passport and having too many'.[32]

The second explanation I have for the allure of feminist internationalism is that it is part of the trenchantly evangelical discipline of international law. The latter is a discipline that aspires to 'make the world a better place'.[33] As David Kennedy has noted, '[f]or many young lawyers and law students, taking up international law, even at its most conventional, is already a gesture of both professional rebellion and personal renewal'.[34] In similar vein, Marti Koskenniemi has claimed that '[t]oday international law remains one of the few bastions of Victorian objectivism, liberalism and optimism'.[35] The fact that international lawyers are alleged to 'mix this with a considerable scepticism of interpretation as an objective enterprise'[36] toughens up their evangelism, arguably making it all the more attractive to domestic feminist legal scholars. And it seems likely that the attractiveness is enhanced by the recent bout of enthusiasm for formalism amongst critical international scholars and, in particular, by Koskenniemi's suggestion that formalism

[29] See further S Ahmed, 'An Impossible Global Justice? Deconstruction and Transnational Feminism' in J Richardson and R Sandland (eds), *Feminist Perspectives on Law and Theory* (London, Cavendish, 2000), 53–70.

[30] See, eg, S Benhabib, 'Sexual Difference and Collective Identities: The New Global Constellation' in S James and J Palmer, above n 17, 137–58, 138 ('If *fragmentation* was the code word of the eighties, *hybridity* is the code word of the 1990s; if *incommensurability* was a master term for the 1980s, *interstitiality* is one for the 1990s; if the *clash of cultures* was the horizon of the 1980s, *multiculturalism* and *polyglotism* are the framework of the 1990s.').

[31] See, eg, R Salih, 'Toward an Understanding of Transnationalism and Gender' in K Knop, above n 15, 231–50; and S Sassen, 'Women's Burden: Counter-Geographies of Globalization and the Feminization of Survival' (2002) 71 *Nordic Journal of International Law* 255.

[32] Above n 30, 157.

[33] D Kennedy, above n 24.

[34] Above n 24. See also R Buchanan and S Pahuja, above n 21, 318 ('One is attracted to international law because it promises a professional domain that will institutionalize or routinize one's critical or humanitarian impulse as a professional practice.').

[35] M Koskenniemi, *The Gentle Civilizer of Nations: The Rise and Fall of International Law 1870–1960* (Cambridge, CUP, 2001), 360.

[36] R Cryer, 'Déjà vu in International Law' (2002) 65 *Modern Law Review* 931, 943 (referring to a point made by M Koskenniemi, above n 35, at 404–406).

may provide a mechanism for curbing any improper influence that moral outrage has on international lawyers.[37]

Yet again, however, I am obliged to concede that an entirely different take on legal internationalism is also possible. There is, for starters, a deep vein of critique in international legal scholarship, alleging *inter alia* that the self-image of international lawyers discourages reflexivity and blocks out criticism.[38] Concern has also been expressed about international legal thought flopping endlessly to and fro between apologetic realism and crude utopianism.[39] In addition, as noted earlier, until recently much international legal scholarship was bedevilled by what Thomas Franck calls 'the constraints of defensive ontology'[40]—in other words, by the question of whether international law is actually law.

The upshot is that I have to admit that there is a dreamy aspect to the above account of the allure of international law's evangelism. Interestingly, however, dreaminess may well be part of the attraction of the international for at least some domestic versions of academic feminism. As Ralph Sandland has noted, there is '[b]road feminist interest with the concept, and political purchase, of utopianism'.[41] Moreover, because postmodern feminists have been playing the most significant role recently in nurturing utopian instincts, it is arguable that there are non-postmodern feminists craving alternative approaches to utopianism. As I see it, these cravings derive from the fact that postmodern feminism tends to invoke the utopian whilst remaining steadfastly and 'notoriously vague when it comes to *specifying* its *own* intended goals or outcomes'.[42] For the non-postmodern feminist, the argument that this vagueness 'is not oversight, but instead conscious political strategy'[43] will also be cold comfort.

Thus far I have suggested international law's grand themes, winning credentials and thorough-going evangelism as key reasons for the allure of the international for domestic academic feminists who are perplexed by the question of who and what feminism is for. If further reasons are required, the internationalist's current

---

[37] See especially, M Koskenniemi above n 35, and K Knop, *Diversity and Self-Determination in International Law* (Cambridge, CUP, 2002).

[38] See, eg, D Kennedy, 'Spring Break' (1985) 63 *Texas Law Review* 1377; D Kennedy, 'Autumn Weekends: An Essay on Law and Everyday Life' in A Sarat and TR Kearns (eds), *Law in Everyday Life* (Ann Arbor, University of Michigan Press, 1993), 191–236; and A Orford, *Reading Humanitarian Intervention: Human Rights and the Use of Force in International Law* (Cambridge, CUP, 2003).

[39] See especially M Koskenniemi, *From Apology to Utopia: The Structure of International Legal Argument* (Helsinki, Finnish Lawyers' Publishing Co, 1989). For Koskenniemi's current position, see above n 35.

[40] T Franck, above n 27, 6.

[41] R Sandland, 'Feminist Theory and Law: Beyond the Possibilities of the Present?' in J Richardson and R Sandland (eds), above n 29, 89–118, 89. A similar view is adopted by N Lacey, 'Feminist Legal Theory and the Rights of Women' in K Knop, above n 15, 13–56, 42–55.

[42] *Ibid*, 89. See also, N Lacey, 'Violence, Ethics and Law: Feminist Reflections on a Familiar Dilemma' in S James and S Palmer, above n 17, 117–36, 134 ('[T]his perspective risks effacing political action. [And] as soon as ... the postmodernist is drawn back into the field of political action, she must confront if not modernist then at least pragmatist ethical questions: what will be the effects of this (rhetorical) strategy; what are the recommendations of the likely outcome?')

[43] R Sandland, above n 41, 91.

trump card—cosmopolitanism—can be invoked.[44] Currently, cosmopolitanism comes in a range of forms, all of which are characterised by a robust effervescence (although in some cases moralistic fervour might be a more accurate description).[45] There is, first, a variant grounded in an ideal of world governance based on universal human rights and global citizenship. Secondly, there is a variant that celebrates cultural hybridity. Finally, there is what was referred to earlier as 'actually existing cosmopolitanism'; in this variant, 'those whose encounter with the wider world is less a matter of choice than compulsion' are brought into sharper focus. And if cosmopolitanism whatever its form seems like a lot of guff, the domestic feminist academic could still find herself captivated by other options available to the internationalist. She could, for example, pursue an internationalism that follows in the footsteps of those who have 'internalised the self-image of the political decision maker's little helper';[46] alternatively she could join those who have moved towards international relations, savouring the latter's 'enthusiasm about the spread of "liberalism"'.[47]

For feminist legal academics working in the United Kingdom (and also perhaps feminists working in jurisdictions with similar legal trends), the allure of the international seems particularly strong. There are, I think, two reasons for this. First, although the international legal system is unable to match its domestic counterparts' ability to enforce law through sanctions, in the UK (as elsewhere) the legal feminist enterprise increasingly seems incomplete where it lacks an international aspect.[48] Cases from the UK go to the European Court of Human Rights in Strasbourg. Moreover, with the coming into force of the Human Rights Act 1998, domestic judges are now bound to uphold 'Convention rights' and 'to take account of Strasbourg jurisprudence'.[49] More generally, as Karen Knop explains, judges—in the UK and elsewhere—'increasingly understand themselves as deeply engaged with international law'.[50] This judicial self-image includes being 'friendly to international law';[51] in other words, invoking international law in a persuasive role as well as when it is binding. The upshot is that, although international law's critics sometimes malign it as 'a process of the universalization of the particular', we need now to be as aware of international law as 'a process of the particularization

---

[44] For discussion, see eg, Kennedy, above n 24.

[45] The three-fold categorisation that follows is taken from R Buchanan and S Pahuja, above n 21.

[46] M Koskenniemi, above n 35, 495.

[47] *Ibid*, 483.

[48] The UK provides an obvious case study for the project, mentioned earlier, of examining who and what *supranational* legal feminism is for and how it relates to other feminist legal projects: see, eg, the extensive reportage and analysis of the European Court of Justice's judgment in *Grant v South-West Trains* Case C–249/96 [1998] ECR I–621 by theorists of gender and sexuality. Much of the latter is summarised or noted in CF Stychin, '*Grant*-ing Rights: The Politics of Rights, Sexuality and European Union' (2000) 51 *Northern Ireland Legal Quarterly* 281.

[49] See respectively ss 6 and 2, Human Rights Act 1998.

[50] K Knop, above n 7, 512 (footnote omitted). For evidence of this relation to England, see M Hunt, *Using Human Rights Law in English Courts* (Oxford, Hart, 1998).

[51] *Ibid*.

of the universal'.[52] This, in turn, means that we need to accept that 'domestic interpretation of [international law] is not everywhere the same nor, indeed, everywhere
good or everywhere bad'.[53] Regrettably, however, the process of particularising the
international is one about which, as yet, we know and understand relatively little.[54]

The second reason for the strong pull of internationalism on UK legal feminism
is that the apparent metanarrative of feminist legal internationalism—namely,
that it should be 'useful to women'—has to be particularly appealing to a domestic legal feminism which has had a bellyful of 'the call to theory'.[55] As Ann
Bottomley has pointed out, the call to theory has sometimes been used 'to chas-
tise and discredit feminists who still address law and still find some purchase in
the law's inadequacies'.[56] This, in turn, has two consequences. The first is that theorising becomes 'deeply apolitical': as Bottomley goes on to explain, 'what ... may
be being reproduced here is a position for theory which simply conforms to and
confirms the position of theory as the pinnacle of the academic project and the
theorist as the "true" academic/scholar'.[57] The second consequence is arguably
more pertinent for the purposes of this essay. It is that the standards to which feminist legal internationalism is held—specifically, 'the real world', 'particular cases'
and 'the facts on the ground'[58]—will be hugely appealing to domestic legal feminists who have felt encased and perhaps belittled by the 'call to theory'. In saying
this, I do not mean to suggest that 'the real world', 'particular cases' and 'facts' are
unproblematic standards.[59] I have read Anne Orford's disturbing account of feminist international legal theory's official *niche* within international law: namely,

---

[52] *Ibid*, 528.

[53] *Ibid*, 524.

[54] See, eg, K Knop, 'Introduction' in K Knop, above n 15, 1–12, 12, noting the relevance of the impact
of international gender norms on a state's private international law; and R Rubio-Marín and MI Morgan,
'Constitutional Domestication of International Gender Norms: Categorizations, Illustrations, and
Reflections from the Nearside of the Bridge' in K Knop, above n 15, 113–52. We also know little about
the gender impact of transnational leanings by domestic judges: see V Jackson, 'Gender and
Transnational Legal Discourse' (2002) 14 *Yale Journal of Law and Feminism* 377, 386–87 ('Further empirical research would be needed ... to know whether courts that engage with the constitutional decisions
of other nations are more open to claims of gender equality. And even if a correlation were found,
further work would be needed to explore whether a causal relationship existed between the two phe-
nomena or whether, alternatively, particular judges or courts, at particular moments in time, were—for
reasons independent of either phenomenon—interested in transnational learning and more open to
gender equality claims.').

[55] J Butler and JW Scott, 'Introduction' in J Butler and JW Scott (eds), *Feminists Theorize the Political*
(New York and London, Routledge, 1992), xiii–xvii, xiii.

[56] A Bottomley, 'Theory is a Process not an End: A Feminist Approach to the Practice of Theory' in
J Richardson and R Sandland, above n 29, 25–52, 38–39.

[57] *Ibid*.

[58] A Orford, 'Feminism, Imperialism and the Mission of International Law' (2002) 71 *Nordic Journal
of International Law* 275, 279.

[59] Nor am I saying that feminist internationalism consistently lives up to the standards; if it did, I
would expect socio-economic issues to feature far more significantly on the international women's
rights agenda. See further D Otto, 'A Post-Beijing Reflection on the Limitations and Potential of
Human Rights Discourse for Women' in KD Askin and DM Koenig (eds), *Women and International
Human Rights Law*, Vol 1 (Ardsley NY, Transnational Publishers, 1999), 115–38.

that 'women from highly industrialised countries' are expected to 'gain access to female "native informants" and produce knowledge about the victimized woman of the Third World', and are also 'authorize[d] to design rules that contribute to the protecting or saving of other women within the realms of international human rights law or international criminal law'.[60] I fully accept, then, that 'the real world', 'particular cases' and 'the facts on the ground' often function as ugly constraints on feminist legal internationalism. My point, however, is that these standards may have significant appeal to the domestic legal feminist who has felt constrained by the 'call to theory', and who is both weary of two decades of regular imports of US feminist theory and also impatient to end 'the indefinite postponement of the utopian moment'[61] that characterises the recent postmodern turn.

Borrowed Theory?

To recap: this essay is centred in a question concerning choice—specifically, in what it means to choose to do feminism 'here' rather than feminism 'there'. My argument is that the choices feminist legal academics make concerning what we might call 'jurisdiction' merit scrutiny by feminists. In the first part, I focused on the following teaser: is it easier today to be a feminist legal internationalist than a domestic feminist? Using Anglo-American legal feminism as a case study, I suggested that the attraction of feminist internationalism is that it seems to ease vexing questions about who and what feminism is for. In the remainder of the essay, I shall be changing tack slightly: the principal question stands but, to explore it further, I shall be digging down into specific practices of feminist legal internationalism and domestic legal feminism.

In this section, my starting point will be the feminist internationalist, and my focus will be on how the internationalist represents herself or himself. What interests me above all else is how the feminist legal internationalist chooses to do theory. I am intrigued by the fact that, in feminist international legal texts, theory tends to be represented as something that is borrowed, not self-generated. Consider the following two examples. First, in *Boundaries of International Law*, Hilary Charlesworth and Christine Chinkin make explicit reference to the term 'borrowing', emphasising that they have drawn on 'the rich literature of feminist theory to study [their] discipline, but ... have not articulated any original feminist theories or methods in the process'.[62] Second, Ruth Buchanan and Sundhya Pahuja, in their article in a recent special issue of the *Nordic Journal of International*

---

[60] Above n 58, 278, 281.

[61] R Sandland, above n 41, 117.

[62] H Charlesworth and C Chinkin, *The Boundaries of International Law: A Feminist Analysis* (Manchester, Manchester UP, 2000), 18. They emphasise that their 'academic training is in international law rather than in feminist theory and [that their] book is primarily addressed to those with an interest in international law'.

Law, note that both particular insights and 'many of the most well worn tools in [their] theoretical toolbox are drawn from feminist theorists'.[63]

It seems to me that there are compelling questions here. Is 'borrowing' exclusive to feminist legal internationalism? Is 'borrowing' a desirable practice for feminist legal internationalism? What is, and is not, being 'borrowed'? With what effect(s)? These and other similar questions coalesce around a concern that the practices of feminist legal internationalism could function to constrain both feminist legal internationalism itself and feminism in general. Ironically, this concern can also be taken as evidence of the emergence of feminist legal internationalism as a distinctive field of scholarship. This latter point is emphasised very clearly by Karen Knop in her introduction to a recent edited collection on gender and human rights:

> The corollary of moulding women's international human rights into a field, however, is that the literature becomes increasingly self-contained. It acquires its own dynamics, the positions in the literature come to be classifiable as majority or minority views, and debates are internalized. In the process, ideas received or adapted from other fields take on a life of their own and to some extent lose touch with their fate in those other fields. The emergence of women's international human rights as an independent subject of inquiry also has the effect of separating it from developments in fields that it takes for granted, or in fields that share some subset of its concerns but have not figured much in thinking about women's international human rights thus far.[64]

In what follows, I propose to look more closely at the practice of borrowing by feminist legal internationalists. I want to begin by emphasising how important it is that my concern about this practice be set in context. We need to remember, for example, that theory has not been a priority for international lawyers in general. Indeed, it is fair to say that there has been a strain of fairly trenchant anti-theoreticism within international legal scholarship.[65] It has been suggested that, historically, international theory did not evolve readily from the languages of political theory and law: the latter deal with 'the realm of normal relationships and calculable results ... International theory [by contrast] is the theory of survival'. In other words, political theory and law 'are the theory of the good life. [Thus] [w]hat for political theory is the extreme case (as revolution or civil war) is for international theory the regular case'.[66]

---

[63] Above n 21, 300, 301. But see the introduction to the issue by A Orford, above n 58, 275 ('Each of the contributions to this issue is an attempt to think through what it means to read and *write* feminist legal theory in an age dominated by internationalist narratives, whether of globalization and harmonization, or of high-tech wars on terror and for humanity.' (emphasis added)).

[64] Above n 15, 2.

[65] See, eg, I Brownlie, *The Rule of Law in International Affairs: International Law at the 50th Anniversary of the United Nations* (The Hague, Martinus Nijhoff, 1998), 11 ('With one exception, theory provides no benefits and frequently obscures the more interesting questions. The exception is produced by the fact that it is often practically useful to understand the theories which have influenced a particular individual or group of decision-makers.').

[66] M Wight, 'Why is There no International Theory?' in H Butterfield and M Wight (eds), *Diplomatic Investigations: Essays in the Theory of International Politics* (London, Allen & Unwin, 1966), 33, cited in M Koskenniemi, '"The Lady Doth Protest Too Much": Kosovo, and the Turn to Ethics in International Law' (2002) 65 *Modern Law Review* 159, 159.

It can also be argued that, more recently, the development of international law theory has been blunted by a new force; what Marti Koskenniemi calls the 'turn to ethics' amongst international law professionals who are focused on the moral necessity of intervention in crises—'[e]very international lawyer today negotiates genocide and war crimes and learns to speak the language of moral outrage as part of a discipline relearning the crusading spirit, and the civilising mission'.[67]

In addition, it seems that international legal scholarship in general and not just feminist legal internationalism owes a heavy debt to domestic innovation. Acknowledgement of this can be found in the introduction to a special issue of the *American Journal of International Law* dedicated to appraising international legal methods:

> Is there some mapping operation to understand or predict the receptivity of our field to innovations in domestic law, or is it a matter of ad hoc individual initiative by certain scholars? Moreover, one can ask if the origin of [numerous international legal] methods in the domestic paradigm means that international lawyers must await new sources of thinking within domestic law before bringing new insights and methods to international law. Perhaps, instead, international legal scholarship can build upon the differences between international law and domestic law to create new methods of inquiry—methods that might, in a reversal of fortune, trickle down (or over) to our domestic law colleagues instead of the other way around ... [In addition] [i]nstead of just defensively asking why international law has not followed certain methodological paths taken in domestic jurisprudence, we can focus on how our own ways of thinking about the law might resonate more among domestic lawyers.[68]

It seems then that the practice of borrowing is not exclusive to feminist legal internationalists; rather, it is endemic in international legal scholarship. This leads me relatively neatly to a second element of context: namely, that if the feminist legal internationalist proclivity for borrowing is evidence of discomfort with theory and theorising, there is a clear parallel here with recent Anglo-American academic feminism. Earlier in this essay, I noted the alienating effect of the 'call to theory' on domestic legal feminists. This seems an appropriate juncture for me to offer further evidence of the trouble that theory can cause for feminists. There is, first, the bewilderment that goes hand in hand with feminism's commitment to 'two powerful, mutually cancelling truths'; namely, that 'on the one hand there is no stable sex or gender and on the other, women too often find themselves unable to escape their gender and the sexual norms governing it'.[69] Then there is the fact that the ensuing question—'[w]hat to do with this double truth that does not even seem paradoxical in its operation?'[70]—is brutally challenging. Given this double blow, it is not

---

[67] M Koskenniemi, above n 66, 160. See also H Charlesworth, 'International Law: A Discipline of Crisis' (2002) 65 *Modern Law Review* 377.

[68] SR Ratner and AM Slaughter, 'Appraising the Methods of International Law: A Prospectus for Readers' (1999) 93 *American Journal of International Law* 291, 301.

[69] W Brown, above n 28, 568.

[70] *Ibid.*

surprising that Anglo-American feminism resonates with what Elspeth Probyn describes as '[t]he agony of the ampersand';[71] that is, the presence of a surplus of 'feminism & ...' publications, suggesting a 'deep anxiety about the right choice of theory'. Nor perhaps is it surprising that theorising about theory has been in such short supply within feminism that important questions have been left largely unanswered:

> [W]hat qualifies as 'theory'? Who is the author of 'theory'? Is it singular? Is it defined in opposition to something which is atheoretical, pretheoretical, or posttheoretical? What are the political implications of using 'theory' for feminist analysis, consider- ing that some of what appears under the sign of 'theory' has marked masculinist and Eurocentric roots? Is 'theory' distinct from politics? Is 'theory' an insidious form of politics? Can any politics be derived from 'theory', or is 'theory' itself a form of political nihilism?[72]

Yet even accepting all of the above, my uneasiness about the feminist legal inter- nationalist practice of borrowing persists. I suspect, first, that if due care is not exercised, borrowing by feminist legal internationalists could shore up a damaging star system within feminism; a system not just of theorists versus users of theory, but one that without justification, or even awareness, prioritises a particular femi- nist theory or a particular feminist theorist. This concern is sharpened by the preponderance of overviews in feminist international legal scholarship;[73] as a gen- eral rule, overviews do not feature ideas that are new or 'at the margins'. A second reason for my uneasiness about feminist legal internationalists' use of borrowing as description of their relationship to theory is that it perpetuates both international law's faltering relationship to theory and feminism's stock role within international legal discourse. It is apposite here to note that Anglo-American feminism came round to the view that naming its own work as theoretical, rather than presenting it as work that utilised the concepts of others (eg, Marxists), was itself a political project: it was a project that contested 'the institutional conditions in which "the- ory" was produced'.[74] And more generally it may be apposite to note that, today, theory itself is in need of support. Theory is under pressure following increased demands from governments and others for 'useful' knowledge and learning. According to these demands, the only theory that is useful is theory that applies, that is true and that sets out to solve 'real' problems. It seems to me therefore that to turn away from theory—whether by borrowing it and thus making others responsible for its production, or in some other way—is to make theory weaker in the face of contemporary anxieties. And, as Wendy Brown points out, this risks

---

[71] E Probyn, above n 3, 270.

[72] J Butler and JW Scott, 'Introduction' in J Butler and JW Scott, above n 55, xiii–xvii, xiii.

[73] L Stanley and S Wise, 'But the Empress has no Clothes! Some Awkward Questions about the "Missing Revolution" in Feminist Theory' (2000) 1 *Feminist Theory* 261, 263.

[74] S Ahmed, 'Whose Counting?' (2000) 1 *Feminist Theory* 97, 100, citing T de Lauretis, 'Displacing Hegemonic Discourses: Reflections on Feminist Theorising in the 1980's' (1988) 3 *Inscriptions* 127.

theory's 'most important political offering'; '[the] opening of a breathing space between the world of common meanings and the world of alternative ones, a space of potential renewal for thought, desire, and action'.[75] My third and final reason for disliking borrowing is more pedestrian. I dislike it because I think that it obscures the question of the relationship between international and local forms of feminism. It does this by turning both into cardboard cutouts of their actual selves—by suggesting, for instance, that feminist legal internationalism is not a 'natural' source of theory either for international feminists, or for their domestic counterparts.

I have a further interest in the practice of borrowing: I am intrigued by the question of *what* is being borrowed. The public/private divide; gender; the perils of essentialism; and the ups and downs of rights' arguments seem the obvious frontrunners. What is not obvious, however, is whether there is sufficient engagement with the fact that domestic feminism contains a range of understandings of these concepts and critiques and that, moreover, the range is not static.[76]

Consider the use of the concept of gender in feminist international legal scholarship.[77] In the US, the fractiousness of recent feminist debates about gender and essentialism has been tempered by lively discussion of whether gender should be ditched in favour of a concept of 'the lived body'. Proponents of the latter concept argue that it has the advantage over gender when it comes to theorising difference.[78] Others, such as Iris Marion Young, accept that this argument has merit but propose a double move as more appropriate: namely, 'the lived body' *plus* a 'resituated' concept of gender. The concept of gender is, they argue, essential 'for theorising social structures and their implications for the freedom and well being of persons'.[79] For me, the question that arises is: to what extent is feminist legal internationalism, with its comparatively longstanding use of the concept of gender, attentive to this unfolding domestic debate? More broadly, to what extent has feminist legal internationalism elaborated criteria to assist it in assessing the need

[75] W Brown, above n 12, 574.

[76] Similar concern has been expressed by J Halley, above n 15, 79, specifically in connection with take-up of the idea that 'sexuality is a distinct domain of women's subordination': 'I don't know what it should mean, inside these international human rights projects, or inside national contexts where these projects have become an element of left/liberal/progressive work, that the core idea—that sexuality is a distinct domain of women's subordination, and that feminism provides the "proper" justice discourse for addressing it—has been elaborated, modified, and contested in the Unitedstatesean intellectually and politically engaged left.'

[77] A second interesting line of enquiry concerns the concept of sexual health. Put to one side the reasons why feminist legal internationalists, like their Anglo-American counterparts, 'have preferred to work with gender rather than face sex' (A Bottomley, 'The Many Appearances of the Body in Feminist Scholarship' in A Bainham, S Day Sclater and M Richards (eds), *Body Lore and Laws* (Oxford, Hart, 2002), 127–48, 142). Instead consider whether feminist legal internationalism is sufficiently alert to what Carol Vance calls 'the complex genealogy' of sexual health. In particular, is it clued up about the following questions: is sexual health 'sexual', and to what extent is it concerned with 'health'? (C Vance, plenary address at *Gender, Sexuality and Law 2*, Conference, Keele University, 27–30 June 2002).

[78] T Moi, *What Is A Woman? And Other Essays* (New York, OUP, 1999).

[79] IM Young, 'Lived Body vs Gender: Reflections on Social Structure and Subjectivity' (2002) XV *Ratio* 410, 419.

for an ongoing infusion of domestic debates into the concepts it has borrowed? For example, would importation of 'the lived body' support elaboration of a universal sexual legal subject (as opposed to 'the homosexual legal subject' of privacy case law, or 'the woman of international legal discourse'), thereby bolstering Michele Grigolo's claim that equality of choices will be guaranteed only when the right to marry and found a family is subsumed within the right to respect for private life?[80] Alternatively, should the feminist internationalist opt for a concept of 'the lived body' plus a modified concept of gender and, if so, how would this impact on current uses of gender in international discourse?[81] Is an emphasis on gender needed to ensure that women as a *group* stay in the picture? Putting that another way, could a combination of concepts—gender and the lived body—help feminist legal internationalism to temper both essentialism and the valorisation of difference? In particular, might it bolster the burgeoning feminist internationalist interest in economic matters and cushion it against the damage that can be caused by inappropriate attention to difference—namely, the tendency to individualise agency to such an extent that gender-based structural differences are obscured?[82]

The Victim Subject: a New Frontier?

I want now to change tack again. In this final part of the essay, my starting point will be domestic feminism, specifically the variant with which I am familiar, Anglo-American feminism. As with the previous part, my approach will be to describe a particular trend within feminist scholarship. In so doing, I aim to bolster the argument that lies at the core of this essay: namely, that the choices feminist legal academics make concerning 'jurisdiction' merit scrutiny by feminists.

I shall begin by sketching some background detail. This is necessary in order to understand more about the context out of which the particular trend with which I am concerned has emerged. I hinted at some of this context earlier in the essay when commenting upon the impact of 'the call to theory' on feminist legal academics. Disputes about 'the call to theory'—or, if you prefer, about theory versus practice—are a constant of Anglo-American feminist legal texts: some texts depict theory/practice as a chicken/egg scenario, but disagree as to which is which; others refuse the chicken/egg scenario, preferring instead to invoke the inter-imbrication of theory and practice. Paradoxically, however, the question 'Just what is meant by the term "feminist theory" and what ideas and ways of working are included or

---

[80] See M Grigolo, 'Sexualities and the ECHR: Introducing the Universal Sexual Legal Subject' (2003) 14 *European Journal of International Law* 1023.

[81] See, eg, A Orford, above n 58, 283 ('How does [the] officially sanctioned desire to "include" women as participants relate to the current enthusiasm for exporting the institutions of the free market in the name of democracy?').

[82] See D Otto in this collection.

excluded from it "by definition"?' is 'surprisingly rarely asked'.[83] Furthermore, definitions of feminism seem to be offered as often, if not more so, by non-feminists as by feminists.[84]

That said, there are definite trends in contemporary Anglo-American feminist debates about 'what counts as feminist theory'. First, there appears to be some anxiety about the hierarchy, or 'star system', allegedly created on the one hand by the burgeoning number of overviews of feminism that purport to translate 'difficult' feminist theory[85] and, on the other, by dubious citation practices.[86] Second, there is increasing anxiety about the traditional stalwarts of feminist theory: about, for example, sexuality as the locus of women's subordination, or the public–private divide as an explanatory tool.[87] Third, there is less enthusiasm for personal narrative or confession as theory. Today, the once-modish 'I' of Anglo-American academic feminism provokes scepticism. In part, this is because the fashion for 'I'—for writing about one's own experience—led inexorably to some horribly indulgent work, '[s]ome of these personal excursions were token and kitsch'.[88] In larger part, however, it is because of the now-widespread realisation that writing about one's own experience is a highly-skilled endeavour; as Lorna Sage pointed out, 'you need to work hard to speak or write cogently in the first person, and to acknowledge that "there is always someone who is not speaking"'.[89] Fourth and finally, for contemporary Anglo-American feminism, 'critical theory' is (for the most part) what is considered desirable and worthwhile. What exactly is covered by 'critical theory' is not (currently) the subject of debate or contention. Moreover, for the most part, even those who claim to be engaged in it either see no need to define it, or prefer not to define it. That said, I think it fair to say that, in general, 'critical theory' reflects an orientation or commitment to what one of its leading US practitioners, Iris Marion Young, describes as 'socially and historically situated normative analysis and argument'.[90] Increasingly, it also seems to correlate with an idea of theory as theorising: theory, not as the last word, but as an ongoing project.

---

[83] L Stanley and S Wise, above n 73, 264.

[84] For criticism of the current position, see eg, B Winter, 'Who Counts (or Doesn't Count) What as Feminist Theory? An Exercise in Dictionary Use' (2000) 1 *Feminist Theory* 105.

[85] L Stanley and S Wise, above n 73.

[86] See, eg, KM Franke, 'On Discipline and Canon' (2003) 12 *Columbia Journal of Gender and Law* 639, 641: 'It is exciting that we can claim, and we can claim credibly, that we are writing in a field called feminist legal theory. But it is exactly these moments in field formation that I think are quite dangerous … Let me just say this: I believe that we disagree badly as feminists. Partly this is because the personal is political. Many of us—and I will include myself in this group—autobiographize our theoretical work. We are writing about ourselves, either explicitly or implicitly. We all risk this kind of standpoint epistemology even as we critique standpoint epistemology. It is what gives passion to our work. But it is something to be careful about. Given the personal stakes in our work, in our ideas, in the values we operationalize in our work, we take disagreements personally. We are hurt by them. And surely at times they become less than scholarly.'

[87] See K Knop, above n 15, especially the chapters by Halley, Knop and Sellers; and D Buss in this collection.

[88] L Sage, 'Mother's Back' (2000) *London Review of Books* (18 May) 37, 37.

[89] *Ibid.*

[90] IM Young, *Inclusion and Democracy* (New York, OUP, 2000), 10.

As noted above, these developments are not of direct interest to me in this essay. I have set them out in some detail because they provide the backdrop to the following question: are there Anglo-American feminists who (wittingly or otherwise) use 'an international orientation' to recreate the glory days of feminism— the days before 'past ideas' were dismissed or corrupted by the postmodern turn in Anglo-American feminism?

An article by Ratna Kapur, in which she pursues a 'friendly critique'[91] of Martha Nussbaum's enthusiasm about the 'good' relationship between theory and practice in Indian feminism, suggests that there is some evidence of the above practice. Interestingly, Kapur's concerns resonate with those put forward seventeen years ago by Chandra Talpade Mohanty.[92] Mohanty suggested that in representing 'third world women'—that is, in speaking of and for them—Western feminists were implicitly engaged in an act of self-representation. In other words, by portraying 'third world women' as a homogenous group (ie, as oppressed and impoverished), and thereby producing 'the image of an "average third world woman"',[93] Western feminists were implicitly authorising a sharply contrasting image of an 'average Western woman'. In effect:

> Third world women come to define not simply what Western women are not (and hence what they are), but also what they once were, before feminism allowed Western women to be emancipated. Third world women become relegated to 'our' pre-history; they embody what 'we' were, before liberation by feminism and modernity.[94]

Ratna Kapur's article points to the ongoing relevance of Mohanty's argument, whilst also suggesting that we may need to add a further layer to it: namely, is it the case that for some contemporary Anglo-American feminists 'third world feminists' are what Anglo-American feminists once were? What we were, that is, *after* 'past' feminism brought emancipation *but before* postmodern feminism tainted the feminist project?[95]

As mentioned above, Kapur's aim is to problematise the way in which US feminist theorist Martha Nussbaum invokes Indian feminism as part of her critique of US postmodern feminist theory (in particular, the variant associated with

---

[91] See R Kapur, 'Imperial Parody' (2001) 2 *Feminist Theory* 79, critiquing M Nussbaum, 'The Professor of Parody' (1999) *The New Republic* (22 Feb), 37, but emphasising, eg, that 'Nussbaum is well known as a sensitive and acute observer and someone who tries to live up to the philosopher's ideal of self-awareness' (p 83). See also R Kapur, above n 22.

[92] CT Mohanty, 'Under Western Eyes: Feminism and Colonial Discourse' (1988) 30 *Feminist Review* 61. For the author's own reflections on this piece, see CT Mohanty, *Feminism Without Borders: Decolonizing Theory, Practicing Solidarity* (Durham CA and London, Duke University Press, 2003), 221–51.

[93] CT Mohanty, 'Cartographies of Struggle: Third World Women and the Politics of Feminism' in CT Mohanty, A Russo and L Torres (eds), *Third World Women and the Politics of Feminism* (Bloomington, Indiana University Press, 1991), 65 (noting that the image is of one who has 'an essentially truncated life based on her feminine gender (read: sexually constrained) and her being "third world" (read: ignorant, poor, uneducated, tradition-bound, domestic, family-oriented, victimized etc.)'.

[94] S Ahmed, *Strange Encounters: Embodied Others in Post-Coloniality* (London, Routledge, 2000), 165.

[95] See eg, CA MacKinnon, 'Points against Postmodernism' (2000) 75 *Chicago Kent Law Review* 687, 710 ('We cannot have this postmodernism and still have a meaningful practice of women's human rights, far less a women's movement.').

Judith Butler, a fellow US feminist). In essence, Nussbaum's argument appears to be that Indian feminist theorising is 'good feminism'. That is, it grows out of the 'material condition' of women's experience of oppression and poverty; it is connected directly to claims for social justice; and, like the theorising of Catharine MacKinnon[96] (and unlike that of Judith Butler[97]), it is driven by the need to find 'practical solutions'. Nussbaum summarises feminist theorising in India as follows:

> In India, for example, academic feminists have thrown themselves into practical struggles, and feminist theorizing is closely tethered to practical commitments such as female literacy, the reform of unequal land laws, changes in rape law (which, in India today, has most of the flaws that the first generation of American feminists targeted), the effort to get social recognition for problems of sexual harassment and domestic violence. These feminists know that they live in the middle of a fiercely unjust reality; they cannot live with themselves without addressing it more or less daily, in theoretical writing and in their activities outside the seminar room.[98]

Kapur takes these conclusions and dissects them with considerable skill. She illustrates how Nussbaum invokes simultaneously the desirability of the way in which Indian feminists do theory and 'the backwardness of women's struggles in India' (the rape laws about which they write and campaign have 'most of the flaws that the first generation of American feminists targeted'). Kapur believes that feminist theorists in India would be bewildered by Nussbaum's depiction of them and their theorising preferences. She offers an account of feminist theorising in India that is very different to Nussbaum's: Kapur's description acknowledges that Indian feminists engage with a range of theories; that they do not rule out theory (even Butlerian theory) being practical;[99] and that they see allegedly practical-oriented solutions as in need of interrogation and historicisation.

Kapur also takes Nussbaum to task for defining Indian women's 'material condition' only in terms of their disadvantage. 'Such an image', Kapur points out, 'exists in the minds of those who require a victim on which to build their theories, rather than to provide a theory with which to empower "the victim"'.[100] This comment leads me to my second point. The point concerns what I see as the comment's chilling resonances. For me, Kapur's comment echoes with the auto-critique levelled by David Kennedy, Anne Orford and other international legal scholars, namely, that the identity of international human rights lawyers relies on

---

[96] See especially CA MacKinnon, *Feminism Unmodified* (Boston MA, Harvard UP, 1987) and *Towards a Feminist Theory of the State* (Boston MA, Harvard UP, 1989).

[97] See especially J Butler, *Gender Trouble* (New York, Routledge, 1990) and *Bodies That Matter* (New York, Routledge, 1993).

[98] M Nussbaum, cited in R Kapur, above n 91, 79.

[99] See, eg, R Kapur, above n 91, 82 ('Discourse theory and postmodernism also provide a more honest politics by complicating the idea of social reform, and seeing it as having the potential to have contradictory results for women. By simply listing these decontextualized and circumscribed reforms as proof of the achievements of Indian feminists, Nussbaum provides a skewed picture. The movements to reform the laws relating to women's rights in India cannot be held out as either a simple success or failure. Nussbaum's analysis does not reveal the complex and contradictory nature of these struggles and their outcomes.').

[100] *Ibid*, 83–4.

constructing others as victims.[101] It also resonates in a troubling manner with what might be called 'victimology'; that is, with the idea of women as victims and men as perpetrators. This idea has come to have overwhelming, even paradigmatic, explanatory force: it is the language we use to speak about rape, sexual slavery, and violence and disorder more generally. But it is a language that, for the most part, does not accommodate the violent feminine, men as victims, or women who do not measure up as 'orthodox' victims.[102] Overall, the point I am making is that, together, these resonances suggest that the door may be wide open for an unhealthy solidarity between feminism 'here' and feminism 'there': a solidarity that could hegemonise women as victims; stunt the development of feminism and of understandings of violence and immorality; and deliver the idea of 'helping women and children' as an endorsement for unwarranted interventions.

Conclusion

This essay has been about choice. As such, it has been about what is arguably the most iconic concept within Anglo-American feminism. That said, the angle taken on choice has been unconventional. The essay contains nothing about abortion. Nor does it have much to say about, for example, the choice between academia and activism, or theory and practice. Instead, in centring choice, the essay argues for consideration of a basic, but pressing, question: namely, what is implicated when a feminist—in particular, a feminist legal scholar—selects an international orientation over a domestic one, or vice versa? Or, in its shorthand version: what does it mean to choose to do feminism 'here' rather than feminism 'there'?

The essay rests on a couple of hunches: first, that there is currently a dynamic of 'here' and 'there' in Anglo-American academic legal feminism (in the courses we teach; in what we write about and whom we choose to reference; in where we aim to publish our writing and in how we picture our audiences); and second, that there is something to be learnt from understanding more about this dynamic. To substantiate these claims, two key arguments were made. The first was that, for a range of reasons, an internationalist orientation arguably has increasing allure for Anglo-American feminist scholars. The second argument concerned a specific trend within feminist legal internationalism on the one hand ('borrowing') and Anglo-American legal feminism on the other ('bringing back the glory days' via reference to foreign feminisms). Taken together, these trends suggest the need for a new critical project within feminism: working 'not from within feminism outward, but from within feminism inward',[103] we need to think more carefully about how domestic and international legal feminism relate to one another.

---

[101] See, eg, work by D Kennedy and A Orford, above nn 38 and 58.

[102] See, eg, R Jamieson, 'Genocide and the Social Production of Immorality' (1999) 3 *Theoretical Criminology* 131; and C Smart, 'Law's Power, the Sexed Body, and Feminist Discourse' (1990) 70 *Journal of Law and Society* 194.

[103] KM Franke, above n 86, 641.

5

Austerlitz and International Law: A Feminist Reading at the Boundaries

DORIS BUSS[*]

International law, like international relations, is a discipline defined in terms of its (presumed) spatial location. It is law that is international; law that governs the relations *between* states. It is law that is not national and law that transcends the nation. Paradoxically, while international law may be defined at the outset by a specific spatial reference, there is also a space-lessness about international law. There is no real international territory, outside a few narrow exceptions, and one would be at pains to *go to* the international. Indeed, we understand international law more in terms of its spatial lack; it is that which is not national.

Part of international law's space-lessness comes through its portrayal in terms of this spatial lack, that is, through the very process of assuming rather than interrogating its spatial claim. Within the international legal academy in particular, there is a sense that we know what we mean by *international* and it is otherwise a trouble-free, neutral space within which the business of legal relations takes place.[1] But what does it mean say that something is international, or, for that matter, transnational, global, local, national? Each of these terms suggests particular spaces and locations, identities and allegiances, relationships and ways of being. And yet, there is a tendency to take for granted[2]—to glide over without comment—'the international' of international law. What assumptions and expectations are we overlooking about how the spaces of international and national are constructed, with attendant implications for what we assume happens or ought to happen in these spaces?

In this chapter, I want to take up the idea of the spaces of international law to consider the implication of spatial construction—the global versus the local, the international and the national—for legal understanding and practice. My interest is shaped by those scholars of law and geography[3] who have emphasised the

Assistant Professor, Law Department, Carleton University, Ottawa, Canada. My thanks to the following people who offered helpful comments and feedback on earlier drafts of this chapter: Ruth Buchanan, Davina Cooper, Dianne George, Welling Hall, Karen Knop, Ambreena Manji, and the participants of the CRAT seminar, Carleton University.

[1] For a further of discussion of the 'aspatiality of legal knowledge' see NK Blomley, *Law, Space, and the Geographies of Power* (New York, The Guilford Press, 1994), ch 2. On the topic of absolute space, see N Smith and C Katz, 'Grounding Metaphor: Towards a Spatialized Politics' in M Keith and S Pile (eds), *Place and the Politics of Identity* (London and New York, Routledge, 1993) 67.

[2] On the taken-for-granted of absolute space, see Smith and Katz, above, n 1.

[3] See, eg, N Blomely, D Delaney, RT Ford (eds), *The Legal Geographies Reader: Law, Power, and Space* (Oxford, Blackwells, 2001), and further citations below.

normative dimensions of the encounter between space and law: the ways in which assumptions about spaces and proper places[4] normalise, and obscure from critical comment 'the assumed divide between law and social and political life that undergirds the soi-distant objectivity of law'.[5] Drawing on the insights offered by the growing scholarship on space and place, I argue for a reading of 'the international' of international law as reflecting 'ideas about what is right, just and appropriate'.[6]

My particular focus here is on boundaries; between public and private spaces, between international and national, between the inside and outside of international law. 'Boundaries *mean.* They signify, they differentiate, they unify the insides of the spaces that they mark.'[7] In this chapter, I am primarily interested in the question of international law's disciplinary boundaries, the ways in which the boundaries of international law regulate who and what is properly international.[8]

Feminist analysis of international law, and particularly the public/private divisions that underpin the discipline, offers an important account of the ways in which international law's spatiality is manifest in the highly gendered process of inclusion and exclusion. In this chapter, I turn to feminist accounts of international law as offering a framework for understanding the normative dimension of international law's spatial ordering. In this analysis, however, I am also interested in troubling what I see as a central tension in feminist theoretical accounts of the international: the question of inside and outside. In feminist accounts, the divides between public and private regulate the in and out of (public) international law, while the discipline's architecture, the boundaries between international and national, state and non-state, and law and not law, regulate the inside and outside of the study and practice of international law. But in sketching the apparatuses of exclusion,[9] feminist theory, I argue, may be offering a restricted political project based on inclusion, whether defined by the movement of disciplinary boundaries or the expansion of legal categories.

---

[4] The idea of proper place is taken from D Cooper, '"And You Can't Find Me Nowhere": Relocating Identity and Structure within Equality Jurisprudence' (2000) 27 *Journal of Law and Society* 249; 'Like Counting Stars: Re-Structuring Equality and Socio-legal Space of Same-Sex Marriage' in R Wintemute and M Andenaes (eds), *Legal Recognition of Same-Sex Partnerships: A Study of National, European and International Law* (Oxford, Hart Publishing, 2001); and T Cresswell, *In Place/Out of Place* (Minneapolis, University of Minnesota Press 1996).

[5] Blomley, n 1 above, at xii.

[6] Cresswell, n 4 above, at 8.

[7] D Delaney, RT Ford and N Blomley, 'Preface: Where is Law?' in Blomley, Delaney and Ford, n 3 above, at xvii.

[8] For a discussion of historiography, colonialism and the erasure effected through international law's disciplinary boundaries, see: N Berman, '"The Appeals of the Orient": Colonized Desire and the War of the Riff' in K Knop (ed), *Gender and Human Rights* (Oxford, Oxford University Press, 2004).

[9] Exclusion in the sense used by feminist international lawyers, and as I use it here, refers to the disciplinary movements by which women, in this case, are overlooked as the subjects of international law, or are otherwise rendered invisible and devalued within the spaces of law. This is a slightly different meaning from that found in some social geography literature, which refers to exclusion as a form of social control and ordering by which certain urban spaces are policed through the removal of groups seen as unclean or undesirable. See, eg D Sibley, *Geographies of Exclusion* (London and New York, Routledge, 1995).

I argue here for an explicit focus on the boundaries between and around spaces as a way to move beyond the limitations of inclusion and exclusion. By looking at the walls, barriers, boundaries that divide legal, political and disciplinary spaces, it may be possible to offer a closer reading of the political movements entailed in spatial allocation. A focus on boundaries has the additional benefit of bringing attention to the materiality of spatial barriers. That is, the spaces of international law and the boundaries of disciplinary fields are more than just metaphors denoting areas of inquiry.[10] The drawing of boundaries around, for example, international law is a structuring process, a means by which particular relationships, subjects, and interests are sited, positioned and prioritised. The definition of the international governs what we see as international law, how we see its impact, and who we see as law's subject. A focus on the boundaries of international law is one mechanism to understand better the acts of power through which we come to know the international.

Thus, while I started this paper by looking at the spaces of international law, I have come to a more particular focus on the architecture of spaces; the boundaries and apparatuses by which space is denoted and ordered. I begin by exploring in more detail the architecture of space through a reading of WG Sebald's acclaimed novel *Austerlitz*.[11] Sebald's discussion of architecture in this novel offers a number of insights into the question of spatial form; the relationship between the shape, size and walls of buildings, the spaces they denote and, in the context of Sebald's novel, the project of European violence. His attention to the materiality of structure, I argue, provides an important framework for a consideration of the structures of international law.

The Architecture of Space

Sebald's novel *Austerlitz* is the story of one man's search for his origins in pre-World War II Europe. Part of the *kinder* transport, Austerlitz as a young child is adopted by a dour and soul-less Welsh minister who insists on the eradication of any mention or memory of Austerlitz's origins. Austerlitz's search is a reclamation and negotiation of fragments; fragments of a life lived and not lived, fragments of a memory.[12] The first half of the novel consists of what appears to be a random

---

[10] For a discussion of the materiality of space, see MP Brown, *Closet Space: Geographies of Metaphor from the Body to the Globe* (London and New York, Routledge, 2000). The issue of the relationship between spatial metaphor and materiality, discussed in Brown, *Closet Space*, ch 1, is not one with which I engage here.

[11] A Ball (trans) (Vintage Press, Toronto, 2001). Many thanks to Ambreena Manji for drawing my attention to this novel.

[12] *Austerlitz* is a complex novel that touches on a number of themes related to memory, representations of the Holocaust, and the conditions of exile. For a nuanced reading of this novel and Sebald's work more generally, see P Schlesinger, 'W.G. Sebald and the Condition of Exile' (2004) 21 *Theory, Culture and Society* 43.

series of diversions from the main story as Austerlitz tutors our narrator on various topics from moths to nocturnal animals. In the first chapter, Austerlitz and our nameless narrator have a chance encounter in Antwerp, and Austerlitz begins his tutorials on European architecture, including train stations and, in this chapter, fortifications.

The focus in the first part of the novel is on the citadel in Antwerp, which, Austerlitz explains, illustrates the 'whole insanity of fortification and siegecraft'.[13] Having been thoroughly demolished in 1832, the fortress was rebuilt at great expense. As the building progressed so did the population of Antwerp. The size of the fortress was extended to accommodate the increase in population. Inevitably, it soon became apparent that in order fully to defend Antwerp, the fortress itself would need to be so large that 'the entire Belgian army would have been insufficient to garrison the fortifications'. The fortress was completed just prior to World War I, and proved to be 'completely useless for the defense of the city'.[14]

Sebald, through Austerlitz, continues on the next page to offer what now can only be seen as a terribly prescient comment on the hubris involved in the building of larger-than-life structures: 'At the most we gaze at it [the Palace of Justice in Brussels] in wonder, a kind of wonder which in itself is a form of dawning horror, for somehow we know by instinct that outsize buildings cast long shadows of their own destruction before them, and are designed from the first with an eye to their later existence in ruins.'[15]

In these extracts, Sebald introduces the first of what I take to be the two main themes traced through his discussion of the Antwerp citadel; the politics of architectural form and the architecture of European violence. Here, Austerlitz's commentary highlights the paradox of size and the limits of a perception of scale in terms of progress. In the case of Antwerp, the size of the fortification was always the wrong issue. Either the citadel was too small to be effective, or too large to be relevant. In either case, the citadel stood as a testament to a conviction about the importance of size or bellicosity in a changing era in which size and bellicosity did not necessarily pertain to security. In revealing the paradoxical insecurity of large edifices that 'cast long shadows of their own destruction', Sebald calls our attention to the form of space; the shape of buildings not as determinant of usage, but as reflecting the pre-occupations and obsessions of a particular world view.

Austerlitz's tutorials on architecture, though seemingly diversionary from the main 'story', can be read against the backdrop of Austerlitz's own experience as a child, as a careful, authorial laying of the groundwork for a consideration of European violence. In these comments, Sebald considers the violence of European architecture as a way to explore what I see as his second theme, the architecture of violence, and European violence in particular.

---

[13] *Austerlitz*, n 11 above, at 17.
[14] *Ibid*, at 18.
[15] *Ibid*, at 19.

I still had an image in my head of a star-shaped bastion with walls towering above a precise geometrical ground plan, but what I now saw before me was a low-built concrete mass, rounded at all its outer edges and giving the gruesome impression of something hunched and misshapen: the broad back of a monster ... I felt reluctant to pass through the black gateway into the fortress itself, and instead began by walking round it on the outside ... From whatever viewpoint I tried to form a picture of the complex I could make out no architectural plan, for its projections and indentations kept shifting, so far exceeding my comprehension ... And the longer I looked at it, the more often it forced me, as I felt, to lower my eyes, the less comprehensible it seemed to become.[16]

In this extract, our narrator tours the citadel in Antwerp the day following his meeting with Austerlitz. The above passage details in part the horror of the building he encounters. Our narrator describes the physical mass in terms of the monstrous. It has the 'broad back of a monster', rises from the soil 'like a whale',[17] and has the 'anatomical blueprint of some kind of alien and crab-like creature'.[18] Its walls are covered in 'open ulcers'.[19] It is a 'monstrous incarnation of ugliness and blind violence'.[20] In this passage, Sebald purposively challenges the form of architecture. Here, the form of the citadel is indeterminable. Up close, one can only see the monstrous. Any beauty or symmetry of the 'star-shaped' design is immaterial, dwarfed by the immensity and ugliness of the walls. As with many of the buildings Sebald introduces in this novel, the citadel becomes, almost inevitably, part of the machinery of European violence.[21]

Sebald's *Austerlitz* suggests for me a number of insights into a reading of the spaces of international law. First, in his account of the Antwerp citadel, Sebald's comments highlight the perils of size and the limits of scale. For Sebald, there is an indulgence involved in the building of large structures, and he invites us instead to consider the peace offered by 'buildings of *less* than normal size'.[22] He goes further to observe that building the perfect citadel brings with it the danger of obsolescence: '[I]n the end you might find yourself in a place fortified in every possible way, watching helplessly while the enemy troops, moving on to their own choice of terrain elsewhere, simply ignored their adversaries' fortresses, which had become positive arsenals of weaponry ... The frequent result, said Austerlitz ... was that you drew attention to your weakest point ...'[23]

Sebald's musings about the paradox of size suggest some caution in assuming the benefits of 'globalising' legal and political spaces. Is there a danger that in

---

[16] *Ibid*, at 25–26.
[17] *Ibid*, at 20.
[18] *Ibid*, at 22.
[19] *Ibid*, at 21.
[20] *Ibid*, at 21.
[21] Our narrator describes accounts of interrogation and torture that occurred in the citadel, *ibid*, at 26.
[22] *Ibid*, at 18
[23] *Ibid*, at 16.

the recent enthusiasm for global citizenship, cosmopolitan democracy[24] and 'cosmopolitan legality',[25] we are taking for granted, rather than interrogating, the nature of global political and legal space? Against the backdrop of Sebald's commentary on the Antwerp citadel, we might question why is it that we imagine the project of renewal[26] in terms of a rebuilding in which the walls of our edifice move ever outwards, or upwards.[27] In our move from the nation to the global, what assumptions about spatial ordering implicit in 'nation' and 'global' are left untroubled? And what small spaces of law and politics might we overlook in our move upwards and outwards?

Through Austerlitz's tutorial on the Antwerp citadel, Sebald makes clear the political nature of spatial form. The size and shape of the citadel is shown to be an act of folly; a commitment to an historic and outdated understanding of international relations. We see the citadel not as architectural expression, but as an overtly political statement; a world view whose violent underpinnings are evident in the monstrous materiality of the structure's walls. Sebald's comments here tease out a tension between the form and use of space. There is a discordance between the citadel's original design as a defensive structure, and its eventual use for torture and interrogation. We come to know the citadel's monstrosity not as a structure that defends, but as a structure that failed to defend. In this portrait of the citadel, Sebald reinforces the arguments made by those working in geography and related fields,[28] that space cannot be read simply as a neutral and unproblematic 'container for social action'.[29] We cannot read social relations off from spatial backdrops.

---

[24] For an overview of this large and growing field, see generally, D Archibugi, D Held and M Kòhler, *Re-imagining Political Community: Studies in Cosmopolitan Democracy* (Cambridge, Polity Press, 1998); D Held, *Democracy and the Global Order: From the Modern State to Cosmopolitan Governance* (Cambridge, Polity Press, 1995); R Falk, *On Humane Governance: Towards a New Global Politics* (Cambridge, Polity Press, 1995). On global citizenship, see generally, BS Turner, 'Cosmopolitan Virtue, Globalization and Patriotism' (2002) 19 *Theory, Culture & Society* 45; April Carter, *The Political Theory of Global Citizenship* (New York and London, Routledge, 2001); A Yeatman, 'Global ethics, Australian citizenship and the "boat people"—a symposium' (2003) 39 *Journal of Sociology* 15–22.

[25] There are clear parallels with my discomfort with 'cosmopolitan legality' and Ruth Buchanan's much more nuanced critical evaluation of this literature. See 'Perpetual Peace or Perpetual Process: Global Civil Society and Cosmopolitan Legality at the World Trade Organization' (2003) 16 *Leiden Journal of International Law* 673, and R Buchanan and S Pahuja, 'Collaboration, Cosmopolitanism and Complicity' (2002) 71 *Nordic Journal of International Law* 297.

[26] For a critical reading of the project of renewal in international law, see N Berman, 'Modernism, Nationalism, and the Rhetoric of Reconstruction' (1992) 4 *Yale Journal of Law and the Humanities* 351; D Kennedy, 'When Renewal Repeats: Thinking Against the Box' (2000) 32 *New York University Journal of International Law and Politics* 335.

[27] For a discussion of scale and perspective in international law that develops this point further, see A Riles, 'The View from the International Plane: Perspective and Scale in the Architecture of Colonial International Law' in N Blomley, D Delaney and R T Ford (eds), *The Legal Geography Reader* (Oxford, Blackwell Press, 2001) 276.

[28] For a discussion of space and international relations, see, eg, YH Ferguson and RJB Jones (eds), *Political Space: Frontiers of Change and Governance in a Globalizing World* (Albany, NY, State University of New York Press, 2002).

[29] T Killan, 'Public and Private, Power and Space' in A Light and JM Smith (eds), *Philosophy and Geography II: The Production of Public Space* (Lanham, CO, Rowman and Littlefield Publishers, 1998) 115 at 117.

Rather the space itself is constructed in and through social relations.[30] In the case of the Antwerp citadel, its original design is ultimately obscured by the monstrosity of its use.

But there is another level at which Sebald invites us to consider the violence of the citadel. In both its design and eventual use, the citadel is an expression of European violence. In the passage cited above, in which the narrator encounters the oozing and ulcerous walls, Sebald draws the reader to the physical materiality of the citadel. Together with the narrator, we see and feel, and are overwhelmed by, the monstrous presence of this building. It takes on its monstrosity, I argue, also in its very creation as an element of European warfare. It might be argued that Sebald is suggesting that Europe cannot escape the violence of its past; that it is doomed to recreate its violence in new and more horrific ways. For my purposes here, Sebald's focus on the materiality of the walls offers two important insights.

First, the walls of the citadel are physical reminders that spaces are not solely metaphoric. The violent presence of the citadel underscores the materiality of oppression.[31] Walls exclude, contain, limit, obscure, and remove. Second, this materiality also signals fixity. While spaces and boundaries by definition are fluid, negotiable and porous, they also endure. Particular spaces or structures can be what David Harvey refers to as 'fixed markers of human memory and of social values'.[32] We might, as Sebald has done here, look more closely at structures themselves as materialisations of dominance and oppression.[33]

In the following discussion, I turn to feminist analysis of the public and private divisions as offering important insights into the spatial framing of international law. This literature, I argue, demonstrates how the boundaries of the discipline are politically drawn and function to regulate who and what is constituted as properly within the remit of international law. My objective here is to consider spatial ordering as part of the process by which, to use the words of David Kennedy, the 'discipline [of international law] participates in keeping a terribly unjust international order up and running, even as it seeks with great passion to be a voice for humanitarian reform, even as it renews itself constantly to be more effective'.[34] If the boundaries of the discipline are seen as a materialisation of the power/knowledge through which dominance is effected, what implications might this have for a project of renewal in which the boundaries are redrawn to better respond to 'injustices'?[35]

---

[30] LA Staeheli and PM Martin, 'Spaces for Feminism in Geography' (2000) 90 *The Annals of the American Academy of Political and Social Science* 135.

[31] MP Brown, n 10 above, at 3.

[32] D Harvey, 'Between Space and Time: Reflections on the Geographical Imagination' (1990) 80 *Annals of the Association of American Geographers* 418, at 429.

[33] MP Brown, n 10 above, at 3.

[34] 'When Renewal Repeats: Thinking Against the Box' in W Brown and J Halley (eds), *Left Legalism/Left Critique* (Durham, Duke University Press, 2002) 373 at 384.

[35] H Charlesworth and C Chinkin, *The Boundaries of International Law: A Feminist Analysis* (Manchester, Manchester University Press, 2000).

Public and Private and the Ordering of Spaces

In the early 1990s, the unfolding feminist analyses of international law focused on the divisions between material and ideological spheres of public and private that were said to underpin and overlay international law.[36] Feminists explored the ways in which international law was structured along a divide between first, public and private international law, with the former dealing with matters between states, and private international law, referring alternately to conflict of laws and/or 'international economic law'. Within the discipline itself, a distinction is made between issues of international concern and those that are 'properly within national, or domestic jurisdiction'.[37] Public/private divisions are additionally evident in the distinctions between, and legal recognition of, public international organisations (such as the UN) and private (non-state) actors; or between state-sanctioned international human rights violations (subject to international legal regulation) and those committed by private, non-state actors (beyond the reach of international law).[38]

With the 'excavation'[39] of each layer of public and private, feminists noted the normative dimension to the gendered division between the spheres, the valuing

[36] H Charlesworth, C Chinkin and S Wright, 'Feminist Approaches to International Law' (1991) 85 *American Journal of International Law* 613; K Engle, 'After the Collapse of the Public/Private Distinction: Strategizing Women's Rights' in D Dallmeyer (ed), *Reconceiving Reality: Women and International Law* (Washington, DC, American Society of International Law, 1993); C MacKinnon, 'On Torture: A Feminist Perspective on Human Rights' in KE Mahoney and P Mahoney (eds), *Human Rights in the Twenty-First Century: A Global Challenge* (Dordrecht, Martinus Nijhoff, 1993); C Romany, 'Women as *Aliens*: A Feminist Critique of the Public/Private Distinction in International Human Rights Law' (1993) 6 *Harvard Human Rights Journal* 87; R Copelon, 'Recognizing the Egregious in the Everyday: Domestic Violence as Torture' (1994) 25 *Columbia Human Rights Law Review* 291; D Buss, 'Going Global: Feminist Theory, International Law, and the Public/Private Divide' in SB Boyd (ed), *Challenging the Public/Private Divide: Feminism, Law, and Public Policy* (Toronto University Press, Toronto, 1997); H Charlesworth, 'Worlds Apart: Public/Private Distinctions in International Law' in M Thornton (ed), *Public and Private: Feminist Legal Debates* (Melbourne, Oxford University Press, 1995); K Engle, 'Views from the Margins: A Response to David Kennedy' (1994) 105 *Utah Law Review* 105; J Mertus and P Goldberg, 'A Perspective on Women and International Human Rights After the Vienna Declaration: The Inside/Outside Construct' (1994) 26 *International Law and Politics* 201; C Romany, 'State Responsibility goes Private: A Feminist Critique of the Public/Private Distinction in International Human Rights Law' in R Cook (ed), *Human Rights of Women: National and International Perspectives* (Philadelphia, University of Pennsylvania Press, 1994); K Walker, 'An Exploration of Article 2(7) of the United Nations Charter as an Embodiment of the Public/Private Distinction in International Law' (1994) 26 *International Law and Politics* 173–99; D Sullivan, 'The Public/Private Distinction in International Human Rights Law' in J Peters and A Wolper (eds), *Women's Rights Human Rights: International Feminist Perspectives* (New York, Routledge Press, 1995); C Chinkin, 'A Critique of the Public/Private Dimension' (1999) 10(2) *European Journal of International Law* 387; H Charlesworth and C Chinkin, n 35 above, 56–9.

[37] H Charlesworth 'Worlds Apart' (1995), at 243.

[38] See, eg, H Charlesworth, 'What are "Women's International Human Rights"?' in R Cook (ed), *Human Rights of Women: National and International Perspectives* (Philadelphia, University of Pennsylvania Press, 1994); Copelon, n 36 above; MacKinnon, n 36 above.

[39] H Charlesworth and C Chinkin, n 35 above, at 18.

and privileging of the (male) public over the (female) private. The focus on the public, and the exclusion of private matters from the remit of international law reinforces as natural a legal system concentrated exclusively on a narrow range of affairs conducted between states that 'reflects male priorities'.[40]

Despite being a rather well-worn area of feminist theory,[41] the public and private dichotomy continues to be an animating topic for feminists and others seeking to understand, among other things, the spatial categorisations of politics and power. While the public/private divide was and continues to be an important focus for some feminist theorising, its theoretical deployment is not without difficulty. In a 1993 article, Nicola Lacey outlined a number of problems inherent in feminist analyses of the public/private divide: the reification of public and private as actual spheres; theoretical collapsing of the descriptive with the normative; a tendency to treat public and private as distinct, bounded spaces that belies their fluidity; and ultimately, a disproportionate and obfuscatory emphasis on the state 'as the touchstone of "the public" and of regulation'.[42] Together, these highlight the difficulty 'that once one engages in a critique of the [public/private] division, one gets sucked into the very categorization one is attempting to undermine.'[43]

With the benefit of hindsight, some of the problems identified by Lacey and others might be found in feminist analyses of the public and private divisions in international law. For example, feminist critical analyses of the gendered operation of international law exposes how the divide between the state/domestic realm and the international/public realm works to position women, their lives and interests within the domestic realm of internal state sovereignty, as beyond the reach of (public) international law. This is certainly a trenchant critique, and yet it relies upon taking public international law at its word; that matters are *either* international *or* domestic/state, and that women's lives are private and not part of public international law. By accepting that the divisions between international and state exist, have some meaning and coherence, and accord, at some level, with the lives of women, feminist analyses may obscure, however unwittingly, the many points at which domestic and international intermingle, or are otherwise unstable categories, particularly in explaining the role of international law in the lives of women.

Additionally, the tendency to describe the domestic character of the state as analogous to the patriarchal family,[44] with the state and its government standing metaphorically for the patriarch, reinforces a conception of public and private

---

[40] *Ibid.*

[41] For an overview of feminist theorising on the public/private divide, see SB Boyd, 'Introduction: Challenging the Public/Private Divide: An Overview' in SB Boyd (ed), *Challenging the Public/Private Divide: Feminism, Law, and Public Policy* (Toronto, University of Toronto Press, 1997); B Cossman and J Fudge (eds), *Privatization, Law and the Challenge to Feminism* (Toronto, University of Toronto Press, 2002); R Fletcher 'Feminist Legal Theory' in R Banakar and M Travers (eds), *An Introduction to Law and Social Theory* (Oxford, Hart Publishing, 2002) 135.

[42] 'Theory into Practice? Pornography and the Public/Private Dichotomy?' (1993) 20 *Journal of Law and Society* 93 at 100–101. See also Boyd, n 41 above; Killan, n 29 above.

[43] Lacey, n 42 above, at 101.

[44] H Charlesworth, 'What are "Women's International Human Rights"?', n 38 above, at 68.

spheres as coherent embodied spaces.[45] John Agnew argues that constructing the state as analytically equivalent to the individual means that states are then treated as 'the moral equivalents to individual persons'.[46] Feminist efforts to challenge the statism of international law may in fact be undermined by its own state-as-patriarch argument. Finally, and perhaps most problematically, the emphasis on unearthing and revealing the ways in which the layers of public and private remove women from the international, carries with it the implication that the answer to this problem is found in the public world of legal regulation and recognition.[47]

Each of these three tendencies—the acceptance of a domestic/international binary, the conflation of the state with the (patriarchal) individual, and the definition of public in terms of (international legal) regulation—is important in understanding the unfolding and possible future directions of feminist engagement with international law. My hesitation with feminist analysis of the public/private divisions in international law is that it tends to a politics framed in terms of inclusion or expansion; altering the category of 'public' so that it includes within it legal recognition of the relations or conditions heretofore (un)seen as private. And with this hesitation about a politics of inclusion, I am left with something of a puzzle. On the one hand, feminist analysis of the public and private in international law offers an important framework for a socio-spatial critique. That is, this literature explicitly recognises and calls our attention to the constitution of spaces— international, national, local, global, public and private—as a political process. And through this recognition is a fundamental challenge to international law; the means by which it delimits the proper place and remit of law and politics. At the same time as recognising the spatiality of international law, some feminist analysis evinces an enduring commitment to the space of international law, so that spatial metaphors— the descriptions of being in and out of disciplines, spaces, places—continue to shape feminist understanding of the possibility of international politics.

This tension is evident in an article by Gillian Youngs[48] on Amnesty International's (AI's) report on violence against women, *Broken Bodies, Shattered Minds: Torture and Ill-Treatment of Women*.[49] In this report, AI makes the case that some private forms of violence against women (such as violence in the home), normally outside of human rights law, could be considered a form of torture and hence attract international sanction under, among other things, the UN Convention against Torture. AI is, in effect, taking up the call of some feminists[50]

---

[45] K Knop, 'Re/Statements: Feminism and State Sovereignty in International Law' (1993) 3 *Transnational Law and Contemporary Problems* 293.

[46] J Agnew, 'Political Power and Geographical Scale' in Y Ferguson and RJB Jones (eds), *Political Space: Frontiers of Change and Governance in a Globalizing World* (Albany, NY, State University of New York Press, 2002) 116, 125–6.

[47] See, eg, H Charlesworth, 'What are "Women's International Human Rights"?', n 38 above, at 71; J Mertus and P Goldberg, n 36 above, at 214.

[48] 'Private Pain/Public Peace: Women's Rights as Human Rights and Amnesty International's Report on Violence against Women' (2003) 28 *Signs* 1209.

[49] ACT 40/001/2001.

[50] See, eg, Copelon, n 36 above.

who have long made this argument. The difficulty, however, is that human rights law generally, and torture in particular, requires a state nexus. That is, international human rights law does not, as a rule, extend to private 'non-state' relationships, and the definition of torture in the Convention requires that the impugned acts be done 'by or at the instigation of or with the consent or acquiescence of a public official'.[51] Indeed, torture is an often-cited example of how the public/private divide functions to erase from international legal scrutiny human rights violations against women. Precisely because of the state nexus, international human rights law and the bodies involved in its promulgation and application, including AI, have, until relatively recently, largely ignored the area of women's rights as falling outside of an international human rights regime focused on a state's actions towards it citizens.[52]

AI's 2001 report, according to Youngs, is thus a breakthrough. It argues, among other things, for a concept of 'due diligence' by which states must 'both actively protect individuals from abuses of their rights and fully address breaches of rights through legal process'.[53] By incorporating a legal obligation for due diligence, 'state accountability [is extended] to the actions of private individuals who deprive a person of his or her human rights'.[54] For Youngs, AI's approach represents a recognition and 'an integrating [of] private as well as public forms of violence against women' into human rights law.[55]

Youngs argues, correctly I think, that the AI report constitutes an important and transgressive approach to 'spatial politics'.[56] AI utilises a number of techniques to forefront the relationship of abuse between men and women, rather than its location. The concept of due diligence, by which the state's legal obligation to protect its citizens is activated, together with an understanding of violence against women as part of a continuum,[57] attempts to collapse, in effect, the divisions between public and private that characterise the legal recognition of violence. By 'breaching the public/private divide in illustrating that wherever the abuse takes place, it remains abuse', AI, according to Youngs, applies a deeply 'structural' understanding of violence and gender discrimination.[58] This move, Youngs argues, is more significant than simply expanding state accountability; it is an act of disruption. By 'writing the body' into 'local politics, international politics, and international political economy', AI, like feminist scholarship, can disrupt those abstractions by which the ordering of 'structures, processes and identities' is made possible.[59]

---

[51] Convention Against Torture and Other Cruel, Inhuman or Degrading Treatment or Punishment, UN Doc A/39/51 (1984), Article 1.

[52] S Bahar, 'Human Rights are Women's Right: Amnesty International and the Family' (1996) 11 *Hypatia* 105.

[53] Youngs, n 48 above, at 1211.

[54] *Ibid.*

[55] *Ibid*, at 1209.

[56] *Ibid.*

[57] *Ibid*, at 1221.

[58] *Ibid*, at 1222.

[59] *Ibid*, at 1215.

In this analysis, both Youngs and AI highlight the way spatial locations and the boundaries between spaces—in this case public and private—are important in the ordering of social relations; the ways in which we accept the location of the social (as distinct from the political or the legal), and the social relationships we identify as properly within the remit of international law and politics. By focusing on the power relationship between men and women through which violence is enabled and naturalised, the AI report weakens the normative grip of public and private ideology on the perception and application of international human rights law.

But there is another aspect of Youngs' analysis that troubles me, and this is what appears to be the enduring hold of spatial sense, in this case of 'in' and 'out', 'within' and 'beyond'. There is an implicit suggestion in this analysis that AI's work in the area of torture and violence against women constitutes a rewriting of the public/private divide. '[I]n line with feminist critiques stressing the political nature of private as well as public forms of violence against women, the report reconfigures state accountability into the expanded sphere of private as well as public domains.'[60] I am troubled by the way Youngs relies on the language and imagery of expansion. The AI report, for example, is described as attempting 'to raise the accountability threshold of states by going beyond the public boundaries of the official arms of the state ... to include private individuals'.[61]

Implicit in this approach is an argument that having revealed the boundaries that divide and regulate, the next step is to redraw or extend beyond the boundary, only this time in a more inclusive way. While I agree that securing greater international attention to violence against women may indeed by a good thing, and in some cases 'inclusion' may be the desired goal, I am unsettled by the unstated here: that inclusion and expansion are necessarily progress. Surely this begs the question: What are we being included in, and under whose terms? For example, we might question torture itself as a framework for thinking about and categorising violence against women. Certainly, acts of violence against women can, and regrettably all too often do, constitute torture as a violation of international human rights law. But why is it that, in order to gain international legal and political recognition, violence against women has to be construed in terms of 'the most severe', whether it be domestic violence as torture or rape as genocide? Is including (some) violence against women within the remit of the Torture Convention the best way forward in securing international recognition of, and action upon, the complex apparatus through which violence against women is enabled?

To this, Youngs might respond that AI and feminists need to work with the tools available to them. The Torture Convention, as a treaty that bridges the gap between international human rights and international criminal law, has strong language, reasonable enforcement and a recognised status under international law. If torture defines the crime, why not use it? And, it is here, I think, that the limitations of AI's approach are most apparent. While seeking to disrupt the pub-

---

[60] *Ibid*, at 1211.
[61] *Ibid*, at 1213.

lic and private divides by which international law orders and defines the relationships it recognises, AI inevitably focuses on a policy of inclusion within, such as
inclusion within the terms of the Torture Convention. In doing so, AI leaves in
place the very logic of the spatial architecture of international law.[62] Violence
against women is understood as a problem that is more than a private matter
between individuals, yet it is ultimately a matter between women and the state.
Through the principle of due diligence the state is paradoxically both the agent primarily responsible for violence against women (by not being diligent enough), and
the chief apparatus for deterring violence against women (by being more diligent).

The limitations of an approach in which the state does 'double duty' as both
cause and solution to violence against women is noted by Youngs, who suggests
that this focus on the state is inevitable given the nature of AI's political mandate
and the limitations of 'working for change within the system'.[63] This may be true,
but it raises questions about how far AI has in fact gone in challenging the spatial
ordering of international law, and how far it has gone in offering a more structural
account of violence against women. For example, by focusing on state responsibility for violence against women, we are left with two main actors in the scenario
of violence: 'the state' and 'the woman'. While the concept of due diligence may
call for a more systemic analysis of the state's own complicity, it leaves intact two
problematic assumptions. First, that violence against women is a domestic state
matter, though one with which the international community *ought* to involve
itself at the level of adjudication. Second, that the state (alone) is responsible for
'women's fate as objects of sexist sexual construction'.[64] There is little room here
for an analysis of the complex factors that might extend beyond the domestic state
but which are deeply entwined with state complicity in violence against women.
There is even less room for considering the interplay between an understanding
of violence against women as a civil and political rights issue (and hence falling
within the weightier human rights treaties), and the social and economic conditions
that shape many women's lives. And the recognition of *international* complicity,
through 'humanitarian intervention', economic insecurity, structural adjustment,
in contributing to violence against women, is well off the map.

The result, I argue, is that while AI's report offers a way of addressing violence
against women that transcends the limitations of the public/private divides, I am
not sure it challenges the architecture of international law by which social relations are placed within or beyond law's remit. In analogous terms, the AI report
might be the equivalent to a rebuilding of the Antwerp citadel to either change its
shape, or extend and bring within its walls more Belgian citizens. But in such a
rebuilding, the structure's own violence is left intact, and we assume, rather than
interrogate, the functional capacity of such a structure. Further, a focus on inclu-

---

[62] Annelise Riles makes a similar argument, which I found persuasive, in her analysis of scale and
perspective in colonial application of international law in Fiji. A Riles, n 27 above, at 283.

[63] G Youngs, n 48 above, at 1223.

[64] W Brown, *States of Injury: Power and Freedom in Late Modernity* (Princeton, NY, Princeton
University Press, 1995) at 170.

sion within, or the expansion of legal categories, does not necessarily address the materiality of the boundary as a mechanism of dominance and oppression. Establishing boundaries, even more inclusive ones, functions to freeze in time particular meanings and social relations.[65] The rebuilding of boundaries might constitute what Doreen Massey refers to as the stabilisation of 'particular envelopes of space-time'.[66] In this case, we might question if the re-established boundaries also stabilise an account of public international law that maintains a problematic and profoundly unequal spatial delimitation between political and economic, public and private law'.[67]

How might we approach a spatial analysis of international law that moves beyond the limits of an analysis based on inclusion/exclusion? Doreen Massey argues for an approach that focuses on 'interrelationships rather than through the imposition of boundaries'.[68] Such an approach might focus on, for example, the interrelationship between violence against women, state complicity, and the broad networks of economic and political power through which violence is enabled and normalised.

Yet another approach might be to eschew international law's disciplinary account of itself (and hence its own spatial delimitations) in favour of accounts of 'the international' and law from outside the discipline. Philip Darby,[69] in his analysis of the colonising effect of 'globalization' knowledge, suggests two possible ways for doing this. One is to challenge the 'line between activism and knowledge'.[70] For example, Darby considers how the protestors at the Seattle demonstrations against the World Trade Conference 'can be seen as revealing the political significance of knowledges about globalization that, for the most part, lay outside the discourse of the academy'.[71] Second, drawing on the work of Jean and John Comaroff, Darby argues that entering 'the lifeworlds of ordinary people and discerning a political salience in their anxieties and aspirations' can lead to thinking about 'the meaning and location of the international'[72] in new ways.

A third possibility, and one I explore in the following section, is to return to the theme of boundaries to look more closely at the borders, walls, lines through which distinctions between the national and international are drawn. Rather than arguing for relocating or rewriting the boundary, I want to focus on the materiality of the boundaries as constituting political and legal spaces through which identity and location may be contested.

---

[65] D Massey, *Space, Place and Gender* (Cambridge, Polity Press, 1994) 5.

[66] *Ibid.*

[67] D Kennedy, 'When Renewal Repeats: Thinking Against the Box' (2000) 32 *New York University Journal of International Law and Politics* 335.

[68] Massey, n 65 above, at 7.

[69] P Darby, 'Reconfiguring "the International": Knowledge Machines, Boundaries, and Exclusions' (2003) 28 *Alternatives* 141–66.

[70] *Ibid*, at 150.

[71] *Ibid.*

[72] *Ibid*, at 159.

Law at the Boundaries

Throughout this chapter, I have referred to 'walls' and 'boundaries', using these terms perhaps indiscriminately to explore the divisions between spaces and categories of knowledge. While both walls and boundaries are often thought of as solid, material masses, my use is not meant to imply the divisions between international and national or law and politics are rigid barriers. I could equally refer to the drawing of lines, or, as Rob Walker[73] does, the 'lines of connection and lines of movement'. In any of these formulations, the point of reference is the distinction between spaces, spheres, levels or places. In this process of distinction is a series of political movements, and possibilities of contestation.

Rob Walker, for example, urges caution in the cosmopolitan turn found in much international studies literature, in which 'historical, ethical, and political destiny' is framed as 'a grand trek from ... polis to cosmopolis, especially from nationalism to some other kind of global/human destiny'.[74] For Walker, the shift from polis to cosmopolis overlooks the question of authority[75]—the 'complexity of problems concerning the authorization of authority'—and by extension the 'limits of modern political possibility/impossibility'.[76] That is, in the urge to move forward, often imagined in terms of an upward climb or a movement of scale, we may overlook and leave unaddressed the foundational political questions which frame the very possibility of politics.

In the context of my analysis, I would argue, drawing on Walker, that investigating the boundary itself allows for a different approach to space and politics, one that insists on examining the political meaning and effect of boundaries. To a large extent, I see feminist analysis, particularly of public and private divisions, as offering the framework for just this sort of inquiry. By drawing attention to the public/private divide, feminists expose how this and other boundaries are important devices by which inequalities are sustained through the processes of ordering. That is, the public/private divide is one mechanism for positioning and ranking who and what belongs where, with implications for the distribution of benefits, access, respect and so on.[77]

But feminist theory, for the reasons discussed above, needs to go further than this. One way forward may be to consider the boundary itself as a site of politics.

---

[73] 'Polis, Cosmopolis, Politics' (2003) 28 *Alternatives* 267 at 281. See also, RBJ Walker, (2002) 'After the Future: Enclosures, Connections, Politics', in R Falk, LEJ Ruiz, RBJ Walker (eds), *Reframing the International: Law, Culture, Politics* (London and New York, Routledge, 2002) 3.

[74] 'Polis, Cosmopolis, Politics', n 73 above, at 269.

[75] On the question of law's authority, see Buchanan and Johnson, this volume; Buchanan, 'Perpetual Peace or Perpetual Process', n 25 above.

[76] 'Polis, Cosmopolis, Politics', n 73 above, at 271.

[77] D Cooper, *Challenging Diversity: Rethinking Equality and the Value of Difference* (Cambridge, Cambridge University Press, 2004), ch 5.

Ruth Buchanan's[78] work on the Maquiladora industries in Mexico provides an example of such an analysis. In her study of the North American Free Trade Agreement (NAFTA), Buchanan considers the industrial development area along the US/Mexico border as the 'borderlands'. Buchanan uses the idea of borderlands to explore the fragmentation and diffusion that may accompany globalising forces, including the liberalisation of trade brought about through regimes, such as NAFTA. In her analysis, NAFTA not only produced economic integration among the three member countries, it 'also further exacerbates differences between localities, industries, and labor markets'.[79] The borderlands became a site at which political, legal and economic identities are formed and contested, and the very meaning of border is subject to redefinition.

Buchanan's concept of the borderlands is instructive also about the enduring and self-referential nature of the dichotomy between international and national where that which is not one is the other.[80] Buchanan's idea of the borderlands helps to disrupt this dichotomy, and to introduce the idea of space that is not necessarily or entirely national or international. Christine Sylvester, in the context of her work on political economy and women's groups in Zimbabwe, takes this further to consider the sites of political economy that might be found in those spaces between the household and the economic. 'Where else are the lines smudged between household places and international political economies in ways that reconstitute identities and redistribute resources? Where should we be looking, in other words, for relations of international political economy, and what transversals of place and knowledge might we find there?'[81]

Both Buchanan and Sylvester provide accounts of boundary that start from a consideration of the activities through which and against which social, political and economic relationships take shape. The boundary then becomes a place in which those relationships are contested, defined and redefined. For these authors, the political space that emerges is not definable solely in terms of international or national. It is both and neither.

For feminist scholarship on international law and politics, the focus on boundaries, with the consequent challenge to the spaces of politics and law, is significant. If the boundary itself is a place of politics, then the redrawing or building of boundaries is both inevitable[82] and a (productive?) place of trouble. Part of the feminist project must be to examine the trouble of boundaries. Perhaps by moving away from an analysis centered on in or out, we might approach boundaries as defining, constituting, and possibly opening up.

---

[78] R Buchanan 'Border Crossings: NAFTA, Regulatory Restructuring and the Politics of Place' in N Blomley, D Delaney and RT Ford (eds), *The Legal Geographies Reader* (Oxford, Blackwell, 2001).

[79] *Ibid*, at 287.

[80] See also R Buchanan, and S Pahuja, 'Legal Imperialism: Empire's Invisible Hand?' in J Dean and P Passavant (eds), *The Empire's New Clothes* (London and New York, Routledge, 2004).

[81] C Sylvester, *Feminist International Relations: An Unfinished Journey* (Cambridge, Cambridge University Press, 2002) at 263.

[82] A Orford, 'Feminism, Imperialism and the Mission of International Law' (2002) 71 *Nordic Journal of International Law* 275, 291.

One area of opening up might be found in Sylvester's consideration of the 'everyday' as a place of politics. By looking at international law and politics in the 'lifeworld'[83] we might offer a further challenge to the enduring binaries of international and national. In a recent interview, for example, Cynthia Enloe argued that terrorism and the identity of terrorists need to be considered in the context of a militarised social system. For her, this means considering the relationship between warlordism and marriage 'as if that connection actually mattered, as if marriages also were a transaction of power ….'[84] Work like Enloe's constitutes a challenge to the spatial delimitation of 'international' in terms of the high politics of state action. It exposes the arbitrariness and inequality of what we commonly accept as properly the weighty matters of inter-state politics. By placing sex and gender,[85] 'passion and play',[86] on the international agenda, feminists are calling attention to their erasure and, one hopes, their importance in a full understanding of 'international' politics.

Conclusion

In this chapter, I have offered a preliminary, and in places tentative, discussion of what an encounter between geography and international law might suggest about the *spaces* of international law. I have argued here for a closer consideration of feminist accounts of the public/private divides in international law as offering a framework for thinking about the way in which the divisions between spaces function normatively to position, prioritise and allocate relationships according to their proper place.

By focusing on the boundaries themselves, I have argued for an approach that questions rather than assumes the location, and hence space, of law and politics. In using terms like 'boundary' or 'walls', I realise that I am on shaky ground. Walls, barriers, boundaries, divisions tend to suggest a permanence and solidity that is counterintuitive to the sense of fluidity often presumed to characterise this particular 'global moment'. While I do not mean to suggest that disciplinary, legal or political barriers are in fact solid walls, withstanding pressure and the erosion of time, I do want to emphasise a materiality of spatial allocation. Divides and divisions may be ideological but they can be remarkably enduring. Part of the puzzle

---

[83] P Darby, n 69 above.

[84] C Cohn and C Enloe, 'A Conversation with Cynthia Enloe: Feminists Look at Masculinity and the Men Who Wage War' (2003) 28 *Signs* 1187, at 1199.

[85] See eg, G Youngs, 'Embodied Political Economy or an Escape from Disembodied Knowledge' in G Youngs (ed), *Political Economy, Power and the Body: Global Perspectives* (Houndmills, MacMillan Press, 2000), at 23.

[86] IM Young, 'Impartiality and the Civic Public: Some Implications of Feminist Critiques of Moral and Political Theory' in JB Landes (ed), *Feminism: The Public and the Private* (Oxford, Oxford University Press, 1998), at 443.

I hope to explore through this and future work is precisely the elements of solidity that seem to accompany spatial awareness, and particularly the political and legal spaces in which we locate the international.

In the latter part of this chapter, I considered the idea of the border or 'borderlands' as possibly opening up an analysis of legal and political spaces. In this respect, I am in agreement with Rob Walker's argument that we need to consider authority as residing in a number of different locations and forms. If we consider state sovereignty, and other forms of authority, as diffuse and variable, the locations at which we contest and/or call on authority are similarly diffuse. And if we consider feminist work, particularly in international relations that explores the everyday lives of women as part of, and relevant to, the conduct of international relations,[87] then the sites at which we might find and explore 'the international' are also variable.

Applied to international law, we might begin to consider law as similarly diffuse and variable rather than as 'a unitary source of ultimate authority'.[88] If we start from an understanding of law as 'a dispersal and fragmentation of authority ... and fluid systems of power sharing',[89] how might this impact upon where we locate law and understand its operation, contestation and transversal? Perhaps one way forward is to begin to challenge the division of international from national spaces; to look for law in those spaces between local and international. How do we account for those spaces where the terms 'local' and 'international' do not appear to have descriptive purchase: the refugee camp, the internationally-funded health clinic, the post-disaster reconstruction zone? How are law, norm, authority and obligation understood and applied in ways that reach beyond hard and soft law, domestic and international?

---

[87] The paradigmatic work in this area is C Enloe, *Bananas, Beaches and Bases: Making Feminist Sense of International Politics* (Berkeley, CA, California University Press, 2000).

[88] J Scott and DM Trubek, 'Mind the Gap: Law and New Approaches to Governance in the European Union' (2002) 8(1) *European Law Journal* 1, at 8.

[89] *Ibid.*

6

Disconcerting 'Masculinities': Reinventing the Gendered Subject(s) of International Human Rights Law

DIANNE OTTO*

For what is important is to disconcert the staging of representation according to *exclusively* 'masculine' parameters.[1]

Introduction

'Women's rights are human rights' is a powerful call for the inclusion of women as full subjects of international human rights law. It became a new rallying point for women's human rights advocates in the late 1980s[2] and was formally adopted by states, first at the 1993 World Conference on Human Rights,[3] and then at the 1995 Fourth World Conference on Women.[4] The claim emanates from feminist analyses of the human rights canon, which reveal that, through a variety of means, women are systematically marginalised or excluded by the dominant masculine standards of the regime[5] and therefore not constituted as fully human for the purposes of guaranteeing their enjoyment of human rights. This critique goes to the heart of the post-World War II discourse of universal human rights, which, as its

---

* Associate Professor, Faculty of Law, the University of Melbourne. Kate Stoneman Visiting Professor of Law and Democracy, Albany Law School, New York, Spring Semester 2004. This chapter is part of a larger work which will partially fulfil the requirements of my JSD candidacy at Columbia University.

[1] L Irigaray, *This Sex Which Is Not One* (Ithaca, Cornell University Press,1985) 68.

[2] FD Gaer, 'And Never the Twain Shall Meet? The Struggle to Establish Women's Rights as International Human Rights' in CE Lockwood, DB Magraw, MF Spring and SI Strong (eds), *The International Human Rights of Women: Instruments of Change* (Washington DC, American Bar Association, 1998) 1, at 19.

[3] Vienna Declaration and Program of Action (Vienna POA), World Conference on Human Rights, UN Doc A/CONF 157/23 (1993), para 18.

[4] Beijing Declaration and Platform for Action (Beijing PFA), Fourth World Conference on Women, UN Doc A/CONF177/20 (1995), Declaration, para 14.

[5] V Spike Petersen, 'Whose Rights? A Critique of the "Givens" in Human Rights Discourse' (1990) 15 *Alternatives* 303; K Engle, 'International Human Rights and Feminism: Where Discourses Meet' (1992) 13 *Michigan Journal of International Law* 517; R Cook, 'Women's International Human Rights Law: The Way Forward' (1993) 15 *Human Rights Quarterly* 230; H Charlesworth, 'What Are "Women's International Human Rights"?' in R Cook (ed), *Human Rights of Women: National and International Perspectives* (Philadelphia, University of Pennsylvania Press, 1994) 58.

most fundamental premise, purports to apply equally, 'without distinction', to 'everyone'.[6] The allegedly universal subject of human rights law also reproduces other hierarchies, including those of race, culture, nation, socio-economic status and sexuality, which intersect in important ways with constructions of gender.[7] While being attentive to these intersections, and the part that feminist human rights claims have played in reproducing other hierarchies, my goal in this chapter is to focus on the lineage of the dualistic production of sex/gender in human rights discourse, and examine how it has functioned to legitimate the exclusionary effects of a discourse that makes the highest claims to inclusivity.

The first part of this chapter outlines the genealogy of the female subjects of international law who antedate the discourse of universal human rights, which emerged in 1945 with the establishment of the United Nations (UN). What emerges is not a unitary trope of 'woman', but three main recurring female subjectivities, which may also overlap and have otherwise complex and productive interrelationships. These subjectivites are, first, the figure of the wife and mother, who needs 'protection' during times of both war and peace and is more an object than a subject of international law; second, the woman who is 'formally equal' with men, at least in the realm of public life; and, third, the 'victim' subject who is produced by colonial narratives of gender, as well as by notions of women's sexual vulnerability. Each of these female personas produces and is dependent upon a binary male representation: the protected subject constitutes her 'protector' in the form of the head of the household and, in times of war, the warrior or combatant; the formally equal subject reproduces the masculine standard of 'equality' against which her claims to equality are assessed; and the 'victim' subject affirms the need for the masculine bearer of 'civilisation' and saviour of 'good' women from 'bad', often 'native', men. Each of these dualistic stagings of masculinity and femininity organises sex/gender as a hierarchy, with the masculine assuming the position of authority. These different representations of men and women achieve a sense of unity from the consistency of the hierarchies they produce; the privileged subject always bears the masculine characteristics of the gendered duality. In fact, his privilege *depends* on his dissimilarity with the discourse's feminine subjects.

In the second and third parts of this chapter, I show how these gendered personas, and their attendant hierarchies, have displayed an uncanny ability to survive in the new era of universal human rights that was founded by the 1945 UN Charter[8] and given content by its progeny of human rights instruments. I examine the efforts of the feminist members of the UN Commission on the Status of Women (CSW) to ensure that the Universal Declaration of Human Rights (UDHR) was inclusive of women. While the CSW sought to promote women's substantive equality, they did

---

[6] Universal Declaration of Human Rights (UDHR), GA Res 217A(III), 10 December 1948, Art 2.

[7] A Harris, 'Race and Essentialism in Feminist Legal Theory' (1990) 42 *Stanford Law Review* 581; LA Crooms, 'Indivisible Rights and Intersectional Identities or, "What Do Women's Human Rights Have to Do with the Race Convention?"' (1997) 40 *Howard Law Journal* 619.

[8] Charter of the United Nations, 26 June 1945.

not prevent the reinvigoration of all three of the marginalised female subjectivities produced by the earlier instruments. These gendered hierarchies persisted, with little change, in the later human rights covenants, and even in the 1979 Convention on the Elimination of All Forms of Discrimination Against Women (CEDAW). I conclude that the differences of gender, even as conceived by feminists, have tended to repeat women's marginalisation and exclusion from full humanity by reproducing the earlier female subjectivities and their masculine counterparts.

Then, in the fourth part, I discuss the women's-rights-are-human-rights strategy and examine the effects of its dual goals: to claim a place for women's specific rights violations in the universal register of human rights, and to mainstream women's human rights in the work of all the human rights treaty committees. I suggest that the new strategy has much in common with that adopted by the CSW in the drafting of the UDHR, which brings feminist efforts during the UN era full circle, back to where they began in 1946. This circularity leads me to the unsettling conclusion that women's full inclusion in universal representations of humanity may be an impossibility so long as the universal (masculine) subject continues to rely for its universality on the contrast with feminised particularities. This conclusion echoes those of many feminist analyses of domestic legal systems: that the exercise of law to empower women may indeed further entrench women's marginality.[9]

While I am not ready to suggest that feminist engagement with human rights law is a futile endeavour, it must be admitted that the enduring nature of these marginalised female subject positions presents a serious conundrum for women's human rights advocates. In the fifth part of this chapter, I offer some initial thoughts on how this conundrum might be addressed. I suggest that strategies that are disruptive of gender hierarchies must be devised in order better to test the potential of human rights law to be fully inclusive. These strategies need consciously to reject constructions of gender as hierarchy and fully embrace the insight that knowledges about sex/gender are socially constructed and therefore open infinite possibilities beyond the relentless dualisms that have been naturalised by so many laws and practices. I also suggest that the largely undocumented histories of women's local resistances to dominating and controlling forms of power, over the centuries, are of critical importance to the project of reinventing strategies to achieve women's full humanity through the discourse of universal human rights, which may yet be possible. Women's histories of resistance may provide the basis for new strategies that will produce empowered and emancipatory female subjects to take the place of the injured and marginalised subjectivities of the present regime, which serve to reproduce masculine, racial and other forms of privilege, in the guise of universality.

---

[9] C Smart, *Feminism and the Power of Law* (London, Routledge, 1989) 161; M Thornton, 'Feminist Jurisprudence: Illusion or Reality?' (1986) 3 *Australian Journal of Law and Society* 5.

The Genealogy of Human Rights Law's Female Subjects

In 1946, when efforts to give content to the UN Charter's references to human rights commenced with the drafting of the UDHR,[10] women had already been constituted as a category, implicitly or explicitly, by international instruments. Early international treaties dealing with the regulation of war,[11] the promulgation of international labour standards[12] and the prevention of trafficking of European women for the purposes of prostitution,[13] took a paternalistic or 'protective'[14] approach to women. Protective representations conceive of women as the property, extension or dependants of men, as primarily mothers and wives, and as innocents, who lack agency or cannot be trusted with it. These female subjects are valued for their chastity, their prioritisation of motherhood and domesticity, their acceptance of the heterosexual family hierarchy and the paternal protection of the state and its laws. By relegating women to a special category, often co-terminus with children, characterised by passivity, dependency, innocence and vulnerability, protective representations feminise the domestic sphere and project a marginalising stereotype of women. Men, in contradistinction, are cast as women's defenders and moral superiors (apart from the often racialised criminals who traffic them), and the active, public, protecting, defending figure of the masculine is produced as the marker of full humanity, who has no need for special rules for his protection.

During the years of the League of Nations, the protective approach was supported by many feminists who drew a parallel with the League's policies on 'natives' and 'minorities', which they understood as laying the groundwork for

---

[10] UDHR, above n 6.

[11] The Geneva Conventions of 1864 made no reference to women, yet there was already a long history of war-time sexual abuse of women. Later instruments referred to women indirectly, in the context of requiring an occupying power to respect 'family honour and rights'. See Convention Respecting the Laws and Customs of War on Land (Hague Convention II), 29 July 1899, Art 46; and Convention Respecting the Laws and Customs of War on Land (Hague Convention IV), 18 October 1907, 36 Stat 2277, 1 Bevans 631, Art 46.

[12] See, eg, International Labour Organization, Maternity Protection Convention 1919 (Convention 3); International Labour Organization, Convention Concerning Night Work of Women Employed in Industry 1919 (Convention 4); and International Labour Organization, Convention Concerning the Employment of Women on Underground Work in Mines of All Kinds 1935 (Convention 45).

[13] International Agreement for the Suppression of the White Slave Traffic 1904, 35 Stat 426, 1 LNTS 83; International Convention for the Suppression of White Slave Traffic 1910, 211 Consol TS 45, 1912 Gr Brit TS No 20 at 267; International Convention for the Suppression of the Traffic in Women and Children 1921, 9 LNTS 415; Convention for the Suppression of the Traffic in Women of Full Age 1933, 53 UNTS 13. See further, J Doezema, 'Loose Women or Lost Women? The Re-Emergence of the Myth of White Slavery in the Contemporary Discourses of Trafficking in Women' (2000) *Gender Issues* 23, at 24.

[14] N Kaufman Hevener, 'International Law and the Status of Women: An Analysis of International Legal Instruments Related to the Treatment of Women' (1978) 1 *Harvard Women's Law Journal* 131, at 133–40, used the term 'protective' as one of three analytic categories she developed to characterise treaty provisions concerned with women's status. Her other two categories were 'corrective' and 'non-discriminatory'.

self-determination and eventual equality.[15] Other feminists, however, disagreed with this approach and instead sought to promote women's equality by way of a commitment to non-discrimination in the enjoyment of rights.[16] The notion of women's equality and rights, as distinct from their tutelage, was formally discussed at the League's 1930 Hague Conference for the Codification of International Law in relation to promoting equal rights for women and men to retain their nationality on marriage.[17] Although the Conference rejected this proposition, it led to the adoption of a resolution that established the League's first ever committee of women to advise it on nationality issues and urged states to study the possibility of 'introduc[ing] into their law the principle of the equality of the sexes in matters of nationality'.[18] In 1935, 10 South American states[19] presented a proposal to the League's 16th General Assembly to promulgate a convention that would promote women's civil, legal and political equality with men.[20] Although action was deferred because many states asserted that the question of women's rights was a domestic issue, two years later the League established a Committee of Experts to undertake a comprehensive enquiry into the legal status of women worldwide.[21] Unfortunately this study was never completed due to the outbreak of World War II.

The point is, however, that by the mid-1930s, a nascent discourse of sex non-discrimination and women's equality was gaining ground. This new account emphasised the common humanity of women and men, constituting the female subject of international law for the first time as autonomous, like men, and claiming for her an equal place in public life. However, the new paradigm proffered a formal, rather than substantive, version of equality because it relied on a comparison with similarly situated men. Therefore it was only effective when the experience of women and men was comparable, which left feminised rights issues, such as gendered violence and reproductive rights, outside the universal register because there was no male comparator against which to claim them by way of 'equality'.[22] The paradigm of formal equality also does not challenge gendered domestic arrangements because its masculine standard limits its scope to equality in the

---

[15] M Lake, 'From Self-Determination via Protection to Equality via Non-Discrimination: Defining Women's Rights at the League of Nations' in P Grimshaw, K Holmes and M Lake (eds), *Women's Rights and Human Rights: International Historical Perspectives* (New York, Palgrave, 2001) 254, at 257.

[16] See ME Galey, 'Forerunners in Women's Quest for Partnership' in A Winslow (ed), *Women, Politics and the United Nations* (Westport Conn, Greenwood Press, 1995) 1.

[17] M Lake, above n 15, at 258.

[18] Resolution on the Nationality of Women, League of Nations, 24 January 1931, reprinted in CE Lockwood et al, above n 2, at 125–26. For a discussion of contemporary issues associated with women's nationality rights, see K Knop and C Chinkin, 'Remembering Chrystal MacMillian: Women's Equality and Nationality in International Law' (2001) 22 *Michigan Journal of International Law* 523.

[19] The Pan-American Union had adopted an equality approach in the Pan-American Convention on the Nationality of Married Women, 26 December 1933.

[20] M Lake, above n 15, at 259–62; ME Galey, above n 16, at 7.

[21] M Lake, above n 15, at 262.

[22] T Loenen, 'Rethinking Sex Equality as a Human Right' (1994) 3 *Netherlands Quarterly on Human Rights* 253.

public sphere. Therefore, despite explicitly rejecting protective representations of women, the formal non-discrimination approach risks leaving them intact in those areas of life where women's experience differs from that of men, which for many women is in most parts of their lives. For the equality principle to achieve women's full inclusion in humanity, it needs to destabilise the masculine universal and work against organising gender as a hierarchy. This, as I have suggested, may prove to be an impossibility, but I will return to this conundrum in the penultimate part of this chapter.

The obvious tension between the gender narrations of protectionism and the embryonic equality principle was, however, not the only historical dynamic that informed the drafting of the UDHR in 1946. There was also the political baggage that had accompanied earlier feminist efforts to improve women's status internationally as part of the 'civilising mission' of European imperialism.[23] As historian Clare Midgley notes, the formative period for modern feminism in Britain coincided with the massive expansion of British imperialism between 1790 and 1850.[24] While early feminists, on the one hand, identified with colonised men and women by drawing on analogies with slavery to describe their own treatment, they simultaneously disavowed any identification with colonised peoples by contrasting the 'progressive' nature of British society with the backwardness of the colonies, in appealing for women's rights.[25] Later, British women campaigning for suffrage drew attention to their social reform agenda for colonised women as a way to justify their inclusion in Parliament, because it would strengthen their capacity to continue the task of civilising black and Indian women, saving them from the 'barbarian' men of the colonies and converting them to Christianity.[26]

Thus a sharp distinction was drawn between the discourse of women's rights, which applied to the enlightened women of the colonisers, and the discourse of salvation, which applied to colonised women who were depicted as victims of the backwardness of their own societies, which helped to justify imperialist interventions.[27] In these ways, the early struggle for women's rights in Europe was heavily implicated in the imperial project. Therefore, early women's rights activists in Europe produced two female prototypes: in their own image they produced the female subject who bears the rights or needs the protections associated with 'civilisation'; and in the image of the women of the colonies they produced the 'victim' subject of her 'uncivilised' culture, whom they could better speak for and save as a result of exercising these rights. The rights associated with 'civilisation' that European women sought to exercise were, however, also committed to the project of patriarchy. Therefore, while European men were full subjects of these rights, European women

---

[23] V Amos and P Parmar, 'Challenging Imperial Feminism' (1984) 17 *Feminist Review* 3.

[24] C Midgley, 'British Empire, Women's Rights and Empire, 1790–1850' in P Grimshaw et al, above n 15, at 3.

[25] *Ibid*, at 7.

[26] *Ibid*, at 12.

[27] R Kapur, 'The Tragedy of Victimisation Rhetoric: Resurrecting the "Native" Subject in International/Post-Colonial Feminist Legal Politics' (2002) 15 *Harvard Human Rights Journal* 1.

were placed in the contradictory position of exercising some of those rights, but as the adjuncts and helpers of 'civilised' men in the mission of imperialism.

Of course many women have resisted their marginalisation in many ways, and their histories provide important accounts of resistance that feminist human rights strategies need to build upon.[28] There have always been women who have been family bread-winners, who have engaged in fighting wars (often disguised as men), who have chosen to work as sex workers, who have participated in public life, and who have resisted the colonial imposition of racial and gender hierarchies. I do not want to suggest that the legal construction of gendered and raced social relations was impenetrable, or that resistance was impossible. The Foucauldian insight that the exercise of power also produces resistance is apt.[29] But the legal construction of social realities was, and is, very powerful, and my interest is to understand how such resistances might impact on the law and challenge its continuing power to marginalise women and other disadvantaged groups.

When the UN Charter was adopted in 1945, it opened a new space for feminist engagement with international law with its assertion of the importance of 'the equal rights of men and women'[30] and its commitment to 'promoting and encouraging respect for human rights and fundamental freedoms for all without distinction as to race, sex, language, or religion'.[31] The vision of the inclusion of all women in the global community, as bearers of 'equal' rights, marked a significant reorientation from the protective and colonial traditions that had preceded it. With the drafting of the UDHR, the stage was set to develop this new idea of human rights that applied to everyone. But the drafters carried with them the trappings of a complicated history of international engagement with the question of women's rights. In addition to the uneasy relationship between the discourses of protectionism and equality, the drafters bore the markings of an imperial history that had bequeathed a woman bifurcated by colonialism. Could the notion of inclusive universality provide a basis for the emergence of a discourse that would jettison the earlier gender tropes of protectionism, colonialism and formal equality in the public sphere, and constitute, instead, a fully inclusive subject in the new law of human rights?

The Persistence of Marginalised Female Representations in the New Era of Universality

The drafting of the UDHR was commenced in 1946 by the newly established Commission for Human Rights (CHR). The CSW, also established by the Economic

---

[28] LA Obiora, 'Panel Discussion: How Does the Universal Declaration of Human Rights Protect African Women?' (1999) 26 *Syracuse Journal of International Law and Commerce* 195, at 208.
[29] M Foucault, 'Two Lectures' in C Gordon (ed), *Power/Knowledge: Selected Interviews and Other Writings 1972–1977* (Brighton Sussex, Harvester Press, 1980) 78.
[30] UN Charter, above n 8, preamble.
[31] *Ibid*, Arts 1(3), 13(1)(b), 55(c) and 76(c).

and Social Council (ECOSOC) in 1946,[32] was an active participant in the drafting sessions, making recommendations aimed at ensuring the inclusion of women in the UDHR's universal coverage. In this, the CSW, which was made up entirely of women, drew directly from the experience of feminists during the preceding years of the League and indirectly on five centuries of women's struggle for emancipation.[33] According to John Humphrey, the first Director of the Division for Human Rights, the early members of the CSW were all 'militants in their own countries' who 'acted as a kind of lobby for the women of the world',[34] which made the Commission an unusually independent body in the Charter's system of state-based representation.

At its first session, CSW members agreed that their goal was to 'elevate the equal rights and human rights status of women, irrespective of nationality, race, language, or religion, in order to achieve equality with men in all fields of human enterprise'.[35] Their particular approach, as reflected in their proposals during the drafting of the UDHR, was to ensure that explicit reference was made to rights that were specific to women's experience, but within the framework of women's equality with men rather than as protective measures.[36] It was a strategy of substantive, rather than formal, equality. As it emerged, their approach clashed with the views of the majority of the CHR, including those of its Chair, Eleanor Roosevelt, who felt that the general prohibition of discrimination based on sex (Article 2) was sufficient to ensure women's equal enjoyment of universal human rights.[37] The detractors argued that explicit references to women would actually weaken the position of women by undercutting the meaning of 'everyone' and introduce rights that were not 'universal' in nature.[38] Therefore, they remained committed to formal rather than substantive equality and strongly resisted the CSW proposals for specificity.

An initial concern for the CSW was the use of masculine descriptors to refer to the generic universal subject, present in the early drafts of the UDHR. Their efforts focused on the opening words of Article 1, which referred to 'all men' and

---

[32] ME Galey, above n 16, at 13–14, records that the CSW was initially established as a sub-commission, answerable to the CHR, until members persuaded ECOSOC to upgrade it to a full Commission three months later.

[33] AS Fraser, 'Becoming Human: The Origins and Development of Women's Human Rights' (1999) 21 *Human Rights Quarterly* 853.

[34] J Humphrey, 'The Memoirs of John P Humphrey: The First Director of the United Nations Division of Human Rights' (1983) 5 *Human Rights Quarterly* 392, at 405.

[35] AS Fraser, above n 33, at 888, quoting from M Galey, 'Promoting Nondiscrimination Against Women: The UN Commission on the Status of Women' (1979) 23 *International Studies Quarterly* 271.

[36] See J Morsink, *The Universal Declaration of Human Rights: Origins, Drafting and Intent* (Philadelphia, University of Pennsylvania Press, 1999) 116–29. For a more critical analysis see H Bequaert Holmes, 'A Feminist Analysis of the Universal Declaration of Human Rights' in C Gould (ed), *Beyond Dominance: New Perspectives on Women and Philosophy* (Totowa NJ, Rowman and Allanheld, 1983) 250.

[37] It should be noted that the Communist delegations, particularly the USSR, were consistent allies of the CSW in the promotion of women's rights. J Morsink, 'Women's Rights in the Universal Declaration' (1991) 13 *Human Rights Quarterly* 229, at 231–32.

[38] M Lake, above n 15, at 265.

went on to prescribe that people should act towards each other 'like brothers'.[39] As Roosevelt later recalled, the CSW representatives argued: 'If we say "all men," when we get home it will be "all men".[40] It took an unprecedented intervention from the UN Secretary-General, at the urging of the CSW, before the CHR agreed to change the opening words to 'all people, men and women', which led to the General Assembly eventually adopting the opening phrase 'all human beings'.[41] The CSW's concern with inclusive language was consistent with their equality approach, because they believed that if women were explicitly included as bearers of all human rights, it would be more difficult to relegate them to special categories requiring protection or salvation.

The CSW's victory on language was only partial as masculine pronouns remained in 14 of the UDHR's 30 articles, which left the CSW with the task of negotiating the wording of every article in order to ensure that the rights of women were included. Despite their efforts, there is only one direct, though very significant, reference to the equal rights of women in the text of the UDHR.[42] This appears in the context of the family. Article 16 recognises the 'equal rights' of men and women 'as to marriage, during marriage, and at its dissolution'. The recognition of equality between women and men in the family was unprecedented because it gave the concept of human rights application in the previously exempted domestic sphere. The efforts of the CSW also resulted in the retention of Article 6 (the right to a legal personality) despite efforts to delete it,[43] and the inclusion of references to equality in a general sense in Article 21 (political participation rights)[44] and Article 23 (the right to the enjoyment of just conditions of work including remuneration).[45] Article 26 (the right to education) also included the CSW proposal that higher education be 'equally accessible to all on the basis of merit'. While it is true that the specific references to equality risk undercutting the meaning of 'everyone', as many members of the CHR feared, they also serve as a reminder of the propensity of the concept of 'everyone' to exclude women and other marginalised groups, and thereby open the possibility of a departure from the approach of formal equality.

Despite these successes, formal non-discrimination remained the predominant approach of the UDHR. The efforts of the CSW to achieve the recognition of women's specific human rights concerns led, unfortunately, to the re-emergence of protective representations of women. For example, in Article 25, 'motherhood' is paired with 'childhood' and recognised as a time of life that requires

---

[39] J Morsink, above n 37, at 232.

[40] FD Gaer, above n 2, at 10, quoting Eleanor Roosevelt, 'Making Human rights Come Alive', Speech to the Second National Conference on UNESCO, Cleveland, Ohio, 1 April 1949, http://www.udhr50.org.

[41] J Morsink, above n 37, at 235–36.

[42] There is a reference to the 'equal rights of men and women' in the preamble of the UDHR.

[43] J Morsink, above n 37, at 243.

[44] *Ibid*, at 250–52.

[45] *Ibid*, at 252–55.

'special care and assistance', while widowhood, but not 'widower-hood', is included as a category that merits social assistance, along with unemployment, sickness, disability and old age. These provisions continue the discursive heritage of representing women primarily as mothers and wives who are domestically focused, vulnerable and dependent on men. This reading is underscored by other wording in Article 25 which recognises that everyone has the right to an adequate standard of living for 'himself and his family', which makes it clear that wives and mothers are not household heads. These provisions conflict with the Article 16 guarantee of equal marriage rights and give renewed life to the protected female subject in the era of universal human rights.

In addition to breathing new life into protective representations of women, the markings of feminism's imperial inheritance also survived in the UDHR. In keeping with their mandate, the CSW sought to promote the rights of women 'irrespective of nationality, race, language or religion'. They argued on several occasions for the inclusion of non-discrimination clauses that made reference to other forms of discrimination, in addition to sex discrimination.[46] Despite this clarity about what would today be described as 'intersectional' forms of discrimination,[47] the CSW's reliance on non-discrimination to do all the work of ensuring the inclusion of women's diversity (beyond gender differences) merited the same critique as the one they applied to the majority's view that prohibiting sex discrimination was enough to ensure women's equal enjoyment of human rights. That is, without specific reference to women's human rights abuses that had race, class or sexuality-related dimensions, universal rights would be limited to those rights that are important to the privileged racial, economic or sexuality group, as well as the privileged gender group.[48]

The privileging of European experience was amply evident in the dominant approach to the drafting of the UDHR, which was to secure individual human rights. This approach excluded group or collective rights from the universal register, despite their importance in most non-European traditions and despite the earlier recognition of the importance of the rights of minority groups in Europe.[49] The privileging of the autonomous individual marked this subject as the highest ideal of 'civilisation', which doubly reinstated the colonial paradigm of masculinity; of European superiority and of the 'victim' subject in need of rescue from her own collective communal culture. The 'spirit' of rights that is present in

---

[46] J Morsink, above n 36, at 244, notes that the CSW supported full equality of civil rights 'irrespective of marriage, race, language or religion' and further, at 251–52, that the CSW supported a Chilean proposal that political participation should be available to everyone 'without discrimination as to race, sex, language, creed or social class'.

[47] K Crenshaw, 'Demarginalizing the Intersection of Race and Sex: A Black Feminist Critique of Anti-Discrimination Doctrine, Feminist Theory and Antiracist Politics' (1989) *University of Chicago Legal Forum* 139.

[48] *Ibid.* See further, A Harris, above n 7, at 242.

[49] N Berman, '"But the Alternative is Despair": European Nationalism and the Modernist Renewal of International Law' (1993) 106 *Harvard Law Review* 1792.

every cultural tradition[50] is thus erased from the text and, along with it, women's histories of resistance to patriarchal arrangements in non-European and colonial societies.[51] Therefore, in privileging European forms of masculinity, the UDHR revives the imperial trope of the 'uncivilised' masculinities of non-Europe and the native woman 'victim' who needs to enjoy the rights and standards of Europe in order to be saved.

In sum, the approach taken by the CSW did not prevent the reinvigoration of all three of the marginalised female subjectivities produced by the earlier instruments; as in need of protection or imperial salvation, or relegated to a position of formal equality with men. This was repeated, with little change, in the translation of the UDHR into legally binding instruments: the International Covenant on Economic, Social and Cultural Rights (ICESCR)[52] and the International Covenant on Civil and Political Rights (ICCPR).[53] Both Covenants, like the UDHR, rely primarily on the prohibition of sex discrimination to ensure women's enjoyment of the rights they enumerate,[54] and therefore fall short of recognising that the full enjoyment by women of human rights requires acknowledging gendered specificities in a way that is consistent with women's equality. Granted, a stronger emphasis on equality between women and men is discernible with the inclusion of common Article 3, which requires States Parties to ensure 'the equal right of men and women to the enjoyment of all … [rights] set forth in the present Covenant'.[55] These articles repeat the UN Charter's reference to the 'equal rights of men and women', which had been relegated to the preamble of the UDHR. Their inclusion suggests general agreement that women's equal rights needed to be given special emphasis within general human rights instruments,[56] and the choice of the word 'enjoyment' indicates that it was substantive rather than formal equality that the drafters had in mind.

However, despite the substantive equality approach suggested by common Article 3, both Covenants repeat the UDHR's use of masculinist language and make few specific references to women. Those that are made either compromise women's equality by taking a protective or imperial approach, or introduce competing narratives that restrict equality to its formal sense. For example, equal matrimonial rights and responsibilities are promoted,[57] but this is contradicted

---

[50] M Mbilinyi, 'Runaway Wives in Colonial Tanganyika: Forced Labour and Forced Marriage in Rungwe District 1919–1961 [1]' (1988) 16 *International Journal of the Sociology of Law* 1, at 3.

[51] LA Obiora, 'Panel Discussion: How Does the Universal Declaration of Human Rights Protect African Women?' (1999) 26 *Syracuse Journal of International Law and Commerce* 195, at 208.

[52] International Covenant on Economic, Social and Cultural Rights (ICESCR), GA Res 2200A (XXI), 16 December 1966, entered into force 3 January 1976.

[53] International Covenant on Civil and Political Rights (ICCPR), GA Res 2200A(XXI), 16 December 1966, entered into force 23 March 1976.

[54] *Ibid*, at Art 2(1) and ICESCR, above n 52, at Art 2(2).

[55] *Ibid*, at common Art 3.

[56] MCR Craven, *The International Covenant on Economic, Social and Cultural Rights: A Perspective on its Development* (New York, Oxford University Press, 1995) 159. Craven refers to the 'preoccupation' of the UN at the time of drafting the Covenants with the issue of sex equality.

[57] ICCPR, above n 53, at Art 23(4), requires States Parties to 'take appropriate steps to ensure equality of rights and responsibilities of spouses as to marriage, during marriage and at its dissolution'.

by protective conceptions of women in association with pregnancy and child-birth,[58] and the continued framing of the right to an adequate standard of living as a right that is due to a man, as the household head.[59] Further, while women's equality with men is asserted with respect to equal pay,[60] this is undermined by the masculine, and European, model of employment that is adopted, which assumes full-time, unbroken patterns of paid work as the norm.[61] This narrow conceptualisation of work does not reflect the many forms of remunerated and unremunerated work done by women, particularly in the informal economy in developing countries and increasingly as migrant workers in developed countries. Further, the weaker enforcement obligations of the ICESCR reveal an underlying commitment to the market economies of capitalism and attribute less importance to economic, social and cultural rights, which impacts disproportionately on poor women, especially in developing countries.

The result is that the main subject of the Covenants, the generic bearer of universal human rights, has remained tenaciously masculine. In contradistinction, the female subjects produced are offered the possibility of enjoying formal equality with men if they can fit themselves into the masculine constructs of work and public life. At the same time, women's secondary domestic position is repeated by the continuing production of the dependent and protected image of the wife and mother. Finally, the imperial heritage of international law, and of feminism in the west, is reflected in the continuing prioritisation of individual rights, constructs of employment that do not include women's unpaid work in family enterprises or in the informal economy, and the lesser importance attributed to economic, social and cultural rights. The specificities of women's lives serve to buttress the production of the masculine universal by operating as the non-universal against which the universal is defined, despite the proclamations of inclusivity in the new era of universal human rights.

The Strategy of a Specialised Women's Human Rights Instrument

The marginalisation of women's rights by the discourse of universal human rights meant that women's enjoyment of human rights was seldom addressed by UN

---

[58] ICESCR, above n 52, at Art 10(2), refers to 'special protection' for mothers around the time of child-birth; ICCPR, above n 53, at Art 6(5), prohibits the death penalty from being applied to 'pregnant women'.

[59] *Ibid*, ICESCR, Art 11(1), recognising the right of 'everyone to an adequate standard of living for himself and his family'.

[60] *Ibid*, at Art 7(a)(i), requires 'women being guaranteed conditions of work not inferior to those enjoyed by men, with equal pay for equal work'.

[61] *Ibid*, at Arts 6 and 7. See further, Expert Group Report, Promoting Women's Enjoyment of their Economic and Social Rights, Abo/Turku, Finland, 1–4 December 1997, UN DAW EGM/WESR/1997/Report, para 46.

human rights bodies in the early years of their operation.[62] Yet it was clear that women's disadvantage was persisting, and in some cases worsening.[63] This state of affairs led to the next major attempt by feminists to promote women's equality using the vehicle of human rights law, which was the promulgation of a specialist women's human rights convention. While this was not an entirely new idea, as women-specific instruments promoting political and nationality rights had already been adopted,[64] it was the first time that a comprehensive instrument was pursued. As a result, the CEDAW was eventually adopted by the General Assembly and opened for ratification in 1979.[65]

The CEDAW urges States Parties to ensure that all discrimination against women is prohibited and that women enjoy 'equal rights with men', or rights 'on equal terms with men' or the 'same rights' as men. Therefore, the new instrument remained in the mould of the earlier instruments, continuing, at least on its face, to promote women's equality in a formal sense, as emanating from women's enjoyment of the same rights as men.[66] The critical issue is how CEDAW addresses women's specificities, and whether the well-worn protective and victim subjectivities are avoided. My assessment is that while CEDAW includes many provisions that have the potential to destabilise marginalised representations of women, their effect is compromised by the continuing survival of all three of the hierarchical gender tropes inherited from the earlier instruments.

On the positive side of the ledger, CEDAW opens up the possibility of understanding women's equality substantively by providing a comprehensive definition of discrimination against women, which includes both direct and indirect forms of discrimination and is clearly concerned with equality in result.[67] This potential is strengthened by an affirmative action provision that allows for the different treatment of women in order to accelerate de facto equality,[68] although the 'temporary' character of such measures must be questioned in light of women's entrenched disadvantage and the long-term nature of the project of dismantling

---

[62] R Cook, 'Women and International Human Rights' (1981) 3 *Human Rights Quarterly* 1; ME Galey, 'International Enforcement of Women's Human Rights' (1984) 6 *Human Rights Quarterly* 70.

[63] See, eg, E Boserup, *Women's Role in Economic Development* (New York, St Martins Press, 1970).

[64] Convention on the Political Rights of Women, GA Res 640(VII), 20 December 1952, entered into force 7 July 1954; Convention on the Nationality of Married Women, GA Res 1040(XI), 29 January 1957, entered into force 11 August 1958.

[65] International Convention on the Elimination of All Forms of Discrimination Against Women (CEDAW), GA Res 34/180, 18 December 1979, entered into force 3 September 1981.

[66] H Charlesworth, C Chinkin and S Wright, 'Feminist Approaches to International Law' (1991) 85 *American Journal of International Law* 613, at 631, 'the underlying assumption of its [CEDAW's] definition of discrimination is that men and women are the same'.

[67] CEDAW, above n 65, at Art 1, requiring, *inter alia*, that women are able to enjoy and exercise human rights.

[68] *Ibid*, at Art 1(4), declares 'temporary special measures aimed at accelerating de facto equality between men and women' not to be discriminatory under the Convention, so long as they do not entail 'the maintenance of unequal or separate standards'.

gender hierarchies through affirmative action. The CEDAW also clearly covers discrimination in the private sphere,[69] thereby challenging the liberal boundaries between public and private that have served to perpetuate protective ideas about women in the family and community.[70] In addition, CEDAW promotes a substantive equality approach in a number of other provisions.[71] With respect to pregnancy and motherhood, CEDAW treats women as full legal subjects and proposes measures in relation to work and health care as a matter of right, rather than as a special benefit or privilege.[72]

The CEDAW Committee has taken advantage of these and other textual opportunities to build a substantive approach to women's equality in its interpretations of the Convention. It has adopted several General Recommendations that attempt to re-imagine the subject of human rights law so that the rights that are specific to women are included in the universal, rather than ignored or marginalised as a special case requiring protective or 'civilising' measures. For example, General Recommendation 16 urges States Parties to recognise and value women's unpaid economic contributions and considers unpaid work in family enterprises to be a form of exploitation of women that is contrary to CEDAW.[73] The CEDAW Committee has also declared their intention to address violence against women as a form of discrimination against women that is prohibited by CEDAW.[74] These interpretations seek to incorporate women's specificities into how gender equality is understood and practiced, directly countering the production of marginalised subject positions as an acceptable response to gender differences.

However, on the other side of the ledger, all three marginalised subjectivities make their appearance in CEDAW. I have already made reference to the subject who is formally equal with men, who is produced by most of CEDAW's substantive provisions. Protective representations of women also survive, for example, in CEDAW's failure to prohibit protective legislation in the field of work, requiring only that States Parties periodically review its continuation 'in the light of scientific and technical knowledge'.[75] This approach does not empower women workers to make their own decisions about where and when they will work, but leaves it in the 'caring' hands of scientists and the legislature. The protected woman can also be discerned in the ambiguous provision requiring the 'suppression … of

---

[69] *Ibid*, Art 1(2)(e), eg, requires measures that eliminate discrimination 'by any person, organisation or enterprise'.

[70] C Romany, 'State Responsibility Goes Private: A Feminist Critique of the Public/Private Distinction in International Human Rights Law' in R Cook (ed), *Human Rights of Women: National and International Perspectives* (Philadelphia, University of Pennsylvania Press, 1994) 85.

[71] CEDAW, above n 65, at Arts 10(f) and 11(1)(d).

[72] *Ibid*, at Arts 11(2)(a) and (b) and 12(2). See further Arts 10(h), 11(1)(f) and 11(2)(d).

[73] CEDAW General Recommendation 16, 'Unpaid Women Workers in Rural and Urban Family Enterprises', 10th Session, 1991, which recognises that unpaid work in family enterprises is a form of exploitation of women that is contrary to CEDAW.

[74] CEDAW General Recommendation 19, 'Violence against Women', 11th Session, 1992, para 6.

[75] CEDAW, above n 65, at Art 11(3), requires that any protective legislation adopted in the field of work 'shall be reviewed periodically in the light of scientific and technological knowledge and shall be revised, repealed or extended as necessary'.

the exploitation of prostitution of women' (Article 6), which clearly does not recognise the rights of women as workers in the sex industry. Instead it seems to cast all prostitution as 'exploitation' and, therefore, all sex workers as needing protection from their 'exploiters'. Such over-simplification of the complexity of women's economic decision-making not only denies women agency, but also reflects gendered anxieties about women's sexuality, as did the earlier anti-trafficking instruments.[76]

The 'victim' subject of the discourse of (neo)colonialism is also evident in CEDAW. She overlaps, to some extent, with the protected figure of the prostitute in that the problem which was driving the adoption of Article 6 in 1979 was no longer the 'white' slave trade but rather the movement of women from developing countries to the west. But Article 6 is not the only means whereby the 'victim' subject is reproduced. The CEDAW devotes Article 14 to addressing the particular problems faced by 'rural women', with women from developing countries in mind. The article constitutes a mini bill of rights within CEDAW, requiring States Parties to ensure rural women's participation in development planning and implementation, their access to adequate health care, social security, training and education, economic opportunities, agricultural credit and loans, and their enjoyment of adequate living conditions. While the intention was to provide a tool that would help to ensure that the development agendas of the UN and the international economic institutions were inclusive of women, the article is a double-edged sword.

On the positive side, Article 14 promotes equality through women's participation in 'development',[77] and requires States Parties to ensure that women enjoy autonomous rights in the areas of health, social security, education, and adequate living conditions.[78] It is significant that none of these rights is premised on the model of equality with men, which effectively removes the universal masculine comparator. On the negative side, the article assumes that the integration of women into the free market economy is the way that development will proceed.[79] The effect is to foist the 'civilisation' of the free market onto rural women as their ticket out of poverty, which denies women the agency that the promotion of their participation in development appears to offer. All too often, attracting women into an uneven and risky market economy through the provision of low-interest loans and credit, has threatened their survival and that of their families, rather than improving their status.[80] The move to draw women into a centralised economy also undermines the economic survival strategies of many poor women, which have been developed in order to resist coercive inclusion strategies. Ambreena Manji refers to this as the 'practice of "exit"', whereby

[76] J Doezema, above n 13, at 40–41.
[77] CEDAW, above n 65, Art 14(2)(a).
[78] *Ibid*, Arts 14(2)(b), 14(2)(c), 14(2)(d) and 14(2)(h).
[79] *Ibid*, Arts 14(2)(e) and 14(2)(g).
[80] A Manji, 'Remortgaging Women's Lives: The World Bank's Land Agenda in Africa' (2003) 11 *Feminist Legal Studies* 139, at 152.

women, in her example of Africa, engage in economic activities in the informal sector, or work as prostitutes or in illegal trading, as a means of escaping state repression.[81] In denying women agency to shape the form that 'development' takes, and in failing to recognise the importance of women's informal economic arrangements, Article 14 rejuvenates the imperial victim subject who needs to be brought into the 'civilising' framework of a formal, liberalised economy in order to be 'saved'.

In addition to repeating the marginalising representations of women, the strategy of a separate women's human rights instrument had the unfortunate effect of further distancing women's human rights from the mainstream for countless other reasons.[82] The other human rights treaty committees left it to the CEDAW Committee to address human rights issues associated with women, which meant that the CEDAW Committee's pioneering General Recommendations had little impact on their work.[83] The continued marginalisation of women by human rights discourse prompted another re-evaluation by feminists, which led eventually to the women's-rights-are-human-rights strategy. The dual goals of the new strategy were to have gender-specific rights abuses recognised as human rights violations, and to counter the ghettoisation of CEDAW by promoting the 'mainstreaming' of women's human rights.[84] This brought the struggle for women's inclusion in the discourse of universal human rights back to where it had begun, to the strategy that the CSW adopted in 1946, which sought to ensure that explicit reference was made to rights that were specific to women's experience within the general framework of equality and universality. Could a renewed focus on women's specificities dislodge the masculine form of the subjects privileged by human rights law, when similar earlier efforts had failed?

The Women's-Rights-are-Human-Rights Strategy

The impetus for this reorientation, away from women-specific instruments and a focus on women-in-development, towards promoting women's rights as human rights, came initially from feminists in Latin America and other developing countries.[85] The move gathered steam by way of feminist reassessments that

---

[81] AS Manji, 'Imagining Women's "Legal World": Towards a Feminist Theory of Legal Pluralism in Africa' (1999) 8 *Social and Legal Studies* 435, at 443.

[82] A Brynes, 'The "Other" Human Rights Treaty Body: The work of the Committee on the Elimination of Discrimination Against Women' (1989) 14 *Yale Journal of International Law* 1.

[83] See further, D Otto, '"Gender Comment": Why Does the UN Committee on Economic, Social and Cultural Rights Need a General Comment on Women?' (2002) 14 *Canadian Journal of Women and the Law* 1.

[84] R Coomaraswamy, *Reinventing International Law: Women's Rights as Human Rights in the International Community* (Cambridge, Harvard Law School Human Rights Program, 1997) at 9.

[85] FD Gaer, above n 2, at 19. See further, B Boutros-Ghali, 'Introduction' in *The United Nations and the Advancement of Women, 1945–1996* (New York, United Nations Department of Public Information, 1996) 1, at 26.

followed the Nairobi Third World Conference on Women in 1985,[86] and was in many ways coalesced by Charlotte Bunch's call for re-visioning women's rights as human rights in 1990.[87] The hope was that making 'universal' human rights more responsive to women's specific human rights violations would not only impact on human rights law, but also provide a new focus for the women-in-development agenda. The call had widespread resonance and, in the years leading up to the 1993 World Conference on Human Rights, thousands of women were mobilised in over 100 countries to claim women's-rights-as-human-rights.[88]

One of the two main goals was to have gender-specific forms of rights violations recognised as violations of universal human rights, like the CSW in 1946. This strategy focused, in particular, on women's specificities associated with gendered violence, reproductive rights and sexuality. While the promotion of women's reproductive and sexuality rights has met with considerable resistance,[89] the anti-violence agenda has, in contrast, achieved extraordinary successes.[90] The concern to address violence against women as a human rights violation has also spilled over into other areas of international law, notably humanitarian law,[91] criminal law[92] and refugee law.[93] In 1993, the UN General Assembly adopted its milestone Declaration on the Elimination of Violence Against Women (DEVAW), which defines violence against women broadly to include violence perpetrated by the state, in the community and, most significantly, in the home.[94] For the first time in an international instrument, the inequality of women is explained as the result of historically unequal power relations between women and men that are perpetuated, *inter alia*, by gendered violence.[95] Even so, the DEVAW fell short of recognising violence against women as a violation of human rights because of states' concerns that to do so would water down their universality.[96] This position, that women's specific rights are not 'universal', echoes the views of members of the

---

[86] J Connors, 'NGOs and the Human Rights of Women at the United Nations' in P Willetts (ed), *The Conscience of the World: The Influence of Non-Governmental Organisations in the UN System* (London, Hurst, 1996) 147, at 163.

[87] C Bunch, 'Women's Rights as Human Rights: Toward a Re-Vision of Human Rights' (1990) 12 *Human Rights Quarterly* 486.

[88] E Friedman, 'Women's Human Rights: The Emergence of a Movement' in J Peters and A Wolper (eds), *Women's Rights, Human Rights: International Feminist Perspectives* (New York, Routledge, 1995) 18.

[89] D Buss, 'Robes, Relics and Rights: The Vatican and the Beijing Conference on Women' (1998) 7 *Social and Legal Studies* 339; SY Lai and RE Ralph, 'Female Sexual Autonomy and Human Rights' (1995) 8 *Harvard Human Rights Journal* 201; A Miller, AJ Rosga and M Satterthwaite, 'Health, Human Rights and Lesbian Existence' (1994) 2 *Journal of Health and Human Rights* 428.

[90] UA O'Hare, 'Realising Human Rights for Women' (1999) 21 *Human Rights Quarterly* 364.

[91] J Gardam, 'Women, Human Rights, and International Humanitarian Law' (1998) 324 *International Review of the Red Cross* 421.

[92] K Askin, *War Crimes Against Women: Prosecution in International War Crimes Tribunals* (The Hague, M Nijhoff, 1997)

[93] A Macklin, 'Refugee Women and the Imperative of Categories' (1995) 17 *Human Rights Quarterly* 213.

[94] Declaration on the Elimination of Violence Against Women (DEVAW), GA Res48/104, December 1993, Art 2.

[95] *Ibid*, preamble, cl 6.

[96] D Otto, 'Violence Against Women: Something Other than a Human Rights Violation?' (1993) 1 *Australian Feminist Law Journal* 159.

CHR in 1946, when the CSW representatives argued for explicit inclusion of women's human rights. It leaves women victims of gendered violence, still, outside the boundaries of universal human rights.

Despite this continued marginalisation, drawing international attention to the endemic problem of gendered violence has had many far-reaching effects, and it is important to acknowledge that many significant reforms in international and domestic legal systems have resulted. However, the focus on women's gendered *injuries* is also problematic because its bases human rights claims on women's vulnerability and pain, which has the unfortunate effect of producing, anew, protective and imperial representations of women. In fact, the compatibility of the anti-violence agenda with conservative ideas about women needing to be 'protected' by the state or 'rescued' from the 'uncivilised' practices of non-western traditions, is one way in which its successes might be accounted for. While this may literally save women's lives in some instances, it casts anti-violence masculinity in a protective mould which repeats, rather than challenges, gender hierarchies.

The strategic focus on gendered violence in its many forms had the potential to be inclusive of women's diverse experiences of gendered violence, but considerably more effort has been directed towards condemning certain 'uncivilised' practices in developing countries, such as genital surgeries[97] and dowry murders,[98] than addressing western forms of violence against women. This orientation has meant that women in the third world have been constructed as 'more victimised' than their western counterparts,[99] which has given new life to the imperial narrative that the non-western woman is a casualty of the misogyny of her own culture. This narrative gives new credence to the 'native victim' subject in need of rescue and rehabilitation, and re-privileges the figure, and the culture, of the European woman as normative. It also leaves no room for the indigenous histories of women's resistances to inform women's human rights strategies because they are erased by essentialising assumptions about the backwardness of non-western cultures.

The second goal of the women's-rights-are-human-rights strategy was to refocus attention back on the general human rights instruments by promoting the 'mainstreaming' of women's human rights.[100] Mainstreaming is understood as consciously considering and taking into account women's, as well as men's, concerns and experiences in every aspect of every plan, action, policy, programme or legislative measure.[101] This goal has also met with considerable success, as reflected in commitments by states at the Vienna World Conference on Human Rights,[102] which were reiterated at Beijing World Conference on Women.[103] For

---

[97] I Gunning, 'Arrogant Perception, World-Travelling and Multicultural Feminism: The Case of Female Genital Surgeries' (1991–92) 23 *Columbia Human Rights Law Review* 189.

[98] R Kapur, above n 27, at 13-18.

[99] *Ibid*, at 2.

[100] See generally, S Kouvo, this volume.

[101] Office of the Special Adviser on Gender Issues and Advancement of Women, *Gender Mainstreaming: An Overview* (New York, United Nations Press, 2002), <http://www.un.org/women-watch/osagi/pdf/e65237.pdf.> (last accessed 22 September 2004).

their part, the chairpersons of the human rights treaty committees agreed to fully integrate gender perspectives into their working methods,[104] by which they were belatedly agreeing to incorporate the pioneering work of the CEDAW Committee, aimed at feminising the subject of human rights law, into their work.

To date, the most tangible outcome has been the adoption of General Comments or General Recommendations that provide authoritative interpretations of the coverage of women's rights by the treaty texts. For example, the Human Rights Committee (HRC), which monitors the ICCPR, adopted General Comment 28 on equality between men and women in 2000.[105] The General Comment works through each of the ICCPR rights, bringing gender-specific violations into the mainstream by re-imagining the subject of the ICCPR as a woman. For example, the right to life (Article 6) is threatened by the need to resort to backyard abortions and by severe poverty, and the right to be free from torture (Article 7) is violated by the infliction of domestic violence.[106] The General Comment clearly promotes women's equality as a substantive concept, and accepts that women's specificities may require different treatment of women and men in order to achieve equality. However, all the problems associated with seeking the inclusion of women by reference to their specificities are also evident. The extensive cataloguing of women's injuries and disadvantages, while progressive in many ways and clearly necessary for making women's human rights abuses legally cognisable, continues to affirm the masculinity of the universal subject who needs no special enumeration of his gender-specific injuries. This illustrates again how the practice of including women by way of drawing attention to their specificities serves to reproduce their marginalisation by resurrecting protective and imperial subjectivities, rather than challenging the hierarchies of gender. For example, only the non-western practices of 'female infanticide, the burning of widows and dowry killings' are listed as illustrative of violations of women's right to life. This is not to say that silence should reign about women's human rights violations outside the west, but that great care needs to be taken in order to ensure that the imperial victim subject is not revitalised by contemporary human rights developments.

General Comment 28 attests again to the tenacity of the supporting tropes which produce masculinity as 'protecting' and 'civilising' in contradistinction to women's vulnerabilities. It reveals how strongly intact the hierarchies of gender have remained, despite over 50 years of feminist engagement with human rights law. The ongoing reinvigoration of marginalised female subjectivities points to the critical question as to whether a focus on women's specificities will ever achieve women's full inclusion in universal representations of humanity, because

---

[102] Vienna POA, above n 3, at paras 37 and 42.

[103] Beijing PFA, above n 4, at paras 221 and 325.

[104] Report of the Sixth Meeting of Persons Chairing the Human Rights Treaty Committees, UN Doc A/50/505 (1995) at para 34(a)–(f).

[105] HRC, 'General Comment 28: Article 3 (Equality of Rights between Men and Women)', 68th Session, 2000, UN Doc HRI/GEN/1/Rev 5, 29 March 2000.

[106] *Ibid*, at para 11.

it is against those very specificities that the privileged figure of the masculine universal is defined. While the specificity approach may improve the conditions of some individual women's lives, which is an important goal it itself, it is limited by its inability to challenge the supporting tropes of the gender hierarchies. Particularising women's injuries serves to strengthen the props that produce protecting, defending, civilising and rescuing forms of masculinity as the universal. This dynamic suggests that, paradoxically, the cost of women's inclusion may be their continuing marginalisation; that the project of disrupting gender hierarchies through human rights law may be impossible.

Rethinking the Strategy of Universalising Women's Specificities

The history of the engagement of women's rights advocates with human rights law, as I have told it, highlights a conundrum. There is little doubt that feminist inclusion strategies need to ensure that the human rights violations that result from women's inequality and disadvantage—'gendered human rights facts'—are reflected in human rights law. In fact, experience has shown that gender-specific violations must be explicitly included in the universal register before they become legally cognisable. However, as I have argued, this method repeats the gendered subjectivities of the hierarchies that are responsible for producing the gendered violations in the first place. The method of attending to women's gendered injuries does not challenge the interdependent underlying scripts of women's marginal gender position and men's gender privilege.

Therefore, unless feminist inclusion strategies find ways to disconcert the continual restaging of women's marginalisation, the most that can be achieved is some improvement in the conditions of that marginalisation. It could be argued that such incremental improvements will multiply and constitute eventually a significant challenge to the persistence of male privilege because the 'gendered human rights facts' will have changed, and this may be right. But this is basically the project that feminists have been engaged in for at least the past five centuries, and the progress to date is not encouraging. Gender hierarchies have not only remained strongly naturalised, but the tropes that they rely upon seem to have barely shifted, despite the recent history of contestation by feminist human rights advocates. In fact, backlashes from fundamentalist forces are presently threatening many of the incremental gains that have been made.[107]

---

[107] On 4 April 2004, the Special Rapporteur on Violence Against Women warned the CSW of 'alarming trends towards political conservatism and backlash which threatened the gains made thus far in the global women's human rights agenda'. Reported in Women's International League for Peace and Freedom, *1325 Peacewomen E-News*, 11 April 2004, <http://www.peacewomen.org/news/1325News/1325ENewsindex.html.>(last accessed 24 September 2004).

So, how could the staging of gender hierarchies in human rights law be re-scripted? How could alternative emancipatory gender dualities be produced? One option may be to reverse the existing gender scripts so that, for example, men are produced as nurturers and carers and women as breadwinners. Such reversals have important symbolic and practical effects in that they immediately compli-cate gender identities and disrupt the naturalness of the dominant gender scripts. However, where such reversals have had some effect on social practices, the priv-ilege associated with masculinity has remained attached to male bodies. For example, male nurses and teachers, despite their relatively recent entry into female-dominated professions in the west, occupy a vastly disproportionate num-ber of senior positions. And despite widespread acknowledgement that women are the breadwinners in many families around the world, their incomes have not shifted to reflect that reality. Therefore, the strategy of reversing the dichotomies appears to offer only a limited challenge to the arrangement of gender as hierar-chy because it can be thwarted by a corresponding reversal of gender privilege, as gendered power follows gendered bodies into the non-traditional gender occupa-tions. However, gender reversals are helpful in revealing the fluidity of sex/gender identities and showing that gender differences are socially, politically and culturally produced, rather than predetermined by nature and biology. This insight has been fundamental to feminist ways of thinking over the centuries.

A second possible method of disrupting the hierarchies of gender might be to particularise the masculine universal in much the same way as the feminine has been made specific in human rights law. This would involve re-imagining men as injured by the hierarchies of gender; casting men as the victims of certain forms of masculinity in a way that would give rise to human rights claims. Conscription into the armed services is one example of enforcing forms of masculinity which many men find coercive and oppressive. While human rights law provides a rem-edy for conscientious objectors, this does not extend to those who object to compulsory service as a form of gender injury. In fact, the discourses that support war have generally constructed objecting men as suffering the injury of gender; as too feminised ('wimpish' or 'gay') to be fighters.[108] If human rights law could produce, instead, the militarised man as the injured subject, the gendered dis-courses that legitimate war as a means of muscular men protecting vulnerable women, or saving non-European women from backward men and cultures, would be seriously disrupted.

But outside an extreme example like military conscription, it seems inaccurate to describe men as 'injured' by their gender privilege. While men's experience of gender power can be contradictory, and may involve pain and alienation,[109] this kind of injury cannot be equated with the injury that comes from lack of gender

---

[108] C Cohn, 'War, Wimps, and Women: Talking Gender and Thinking War' in M Cooke and A Woollacott (eds), *Gendering War Talk* (Princeton, Princeton University Press, 1993) 227.

[109] M Kaufman, 'Men, Feminism, and Men's Contradictory Experiences of Power' in H Brod and M Kaufman (eds), *Theorizing Masculinities* (London, Sage, 1994) 142.

privilege, not least because male gender injury does not benefit women. In fact, if the injuries associated with masculinity were to be enumerated—like those associated with competitiveness, aggression and dominance—the list would be likely to bear a resemblance to the UDHR, although it would be different in the important sense of having identified the *cause* of the injuries as dominating forms of masculinity. So, while there are many disruptive possibilities in the idea that men's injuries resulting from their male privilege could be made legally cognisable, turning the attention back on men in this way runs the risk of shifting the focus away from the operation of gender hierarchies and erasing women all over again. At the same time, if masculinity is only conceptualised as a dominating form of power in human rights law, it leaves the female subject trapped in the gender-subordinate position and precludes any hope for change.

Neither the reversal of the gender duality, nor the strategy of particularising the masculine, seems to produce emancipatory dualities that directly challenge gender hierarchies. Perhaps then we should be searching for ways to conceptualise gender as something other than a dichotomy. Could human rights law produce gender as a fluid and shifting set of ideas, practices, relationships and possibilities, and in this way succeed in producing gendered subjectivities that are liberatory or 'resistive'?[110] The notion of gender hybridities usefully illustrates this idea; that human beings are a rich and varied multiplicity of characteristics that are culturally associated with masculinity and femininity, rather than predetermined as either 'male' or 'female'. Gender-identity, then, becomes the hybrid result of choices and desires, rather than either male or female. Such an approach would be consistent with the knowledge that gender is a socio-cultural construction, and also the poststructural insight that the perception of biological difference (sex) is itself the result of a culturally specific set of ideas.[111] If a multiplicity of gendered subject positions could be brought into the legal lexicon, the full range of gender possibilities would be opened to both women and men as never before, and the two-sided comparative model of gender equality would be superceded. But the rejection of gender as dichotomy and hierarchy would also mean the loss of conceptual tools that are necessary to make legal sense of 'gendered human rights facts', at least for the foreseeable future. Therefore, while visionary, this approach also threatens the erasure of the female subject and her gender-specific human rights violations, and it may still reassert the masculine as the universal in the image of the hybrid.[112] These difficulties suggest that women's full inclusion in the universal register of human rights law may indeed be an impossibility.

---

[110] R Kapur, above n 27, uses the term 'resistive subject'.

[111] J Butler, *Gender Trouble: Feminism and the Subversion of Identity* (New York, Routledge, 1990) 8, states that 'sex, by definition, will be shown to have been gender all along'. See further S de Beauvoir, *The Second Sex* (New York, Vintage Books, 1974) 38, describing the body is a 'situation' which has 'always already been interpreted by cultural meanings'.

[112] For discussion of some of these difficulties, see S Baden and AM Goetz, 'Who Needs [Sex] When You Can Have [Gender]? Conflicting Discourses on Gender at Beijing' in C Jackson and R Pearson (eds), *Feminist Visions of Development: Gender Analysis and Policy* (New York, Routledge, 1998) 19.

But rejecting the discourse of universal human rights as an irredeemably masculinist endeavour is premature. If the project of women's equality is reinvented as a project concerned with dismantling gender hierarchies, and reproducing gender as hybrid and multiplicitous rather than duality, then it has barely begun, and it is hard to predict what new opportunities and insights might emerge. This reinvention would make available many more tools for contesting gender hierarchies than those provided by the paradigm of gender equality, although I am concerned that I may have depicted the opportunities p rovided by the existing framework too statically in the preceding discussion. In highlighting the recurrence of three primary gender dualities in human rights law, my point was to illustrate the tenacity of hierarchical conceptions of gender differences, not to deny that these gender scripts are being continually contested through women's various engagements with law, and not to suggest that these are the only productions of gender that are available to us. I have highlighted their tenacity in order to illustrate the need to tackle the hierarchies of gender and, in particular, the need to disrupt the discourse of masculine superiority, which is dependent on the marginalising production of injured women needing legal/masculine protection, the salvation of 'civilisation', or formal equality with men. The persistence of marginalised representations of women can be accounted for by this relationship of interdependence. If the focus of feminist human rights advocates remains only on the way that law produces women, the problem will continue to be misunderstood as a problem of gender difference rather than one of gender hierarchy. Women will not assume the status of full subjects, in a field that has been built on their marginalisation and erasure, without first dismantling its founding hierarchies. The recent efforts of the CSW to promote discussion about the role of men and boys in achieving gender equality, may be a useful initiative in this regard.[113]

An important aspect of such a reinvention is to recover women's lost histories of grass roots resistance. This recovery effort will help to constitute emancipatory female subjectivities who are not defined by their gendered injuries and colonial victimhood, but have the agency to struggle for their rights. I have in mind the 'runaway wives' of colonial Tanzania, who resisted both the colonial and customary restrictions placed on them as married women;[114] the women who 'exited' the free market economy in Nigeria in order to resist the coercive economic policies of the state and ensure the economic survival of their families;[115] and the sex workers in India who resisted the oppressive policies the recent right-wing Hindu nationalist Government.[116] It is notable that in all of these examples, women pursued empowerment through strategies that evaded or manipulated the law, rather than by engaging the law. This reminds us to be wary of the rights that formal law

---

[113] See Division for the Advancement of Women, The Role of Men and Boys in Achieving Gender Equality, EGM/MEN—BOYS—GE/2003/REPORT, 12 January 2004, prepared for the 48th session of CSW, March 2004.

[114] M Mbilinyi, above n 50.

[115] AS Manji, above n 81.

[116] R Kapur, above n 27, at 32.

can offer and engage also with the 'laws' that operate outside and alongside formal legal systems as offering important resistive possibilities, especially for non-elite women.[117]

Conclusion

The international struggle for the full inclusion of women in the paradigm of universal human rights has reached a point where it needs reinvention. The problem is that strategies that draw attention to women's specificities risk restaging the masculinity of the universal subject of human rights law, as do strategies of equality which emphasise women's similarity with men. Therefore, seeking women's equality through the inclusion of women's specific rights in the universal register, while shifting some of the exclusionary boundaries of the paradigm, has not been successful in eliminating the long-standing gender hierarchies that reproduce the enduring tropes of women in need of protection or salvation, and offer, mostly, a formal version of equality with similarly situated men. By reproducing these marginalised female personas, feminist inclusion strategies have unwittingly sustained the masculine image of the universal subject as the protector and civiliser of women, and the standard of equality. Feminist efforts to engage human rights law may well have had the unintended effect of further entrenching women's inequality and of giving sustenance to other hierarchies that intersect with those of gender, like hierarchies associated with imperialism and race.

The reinvention of the struggle for women's equality needs to focus attention on disconcerting the hierarchical binary of gender, which means changing how masculinity, as well as femininity, is understood. It means drawing on women's long histories of resistance in order to replace the injured subjectivities produced by human rights law with subjects who have agency to struggle for their rights. Such a reinvention also requires fully accepting the constructed and fluid nature of gender differences. Therefore, while it continues to be important to achieve the recognition that human rights violations that are specific to women are universal, it must be recognised that this alone will not challenge the hierarchical arrangements that flow from conceiving gender as a duality. Fully accepting the socially constructed nature of sex/gender, and the possibilities for equality that flow from it, means bringing into being universal subjects of human rights law that are a hybrid of sex/gender potentialities, who dis-concert the staging of gender as hierarchy.

The project of destabilising and particularising the masculine universal, producing emancipatory gender subjectivities, and developing a framework in which sex/gender can be more completely understand as a fluid social construction, has

---

[117] AS Manji, above n 81.

barely begun, and it is hard to predict what new opportunities and insights might emerge. This project is an interdisciplinary endeavour that requires drawing on new theoretical paradigms, as well as old histories, in order to reconceive gender differences as non-hierarchical. But in the meantime, we feminist human rights advocates need to be wary of legal constructions that cast women as victims, as in need of protection, and as solely needing to enjoy the same rights as similarly situated men. We need to find the courage to break new ground in an old struggle that has never lost its urgency.

7

The 'Unforgiven' Sources of International Law: Nation-Building, Violence, and Gender in the West(ern)

RUTH BUCHANAN AND REBECCA JOHNSON[*]

Introduction: The Force of Law's Stories

The rules and principles of justice, the formal institutions of the law, and the conventions of a social order are ... but a small part of the normative universe that ought to claim our attention. No set of legal institutions or prescriptions exist apart from the narratives that locate it and give it meaning ... Once understood in the context of the narratives that give it meaning, law becomes not merely a system of rules to be observed, but a world in which we live.[1]

In his classic work, 'Nomos and Narrative', Cover reminds us that legal traditions form part of a complex normative world—a 'nomos'—a world of language and myth.[2] Because precept and narrative operate together to ground meaning, one cannot truly inhabit any given nomos without a rich understanding of its narratives. The very intelligibility of behaviour within the nomos inheres in the communal nature of common scripts or narratives for that behaviour. International law is also supplied with 'history and destiny, beginning and end, explanation and purpose' in and through narratives.[3] In contrast with conventional approaches, new scholarship in international law has begun to reveal the

---

[*] Associate Professor, Law Faculty, University of British Columbia, and Associate Professor, Law Faculty, University of Victoria. The authors wish gratefully to acknowledge Doris Buss, Ambreena Manji, Peter Fitzpatrick, Sundhya Pahuja, Sara Ramshaw, Renisa Mawani and Jeremy Webber for reading and offering generous comments on earlier versions of this essay.

[1] R Cover, 'Nomos and Narrative' (1983) 97 *Harvard Law Review* 4, at 4.

[2] *Ibid,* at 6. See also J Tully, *Strange Multiplicity: Constitutionalism in an age of Diversity* (New York, Cambridge University Press, 1995) at 60, and P Berger, *Sacred Canopy: Elements of a Sociological Theory of Religion* (Garden City NJ, Doubleday, 1967).

[3] A Orford, *Reading Humanitarian Intervention : Human Rights and the Use of Force in International Law* (Cambridge New York, Cambridge University Press, 2003) at 36.

extent that the discipline 'operate(s) not only, or even principally, in the field of state systems, rationality and facts, but also in the field of identification, imagination, subjectivity and emotion'.[4] In this paper, we suggest that the 'nomos' of which Cover speaks and international law are connected through a shared reliance on a set of narratives concerning the origins of law.[5] This can be seen most clearly in the context of interventions, both military and monetary, that are conducted under the auspices of nation-building.[6]

Although 'perhaps no concept is more fundamental to international law than sovereignty',[7] investigations of the source or foundation of sovereign law are not a common subject of mainstream international legal discourse.[8] At the margins, however, critical and feminist scholarship in international law has begun the daunting task of untangling the interwoven strands of imagination, memory and desire that bind sovereign nations into a 'nomos of the earth'. So too, contemporary 'apocryphal jurisprudence'[9] attends to stories of the origins (both mythical and actual) of modern law, and to the regulation of subjectivity effected through these narratives. In apocryphal jurisprudential accounts, modern law tells the story of what it *is* through a sequence of exclusions; that is, accounts of what it is *not*. Two sets of these exclusionary narratives concern us here. The first are originary accounts in which the violent and savage order is displaced, even vanquished, by the arrival of sovereign law. As the story goes, law's authority is secured through its exclusion of violence, though, as we will see, this exclusion can never be realised.[10] The second set of narratives are those which produce the legal order as masculine, and the legal subject as male,

---

[4] *Ibid*, at 36.

[5] On the connection between law, nation and the international, see R Buchanan and S Pahuja, 'Legal Imperialism: Empire's Invisible Hand?' in J Dean and P Passavant (eds), *The Empire's New Clothes* (London, Routledge, 2004).

[6] While this paper had its genesis in a consideration of the events immediately surrounding the US led invasion of Iraq in 2003, we believe that the analysis begun in this paper is more broadly applicable. Indeed, as Ambreena Manji pointed out to us in a comment on an earlier version of this paper, monetary interventions such as those authorised by the World Bank employ the language of nation-building and rule of law with greater legitimacy and more universality than the US or even the UN. Space constraints (and good sense) foreclosed further consideration of this topic in this paper, however. On the World Bank and rule of law, see R Buchanan and S Pahuja, above n 5.

[7] K Knop, 'Re-Statements: Feminism and State Sovereignty in International Law' (1993) 3 *Transnational and Contemporary Problems* 292, at 343.

[8] A Orford, above n 3, at 72. She puts it this way, 'International lawyers do not usually conceive of international law as embodying or enacting sovereign power. Indeed, the question "is international law really law?," a question that haunts legal theory, is a manifestation of the sense that international law lacks this sovereign force.' Of course, there are many notable exceptions in critical international law scholarship, such as EM Morgan, 'The Hermaphroditic Paradigm of International Law: A Comment on Alvarez-Machain' in *State Sovereignty: The Challenge of a Changing World: New Approaches and Thinking on International Law* (Proceedings of the 21st Annual Conference of the Canadian Council on International Law, October 1992) at 237.

[9] By this, we refer to jurisprudence concerned with the circulation of stories in a culture. See D Manderson, 'Apocryphal Jurisprudence' (2001) 23 *Studies in Law, Politics and Society* 81.

[10] J Derrida, 'Force of Law: The "Mystical Foundation of Authority"' in D Cornell, M Rosenfeld and DG Carlson (eds), *Deconstruction and the Possibility of Justice* (New York, Routledge, 1992).

while displacing both the feminine and the female subject to a space that is outside the law.[11] We see these displacements effected in a myriad of ways, from the narratives of 'muscular' humanitarian intervention in which the masculinised hero (the UN, NATO or the US) rescues the feminised developing state, to the familiar account of the relegation of women to (unregulated) private space and their (implicit or explicit) exclusion from regulated public spaces. These two sets of narratives implicate each other, although they are often considered separately.

Modern law has much at stake in maintaining these boundaries: between male and female, inside and outside, law and violence, civilisation and savagery. In our postmodern era, we know that the stability of these modernist categories is largely a chimera. Yet law, including international law, is one realm in which the rearguard action of shoring up these categorisations takes place. The public and scholarly debates concerning the 'legality' of the Anglo-American invasion of Iraq in 2003 provide one illustration of this process at work—a fervent effort to reinforce the hopelessly blurred boundary between law and violence.[12]

That international law may function as a conservative force rather than, as its disciplinary self-representations would have it, a liberating one is not necessarily a new insight.[13] What we think is useful to explore further, however, is how this comes to happen. And how we, in the developed Western world, are made complicit in this process.[14] How we are caught up in the stories, for example, that portray people trapped in various conflicts in the developing world as victims, and international humanitarian law as the agent of their rescue. Or why we continue to rely on portrayals of the sovereign state as the bounded and masculine subject of public international law, erasing women's agency and identity within international legal discourse. We are apparently unable to resist the appeal of these stories, even though they naturalise divisions we would seek to put in question.

It is of no small interest to us that the concerns of apocryphal jurisprudence—concerns with the sources of modern law and its place in maintaining the categorisations and exclusions of our nomos—are also concerns of the Western. The Western provides a mythic location, the frontier, in which anxieties

---

[11] N Naffine and RJ Owens, *Sexing the Subject of Law* (North Ryde NSW, LBC Information Services, 1997). Also, D Dallmeyer (ed), *Reconceiving Reality: Women and International Law* (Washington DC, American Society of International Law, 1993); H Charlesworth and C Chinkin, *The Boundaries of International Law: A Feminist Analysis* (Manchester, Manchester University Press, 2000).

[12] On the public discussions regarding the 'legality of the war' see Open Letter by Law Professors, 'War Would be Illegal', 7 March 2003, online: *Guardian,* <http://www.guardian.co.uk/letters/story/0,3604,909275,00.html> (last accessed 17 September 2004); R Singh and A Macdonald, 'Legality of Use of Force Against Iraq', online: Lawyers' Committee on Nuclear Policy <http://www.lcnp.org/global/IraqOpinion10.9.02.pdf> (last accessed 17 September 2004).

[13] M Koskenniemi, *From Apology to Utopia: The Structure of International Legal Argument* (Helsinki, Finnish Lawyers Publishing Co, 1989).

[14] For more on complicity, see R Buchanan and S Pahuja, 'Collaboration, Cosmopolitanism and Complicity' (2002) 17 *Nordic Journal of International Law* 297.

about law's foundations, nation-building, and sexual and racial differences, can be played out.[15] In both fiction and film, the Western has been a powerful site for the ongoing working and reworking of these anxieties. Its fecundity has made it the most loved genre in American popular culture: influential Americans, from Presidents Roosevelt, Eisenhower and Nixon (one could probably add Reagan and Bush Senior and Junior to this list) to Douglas MacArthur and Henry Kissinger, have been avowed fans of the Western.[16]

In an earlier paper, we argued for the importance of taking the intersection of law and popular culture in film seriously.[17] To the extent that films participate in constructing as well as in reflecting upon our nomos, they can and should be read as jurisprudential texts.[18] In this paper, we are arguing for a reading of the Western genre, and of one exemplary Western in particular, as a source of insight about the nomos of law and of the international. Not only does the cinematic Western deal explicitly with questions about the foundation of law, nation and sovereignty, it does so in ways that invite commentary. Indeed, the cinematic Western is one of our nomos' most prolific and powerful genres for the exploration of accounts of law's origins, masculinity and violence.

In this chapter, we turn our attention in particular to Clint Eastwood's film, *Unforgiven*. We seek to illustrate the ways in which the film opens up for our consideration several key insights about the operation of modern law. The most central and perhaps obvious of these is, of course, the inescapable link between the founding violence of frontier justice and the (American) ideal of the rule of law. Intertwined with these is the narrative of the masculinised hero rescuing the feminised victim. While *Unforgiven* can be read as faithfully reproducing these familiar storylines, it also subverts them; refusing to glamorise or 'forgive' its violence, giving agency to its female characters, and undermining the machismo of its outlaw hero, William Munny.

We offer a reading (or rather, an intentional mis-reading)[19] of *Unforgiven* in conjunction with a theoretical account of law's foundation, and contemporary debates over calls for intervention into the affairs of sovereign states. *Unforgiven* draws our attention to the many erasures still at work in our conceptions of law,

---

[15] R Slotkin, *Gunfighter Nation: The Myth of the Frontier in Twentieth-Century America* (New York, Atheneum, 1992).

[16] LC Mitchell, *Westerns: The Making of the Man in Fiction and Film* (Chicago, Chicago University Press, 1992) at 15.

[17] See R Johnson and R Buchanan, 'Getting The Insider's Story Out: What Popular Film Can Tell Us About Legal Method's Dirty Secrets' (2001) 20 *Windsor Yearbook of Access to Justice* 87. The argument is that in our society, film, like law, enjoys a 'licence to arbitrate the social imaginary'. Both law and film engage in the practice of 'world-making' in the making of meaning through the telling of stories.

[18] See O Kamir, 'X-Raying *Adam's Rib*: Multiple Readings of a (Feminist?) Law-Film' (2000) 22 *Studies in Law, Politics and Society* 103.

[19] By misreading, we mean an intentional reading 'against the grain'; subjecting a text to an interpretation that cuts against both conventional understandings and the likely intentions of its authors. See also Anne Orford's misreadings of the texts of international law (above n 3, ch 2) and Spivak's misreadings of the canons of philosophy in GC Spivak, *A Critique of Postcolonial Reason: Toward a History of the Vanishing Present* (Cambridge, Harvard University Press, 1999).

violence and gender. It helps us to identify the exclusions operating at 'the source' in the stories we believe about the origins of law, whether in the mythic past of the American West, or in the mythic future of a 'liberated' Iraq.

We begin by providing an elaboration of the ground on which we seek to situate the discussion that follows. First, we suggest that the frontier myth, as encapsulated in the genre of the Western in twentieth-century American letters and film, can usefully be read as one version of the account of modern law's foundations, one which is particularly relevant to contemporary considerations of the international. Both the Western and modern law establish themselves through the construction of ostensibly stable categories, most importantly, the distinctions between law/violence, civilised/savage, masculine/feminine, which we will take up in some detail. In the second part, we turn to an examination of *Unforgiven*, to consider more carefully how it manages both to invoke and subvert these modernist dichotomies. Our critical exegesis of *Unforgiven* will reveal the contours of some of the deep social narratives about justice, gender and violence at issue in modern law. We suggest in our concluding section that this line of inquiry is particularly suggestive in relation to current debates over the legitimate use of force and humanitarian intervention in international law.

Stories of Legal Origins[20]

The origin has to 'be' before and after the point of origination.[21]

There are many stories upon which one might draw to provide an account of the source and legitimacy of modern law, including Freud's account of patricide in *Totem and Taboo*, or Hobbes's account of the transition from a 'state of nature' to sovereignty.[22] We focus here on the mythical West, and the stories told in the Western genre of books and films of outlaws and lawmen on the American frontier. As an origin myth, the Western shares much with these other examples, including most obviously their violent and masculinised nature. But, of course, there is always more to the story (of origins). Origin myths don't work, as they claim, by providing us with a definitive account of 'how it all got started'. Rather, as Peter Fitzpatrick has argued, it is the failure of modern law's accounts of its own

---

[20] We thank Sundhya Pahuja and Jennifer Beard for originally piquing our interest in this line of inquiry. See S Pahuja and JL Beard, 'Before the Beginning: Disclosing Law's Foundation' (2003) 19 *Australian Feminist Law Journal*.

[21] P Fitzpatrick, 'Breaking the Unity of the World: Savage Sources and Feminine Law' (2003) 19 *Australian Feminist Law Journal* 47.

[22] On *Totem and Taboo*, see P Fitzpatrick, *Modernism and the Grounds of Law* (Cambridge, Cambridge University Press, 2001), ch 1. On Hobbes, see K Shaw, 'Feminist Futures: Contexting the Political' in R Falk, L Ruiz and RBJ Walker (eds), *Reframing the International: Law, Culture, Politics* (New York, Routledge, 2002) at 224.

origins definitively to 'settle' the matter that is telling. The irresolution of these accounts is their most revealing aspect.[23]

Modern law's narratives of origin undertake an impossible task, for they must somehow reconcile the realms of the universal and the particular, inside and outside, savage and civilisation, law and violence. For this reason, many legal theorists have felt compelled to describe law's foundation in paradoxical terms. So, for Robert Cover, 'Every legal order must conceive of itself in one way or another as emerging out of that which is itself unlawful.'[24] For Agamben, the paradox is that 'the sovereign is at the same time both inside and outside the juridical order'.[25] Or, as Fitzpatrick pithily pronounces, 'law, in short, constituently combines a self-grounding with grounds other to it'.[26] The resolution of modernity's dilemma, it seems, requires the impossible artistry of law in order to 'suture the great chasm between the finite and the infinite in a line of zero width'.[27] This line is, of course, sovereignty; that which underpins and connects the modern nation and the modern subject.

> Instead of a world we vaguely remember and castigate for worrying about the number of angels dancing on the head of a pin, we have become used to a world that dances on razors, on the edge of the state, on the edge of the modern subject.[28]

Indeed, the question of sovereignty is central to each of these formulations, although not necessarily in a way that would be familiar to international law scholars. Nevertheless, so much has been written so well on the subject of modern law's problem with 'grounds' that a reader might legitimately ask what could possibly justify a return to this well-trod terrain. Indeed, one might even suggest that the obsession with origins is itself a pre-occupation of modernism, and one that we might do well to get beyond.[29]

But can we simply 'get past' the paradox of law's self-founding? The implication of the above accounts is that the story of law's foundations is not an 'old' story, in the sense that it cannot be expected to 'fade into annals of history'. Rather, the story, of law's foundation is a story that is always with us; it must constantly be re-enacted. This is what Derrida calls the 'paradox of iterability': 'Iterability requires the origin to repeat itself originarily, to alter itself so as to have the value of origin.'[30] In the context of an extended discussion of Freud's *Totem and Taboo* as an account of law's origins, Peter Fitzpatrick formulates this iterability in terms of the mythic dyad of the savage and civilisation, which he concludes by observing: 'Civilization, then, has "repeatedly" to be made permanent.'[31]

---

[23] P Fitzpatrick, *Modernism*, above n 22, at 12.
[24] R Cover, above n 1, at 23–24.
[25] G Agamben, *Homo Sacer* (Stanford, Stanford University Press, 1998) at 15.
[26] P Fitzpatrick, *Modernism*, above n 22, at 12.
[27] RBJ Walker, 'Polis, Cosmopolis, Politics' (2003) 28 *Alternatives* 267.
[28] *Ibid*, at 270.
[29] M Antaki, 'Leading Modernity (to) A-ground' (2003) 19 *Australian Feminist Law Journal* 115.
[30] J Derrida, 'Force of Law', above n 10, at 43.
[31] P Fitzpatrick, 'Breaking the Unity of the World', above n 21.

Similarly, regarding the narratives that served to hold colonial relations in place, Homi Bhabba has observed that 'the same old stories ... must be told (compulsively) again and afresh, and are differently gratifying and terrifying each time.'[32] In the seemingly endless repetition of the 'same old stories' one finds a reconciliation of sorts of the demands for both stability and flexibility, or determination and responsiveness, to use Fitzpatrick's language:

> It is in this paradox of iterability, then, in the repetition of the competing yet complementary pulls of sameness and difference that law finds its ground and order unendingly forms.[33]

Re-enactments of the perplexing moment of sovereign law's self-founding are all around us, from the stalled negotiations over aboriginal title in British Columbia to the unfolding events of the War on Terror. They are narrated through the morning news, the afternoon lecture on property law, and the evening trip to the cinema. We need to attend to each of these retellings, for as RBJ Walker reminds us, the problem of sovereignty 'cannot be detached from the most pervasive cultural, social and political practices of modern life, especially those practices that encourage us to assume that all the questions about the authority of authority have already been answered with some authority.'[34] The endlessly repeated stories of law's founding authority—both what they reveal and what they conceal—literally make 'the world in which we live'; they not only demand our attention, they call us in. That is, they call upon us to take our (proper) places so that the action may begin (again).[35]

The Western as a Founding Myth

The hunger Westerns satisfy is a hunger not for adventure but for meaning.[36]

The Western as a genre shares with other myths of origin this (paradoxical) iterability, that is, the combination of stability and flexibility that comes with repetition. Tompkins notes that the genre appears to operate within 'a terribly strict set of thematic and formal codes', in which the 'same manoeuvres are performed over and over'.[37] Westerns share a predictably unforgiving yet austerely beautiful

---

[32] HK Bhabba, *Location of Culture* (New York, Routledge, 1994) at 77, quoted in A Orford, above n 3, at 183. See also G Deleuze, *Difference and Repetition* (New York, Columbia University Press, 1994).

[33] P Fitzpatrick, above n 22, at 79.

[34] RBJ Walker, above n 27, at 274.

[35] On women in international law and their proper places, see D Buss, 'Feminist Theory and the State of International Law: Rethinking Public and Private Spheres', talk at The New International Law Workshop, Birkbeck University, June 2003.

[36] J Tompkins, *West of Everything: The Inner Life of Westerns* (New York, Oxford University Press, 1992) at 15.

[37] *Ibid*, at 27.

wilderness setting. Their heroes are lean, taciturn, white men; men who speak little but can see far. They are subjected to extraordinary physical suffering; from rain and cold, exhausting journeys, to brutal beatings, all of which they endure stoically. The supporting characters are almost always white men as well. Women and native people may function as extras, but are rarely if ever real characters with whom we become acquainted. The indoor setting is usually a saloon, bringing with it the attendant themes of drinking, gambling and prostitution. The stories almost always culminate in an ecstatic scene of violent retribution, in which the audience is expected to identify with the hero.[38] For the viewer, the violent culmination is read as justifiable not only because it is the resolution of a vengeance plot, but also because it is seen to clear the way for 'the possibility of a new beginning, of re-founding, of establishing governments from reflection and choice, rather than mishaps of birth and tradition'.[39] Through the familiar yet remote canvas of setting, characters and plot, Western films have told and retold, to generations of viewers, a mythic tale of the violent foundations of law on the frontier.

Even if Westerns all tell 'the same old stories,' the genre has also proven highly adaptable in response to changing social and political contexts. Lee Clark Mitchell argues that the Western has been successful both because it was open to multiple interpretations, and because it was such a flexible form that plots were able to shift in accordance with 'the altering winds of cultural anxiety and popular ideals'.[40] Similarly, William Handley suggests that the Western provides a space 'where open questions about national identity, the meaning of American history and democracy and the struggle of the nation's present and future are worked through ... in both the political and artistic sense.'[41] Just what allows the genre to be so productive in this way is not explained in these accounts.

Westerns produce meaning in the same way that modern law does—through the invocation of a series of 'classic' oppositions, 'parlour versus mesa, East versus West, women versus men, illusions versus truth, words versus things'.[42] Indeed, like modern law, the Western claims to depict a world of clear (even obvious) choices. And, as with law, as we begin to look more closely at the alternatives laid out for us in the Western, we see that the distinctions are less clear than they at first appear:

---

[38] *Ibid*, at 229. Tompkins describes this moment as one of 'moral ecstacy'.

[39] J Marini, 'Western Justice: John Ford and Sam Peckinpah on the Defense of the Heroic' (2001) 6 *Nexus: A Journal of Opinion* 57-65, at 57. For a slightly different take that reads Western history and Westerns together, see J Walker's Introduction to *Westerns: Films Through History* (New York, Routledge, 2001).

[40] LC Mitchell, above n 16, at 5. For an exploration of the various sub-genres of the Western, one which places the sub-genres in their socio-cultural-historical contexts, see W Wright, *Six Guns and Society: A Structural Study of the Western* (Berkeley, University of California Press, 1975).

[41] WR Handley, *Marriage, Violence, and the Nation in the American Literary West* (Cambridge, Cambridge University Press, 2002) at 33.

[42] J Tompkins, above n 36, at 48.

What is most characteristic of these oppositions is that as soon as you put pressure on them they break down. Each time one element of a pair is driven into a corner, it changes shape and frequently turns into its opposite. It's as if the genre's determination to have a world of absolute dichotomies ensures that interpenetration and transmutation will occur.[43]

The inherent instability of the categories it purports to establish is one key to the genre's ability to function as a vehicle for containing and mediating a variety of social tensions, and hence its enduring appeal. For example, Jane Tompkins asserts: 'Westerns strive to depict a world of clear alternatives—independence versus connection, anarchy versus law, town versus desert, but they are just as compulsively driven to destroying these opposites and making them contain each other.'[44] Through this fundamental ambiguity, the dual tendency towards distinction and the erasure of distinctions, the Western, like law, opens itself to a variety of alternative readings, providing a fertile space for cultural critique of continuing relevance.[45]

Indeed, if we turn to the narration of contemporary events in the popular media, we can see that these tensions and anxieties, and their apparent resolution in mythic narratives of the frontier, remain a powerful part of the American (and hence global) cultural frame of reference. As Nick Blomley observes, 'the trope of the "frontier" that separates the West from the savage is still powerfully operative.'[46] In this era in which the real and the spectacle have become improbably reversed,[47] it seems hardly remarkable that the press room in the White House seems to recount the familiar Western plot line in which a lawless outlaw must be ruthlessly killed, and his bad deeds avenged, in order that a just, free and democratic legal order can take its rightful place on the frontier.[48]

To be sure, observations about the 'cowboy' in the White House, or the sense of 'frontier justice' embodied in America's increasingly unilateralist stance on foreign policy, are often made disparagingly, in passing, by critics dismayed by the retreat from a liberal internationalist order whose moral and legal superiority is taken to

---

[43] *Ibid.*

[44] *Ibid.*

[45] So, eg, Kamir argues that the social functions of what William Wright calls the professional plot Western (above n 40, at 168) are now performed in a sub-genre of lawyer movies. See O Kamir, 'Towards a Theory of Law-and-Film: A Case Study of Hollywood's Hero-Lawyer and the Construction of Honor and Dignity' (February 2004), University of Michigan Law, Public Law Working Paper No 34, <http://ssrn.com abstract = 5068027> (last accessed 17 September 2004). On the links between the Western and the Road Film, see S Roberts, 'Western Meets Eastwood: Genre and Gender on the Road' in S Cohan and IR Hark (eds), *The Road Movie Book* (New York, Routledge, 1997) 45.

[46] N Blomley, 'Law, Property, and the Geography of Violence: The Frontier, the Survey, and the Grid' (2003) 93 *Annals of the Association of American Geographers* 121, at 125.

[47] See, eg, S Zizek, *Welcome to the Desert of the Real* (London, Verso, 2002).

[48] As Susan Faludi observed, 'On the eve of the Iraqi invasion, the president's advisors were working hard to embed George W Bush inside the script of the American Western, as if we had missed the "subtext" of the president's own statements over the past year or so about "smoking them out of their holes" and "wanted: dead or alive"': 'An American Myth Rides Into the Sunset' (30 March 2003), *New York Times*, D13.

be self-evident. We argue, however, that the narrative of 'frontier justice' is embedded much more deeply in internationalist discourse than reflections on the tenure of the most recent Texan in the White House might reveal. In our view, the contradictory legacy of frontier justice manifests itself both in the (American) ideal of the 'rule of law' and the interpenetration of that ideal with the presumptions of liberal internationalism.[49]

Law and Violence on the Frontier

The construction of that which is deemed law thus rests on the violent world of non-law. The inscription of a frontier—which may be figurative, temporal and spatial—is integral to this process.[50]

The genre of the Western in both fiction and film mythologised the settlement of the American frontier—that is, a frontier imagined both in terms of a particular territory and in relation to a particular nation.[51] It didn't seem to matter that its landscape was not always exclusively or recognisably 'Western'.[52] Rather, the frontier has served as a (peculiarly American)[53] mythic boundary between civilised and uncivilised, between a 'masculinised' West and a 'feminised' East; a liminal site in which the anxieties about nation-building and identity, particularly gender, but also racialised identities, could be worked out.[54] For this reason, the frontier can profitably be thought of as a 'spatialisation'—that is, a spatial concept that is always at its root bound up with social relations—rather than as either a particular territory or a spatial metaphor.[55] As Mitchell puts it, the 'West of free speaking was thus never an actual place, first discovered, then explored, but has always been

[49] On rule of law, see R Buchanan and S Pahuja, above n 5.

[50] N Blomley, above n 46, at 124.

[51] For an illuminating, if brief, discussion of the particularities of this American notion of the frontier, see P Fitzpatrick, 'The Immanence of *Empire*' in J Dean and P Passavant, above n 5, at 49–50.

[52] LC Mitchell, above n 16.

[53] To say that the Western is a peculiarly American product is not to deny that other nations and cultures have their own engagements with the genre. The 'spaghetti Westerns' of Sergio Leone are likely the best known examples, but there is a German fascination with the Western. See, eg, UG Poiger, 'A New, "Western" Hero? Reconstructing German Masculinity in the 1950s' (1998) 24 *Signs* 147; and T Schneider, 'Finding a new Heimat in the Wild West: Karl May and the German Western of the 1960's' in E Buscombe and RE Pearson, *Back in the Saddle Again: New Essays on the Western* (London, British Film Institute, 1998).

[54] S Roberts, above n 45, focuses on this phenomenon in her argument that the American Road Movie is one of the modern incarnations of the Western, saying, at 45: 'What ultimately links the road movie to the Western is this ideal of masculinity inherent in certain underlying conceptualizations of American national identity [revolving around individualism and aggression] that have persisted, if only through continual ideological struggle.'

[55] N Blomley, above n 46, at 123. In focusing here on 'the idea' of the frontier, we do not go so far as to deny its materiality. We agree with Buss that the frontier is *both* metaphor and material space. As Brown argues, the spaces we construct through social relations are the spaces of power/knowledge; to deny the materiality of those spaces would risk a denial of the power/knowledge enacted by and

instead an ideological terrain reinvented with each generation of fears and hopes.'[56] The frontier is necessary to our legal imaginations because of its capacity to combine opposites: it is both violent and law-abiding; it is both East and West; it is the edge of the civilisation and the edge of the wilderness. The frontier stands in here as the 'razor's edge', the impossible line on which 'law' and 'not law' are balanced. To the extent that modern law must always be able to 'maintain itself in relation to an exteriority', an idea of the frontier is essential.[57]

The frontier narrative of the Western shares with other modernist accounts of law's origins a troubled and slippery relationship between law and violence. While the arrival of law on the frontier is said to herald the cessation of violence, and the inauguration of a society governed by rules rather than force, that very arrival is always predicated on a violent act.[58] Although it cannot be said that the violence done 'before the law' is 'legal', 'this law to come will in turn legitimate retrospectively, the violence that may offend the sense of justice, its future anterior already justifies it.'[59] Conventional accounts, recognising the difficulty arising from law's simultaneous association with and disavowal of violence, would draw a line in the sand here between law's reluctant or exceptional resort to violence and the savage violence that remains still outside the law. The problem is that the 'founding' violence, the pre-legal violence of the origins of law, does not fall on either side of that imaginary line.

Rather, in the founding moment, that which is set apart from law, violence, is also deeply embedded within it.[60] As Agamben explains, 'the juridico-political

---

through space. See MP Brown, *Closet Space: Geographies of Metaphor from the Body to the Globe* (London Routledge, 2000). It is important not to lose sight of the ways in which the 'materiality' of the actual frontier, as the 'razor's edge' of law and not law, has had and continues to have a very real impact upon American Indian and First Nations communities.

[56] LC Mitchell, above n 16, at 6.

[57] G Agamben, above n 25; P Fitzpatrick, above n 22.

[58] The dilemma presented by the commingling of law and violence on the frontier is well illustrated in John Ford's last Western, *The Man Who Shot Liberty Valence* (1962). In this film, John Wayne and Jimmy Stewart play the contrasting characters of Tom Doniphon (the Western gunfighter) and Ranse Stoddard (the Eastern lawman). The legal order transplanted from the East in the persona of Ranse Stoddard is feeble, and threatened by the lawless violence of the West, personified by the outlaw, Liberty Valence (played by Lee Marvin). Law on the frontier is established only once Liberty Valence is shot dead, ostensibly by Ranse. That shot, the act of heroism for which Ranse becomes famous, was in fact the act of Tom Doniphon, the hero of the 'old' West. Tom, hidden in shadows, made the shot that both saved Ranse's life and made him a hero. But in order for modern and civilised law to establish itself on the frontier, that fact must be concealed lest law and violence become indistinguishable. As Ryan notes, *Liberty Valence* poses the question: 'To what extent does the legal order necessarily find its origins in kinds of violence that compromise its very legitimacy?' See C Ryan, 'Print the Legend: Violence and Recognition in *The Man Who Shot Liberty Valance*' in J Denvi (ed), *Legal Realism: Movies as Legal Texts* (Urbana, University of Illinois Press, 1996) at 24.

[59] J Derrida, above n 10, at 35.

[60] 'Violence is not exterior to the order of droit. It threatens it from within.' J Derrida, above n 10, at 34. See also N Blomley, above n 46: 'The constitutive outside is at once radically set apart and deeply embedded within law.' G Agamben, above n 25, speaks of the capacity of law to maintain itself in relation to an exteriority, pointing in particular to that violence which is imagined as 'beyond state sovereignty and yet captured within it.'

order has the structure of an inclusion of what is simultaneously pushed outside.'[61] This occurs because of the necessity of the re-iteration of the (violent) origins. As we've already observed, the self-founding narrative of law doesn't stand on solid ground, but rather acquires its aura of stability from its continual repetition. It is through these repetitions that violence, although cast out, returns to infuse law.

From this it also follows, as Nick Blomley astutely observes, 'the frontier is not closed'.[62] This observation is made in contrast with the classic account of Frederick Jackson Turner, which provides the American frontier with meaning and historical trajectory (telos) from 'open and empty' to 'settled and civilised'. In our account of the mythic West, however, the frontier can never be closed, as the divide that it purports to maintain between the 'civilised' inside and the 'violent' outside of law requires it to be continually open, perpetually enacting the violence that it would purport to exclude.

Locating Women in the Western

Without a woman, the story wouldn't work.[63]

The Western seems preoccupied with a world of rugged masculinity, where women figure as marginal characters. It is thus not surprising that it has been rated as women's least favourite movie genre.[64] As we observed above, one can think of the frontier as a spatialisation—a concept that is simultaneously social and spatial in its ordering effects.[65] Those ordering effects are not genderless. In the Western, particular spaces are not only represented as lawful or lawless, they also encode social ideas about gender, and the 'proper places' of women.[66] And what are those proper places? In the world of the Western, women appear almost exclusively in

---

[61] G Agamben, above n 25, at 18.

[62] N Blomley, above n 46, at 124.

[63] Anthony Mann, quoted in R Bellour, 'Alternation, Segmentation, Hypnosis: Interview with Raymond Bellour', conducted by J Bergstrom in C Penley (ed), *Feminism and Film Theory* (London, Routledge, 1988) at 187.

[64] Even in the heyday of the Western, women did not make up any significant part of the audience for the Western, ranking it as their least favourite genre. See L Handel, *Hollywood Looks at Its Audience: A Report on Film Audience Research* (Champaign, University of Illinois Press, 1950) at 124, cited in VW Wexman, *Creating the Couple: Love, Marriage, and Hollywood Performance* (Princeton NJ, Princeton University Press, 1993) at 69.

[65] N Blomley, above n 46.

[66] D Buss, above n 35. On 'proper place,' see: T Cresswell, *In Place/Out of Place* (Minneapolis, University of Minnesota Press, 1996); D Cooper, 'Like Counting Stars: Re-Structuring Equality and Socio-Legal Space of Same-Sex Marriage' in R Wintemute and M Andenaes (eds), *Legal Recognition of Same-Sex Partnerships: A Study of National, European and International Law* (Oxford, Hart, 2001). On gender and space generally, see D Massey, *Space, Place, and Gender* (Minneapolis, University of Minnesota Press, 1994); LA Staeheli and PM Martin, 'Spaces for Feminism in Geography' (2000) 571 *The Annals of the American Academy of Political and Social Science* 135–50.

one of two locations: the homestead and the saloon. Both the good woman and the bad woman have their proper place on the frontier. In its flattened representations of women, the filmic Western seems merely to play out the madonna/whore dichotomy found in much of Western civilisation's art and literature.[67] But the flattened gendered dimensions of the genre bear further critical attention.

Attending to gender, in *West of Everything*, Tompkins argues that the inner life of the Western is fundamentally about the rejection of the feminine and the reclaiming of all things masculine. She dismisses the notion that the Western is primarily about the encounter between civilisation and the frontier, or even that it has anything to do with West as such: 'It is about men's fear of losing their mastery, and hence their identity, both of which the Western tirelessly reinvents.'[68] She asserts that the genre needs to be understood at least in part as a reaction against the dominance of the nineteenth-century sentimental novel (a genre dominated by women).[69] As she puts it:

> The Western owed its popularity and essential character to the dominance of a women's culture in the nineteenth century and to women's invasion of the public sphere between 1880 and 1920. For most of the nineteenth century the two places women could call their own in the social structure were the church and the home. The Western contains neither. ... Given the enormous publicity and fervor of the Women's Christian Temperance Union crusade, can it be an accident that the characteristic indoor setting for Westerns is the saloon?[70]

But if the Western involved a rejection of femininity and of all things related to the nineteenth-century sentimental novel, Tompkins notes that it was in many ways a surface rejection. The Western retained (in a form inflected with masculinity rather than femininity) the sentimental novel's same disciplinary model of heroic selfhood: a model involving renunciation of self; a regime of silence imposed where expression is most needed; the equation of repression with

---

[67] There is a significant literature on such representations in film generally. See, eg, A Kuhn, *The Power of the Image: Essays on Representation and Sexuality* (London, Routledge, 1985); MA Doane, *Femmes Fatales: Feminism, Film Theory, Psychoanalysis* (New York, Routledge, 1991). For an engaging visual collection of examples from the 19th century, see B Dijkstra, *Idols of Perversity: Fantasies of Feminine Evil in Fin-de-Siècle Culture* (Oxford, Oxford University Press, 1986).

[68] J Tompkins, above n 36, at 45.

[69] The argument parallels in some ways Harold Bloom's theory that patterns of imagery in poems represent both a response to and a defence against the influence of precursor poems. See H Bloom, *A Map of Misreading* (New York, Oxford University Press, 1975) and H Bloom, *Anxiety of Influence* (New York, Oxford University Press, 1973). It is worth noting that Tompkins's thesis is consistent with that advanced by A Douglas, *The Feminization of American Culture* (New York, Anchor Books, 1988). See also Schaum's exploration of the view in this period that the predominance of women authors in literature had produced 'a nation literally unmanned of its intellectual and creative strength'. M Schaum, 'HL Mencken and American Cultural Masculinism' (1995) 29 *Journal American Studies* 379, at 381. For a collection of articles exploring the complexities of manhood and masculinity during the Victorian era, see MC Carnes and C Griffen (eds), *Meanings for Manhood: Constructions of Masculinity in Victorian America* (Chicago, University of Chicago Press, 1990).

[70] J Tompkins, above n 36, at 44.

integrity and authenticity. What appeared to be a rejection of the feminine as articulated in the sentimental genre was often little more than a rearticulation of the same set of disciplinary codes from a different gender direction.[71] Gender, she asserts, functions in the Western in a more complicated fashion than its surface indicates. While we do not agree with the strong version of the claim that the Western has nothing to do with civilisation, we do agree that gender must be taken into account. And certainly, Tompkins's gender analysis also resonates with the oft-articulated feminist insight that, when attempting to read gender into the art and literature of Western civilisation, it is important to attend to the seeming silences, gaps and repressions.[72] Even the absent woman (as we will later see in our discussion of *Unforgiven*) may continue to function as a crucial structuring element.

Wexman, also taking gender seriously, asserts that while the Western seems preoccupied with questions of law and violence on the frontier, and while the act of founding a (modern) legal order is generally represented as a necessarily masculine endeavour, woman nonetheless remain central to the genre itself.[73] In a related vein, Bellour argues that Westerns are 'subtended from one end to the other by the problematic of marriage'.[74] This theme is pushed to the centre in William Handley's work, *Marriage, Violence, and the Nation in the American Literary West*.[75] Handley points out that the literary west (if not the west of the Western film) was preoccupied with marriage. Indeed, he argues that it is nearly impossible to unpick the braiding of marriage and nation in the Western. As he puts it, people presumed that marriage of the proper sort would create the right kinds of citizens.[76] If the Western is often explicitly about the legitimacy of law, and the meaning of the foundational violence, it is also the case that the meaning of marriage is often being constructed in tandem with the meaning of citizenship, nation and law itself. The convention is to have a woman central to nation-building, to the bringing of civilisation to the frontier, to the project of expelling violence from the spaces of civilisation.[77] That is, as in the Mann epigraph above,

---

[71] *Ibid*, at 127: ' ... women cannot express their rage because to do so marks them as unfeminine. Men cannot register their pain because to do so marks them as unmanly. The gender system works to enforce codes of behaviour that are, in their different ways, excruciating.'

[72] A classic remains A Rich, *On Lies Secrets and Silence: Selected Prose, 1966-1978* (New York, Norton, 1979).

[73] VW Wexman, above n 64, at 70. In one chapter, she presses this point: 'Star and Genre: John Wayne, the Western, and the American Dream of the Family on the Land.'

[74] R Bellour, above n 63, at 187.

[75] WR Handley, above n 41.

[76] *Ibid*, at 3.

[77] Again, *The Man Who Shot Liberty Valance* well illustrates this point. In the film, both Ranse and Tom are in love with Hallie. She is the prize in the contest not just between two men, but also between the orders of positive and natural law. In the story, the very foundation of modern (legal) civilisation is, at the end, contingent on the struggle over a woman, and the question of who is the better man for Hallie. Tom leaves Ranse to take the credit for shooting Liberty Valance, but only because Tom has decided that Ranse *is* the better man for Hallie: 'You taught her to read and write. Now give her something to read and write about.' As Wexman points out, above n 64, at 124: 'This formulation of the issue places not an abstract notion of justice or even the welfare of the town as the crucial motivating factor in the murder of Valance, but rather the possession of a Northern European woman who has been made literate and who now must be provided with laws to protect the group interests that she represents.'

'Without a woman, the story wouldn't work.' And, as per the conventions, not just any woman will do: it is only the pure white woman who has the capacity for being a civilising force.[78]

Reading Nation, Violence and Gender through *Unforgiven*

We turn now to *Unforgiven,* the 1992 Clint Eastwood film that won Academy Awards for best picture and director,[79] and which generated a significant body of academic writing.[80] It is widely held as an iconic text, one that is celebrated as an achievement both in the genre of the Western, and in film generally.[81] The film sums up the genre of the Western by invoking, thematically and stylistically, countless prior Westerns, including many featuring Eastwood himself.[82] It continues to rework the familiar themes of masculinity, justice and the civilisation of the frontier, albeit by revealing more overtly the uncertainties and contradictions that attend the creation and maintenance of these categories. It both draws on and deviates from the genre in ways that speak to the anxieties of the time in which it

---

[78] For more on 'Racial Difference and the Threat of Miscegenation', see VW Wexman, above n 64, at 89–105.

[79] *Unforgiven* (Malpaso Productions/Warner Brothers, 1992). The transcript of the film is available online at <http://www.clinteastwood.net.> (last accessed 17 September 2004). Click on 'Filmography', then on 'Unforgiven', then on 'Script'.

[80] See, eg, O Kamir, above n 45; A Sarat, 'When Memory Speaks: Remembrance and Revenge in Unforgiven' (2002) 77 *Indiana Law Journal* 307–29; W Beard, '*Unforgiven* and the Uncertainties of the Heroic' (2002) 3 *Canadian Journal of Film Studies* 41; M Whitlock Blundell and K Ormand, 'Western Values, or the Peoples Homer: "Unforgiven" as a Reading of the "Iliad"' (1997) 18 *Poetics Today* 533; WI Miller, 'Clint Eastwood and Equity: Popular Culture's Theory of Revenge' in A Sarat and TR Kearns (eds), *Law in the Domains of Culture* (Ann Arbor, University of Michigan Press, 1998) at 161; C Plantinga, 'Spectacles of Death: Clint Eastwood and Violence in *Unforgiven*' (1998) 37 *Cinema Journal* 65.

[81] It is helpful to distinguish the typical from the iconic. In his discussion of genre, Ryall points out that the iconic or 'canonical' Westerns are, in many senses, not typical of their genre. Indeed, if one wants best to understand the norms of the genre, he asserts that one needs to go to the 'B' pictures rather than the Hollywood 'A' list. See T Ryall, 'Genre and Hollywood' in J Hill and P Church Gibson (eds), *The Oxford Guide to Film Studies* (New York, Oxford University Press, 1998) at 334. Certainly, audiences for Hollywood films, just like audiences for other cultural products, 'read them according to a detailed set of assumptions—an intertextual consciousness—derived from a regular viewing of related films and an awareness of the various secondary discourses.' Further, the pleasures of the viewer are derived in large measure (at 334) 'from such qualities as the ritualistic predictability of the narratives and the nuancing of familiar conventions'.

[82] The co-mingling of influences is also marked in the film's final dedication, 'for Don and Sergio.' The latter is, of course, 'spaghetti western' director Sergio Leone, responsible for Eastwood's transformation into The Man With No Name. He worked with Eastwood in *Fistful of Dollars* (1964), *For a Few Dollars More* (1965) and *The Good, The Bad and the Ugly* (1966). The former, action-movie director Don Siegel, directed Eastwood in *Dirty Harry* (1971), as well as in *Coogan's Bluff* (1968) and *The Beguiled* (1971).

was produced, and the time in which we read it.[83] In particular, we read it as a story about humanitarian interventions and projects of nation-building.[84]

Unforgiven draws together the threads explored above. In the exegesis that follows, we discuss key scenes in the film to illuminate the ways in which it functions both as a meditation upon and reflection of contemporary dilemmas of law, violence, gender and nation. Our (mis)reading of *Unforgiven* aims to utilise it as a vehicle for the recognition of the ways in which certain powerful stories in Western culture exert a 'pull' upon our sensibilities, positioning us both to identify with certain types of agents and to respond to certain types of injuries, to the exclusion of other narratives, other agents and other possible harms.

The Injury

The opening scene of the film links together law, violence and gender in the symbolically important site of the saloon. In the opening minutes of the movie, Delilah, one of the whores working in Greeley's Saloon and Billiards, is viciously attacked with a knife by cowboy Mike, assisted by his friend Davey. The cause of the trouble? A woman's laughter. When Sherriff Little Bill arrives on the scene, Strawberry Alice, another of the whores, reports: 'She didn't steal nothing. She didn't even touch his poke. All she done, when she seen he has a teensy little pecker, is give a giggle. That's all. She didn't know no better.' This opening act of violence is thoroughly gendered. Not only is it enacted on the body of a woman, it is justified because of the gendered assault of her laughter on the body of a man.[85] Through her laughter, she has assaulted the core of his sexualised masculinity. Mike's return of violence is similarly sexualised and gendered, targeting her face and breasts, the parts of her body which signify her beauty and desirability in the sexual economy of the brothel/saloon.

In such a context, what penalty is appropriate? Strawberry Alice makes it clear that she sees the injury to Delilah as deserving of the maximum sanction possible at law: 'Going to hang them, Little Bill?' Little Bill initially indicates his own view that the punishment required is something short of death, telling his deputy to go fetch his bullwhip. Strawberry Alice's expression of outrage is matched by that of

---

[83] David Peoples' script was originally written in 1984. Eastwood produced it nearly a decade later. For a useful discussion of the legitimacy of readings which speak less to authorial intent than to reader response issues, see Kamir's discussion of modern Western legal understandings of *Rashomon*, a Japanese film produced in the 1950s, set in feudal Japan, in O Kamir, 'Judgment By Film: Socio-Legal Functions of *Rashomon*' (2000) 12 *Yale Journal of Law and the Humanities* 39.

[84] Further, that this re-reading has been prompted, in part, by recent events in Iraq should not seem extraordinary when one considers that the film appeared in the year following what is now know as Gulf War I.

[85] For a discussion of women's laughter, see J Elsley, 'Laughter as Feminine Power in *The Color Purple* and *A Question of Silence*' in R Barreca (ed), *New Perspectives on Women and Comedy* (Philadelphia, Gordon and Breach Science Publishers, 1992) at 193–99; see also T Modleski, 'Rape vs. Mans/laughter: Blackmail' in T Modleski, *The Women Who Knew Too Much: Hitchcock and Feminist Theory* (New York, Routledge, 1989) at 17–30.

Skinny, the brothel owner, who asserts that *he himself* is the victim. The injury is here re-inscribed to focus not on the body of Delilah, but on Skinny's damaged property interests: he has invested in Delilah, and the slashing of her face has made her economically unprofitable.[86] An economic injury cannot be redressed through a whipping, but requires economic recompense. Little Bill is persuaded by the argument, and directs Mike and Davey to deliver a certain number of ponies to to Skinny before the spring.

To Alice's expression of outrage that the cowboys are not even to receive a whipping, Little Bill grabs her and pulls her close, saying: 'Haven't you seen enough blood for one night, Huh? Hell, Alice, it ain't like they were tramps, or loafers or bad men, you know they were just hard working boys who were foolish. If they was given over to wickedness in a regular way then I could see…' Alice interrupts, finishing his sentence with, 'Like whores?' The movie positions the viewer, like Alice, to understand the double standard all too clearly. 'Given over to wickedness in a regular way,' the whores are visible to the law only through the property interests of those who, like Skinny, profit from the women's location in the sexual economy. Through their emplacement in the sexual economy of the brothel, they do not merit the full protection of the law. Such protection apparently extends only to the right kind of woman, potential wives and mothers, women on the homestead, women who advance the nation-building cause.

In the face of law's failure/refusal to expel violence from their space of work, and to see them as the appropriate subjects of law, they take the law into their own hands. They pool their savings and offer a reward of one thousand dollars for anyone who will kill Mike and Davey. And we see how the nature of the injury has again changed. Their outrage over the cutting of Delilah has been surpassed by their outrage over the gendered violence of the law's erasure of their collective status as persons: 'Just because we let them smelly fools ride us like horses doesn't mean we gotta let them brand us like horses. Maybe we ain't nothing but whores but, by God, we ain't horses.'

But as viewers, we find ourselves in a bind with respect to the injury, and the whores' efforts to find redress. Though sickened by the violence done to Delilah, and outraged by the injustice of the law's response, we are left uncomfortable with the whores' desire to have the heads of the two cowboys.[87] Indeed, we begin to see the ways in which their desire for vengeance erases Delilah's subjectivity as effectively as did Mike with his blade and Little Bill with his 'law'. Further, though we as viewers reject the vision that their status in the sexual economy might leave them outside the protection of law, we also see that they are, nonetheless, danger-

---

[86] Skinny's legal argument is articulated thus: 'This here is a lawful contract between me and Delilah Fitzgerald, the cut whore. I brought her clear from Boston, I paid her expenses and all, and I've got a contract here that represents an investment of capital. … Damaged property. Like if I was to hamstring one of their cow ponies. … maybe she can clean up the place or something, but nobody's going to pay good money for a cut up whore.'

[87] And indeed, their refusal to allow Davey to make reparations directly to Delilah emphasises the injustice of their response to the injury.

ous women. They are *femmes fatales,* who, Pandora-like, have opened the door to lawlessness and violence that will bring suffering and death to the town of Big Whiskey.

The Flawed Call for Justice

As expected, news of the bounty spreads quickly, and men of 'notoriously vicious and intemperate disposition' are drawn to the town. Amongst them, three well-known assassins of the 'old West', English Bob, William Munny, and Ned Logan. Bob, the first to arrive, is promptly apprehended and savagely beaten by Little Bill, in a scene that is shot in such as way as to leave viewers deeply discomfited. Little Bill makes it clear that the public and vicious nature of his punishment is intended to have a deterrent effect:

> I guess you think I'm kicking you, Bob. It ain't so. What I'm doing is talking. You hear? I'm talking to all those villains down there in Kansas. I'm talking to those villains in Missouri. And all those villains down there in Cheyenne, and I'm telling them there ain't no whore's gold. And even if there was, well they wouldn't want to come looking for it anyhow.

The effect of the scene on the viewer, however, is to put in question the legitimacy of Little Bill's legal order. The legitimacy is further broken down during the beatings Bill subsequently administers to Munny and then Ned. While Bill is unaware who Munny *is* while beating him for violating the 'No Guns' bylaw, it is also clear that he is taking great pleasure in the brutal beating, grinning as he allows the ill and beaten Munny to crawl on his belly out of the saloon. Later in the film, after the first of the contract killings has been completed, Bill administers a third vicious beating. This time, the victim is Ned. Stripped to the waist, wrists tied to the bars of the jail cell, Ned is whipped again and again in a beating that proves ultimately to be fatal.

In the vicious beatings Little Bill gives to English Bob, Munny and Ned, the lawmaker is revealed as equally violent and unforgiving as the alleged outlaws. In the character of Little Bill, the film brings us face to face with the insight that the violence that the founding of law has attempted to cast out inevitably returns to suffuse it. It is the women in the brothel who have implemented just such a dangerous return, exposing the tenuous violent foundations of the legal order that Little Bill is straining to hold in place in Big Whiskey. In so doing, however, they are not unequivocally on the side of 'justice' themselves. Indeed, if we are made uncomfortable by the violence of Little Bill, the violence of the contract is equally painful.

Indeed, there is no easy place from which to watch the unfolding of the film's apparently irrevocable sequence of violence. Both the contract killings are myth-shattering, in that they confound both our genre expectations (as well as those of The Kid) about the quick, clean and heroic nature of violence in the frontier mythology of the old West.[88] The first of the cowboys to be shot is Davey, the cowboy shown to be less than deserving of the sentence placed on him. And when he is finally shot by Munny, it is a 'gut shot' which fails to kill, but leaves a wounded and groaning victim to die slowly in the sun, begging for water. The movie allows the viewer no distance from its brutality, just as Munny can find no relief from his haunting memories of killings past. The film's motto, 'Deserve's got nothing to do with it', underlines both the connection between law and violence and the disconnection between law and justice. The second of the two killings, though less painful to watch, is equally unsatisfying. In neither of the two killings is there a strong sense of justice being done. Though the whores may have been responding to an injustice, their call for retribution opens a Pandora's Box of new injustices and inequity. Far from re-establishing law's relationship to justice, their call both destabilises law and gives rise to new injustices.

Authorising Heroic Intervention

If the gendered injury involves women in the saloon, the development and resolution of the tale is integrally linked with a dead woman who had once occupied the homestead, Munny's wife, Claudia Feathers. She is, one might say, an absent presence: though dead, she is invoked and re-invoked throughout the movie. Munny's actions and re-actions are not meaningful without an understanding of the role played by Claudia. Indeed, the architecture of the movie places Claudia at the foundation. Using the structural device of a framing story, the movie opens and closes with the same scene: a backlit shot of a homestead on the desolate prairie; one gnarled tree stands beside a lone log cabin. In the first of these two bookend pieces, the silhouette of a man can be seen in the distance, digging a hole in the earth behind the cabin. A haunting melody plays while the following text scrolls slowly over the screen:

> She was a comely young woman and not without prospects. Therefore it was heartbreaking to her mother that she would enter into marriage with William Munny, a known thief and murderer, a man of notoriously vicious and intemperate disposition. When she died, it was not at his hands as her mother might have expected but of smallpox. That was 1878.

---

[88] Giroux describes this kind of violence as 'symbolic violence'. Such violence 'attempts to connect the visceral and the reflective. It couples the mobilisation of emotion and the haunting images of the unwelcome with an attempt to "give meaning and import to our mortal twitchings". ... Instead of providing the viewer with stylistic gore that offers the immediacy of visual pleasure and escape, symbolic violence probes the complex contradictions that shape human agency, the limits of rationality, and the existential issues that tie us to other human beings and a broader social world.' See HA Giroux, 'Racism and the Aesthetic of Hyper-Real Violence' in HA Giroux, *Fugitive Cultures: Race, Violence, and Youth* (New York, Routledge, 1996), at 62.

At the end of the movie, we are returned to the same desolate, backlit shot of the homestead. This time the text reads:

> Some years later, Mrs Ansonia Feathers made the arduous journey to Hodgeman County to visit the last resting place of her only daughter. William Munny has long since disappeared with the children. ... some said to San Francisco where it was rumoured he prospered in dry goods. And there was nothing on the marker to explain to Mrs Feathers why her only daughter had married a known thief and murderer, a man of notoriously vicious and intemperate disposition.

In this way, the film begins and ends with the question of Claudia. This narrative framing makes it clear from the beginning that marriage, its meaning and function are central to the story being told. As we have already suggested, in the Western, a marriage of the proper sort can create the right kinds of citizens. Nation-building, the excising of violence and the bringing of civilisation all are tasks that require the right sort of woman in her proper place.

And Claudia is just such a woman. She has a profound effect on Munny's behaviour and his psyche. It is because of her that, as he constantly tell us, 'I ain't like that no more. Claudia, she straightened me up, cleared me of drinking whisky and all.' Claudia's order disavows drinking, gambling and killing, and offers up settled family life and farming as a preferable alternative to riding the range. It is Claudia who transforms Munny from villain to potential hero. Yet his heroic potential is not immediately obvious to the viewer. Indeed, our initial suspicion is that Claudia may be responsible for his emasculation. We first meet Munny in a pigsty, prone and covered in filth. The widowed father of two young children, he is clearly inadequate as a farmer. Like 'The Kid,' soon to be one of Munny's partners in the quest for the bounty, we have a hard time reconciling this picture with Munny's reputation as the 'meanest god damned son of a bitch alive'. It is, indeed, his desperate need for money for his children that eventually leads Munny to respond to the whores' bounty.

Both Claudia and her moral order are fundamentally tied to the homestead and the project of nation-building. Good men, like good women, are deeply connected to the home. And it is in the home that we encounter Claudia's ghostly traces, traces that identify her as continuing to occupy her roles as wife and mother. Indeed, it would seem that even death does not release her from her childcare obligations: when Munny rides off to pursue the bounty, he still charges her spirit with the task of watching over the children.[89] And further, Claudia's death does not release Munny from his obligations of sexual fidelity. Unlike his partners, he turns down the offer of 'free-ones' from the whores.

Claudia's order does reject the saloon and the peddling of flesh, but this rejection does not seem to focus on the immorality of the women selling their services.

---

[89] Munny leaves the two small children on their own, telling them, 'I'll be back in a couple of weeks. You remember how the spirit of your dear departed Ma watches over you.'

Rather, it focuses on the dangers of the saloon to the nation itself—the threat posed to the most important of men, fathers.[90] The saloon, with liquor and sex for sale, is a site of potential contagion. Claudia's moral order creates an enlightened man who is somehow able to see the immorality of prostitution while continuing to acknowledge the full humanity of the whores. Indeed, other than Davey (who had attempted to make direct reparations through the offer of her own pony), Munny is the only person to speak 'to' Delilah, and to do so in ways that address her 'self'. And, in riding away at the end, his final words of warning are directed at those who would hurt the whores. So it is that, even after her death, Claudia continues to exert a civilising moral influence upon Munny.[91] We as viewers are made to understand that marriage to the right kind of woman is crucial for the reformation/construction of a re-imagined civilised masculine citizen.

But again, it must be the right kind of woman, as the film reinforces through its treatment of The Other wife in the movie. She is Ned's Indian wife, Sally Two Trees. If Claudia is an absent presence in the movie, one might make the argument that Sally is her dark double, that is, a present absence. Though physically present, she is silent, speaking no lines of text. Sally is not shown to have Claudia's power as a source of moral authority for Ned. Ned understands that Munny wouldn't be seeking the bounty if Claudia were alive. Sally Two Trees *is* alive, and clearly disapproves, but her moral authority is insufficient to prevent Ned from joining Munny on this problematic voyage. Further, the dead Claudia's moral force was such that Munny put aside the pleasures of the flesh. Sally Two Trees has no such authority: Ned willingly takes up the whores' offers of 'a free one'. Although there are two wives in this story, they are positioned quite differently with respect to the task of 'nation building'. In this respect, it is significant that Sally is textually marked as 'an Indian'.

It is also interesting to reflect on the relationship between what the film does at the levels of script and of casting. Morgan Freeman was cast in the role of Ned. This was an open option: though it may be a Hollywood convention to cast white actors where race is not 'in issue', nothing in the text of the script identifies Ned's racial background one way or the other. Here, the casting of a black man in the role adds significant depth to the film. It makes the scene where Ned is whipped to death all the more brutal, since it is inevitably coloured by our cultural knowledge of racialised violence against black men. Such a choice was not open with respect to the character of Sally Two Trees. Not only does her name mark her as Indian, Ned also uses her race as an explanation for her seeming rudeness to Munny, for her having given him evil eye. Ned says, 'Sally's an Indian, and Indians aren't over-friendly.'

---

[90] 'That ain't right, peddling flesh. Claudia, God rest her soul, would never want me doing something like that, me being a father and all.'

[91] Indeed, it might be argued that she functions as such a powerful moral force precisely because she *is* dead. In death, Claudia is able to combine both particularity, that is, her embodied white woman-ness, and universality, as the quintessential wife and mother of the nation. This 'combination of determination and what is beyond determination' resonates with Fitzpatrick's account of the origin of law, to which we alluded earlier, P Fitzpatrick, above n 22, at 76.

But *why* does the story mark her textually as an Indian? Apart from taking its place in a long history of unflattering and flattened representations of First Nations peoples in the genre, this marking draws into the film a set of racialised discourses about the kinds of women who could serve as the cornerstones in the creation of a just and civilised nation.[92] In marking her as Indian, the film itself performs a judging act:[93] Sally is found incapable of occupying that space which is inhabited by Claudia. In marking her as an Indian, the film also provides us with the explanation for Sally's failure: she is quite simply not the right kind of woman.

The film's portrayal of the two wives offers up as the most persuasive source of legitimacy, or grounds, for law and nation the internal, self-regulative, conscience-binding authority of a very specific racialised (white) mother rather than the authoritative, 'power over' authority of the father. In so doing, it may provide us with insight into the gendered and racialised content of the (ostensibly universalised) discourses of 'nation-building', particularly to the extent that they take shape within and as disseminated by an American-led 'coalition of the willing'.

The Showdown

We conclude this section with a discussion of the showdown, the climactic final scene of ecstatic violence, which again takes place in the saloon. The initial injury occurred there, and it is to the saloon that we return. And if much of the film to this point could have been called an anti-Western, here it becomes rather an *uber-*Western. The film pulls its punches, and we end with something much closer to a generic climax.

At this point, the two killings having been completed, the women deliver the bounty money to Munny and The Kid, along with the news that Ned was caught, beaten to death by Bill, and is now on display outside of the saloon. This news has a dramatic effect on Munny and inaugurates the final act. Claudia's civilising influence is set to the side, and he begins taking long swigs from a nearby bottle of whisky. He also says, 'So they killed Ned for what I done?' Here, though he will later utter the line 'Deserve's got nothing to do with it', it is clear that deserve has everything to do with it.[94] He rides back into town to avenge his friend's death, bottle in hand.

Munny enters the saloon and shoots Skinny, the unarmed bar owner, saying 'he should have armed himself if he was going to decorate his saloon with my friend.'

---

[92] For a delicious fictional playing with this flattened history of Cowboys and Indians in the Western, see T King, *Green Grass, Running Water* (New York, Bantam Books, 1994).

[93] On the ways in which film both performs act of judgement and positions its viewers to do likewise, see O Kamir, 'Judgment By Film: Socio-Legal Functions of *Rashomon*' (2000) 12 *Yale Journal of Law and the Humanities* 39. See also O Kamir, *The Rule of Law-Films: How Law on Screen Constructs Guilt, Gender, Dignity and Honor* (Durham, NC, Duke University Press, forthcoming).

[94] For a reading of the film with takes very seriously the notion of 'desert' and revenge, see WI Miller, above n 80.

At this, Little Bill recognises who he is, and says, 'You'd be William Munny out of Missouri. Killer of women and children.' Up to this point in the film, Munny has consistently responded to such assertions by saying 'I ain't like that no more.' But he no longer disclaims this aspect of his past, or, indeed, his personality. This time, he says, 'That's right. I've killed just about anything that walked or crawled at one time or another, and I'm here to kill you, Little Bill, for what you did to Ned.' Then, in a piece of balletic violence, Munny manages single-handedly to shoot down five armed men, including Little Bill. The saloon now empty, Munny goes to the bar, and pours another drink. Although some viewers may experience in this scene a disquieting shift, it is satisfying, even pleasurable for most viewers, fulfilling genre expectations of what the Western outlaw hero is supposed to be doing.[95] We *want* him to kill Little Bill, and he does it with the *panache* that we would expect from The Man With No Name, or even Dirty Harry Callahan. The final exchange between Munny and Little Bill invokes a long tradition of laconic Western heroes. Bill says 'I don't deserve to die like this. I was building a house'; to which Munny replies 'Deserve's got nothing to do with it,' and shoots him point blank. This piece of violence stands in sharp contrast with the acts of violence that preceded it. As viewers, we are now positioned to identify with and even cheer the killing of Little Bill and Skinny. In part, this is facilitated by the filmic techniques deployed for the various portrayals of violence. The earlier violent moments are filmed in a manner that emphasised realism. We are forced to confront the ugliness and pain of actual slashing and killings. But in this final scene, we retreat from what Giroux calls 'symbolic violence' back into the less textured world of what he labels 'ritualistic violence'. [96] This is action-adventure violence of the kind typical of much Hollywood fare. The suffering of victims is no longer at issue. The sense of complexity and ambivalence cultivated earlier in the film is erased. We are now called upon to believe wholly that this killing is indeed deserved. As in the classic Western, there is no moral ambiguity in the portrayal of paroxysm of vengeance that provides the culminating moment of the film.[97]

Thus, in its final moments, the film makes a dramatic 'swerve' to a mythic narrative that embeds a quite different (and much less equivocal) account of the outlaw hero and his role in law's violent foundations. What should we make of

[95] Our observations here are based on an informal and assuredly unscientific 'survey' of viewer responses to the film, including our own, our students, and the many friends and colleagues who have had to endure our (perhaps somewhat myopic) fascination with it for too long.

[96] Ritualistic violence is that 'at the centre of the genres that produce it—horror, action-adventure, Hollywood drama—utterly banal, predictable, and often stereotypically masculine. This type of violence is pure spectacle in form and superficial in content. Audiences connect with such depictions viscerally; yet it is not edifying in the best pedagogical sense, offering few insights into the complex range of human behavior and struggles. Ritualistic violence is racy, sensationalist, and testosterone laden. ... it glows in the heat of the spectacle, shock, and contrivance, yet it is entirely formulaic.' HA Giroux, above n 88, at 61.

[97] As Tompkins emphasises, above n 36, the entire film works towards the final act of violent retribution. The moment of violent retribution is in fact a central point in the entire rape-revenge genre. For an extended exploration of that genre, see CJ Clover, *Men, Women, and Chainsaws: Gender in the Modern Horror Film* (Princeton NJ, Princeton University Press, 1992), particularly ch 3, 'Getting Even'.

this abrupt change of direction? We observed at the outset that the Western negotiates the paradox of modern law's self-founding through its iterability, that is, the
ability to combine sameness and difference through repeated retellings.
Unforgiven performs our modern dilemma for us, capturing the problem of how
we—as moderns—must grapple with our need both to disavow the violence that
is endemic to our legal order and yet, somehow, also affirm it.

Unforgiven is not an anti-Western, but it is a Western of its time. It appears initially to deconstruct the place of both gender and violence in the Western. But at
the end, it does neither. Claudia, as the central female character, is emphatically
kept in her 'place'. In the final scene, violence is also put back into its proper place
as well.[98] *Unforgiven* shows us both our loss of faith in the myth of law's foundations, as well as our unfailing capacity to continue, in the face of this cynicism, to
stake all claims on its continued potency. Indeed, our cynicism is far from debili-
tating here, as Žižek has pointed out.[99] Rather, by enacting the denial of the myth's
potency, by claiming that it no longer has the hold that it once had, we give it even
greater power over us. And perhaps this explains, in part, the film's great success.
By enacting a profound and gut-wrenching critique of violence throughout most
of its duration on screen, the film heightens many viewers' pleasure in the climactic
return of the mythic hero, and reinforces the efficacy of the masculine myth of law
and its violent origins.

Reading the International

*International legal stories participate in creating worlds inside which we live life everyday.
These stories at once make us feel less anxious about our own insecurity and more
complacent about the insecurity and suffering we inflict upon others.[100]*

We propose that our reading of *Unforgiven* opens an avenue for re-examining the
way international law may also function, despite itself, as a conservative force—
one that helps to hold in place the divisions and inequalities of our modern era.[101]
There are two avenues through which we think this might happen. The first is
through an examination of the substance of the narrative itself, how it provides

---

[98] Of course, this is not atypical for Hollywood films. See, eg, 'Seduction and Betrayal in *The
Bodyguard*' in B Hooks, *Outlaw Culture: Resisting Representations* (New York, Routledge, 1994), where
she argues the film seduces us with the promise of a taboo-exploding, inter-racial love affair between
Whitney Houston and Kevin Costner, only to betray that expectation by pushing the actualisation of
the relationship out of the characters' reach in the final scenes.

[99] S Žižek, *On Belief* (London, Routledge, 2001).

[100] A Orford, 'Muscular Humanitarianism: Reading the Narratives of the New Interventionism'
(1999) 10 *European Journal of International Law* 679, at 708.

[101] On this point, S Pahuja and R Buchanan, 'Law, Nation, and (Imagined) International Communities'
in *Law, Text, Culture* (2004).

a particularly persuasive (even hegemonic) account of the links between law, violence, gender and nation that inform contemporary debates in international law. We argue, along with many feminist scholars working in the field, that the violent, gendered and racialised content of this peculiarly Western story needs to be revealed as such, and reckoned with more directly than is currently the case. The second is by drawing attention to the function of narrative itself, as it plays out in the international sphere. As we observed earlier, the stories of law's founding authority are necessarily repeated in our public spheres, shaping our increasingly transnational 'nomos' while making particular demands on us as viewers/listeners. We do not stand outside these narratives. They draw us in, and attempt to position us, just as a film endeavours to position its viewers through the use of camera angles, editing and sound. Understanding how we, as citizens in the West, as well as legal scholars, can find ourselves complicit in these stories is another crucial task to which we aim to contribute.[102]

We've suggested in particular that our analysis might be relevant to reconsiderations of the approach taken by international lawyers to the question of humanitarian interventions. We think it is possible to read *Unforgiven* as a mythic account of humanitarian intervention, in which feminised victims seek justice from a source outside the oppressive legal order in which they are confined. The film subverts the myth's moral clarity, however, for neither the call for justice itself nor the response can be experienced unequivocally. The film does indeed draw to a conclusion, however, and in its final moments, as William Munny rides out of town, he admonishes the townsfolk not to disrespect or otherwise injure the whores. As Orit Kamir has argued, the whores appear to be the primary beneficiaries of the shooting of Skinny and Little Bill, being reinscribed as the possessors of human dignity.[103] And certainly, a dominant reading of the film does suggest, on one level, that the whores can now take their rightful places as full members of the community. While our reading of the gendered exclusions throughout the film leads us to be less than hopeful about the collective fate of the whores, we do agree with Kamir that there is something quite seductive about the emancipatory possibility held out by the 'rescue' narrative in the film's conclusion.

Indeed, we have argued in this paper that Westerns, and *Unforgiven* in particular, can assist us to recognise more clearly the ways in which certain powerful stories in Western culture exert a 'pull' upon our sensibilities, positioning us both to identify with certain types of agents and to respond to certain types of injuries, to the exclusion of other narratives, other agents and other harms. We suggest that one can read contemporary accounts of the international as analogous to a cinematic narrative, one that has many of the characteristics of the Western. The story is told largely through images in the popular media, although scholarly accounts,

---

[102] R Buchanan and S Pahuja, above n 14.

[103] O Kamir, "Deserve's got nothing to do with it": Deterrence and Retribution, Honour and Dignity in Clint Eastwood's Unforgiven', Presentation at the Annual Meeting of the Association for the Study of Law, Culture and the Humanities, New York, March 2003.

documentaries and fictional retellings of events trace and retrace these familiar storylines. The accounts usually involve 'characters' such as NATO, the 'international community', the US and rogue states, with and against whom we are invited to identify.

An illuminating and sympathetic effort to reveal the narratives that help to contain our responses to the tragic and morally ambiguous terrain on which humanitarian interventions take place can be found in the work of Anne Orford. In *Reading Humanitarian Intervention*, Orford argues that the international has increasingly been understood as a realm of danger, instability and insecurity.[104] In this realm, heroic, masculinised subjects encounter threats from rogue states, terrorists and other outlaws. The heroic role in which these subjects are positioned requires them to face down these threats of violence, lawlessness, and even savagery, with force if necessary, in order to establish order, civilisation and, most importantly, the rule of law. The central heroic figure with which we are called to identify is 'tough, aggressive, decisive, benevolent' white masculinity.[105] While Orford depicts these figures as knights in white armour, it should be clear from our preceding analysis that the cowboy—that other familiar trope of mounted masculinity—is equally, if not more, apt. We suggest that the dangerous realm of the 'international' can be seen as an imagined space very like the frontier West. As in the cinematic Western, Orford observes that contemporary discourses of humanitarian intervention call upon us to identify with the hero, and to support his inevitable use of force to accomplish what we are made to believe are necessary and morally desirable ends. In both narratives, through the actions of morally superior white 'men', law paradoxically both uses 'legitimate' violence to banish (illegitimate) violence, and restores (or bestows) a just legal order to a formerly dangerous and lawless realm.

In both Orford's account of international humanitarian intervention and our account of the cinematic Western, it is the distinction between law and violence that is centrally in issue. This distinction, however, is deeply interpenetrated with the heroic narrative of (white) masculinised agency and feminised/racialised victimisation. As we've seen in our close reading of *Unforgiven*, the law and violence distinction depends on other unequally weighted binaries, such as male and female, civilised and savage, to hold it in place, and vice versa.

The most significant convergence between our account and Orford's, however, is the focus placed in each on the ways in which we are positioned as viewers. Film theory is, of course, particularly instructive in this respect. We can all too readily see how films like *Unforgiven* work on their viewers, using filmic effects to encourage specific types of identifications and responses.[106] We saw how, in the early part

---

[104] A Orford, above n 3.

[105] *Ibid*, at 692.

[106] To say that a film encourages specific types of identification or response is not to assert a causal relation, or to claim that film works unproblematically on the viewer. For more on the importance of attending to audience response, see R Buchanan and R Johnson, above n 17, at 103–107. Certainly, films can be read with or against the grain; we are arguing for the importance of acknowledging the pull of the standard story in order to read it differently. On reading against the grain, see O Kamir, '*Rashomon*', above n 93.

of the film, the violence was discomforting, destabilising; while in its cathartic concluding sequence, we were thrilled and relieved that our troubled hero, Munny, with whom we have now come to identify totally, has finally acted decisively to right prior wrongs and inaugurate a new, just legal order in the town of Big Whiskey. We no longer question the justice or authority with which he acts, because of how we have been positioned as complicit in his actions. Orford argues similarly that we (as international law scholars in the West) fail to question the justness or humanity of 'humanitarian interventions' because we have already been positioned to identify with the heroic intervenors on behalf of the feminised and presumed-to-be helpless victims.

Conclusion

Our reading of *Unforgiven* reveals some of the gendered and racialised narratives at work in the contemporary discourses of the international, and their connection to even deeper and affect-laden gendered and racialised narratives of the source and authority of law.[107] We have done this by suggesting that the Western, and *Unforgiven* in particular, traces an account of the founding of law on the frontier that resonates strongly with the mythological foundations of modern law in the West. Both sets of stories reveal acts of founding as a twofold process of inclusion and exclusion. The dominant, generic account of the Western tells a story of itself as being about neither race nor gender, but about individual freedom and the search for justice, and the shaping of the nation out of the savage and lawless frontier. Though women seem to be absent, they are actually central to the story. And the people who can take their proper place in the nation are specifically marked by race (here, whiteness). In its act of self-founding, nation defines its Others as it defines itself. That act of demarcation, the particularity of the foundation of law and nation, must immediately be erased, so that law and nation can both be seen as responsive to the universal demands of justice and equality.[108] We've shown how the Western generally, and *Unforgiven* in particular, gives content to both the insiders and the outsiders framed by the account of law's foundations. We have further suggested that these narratives are not confined to film, but rather are central to the construction of our 'nomos' in the West. Their endless replication in film, and in popular culture more generally, is part of what makes them so persuasive and intuitive. By articulating the narratives of exclusion embedded in the generic accounts, we hope to make it possible to imagine how the story could be told differently.

---

[107] For an exploration of the significance of the visceral register of being to thinking, judgement and public culture, see WE Connolly, *Neuropolitics: Thinking, Culture, Speed* (Minneapolis, University of Minnesota Press, 2002).

[108] See P Fitzpatrick, above n 22.

Unforgiven, in the ways that it simultaneously enacts and deconstructs the genre of the Western in which these exclusionary narratives are powerfully inscribed, also helps to reveal the unstable and contradictory nature of many of these stories. Reading law through film in this way reveals how we might be called or interpolated by these narratives to identify with certain (white, male, macho) subject positions instead of others. *Unforgiven* helps to make this process visible by making the usual identification with the white male hero extremely uncomfortable at first: instead of taking pleasure in our identification with the powerful, macho hero, we are made to squirm through the techniques that the film uses to deglamorise its violence and to humanise/feminise its macho hero. We seek to use the film's deconstructive moves to parallel our own efforts at reflexively repositioning ourselves in relation to the heroic narratives of international intervention and the holistic narrative of law's founding certainties.

Neither the idea of law's violent foundations, nor that of the violence endemic to the masculinised hero (whether played out in the Cineplex or on CNN), will have come as a revelation to most readers. A more potent question is this: How is it that the erasure of the various violences which fracture our international legal order continues to be effected so readily? That is, how can we, knowing of the violence, somehow forget, or too readily accept it? The insight about erasure comes from our reading of film more generally—thinking about how film works on us as subjects and make us complicit. Narratives work in somewhat the same ways in the international public sphere —through media coverage of crises in the developing world, through the distressing slippage between movies, CNN and the 'desert of the real'.[109] We argue for a practice of reading the public sphere as we might read a film, indeed, by reading these artefacts alongside one another. Such practices might well move us in the direction of a better understanding of our nomos, of how we are made complacent about the suffering and insecurity inflicted on others and, hence, become complicit subjects of both law and the international. As we also argued, narratives only cohere or sustain themselves through endless repetition. And with re-iteration comes the possibility of reading against the grain, of writing things differently. Each reading re-inscribes, but also potentially alters, these categories.[110] We have shown how re-inscription exists alongside subversion in *Unforgiven*. So, then, to know and understand the narratives of our nomos opens space for shifts: both in the shape of the narratives, and in their direction.

---

[109] This currently popular phrase is spoken by the character 'Morpheus' in the Wachowski brother's film, *The Matrix* (1999), and is taken as a point of departure in S Žižek, *Welcome to the Desert of the Real* (London, Verso, 2002).

[110] For a discussion of the productive possibility of repetition, see the interchange between TT Minh-ha and H Bhabha, 'Painted Power' in TT Minh-ha, *Cinema Interval* (New York, Routledge, 1999), at 17–31.

8

'The Beautyful Ones' of Law and Development

AMBREENA MANJI*

Introduction

Consider these book reviews of Ayi Kwei Armah's novel *The Beautyful Ones Are Not Yet Born*.[1] The first:

> This novel is a powerful testimony to the horrors of corruption which blight Africa. A bloated civil service characterised by graft exists alongside widespread poverty and despair. Kwei Armah does more to prove the need for good governance and the rule of law in Africa than any World Bank official report. (World Bank in-house magazine circa 2001)

Next:

> Kwei Armah portrays the deadening effect of material desire on an entire society. Solidarity is unknown in a post-colonial Ghana in which material possessions are the only source of status and everyone is fighting for a piece of 'the gleam'. ('no global magazine' distributed at Cancun, 2003)

Both these imaginary reviews (I confess to making them up) might function as political manifestos, the first for the World Bank's governance programmes and the second for civil society groups at Seattle, Genoa, Doha or Cancun. Both are arguably accurate renditions of Kwei Armah's seminal novel published in 1968. It is perhaps the possibility of these radically different, indeed conflicting, readings which led to Kwei Armah's reported rejection of this his first literary child. In the

* Law Department, University of Keele, UK. This paper began life as a presentation to a Gender, Sexuality and Law Workshop at the University of Keele in October 2003. I benefited from discussing it at a seminar at Kent Law School and at an ESRC workshop on the Anthropology of Law at Birkbeck College. My thanks to the participants on all three occasions for their stimulating comments and encouragement, and to Upendra Baxi, Doris Buss and John Harrington for reading the paper in its various incarnations.

[1] A Kwei Armah, *The Beautyful Ones Are Not Yet Born* (Nairobi, East African Educational Publishers, 1968).

1980s he was to dismiss his novel as Eurocentric, the product of a conflicted youth before he reached Pan-Africanist maturity.

Rumour has it that we are currently witnessing a rebirth of law and development. If this is so, (re)consideration of this brat of a novel may well repay scholars and practitioners at, and of, this global moment. If, in an era of economic globalisation, the terms of which are imposed on the global South by the wealthy North and its financial institutions, the novel might function as a manifesto for intervention in African governance (assuming of course a literary bent on the part of World Bank, IMF and US Treasury bureaucrats) then, in the words of Baxi,

> how may we feminize the dominant patriarchal conceptions of global 'development' and 'impoverishment'? In other words, how may we construct descriptions of the emergent legal patriarchy of contemporary globalisation?[2]

'The Beautyful Ones Are Not Yet Born'

The novel begins with the first of many authorial reflections on 'victorious filth'.[3] The protagonist, known to us only as 'the man', walks to work through the capital, Accra. On a waste bin placed in the street by the city council he reads, 'Keep your country clean by keeping the city clean' and recalls:

> The radio had run a program featuring a doctor, a Presbyterian priest, and a senior lecturer from the University of Legon. The three had seemed to be in agreement about the evil effects of uncleanliness.[4]

The remainder of the novel consists in exploring this richly suggestive metaphor. The story ends with another walk, one which takes place after the man's ritual cleansing in the sea. In 'the space, or more correctly, the distance between these two points'[5] the man struggles against the temptations of corruption in which those around him wallow. As all his acquaintances learn 'to eat' (in the startling Kenyan phrase), the man's disgust at his surroundings and his fellow citizens grows.

Much has been written about Kwei Armah's novel since its publication in the immediate aftermath of Ghanaian independence. To my mind the most appealing reading has come from Lazarus, who has attempted to recapture from Armah the residual sense of possibility, of optimism which might be found in the 'not yet' of the novel's title. Lazarus has read the *Beautyful Ones* as a dialectical work whose

---

[2] U Baxi, 'Global Development and Impoverishment' in P Cane and M Tushnet (eds), *Oxford Handbook of Legal Studies* (Oxford, Oxford University Press, 2003).

[3] Above n 1, at 12.

[4] Above n 1, at 7–8.

[5] N Lazarus, *Resistance in Postcolonial African Fiction* (New Haven, Yale University Press, 1990).

'reciprocity is first heralded in the "not yet" of its title and is most clearly demonstrated in the complex relationship between the affirmative vision, which is
implicit in the man's search for authentic values, and the blasted landscape within
which the novel's action is staged.'[6]

The novel is heavy with images of filth, of vomit, faeces and dirt. Sweat and
grease are polished into the very grain of the wooden banisters in the man's down-
town Accra office block:

> The touch of the banister on the balls of his fingertips had something uncomfort-
> ably organic about it ... The wood underneath would win and win till the end of
> time ... it would convert all to victorious filth ...[7]

He watches as his acquaintances enjoy their new found positions as government
servants in the new state, a postcolonial ruling class who drink only imported
beer, live on the hills surrounding Accra and relieve their children of the burden
of African names. Postcolonial Ghana instead names its children 'Princess', takes
surnames such as 'Acromond' (Kwei Armah asks: 'what Ghanaian name could that
have been in the beginning, before its civil servant owner rushed to civilise it ...?').
In a rare moment of humour, Kwei Armah narrates a list of names: ' "Grantson"...
more and incredible they were getting. There was someone calling himself
"Fengtengson" in this wide world, and also a man called "Binful" '.[8]

There are plenty of opportunities for the man to participate in this new wealth-
seeking. In his job at the railway offices he is offered money by businessmen looking to hurry on a delivery of cargo. He resists. The meals his family eats grow
smaller. His wife sings mockingly at him 'Onward Christian Soldier', even as Kwei
Armah makes apparent the man's lack of religion. Contemptuously she likens him
to a chichidodo bird which 'hates excrement with all its soul ... but only feeds on
maggots, and you know the maggots grow best inside the lavatory'.[9] Still he will
not participate in what Kwei Armah describes as 'the national game'.[10]

For those 'whose entrails are not hard enough for the national game',[11] such as
the man, it remains only to marvel at the progress of 'big names'.[12] One such is
Koomson, formerly a railwayman and docker. The man remembers him '... pulling
ropes ...[b]listered hands, toughened, callused hands'.[13] Now he sits in government in Accra, a 'Party man'.[14] When the coup which overthrows the government of
Kwame Nkrumah comes, Koomson, no longer 'beaming with self-esteem',[15] fears

---

[6] *Ibid*, at 46.
[7] Above n 1, at 12.
[8] *Ibid*, at 126.
[9] *Ibid*, at 45.
[10] *Ibid*, at 55.
[11] *Ibid*.
[12] *Ibid*, at 56.
[13] *Ibid*, at 88.
[14] *Ibid*, at 178.
[15] *Ibid*, at 147.

the army will arrest him and seeks the man's help to escape. Together they flee down the hole of a pit latrine which the man has torn up, rescuing Koomson by forcing his bloated body through the hole in the ground, retching against the smell and filth. As they travel through the darkened city to the fishing harbour where Koomson is safe, we are left wondering at the man's willingness to lead this rescue.

Birth and Rebirth

In the face of this brief summary, it should not surprise us that most commentators on the novel have found in it despair and disgust, and little possibility of hope. Out of this, Lazarus has forged a critique which shows the novel to be one of resistance and struggle, and which urges us to reconsider the possibilities of the novel, the hope encapsulated in the words 'not yet'.

Unexplored by critics and advocates of the novel alike have been its themes of birth and rebirth, suggested in that part of the novel's title neglected by Lazarus: 'not yet *born*'. What are the novel's possibilities for rebirth, for law and development's resurgence? Can we capture from Kwei Armah a more radical ideal of rebirth that goes beyond, indeed rejects, current appeals? That Thabo Mbeki uttered calls for an African renaissance even as his government tightened its embrace of a neo-liberal economic and political agenda should keep us from the seductive shores of such conceptions.[16]

Themes of birth and rebirth recur throughout Kwei Armah's novel. The man wonders self-critically if he is a 'soul born without the luck of other souls'.[17] Just as the man is disgusted by the distorted birth of his country, by the wasted potential of independence, he tries to avoid the mocking birth scar across his wife's belly. He turns away from glimpsing its flesh not (only) because of his disgust at her. Her words emasculate him, alert him to the unmanliness of being unable to participate in corruption, but her body also recalls something more. Her body, like the body politic, is scarred by birth. His wife's is thus not the only 'scar he has not learned to live with'.[18] Her emotional betrayal in seeking to force him 'to eat' recalls Ghana's postcolonial betrayal. Independence was marked in remarkably similar ceremonies across the continent, indeed across the decolonising world, and hard on the heels of these ceremonies flowed remarkably similar disillusionment with the postcolonial project. As such, Kwei Armah's novel speaks to, and of, postcoloniality—or more accurately, neocoloniality—in general.

Samir Amin has characterised the developmental state as a national bourgeois construction,[19] and it is within this framework that Kwei Armah's novel must be

---

[16] See T Ngwane, 'Sparks in the Townships' (2003) 22 *New Left Review* 37.
[17] Above n 1, at 98.
[18] *Ibid.*
[19] S Amin, *Capitalism in the Age of Globalization: The Management of Contemporary Society* (London, Zed Books, 2000), at 17.

understood. The impossibility of resisting 'the gleam' is the novel's central theme. In contrast to the degradation and dirt of the man's home and district, up on the hills around Accra stand the shining, white buildings of the 'Atlantic Caprice Hotel' and the University of Legon. The former frequented by Ghana's postcolonial, Anglophile elite, the latter mocked by these same people who having acquired their educations at the English Bar, deprecate Nkrumah's plans for African education.[20] The sunlight shimmering on the clean white facades of these buildings, neither of which the man has succeeded in entering, is described by Kwei Armah as 'the gleam'. It symbolises the bright light of wealth and material possessions, and the corruption in which one must inevitably engage to acquire them. The seduction of 'the gleam' is epitomised in the voluptuous modernity of this architecture. Those who resist 'the gleam' are condemned variously to madness, retreat or isolation, but always to squalor.

Madness, retreat and religion are the responses of three characters in the novel to the call of 'the gleam'. Maana, who fought with the man for the nation's independence, appears in the novel as a prophetic madwoman (elsewhere in the novel, possibly with her in mind, Kwei Armah refers to 'the keen, uncanny eyes and ears of lunatic seers').[21] The man's friend, whom we know only as 'teacher', retreats from the world, living alone in a bare room with only Radio Ghana for company. A former comrade turns to religion, taking refuge in the poetry of Gibran. The man's response is social isolation. Repelled by 'the gleam', he is a misfit in social life. He finds it almost impossible to carry out the mundane tasks of everyday life. In the new Ghana, Kwei Armah seems to be suggesting, this includes having the necessary social grace to accept bribes. He thus deprives his family of the very things they desire.

Global Moments

I suggested at the beginning of this paper that, read in one way, the novel might give heart to international financial institutions and bilateral agencies (such as Britain's Department for International Development and the United States Agency for International Development) who, as part of their structural adjustment programmes and since, have sought to promote policies of good governance and the rule of law in the global South.[22] The corruption depicted by Kwei Armah

---

[20] For a first-hand account, see C Cruise O'Brien, *Memoir: My Life and Themes* (London, Profile, 1998). Cf 'Message from Osagyefo The President on the Occasion of the Enrolment of the First Group of Lawyers at Ghana School of Law on Saturday 22 June 1963' (1964) 1 *University of Ghana Law Journal* 2; and G Bing, *Reap the Whirlwind: An Account of Kwame Nkrumah's Ghana from 1950 to 1966* (London, Macgibbon and Kee, 1968).

[21] Above n 1, at 12.

[22] For the most recent manifestation of such efforts, see the account in P McAuslan, 'The International Development Act 2002: Benign Imperialism or Missed Opportunity?' (2003) 66 *Modern Law Review* 563. See also H Benn, 'Why Britain Leads the Way in Aid', <http://www.guardian.co.uk/comment/story/0,3604,1119141,00.html> (last accessed 1 October 2004).

might be argued to play into the hands of 'donors' whose thinly veiled racism seeks always new policy prescriptions for the South's perceived ills. In this economic and social pessimism the 'managerial functionaries of the world system' are joined by the South's ruling classes.[23] Structural adjustment programmes have led to brutal impoverishment, destroying the fledgling achievements of many countries in the provision of primary health and education.[24]

Civil society groups such as non-governmental organisations have proved incapable of launching meaningful critiques. Themselves composed of a compradorial elite taking their orders directly from their funders in the North, they have been fatally incapable of locating the problems of structural adjustment in capitalism. Instead, their criticisms have been purely moral. Wrong-headed policies, not the system from which they emanate, are accused of causing poverty.[25] The new-fangled 'poverty reduction strategies' of international 'donors' are themselves at once a response to and a furtherance of impoverished analyses.[26] Nonetheless, poverty reduction has now found a legal basis in Britain's International Development Act 2002, which stipulates that '[t]he Secretary of State may provide any person or body with development assistance if he is satisfied that the provision of the assistance is likely to contribute to a reduction in poverty'.[27] It is difficult to see how this aim is to be reconciled with Britain's support for the World Bank's emerging global land policy, which is built on the exploitation of women's unpaid labour and will serve only to entrench poverty.

This preoccupation with issues of good governance, as an element of which developing states are forced to show how they have tackled corruption, must, however, be placed in its proper historical perspective. Kwei Armah wrote his novel as Ghana experienced its first decade of independence, a time when her first president, Kwame Nkrumah, perhaps more than any other in Africa, succeeded in mystifying the West with his political and economic plans.[28] He embraced a strategy of commercial non-alignment and entered into trade and aid agreements with the Soviet bloc. In Britain, this was interpreted as 'a hostile challenge or a dastardly betrayal'.[29] Conservative newspapers wrote of a red shadow hanging over the former Gold Coast. In perpetual fear that Nkrumah would go over to the Soviets, the United States, together with Britain, its constant companion, sought ever-closer relations with Ghana. The funding of the completion of Ghana's Volta Delta Dam

---

[23] S Amin, above n 19, at 17.

[24] See J Harrington, 'Law and the Commodification of Health Care in Tanzania' (2003) Law, Social Justice and Global Development Journal, available at <http://elj.warwick.ac.uk/global/issue/2003-2/harrington.html> (last accessed 1 October 2004).

[25] See above n 23.

[26] See generally P Cammack, 'Making Poverty Work' in L Panitch and C Leys (eds), Socialist Register 2002: A World of Contradictions (London, Merlin Press, 2001); and R Young, 'New Labour and International Development' in D Coates and P Lawler (eds), New Labour in Power (Manchester, University of Manchester Press, 2000).

[27] See s 1, International Development Act 2002.

[28] B Davidson, Black Star: A View of the Life and Times of Kwame Nkrumah (London, Allen Lane, 1973).

[29] Ibid, at 172.

by the US figured, like many dam projects around the world, as part of a wider international relations strategy.[30] Attempts to mitigate the corruption of which Kwei Armah writes in *The Beautyful Ones,* nowhere featured on the agenda of foreign powers. As in the rest of Africa, it was only with the end of the Cold War that demands for good governance and the rule of law came to prominence as part of World Bank and bilateral aid conditionalities. Is it possible that despite this historical blind eye, Kwei Armah's novel might be read as a manifesto for the patriarchal economic and political prescriptions of international financial institutions?

A close reading of *The Beautyful Ones* suggests not. The reminder of this paper is an attempt to argue that we need to be alert to the gendered nature of endeavours to encourage 'economic man'[31] and to construct the subjectivity of the people of peripheral and semi-peripheral countries. I hope to show that the project to release the 'entrepreneurial spirit' of the poor is parasitic upon, and threatens to worsen, unequal gender relations. Women's unpaid labour will underpin the formalisation of property rights. The argument that ways must be found to 'bring the assets of the poor into the legal system so that they can be used as collateral for loans'[32] is founded on a figurative 'sexual contract'[33] under which women's labour in the home (and on the land) is an extension of their reproductive labours.

If we fail to formalise land relations, we are told, we condemn land to the status of 'dead capital'.[34] In the view of the World Bank, and of the third world governments which have embraced this vision of their own future, land which is used only for subsistence is a 'dead asset'[35] which holds back economic development. By releasing such dead capital we will liberate peasant farmers into the world of the market where they can use their assets to raise loans. In the characteristically succinct words of *The Economist:*

> ... Africans find it hard to use what they have to best advantage because they lack secure property rights. Very few can prove that they own their land or their homes, because they do not have title deeds. This matters, because without a reliable system for ascertaining who owns what, assets cannot be used as collateral. In rich countries, if a farmer wants to invest in better seeds or bigger tractors, he can probably borrow the necessary cash using his land as security. If he fails to honour his debt,

[30] The British Government's involvement in funding the Pergau Dam is a well-known example. See *R v Secretary of State for Foreign affairs ex parte World Development Movement Ltd* [1995] 1 All ER 611. See also C Palit, 'Monsoon Rising: Mega-Dam Resistance in the Narmada Valley' (2003) 21 *New Left Review* 81; and A Roy, *The Algebra of Infinite Justice* (London, Flamingo, 2002).

[31] See also D Otto, 'Disconcerting Masculinities: Reinventing the Gendered Subject(s) of International Human Rights Law', in this volume.

[32] Former US President Bill Clinton's Address to the Labour Party Conference, October 2002. Full text available at <http://politics.guardian.co.uk/labour2002> (last accessed 1 October 2004).

[33] C Pateman, *The Sexual Contract* (Cambridge, Polity Press, 1988).

[34] H de Soto, *The Mysteries of Capital: Why Capitalism Triumphs in the West and Fails Everywhere Else* (New York, Basic Books, 2000), at 15.

[35] World Bank, *Land Policies for Growth and Poverty Reduction* (Oxford, Oxford University Press, 2003).

the bank takes the land. If all goes well, however, his easy access to credit allows him to make his land more productive, which in turn increases its worth. Asset-backed lending is a crucial element in the dynamism of advanced capitalist countries. In America, for example, the most common way for an entrepreneur to raise start-up capital is by mortgaging the family home.[36]

Transparently taking its cue from the recently published World Bank global land policy, *The Economist* argues that the future lies in a transition from peasant subsistence to petty bourgeois entrepreneurship. If it is clear-sighted about capital, however, it fails to make any mention of labour, the other pillar on which the World Bank's land policy rests. In particular, the notion of 'non-contractible labour'[37] is crucial to the World Bank. According to its global land policy report, 'family members have higher incentives to provide effort than hired labor. They ... can be employed without incurring hiring or search costs.'[38] The objective is to avoid the employment contract in favour of the 'non-contractible', flexible, willing and unpaid labour of women. Similar concerns had arisen in the industrial context, where reliance on domestic labour through the putting-out system was a means of evading the need for management.[39] As Braverman showed,

> functions of management were brought into being by the very practice of cooperative labor. Even an assemblage of independently practicing artisans requires coordination, if one considers the need for provision of a workplace and the ordering of processes within it ... [this] required conceptual and coordination functions which in capitalist industry took the form of management.[40]

The notion of non-contractibility employed by the World Bank in the agricultural context takes the private sphere of the household to be characterised by affective ties of community, which give rise to solidarity between individuals. In contrast, feminist theorists have revealed how the private sphere is often based on quasi-feudal domination and on coercion rather than freedom.[41]

---

[36] *The Economist*, 'Breathing Life into Dead Capital: Why Secure Property Rights Matter' in *How to Make Africa Smile: A Survey of Sub-Saharan Africa*, 17 January 2004, at 10–11.

[37] The phrase 'non-contractible labour' was employed in the first draft of the World Bank's Policy Research Report. For a detailed analysis, see A Manji, 'Remortgaging Women's Lives: The World Bank's Land Agenda in Africa' (2003) 11 *Feminist Legal Studies* 139. Although the term was removed from the World Bank's final document 'Land Policies for Growth and Poverty Reduction', the notion of non-contractible labour continues to underpin the Bank's plans for agricultural productivity.

[38] Above n 36, at 81.

[39] S Pollard, *The Genesis of Modern Management: A Study of the Industrial Revolution in Britain* (Cambridge, Harvard University Press, 1965).

[40] H Braverman, *Labor and Monopoly Capital: The Degradation of Work in the Twentieth Century* (New York, Monthly Review Press, 1998), at 42.

[41] See the literature cited in J Stacey, 'The Family is Dead, Long Live Our Families' in N Holmstrom (ed), *The Socialist Feminist Project: A Contemporary Reader in Theory and Politics* (New York, Monthly Review Press, 2002).

Drawing on the debates surrounding feminist demands that women should be paid for housework,[42] it is possible to assess the impact on agricultural productivity of women being remunerated for their household and agricultural labour. Labour constitutes the greatest cost on small farms. If family labour were waged, this would constitute a cost rather than a saving, reducing the productive and competitive advantage of the unit. The entire notion of the productivity—which is central to *The Economist's* assessment cited above—is founded on the availability of the labour of women, which is taken to be free, flexible and willing.

Seen in this light, plans to enable and encourage the use of land as collateral are built on the backs of women. The capital raised by the household, whilst not necessarily accruing to women, is made available on the assumption of the continuing availability of women's labour. The household is taken to be an undifferentiated unit in which the needs and interests of men and women converge. This neglects entirely the ways in which the family 'functions as an ideological and economic site of oppression'.[43] Apparently in spite the efforts of femocrats within the institution, the patriarchal power of kinship structures seems to be a prerequisite for the World Bank's plans for increased agricultural productivity in the developing world.[44] In the hope-filled account of *The Economist* presented above, no mention is made of women's role in servicing rural debt, or the part their labour will play in providing a cushion against the vagaries of the market. This is reminiscent of peasant smallholders' responses to the introduction of coffee cultivation in colonial Tanganyika, a development which integrated them into an unstable, fluctuating world economy. Colonial intervention in the countryside made the labour of women in urban prostitution crucial to the household economy, for 'daughters' earnings, if used judiciously, could keep the market at a distance'.[45]

It is at this neo-liberal historical juncture that I believe we should reconsider Kwei Armah's novel. It is clear that 'the man' is in fact the diametric opposite of the image of the ideal market actor so vigorously propagated by institutions such as the World Bank, a far cry indeed from the World Bank's vision of a universal economic subjectivity.[46] It is precisely in this fact that I believe the novel's regenerative potential lies. Here, I am with Lazarus in reading the man's incorruptibility as a sign of his steely resistance. But I would go further and interpret the man's disgust

---

[42] See, eg, A Oakley, *The Sociology of Housework* (Oxford, Blackwell, 1985); and M Mies, *Patriarchy and Accumulation on a World Scale: Women in the International Division of Labour* (London, Zed Books, 1986).

[43] C Smart, *The Ties That Bind: Law, Marriage and the Reproduction of Patriarchal Relations* (London, Routledge & Kegan Paul, 1984).

[44] This approach was manifest in the early initiatives of the World Bank and other development agencies: 'Patriarchal and liberal discourses, at both national and international level, left unchallenged the question of gender relations in society, and often made these attendant upon a sexual division of labour and individual negotiation within the family.' See S Rai, *Gender and the Political Economy of Development* (Cambridge, Polity, 2002), at 58.

[45] See L White, *The Comforts of Home: Prostitution in Colonial Nairobi* (Chicago, University of Chicago Press, 1990), at 225.

[46] A Manji, 'Liberalising Land, Fetishising Law: The Struggle for Women's Land Rights in Uganda' (2003) 19 *Australian Feminist Legal Studies* 81.

for the 'gleam' as itself containing the novel's regenerative vision. The man's lack of desire, his almost pathological awkwardness in the face of his fellow citizen's striving after the material, contain the seeds of some future hope. In the title of the novel, Kwei Armah seeks to foretell the birth of *The Beautyful Ones*—in the plural. The man is alone, condemned to social isolation because be can't (won't) play the role of a normal market actor. His is 'the mind unable to decide to do what everyone was saying was the necessary thing, what everyone was doing'.[47] The subversive potential of the novel is in its suggestion that it is those who are corrupt, those who have taken to capitalist relations however skewed by corruption, whom we are forced to count as normal. It is the man who is abnormal, who inhabits a world free from desire for material things.

I want to suggest that the regenerative vision of the novel is its suggestion that one day the man will not be alone. Many beautiful ones will be born. They will sustain him and each other. At the end of the novel, in the escape, Koomson emerges 'head first through the hole of a pit latrine, the man standing over him shouting "push"'.[48] Is Kwei Armah enacting a decidedly unlovely (re-) birth scene? All that is certain is that this time there will be no scars. No child has 'had to be dragged out of its mother's womb'.[49]

'The Beautyful Ones' of Law and Development

As an area of scholarship and practice, the birth of law and development itself coincided with 'the agonising birth'[50] of the developmental state in the late 1960s.[51] Newly independent African states embraced an ideology which gave the state a central role in bringing about economic growth. Scholars of law and development, many of whom were based in African law schools and also in the United States, looked to development studies, economics and politics to inform their work. They saw law as a discipline whose ends should be determined by other disciplines.[52] The main concern of these scholars was to provide technical assistance to government ministries and to boost their administrative efficiency.

The law and development movement had a pragmatic and instrumentalist view of the role of law. Lawyers played a central role in what Samir Amin has characterised as a 'bourgeois national project' of developmentalism,[53] but by the mid-1970s, it seemed that both as an area of scholarship and as a policy-oriented

---

[47] Above n 1, at 98.

[48] *Ibid*, at 167–68.

[49] *Ibid*, at 98.

[50] P Hanafin, 'D(en)ying Narratives: Death, Identity and the Body Politic' in (2000) 20 *Legal Studies* 393.

[51] Y Ghai, 'Law, Development and African Scholarship' (1987) 50 *Modern Law Review* 750.

[52] J Harrington and A Manji, 'The Emergence of African Law as an Academic Discipline in Britain' (2003) 102 *African Affairs* 109.

[53] Above n 19, at 32.

practice, the methods, outlook and objectives of law and development had been abandoned.[54]

Today, law and development scholarship and practice are widely held to have been reborn[55] as economic globalisation witnesses a 'market-oriented development model'[56] imposed on peripheral and semi-peripheral countries. For Sousa Santos, the main features of economic globalisation include requiring national economies to open up to trade and to privatise productive state enterprises, as well as to ensure that private property rights are clear and inviolable.[57] Simultaneous battles for the formalisation of property rights and against corruption are at the core of the contemporary neo-liberal economic programme. Emerging from the wilderness years, law in development has come once again on to the international agenda, its original concern with the economic growth of the developmental state having been transmogrified into the promotion of good governance and the rule of law and, in the words of Sousa Santos, 'formal democracy as a political condition for international assistance'.[58] International financial institutions and bilateral donors have poured millions into what is referred to as 'rule of law aid' or 'rule of law reform'.[59] Estimates of the amount of assistance disbursed as rule of law aid vary: it is thought to have been US$500 million from Multilateral Development Banks in the late 1990s,[60] and US$9 billion from all development agencies and multilateral banks in the last decade.[61]

Writing of the revival of law and development, Kennedy offers an insightful characterisation of the contemporary embrace of the rule of law, arguing that there is an unarticulated hope amongst practitioners and scholars that opting for law might substitute for, and thus avoid confrontation with, 'perplexing political and economic choices'.[62] Similarly, Cutler has argued for the need 'to recognise that law is not external but internal to and constitutive of social, political, and economic worlds and is thus inescapably implicated in the politics of "who gets what"'.[63] For Kennedy, the failure to interrogate 'the idea that building the rule of

[54] See D Trubek and M Galanter, 'Scholars in Self-Estrangement: Some Reflections on the Crisis in Law and Development Studies in the United States' (1974) *Wisconsin Law Review* 1062; and J Merryman, 'Comparative Law and Social Change: On the Origins, Style, Decline and Revival of the Law and Development Movement' (1977) 25 *American Journal of Comparative Law* 457.

[55] T Ginsburg, 'Does Law Matter for Economic Development: Evidence from East Asia' (2000) 34 *Law and Society Review* 829; M Chibundu, 'Law in Development: On Tapping, Gourding and Serving Palm-Wine' (1997) 29 *Case Western Reserve Journal of International Law* 167.

[56] B Spalling, *Development with Equity in the 1990s: Policies and Alternatives* (Madison, Global Studies Research Programme, 1992).

[57] B de Sousa Santos, *Toward a New Legal Common Sense* (London, Butterworths, 2002), at 167.

[58] *Ibid*, at 167.

[59] T Carothers, 'The Rule of Law Revival' (1998) 77 *Foreign Affairs* 95.

[60] D Trubek, 'Rule of Law Projects Yesterday, Today and Tomorrow', paper presented at a Conference on 'Law and Economic Development: Critiques and Beyond', Harvard Law School, April 2003.

[61] R Messick, 'Judicial Reform and Economic Development: A Survey of the Issues' (1999) 14 *World Bank Research Observer* 117.

[62] D Kennedy, 'Laws and Developments' in A Perry and J Hatchard (eds), *Law and Development: Facing Complexity in the 21st Century* (London, Cavendish, 2003), at 17.

[63] AC Cutler, 'Historical Materialism, Globalization, and Law: Competing Conceptions of Property' in M Rupert and H Smith (eds), *Historical Materialism and Globalization* (London, Routledge, 2002), at 233.

law might *itself* be a development strategy'[64] has meant that law and development practitioners and scholars have excluded, rather than encouraged, contestation over economic and political choices:

> ... this places law, legal institution building, the techniques of legal policy-making and implementation—the 'rule of law' broadly conceived—front and centre.[65]

The 'turn to law all too often in flight from economic analysis and political choice'[66] is nowhere more manifest than in contemporary African land reform. With the flowering of what might be described as new wave law and development in the era of neo-liberalism,[67] land reform has come in practice to mean land *law* reform.[68] Controversy about consent clauses[69] has taken the place of contestation over 'distributional choices'.[70]

In an age of 'neo-liberal triumphalism', is it possible to imagine a different rebirth for law and development? What might be the alternatives to a law and development scholarship which is suffused with technocratic aspirations, which is too often 'episodic and contingent, and ... corrupted (from the worm's eye perspective) by the infinitely, and expediently, shifting agenda of intergovernmental aid agencies ...'?[71] What are the prospects for contemporary law and development, dragged from the womb this time not by the Cold War but by economic globalisation?

I suggested at the start of this paper that reconsideration of Kwei Armah's novel might provide a starting-point for constructing an alternative to dominant conceptions of law and development and for recapturing law and development as 'a broad vocabulary for political struggle'.[72] The impulse for such a task comes from Kennedy's observation, rooted in a description of the ever-changing experience of teaching the subject through different political times, that the current revival of law and development presents us with an opportunity—most often lost—to interrogate

---

[64] Above n 62, at 17 (author's emphasis).

[65] *Ibid*, at 18.

[66] *Ibid*.

[67] I have adapted this phrase from H Bernstein, 'Land Reform: Taking a Long(er) View' (2002) 2 *Journal of Agrarian Change* 433. Bernstein draws the term 'new wave land reform' from an International Fund for Agricultural Development report which asserts: 'Previous land reform programmes have been unduly confiscatory, statist or top-down. "New wave" land reform, which is decentralised, market-friendly and involves civil society action or consensus is sometimes feasible and consistent with just and durable property rights.' See International Fund for Agricultural Development, *Rural Poverty Report: The Challenge of Ending Rural Poverty* (Rome, IFAD, 2001), at 75.

[68] P McAuslan, *Bringing the Law Back In: Essays in Land, Law and Development* (London, Ashgate, 2003); A Manji, 'Cause and Consequence in Law and Development' (forthcoming (2005) 43(1) *Journal of Modern African Studies*.

[69] H Busingye, 'Lobbying and Advocacy on Women's Land Rights: The Experience of the Uganda Land Alliance' in M Rugadya and H Busingye (eds), *Gender Perspectives in the Land Reform Process in Uganda* (Kampala, Uganda Land Alliance, 2002).

[70] Above n 62, at 19. See also D Kennedy, 'The Stakes of Law, or Hale and Foucault' (1991) 15 *Legal Studies Forum* 327. For an account of Tanzania's experience of this sleight of hand, see I Shivji, 'Land: The Terrain of Democratic Struggles' (1997) 5 *Change* 4.

[71] U Baxi, above n 2, at 476.

[72] D Kennedy, above n 62, at 17.

difficult political choices. The task is to reveal the existence of a range of possible legal arrangements, all of which are associated with different political ideas.[73] Kennedy offers a vision of how in scholarship and teaching we might overcome a seeming powerlessness in the face of neo-liberal, bureaucratic ideas of both 'development' and 'law'.

I would like to suggest that at this time more than at any other, law and development need 'the keen, uncanny eyes and ears of lunatic seers'.[74] The 'beautiful ones' of law and development will be those whose analyses show that '[a] global capitalist order is always a contingent social construct' and that 'the actual development and continuity of such an order must be problematized'.[75] One possible point of departure is to recognise that, although it has quickly achieved the status almost of common sense, the rhetoric of new economic rationality barely disguises the project for the ever deeper penetration of capital into the African continent. This paper has attempted to show how Kwei Armah's vision might assist: literature, unlike law, admits of, and on occasion celebrates, such contingency.[76]

Conclusion

In recent years, resistance to the neo-liberal projects of the World Trade Organisation, the European Union and the World Bank has forced a reconsideration of the inevitability of global capitalist triumph.[77] This paper has attempted to heed Baxi's call to provide 'descriptions of the emergent legal patriarchy of contemporary globalisation'.[78] As John Saul has reminded us,

> The abject failure of neo-liberal 'reforms' since the 1980s, the malignant nature of capitalism's continuing grip upon Africa, and the deepening conditions of poverty that face most Africans suggest that the search for genuine alternatives—revolutionary, socialist— must, with ever renewed force, find its way back onto the continental agenda.[79]

Written at the end of one imperial age, Kwei Armah's literary endeavour in *The Beautyful Ones* remains richly suggestive of new means of collective action in the one presently before us. Continued critiques of dominant but barren discourses of law and development should constitute one such collective endeavour.

---

[73] *Ibid*, at 19–20.

[74] Above n 1, at 12.

[75] L Panitch and S Gindin, 'Global Capitalism and American Empire' in L Panitch and C Leys (eds), *Socialist Register 2004: The New Imperial Challenge* (London, Merlin Press, 2004), at 5. Meiksins Wood also reminds us from a historical materialist perspective that 'we can explore a development like globalisation not as some ahistorical natural process but as a truly historical one'. See E Meiksins Wood, 'Global Capital, National States' in M Rupert and H Smith (eds), *Historical Materialism and Globalization* (London, Routledge, 2002), at 18.

[76] See M Aristodemou, *Law and Literature: Journey's From Her to Eternity* (Oxford, Oxford University Press, 2002).

[77] See I Wallerstein, 'New Revolts Against the System' (2002) 18 *New Left Review* 29.

[78] Above n 2, at 473.

[79] J Saul, 'Poverty Alleviation and the Revolutionary Socialist Imperative: Learning from Nyerere's Tanzania' (2002) 57 *International Journal* 193, at 193.

9

Feminist Perspectives in International Economic Law

FIONA BEVERIDGE*

Introduction

The object of this essay is to explore potential foundations for feminist critiques of international economic law. It focuses in particular on the near-complete absence of gender considerations from the discourses of the World Trade Organisation (WTO), on the reasons for that absence and on the grounds for 'engendering' that discourse. To achieve this, this contribution draws on possible intersections and synergies between political science, international relations and development studies, and feminist legal studies in relation to international economic law. First general arguments about the relationships between gender and the economy, gender and trade, and gender and trade law are examined. Then the accommodation of gender concerns in two major international institutions—the WTO and the World Bank—is examined. Although both deal at the highest level with issues of economy and development, their track records on addressing gender issues are vastly different. This chapter considers this observation and possible explanations for this state of affairs, then concludes by outlining some possible contours of a 'gender agenda' for international trade law.

Background

International economic law is a field of study which has risen to prominence in the US and the UK only in the last decade or two. Though the General Agreement on Tariffs and Trade (hereafter GATT) has existed since 1947, public international lawyers have on the whole ignored this sub-system of law. Instead, a small

* Reader in Law, University of Liverpool. Thanks are due to Dominic McGoldrick, University of Liverpool and Jo Shaw, University of Edinburgh, and to the editors, for their helpful advice and encouragement. The usual disclaimer applies.

number of international lawyers in the UK and elsewhere in Europe have, since the 1960s, pursued questions concerning the role of law in development, looking at international institutions and legal regimes such as the International Monetary Fund (hereafter IMF), the World Bank and the GATT, and aligning themselves closely with interdisciplinary schools in development studies.[1] Studies often focused on the tension between the (formal) equality and the (real) inequality of states in these systems, and on case-studies of the legal position of peripheral economies.[2] From the perspective of public international law, this 'Law and Development' movement appeared to remain small and diffuse, with initiatives such as the claim for a New International Economic Order making little impact within public international law.[3] And in reality it seems Law and Development scholars in Western Europe and North America often focused their attention elsewhere, on internal law reform, on good governance, or on human rights issues.[4]

Coinciding with the Uruguay Round of trade negotiations (from 1986), the World Trade Organisation (hereafter WTO) agreements in 1994, and such high-profile GATT cases as Tuna/Dolphin,[5] EC Bananas[6] and Shrimp/

---

[1] For discussion cf D Kennedy, 'Laws and Developments' in A Perry and J Hatchard, *Law and Development: Facing Complexity in the 21st Century* (London, Cavendish, 2003) 17–26; JH Merryman, 'Comparative Law and Social Change: On the Origins, Style, Decline and Revival of the Law and Development Movement' (1977) 25 *American Journal of Comparative Law* 457; BZ Tamanaha, 'The Lessons of Law-and-Development Studies' (1995) 89 *American Journal of International Law* 470.

[2] This approach is exemplified in the collection of materials drawn together in Y Ghai , R Luckham and F Snyder, *The Political Economy of Law: A Third World Reader* (Oxford, OUP, 1987). For more recent examples, see eg, J Faundez, ME Footer and JJ Norton, *Governance, Development and Globalization: a Tribute to Lawrence Tshuma* (London, Blackstone Press, 2000); A Seidman, RB Seidman and TW Wälde (eds), *Making Development Work: Legislative Reform for Institutional Transformation and Good Governance* (The Hague and London, Kluwer Law International, 1999).

[3] Typical examples of work exploring the status of NIEO norms in public international law include FV Garcia-Amador, *The Emerging International Law of Development* (New York, Oceana 1990); K Hossain and SR Chowhury (eds), *Permanent Sovereignty over Natural Resources: Principle and Practice 1984*; O Schachter, 'The Evolving International Law of Development' (1976) 15 *Colombia Journal of Transnational Law*; T Wälde, 'A Requiem for the "New International Economic Order": The Rise and Fall of Paradigms of International Economic Law' (1997) 1 *Center for Energy, Petroleum & Mineral Law and Policy Online Journal*, <htpp//www.dundee.ac.uk/cepmlp/journal> (last accessed 28 September 2004); G White, 'The New International Economic Order: Principles and Trends' in H Fox (ed), *International Economic Law and Developing States: An Introduction* (London, British Institute of International and Comparative Law, 1992) at 27–57.

[4] See eg J Faundez et al, above n 2; A Seidman et al, above n 2; SR Chowdhury, EMG Denters and PJIM de Waart, *The Right to Development in International Law* (Dordrecht, Nijhoff, 1992); PJIM de Waart, *International Law of Development* (Dordrecht, Nijhoff, 1988). The point is well-made by Yash Ghai that any crisis in the Law and Development 'movement' in the West had little impact in Africa: 'A continuing concern with development seemed natural to African researchers.' Y Ghai, 'Law Development and African Scholarship' (1987) 50 *Modern Law Review* 750, at 769. For discussion of a more recent revival of Law and Development Scholarship, see A Manji in this collection; also D Kennedy, above n 1.

[5] US—Prohibition of Imports of Tuna, 18 February 1992, GATT BISD (39th Supp) (1993) 30 *International Legal Materials* 1598; US—Restrictions on Imports of Tuna, 16 June 1994, DS29/R, (1994) 33 *International Legal Materials* 839.

[6] EEC—Import Regime for Bananas, Report of the Panel, 11 February 1994, DS38/R.

Turtle,[7] a growing number of lawyers have turned their attention to what is increasingly seen as a separate and distinct sub-system—international economic law. In one sense the field of enquiry is narrowing, with scholars choosing to focus almost entirely on the WTO system and its rules, at the expense of the World Bank, UNCTAD, etc. But in other senses the discipline is expanding, both to new subject areas and to new forms of scholarship. In terms of subject matter, the new WTO agreements themselves cover an increasing number of areas; and at the same time, the WTO is being called upon to take on board 'trade-and' issues (trade-and-environment, trade-and-labour, trade-and-human rights). In terms of scholarship, the previous generation of trade practitioners, focusing on the technical/doctrinal aspects of the rules,[8] have been joined by a new generation of scholars harnessing a wider range of academic approaches and methodologies to the field. Hence, alongside technical/doctrinal expositions of the laws and procedures, a broad range of critical approaches are now found in the emerging field of international economic law. The types of governance and constitutionalist questions that have previously been asked of national governments and of the EU are now asked, rightly or wrongly, of the WTO.[9] A final development is that international economic law is increasingly seen as of wider importance within international law.[10]

Outside the academy the WTO is also receiving increased attention from governmental, non-governmental and market actors seeking to utilise WTO or anti-WTO discourses to further their interests. Whether the highly visible anti-globalisation

[7] US—Import Prohibition of Certain Shrimp and Shrimp Products, Report of the Panel, 15 May 1998, WT/DS58/R, 98–1710; Report of the Appellate Body (AB–1998–4), 12 October 1998, WT/DS58/AB/R, 98–3899. Further relevant documents can be located on the WTO disputes website at <http://www.wto.org/english/tratop_e/dispu_e/dispu_e.htm> (last accessed 28 September 2004).

[8] See eg R Hudec, *Enforcing International Trade Law: The Evolution of the Modern GATT Legal System* (Salem (NH), Butterworth Legal, 1993); JH Jackson, *World Trade and the Law of GATT* (Indianapolis, Bobbs-Merrill, 1969); JH Jackson, *The World Trading System*, 2nd edn (Cambridge Ma, MIT Press, 1997); EU Petersmann, *International Trade Law and the GATT/WTO Dispute Settlement System* (London, Kluwer Law, 1997); MJ Trebilcock and R Howse, *The Regulation of International Trade* (London, Routledge, 1999).

[9] MCEJ Bronkers, 'Better Rules for a New Millenium: A Warning Against Undemocratic Developments in the WTO?' (1999) 2 *Journal of International Economic Law* 547; DZ Cass, 'The "Constitutionalization" of International Trade Law: Judicial Norm-Generation as the Engine of Constitutional Development in International Trade' (2001) 12(1) *European Journal of International law* 39; G de Búrca and J Scott (eds), *The EU and the WTO: Legal and Constitutional Issues* (Oxford, Hart Publishing, 2001); J Jackson, 'Sovereignty, Subsidiarity, and Separation of Powers: The High-Balancing Act of Globalisation' in DLM Kennedy and JD Southwick (eds), *The Political Economy of International Trade Law: Essays in Honour of Robert E Hudec* (Cambridge, CUP, 2002); M Krajewski, 'Democratic Legitimacy and Constitutional Perspectives of WTO Law' (2001) 35 *Journal of World Trade* 167; JHH Weiler (ed), *The EU, the WTO and the NAFTA: Towards a Common Law of International Trade?* (Oxford, OUP, 2000).

[10] See eg M Lennard, 'Navigating by the Stars: Interpreting the WTO Agreements' (2002) 5 *Journal of International Economic Law* 17; DM McRae, 'The WTO in International Law: Tradition Continued or New Frontier?' (2000) 3 *Journal of International Economic Law* 27; EU Petersmann, 'Dispute Settlement in International Economic Law—Lessons for Strengthening International Dispute Settlement in Non-Economic Areas' (1999) 2 *Journal of International Economic Law* 189; K Raustiala, 'Rethinking the Sovereignty Debate in International Economic Law' (2003) 6 *Journal of International Economic Law* 841.

protests at Seattle or Turin, the loud criticism of the GATT/WTO dispute settlement bodies for their apparent failure to give sufficient protection to pro-environmental policies of Members, the tough economic posturing of the US over tariffs on steel imports, or the resort to the WTO Dispute Settlement Body for strategic gains in the arguments over the US use of extra-territorial jurisdiction in relation to Cuba, the WTO is increasingly viewed in political terms and as a site for political struggles.

Despite these developments, feminist legal critiques of international economic law have so far been fairly muted.[11] Mariama Williams, seeking to advance a gender perspective on the Doha Ministerial Declaration (the negotiating agreement concluded at the Doha Ministerial Meeting of the WTO in November 2001),[12] concluded:[13]

> [G]ender advocates should be very concerned, especially in the areas of food security, TRIPs, and the GATS negotiations, which will further liberalize services. These continue to pose serious implications for access and affordability of food and nutrition, access to public health including reproductive health for women and basic social services such as health and education as well as critical natural resources such as water. The full implications of GATS, which covers just about everything except agriculture and goods, TRIPs and TRIMs, and involves issues of procurement and investment, has yet to be fully recognized by feminist activists working on issues of health, reproductive health, women's economic and social empowerment and women's rights.

These claims, based on established development-centred critiques[14] and perspectives,[15] represent a significant challenge to scholars in international economic law, calling into question the vision of growth-centred development which the WTO agreements embrace and evoking other international legal norms—on good governance, human rights, gender equality, people-centred development, for example—in the process. The near-absence of any gender discourse from the day-to-day operations of the WTO, and indeed from the Doha round of multilateral trade negotiations, coveys the impression that trade, or at least trade law, is

---

[11] See R Buchanan and S Pahuja, 'Collaboration, Cosmopolitanism and Complicity' (2002) 71 *Nordic Journal of International Law* 297, at note 4.

[12] WT/MIN(01)/Dec/1, Ministerial Declaration of 20 November 2001; see further the Ministerial Statement adopted at the conclusion of the Cancún Round of trade talks in September 2003: WT/MIN(03)/20, Ministerial Declaration of 14 September 2003.

[13] M Williams, 'The Doha Ministerial: Not Good for Development, Not Good for Gender Equality, Commentary and Perspective' (2002) 2 *International Gender and Trade Network January 2002*, http://www.genderandtrade.net/Bulletins/Jan02.pdf (last accessed 8 February 2005).

[14] Examples include N Cagatay, *Trade, Gender and Poverty* (New York, UNDP, 2001); C Grown, D Elson and N Cagatay (eds), 'World Development: Special Issue on Growth, Trade, Finance and Gender Inequality' (2000) 28(7) *World Development* and contributions therein; MH Marchand and JL Parpart, *Feminism, Postmodernism, Development* (London, Routledge, 1995) and contributions therein.

[15] See, for instance, the materials available as the Financing for Development Gender Policy Briefing Kit on the Women's Environment and Development Organisation website: <htpp://www.wedo.org/ffd/> (last accessed 28 September 2004).

gender neutral.[16] This chapter challenges that views and presents a case for inclusion of a gender perspective in international economic law.

Gender and the Economy

The relationship between gender and the economy has been addressed most thoroughly in the development studies field, where the need to take account of the gendered organisation of societies has been recognised as central to the effectiveness of development programmes and development assistance strategies. In 1997, the United Nations Commission on the Status of Women recommended that '[d]evelopment policies should focus on the economic empowerment of women. The interlinkage between national policies at the macrolevel and economic and social gender roles and relations at the microlevel should be clear in order to make the policies more effective.'[17] In the Platform of Action adopted at the 1995 Beijing Conference, UN Members were exhorted to:

> Analyze, from a gender perspective, policies and programmes—including those related to macroeconomic stability, structural adjustment, external debt problems, taxation, investments, employment, markets and all relevant sectors of the economy—with respect to their impact on poverty, on inequality and particularly on women; assess their impact on family well-being and conditions and adjust them, as appropriate, to promote more equitable distribution of productive assets, wealth, opportunities, income and services.[18]

Gender-based analyses of poverty have been particularly important in the development of gendered economic perspectives. As summarised by Nilufer Cagatay:

> Viewed from the lens of human poverty, women and girls can be poorer relative to men within households that are classified as poor according to income poverty criteria. There can also be women and girls who are poor from a human poverty perspective in households that are classified as non-poor by these criteria. While it is clear that women should not be viewed as passive victims, and their agency should

---

[16] In this context the Report, issued as this chapter was going to press, of the UN Inter-Agency Task Force on Women and Gender Equality, Task Force on Gender and Trade, *Trade and Gender*, represents an important new development and opportunity to begin to address this omission in trade law and policy-making: *Opportunities and Challenges for Developing Countries* (New York, United Nations, 2004) (UNCTAD/EDM/2004/2) (hereafter 'UN Task Force' and *Trade and Gender*).

[17] Commission on the Status of Women, Agreed Conclusions on Women and the Economy, March 1997; see also Commonwealth Secretariat, *Engendering Adjustment for the 1990s* (London, Commonwealth Secretariat, 1989).

[18] United Nations, *Fourth World Conference on Women, Declaration and Platform for Action 1995*, UN Doc A/CONF 177/20, 15 Sept 1995, 58(b).

be recognised, gender relations cause women and men to experience poverty differently within households.[19]

More recently, reports by the UN and the World Bank have highlighted the links between poverty and gender inequality.[20] These insights have in turn fuelled gender-based analyses of economic policies, leading to the conclusions, first, that economic policies will impact differently on men and women, and, secondly, that gender will influence the outcome of economic policies.[21]

Gender and Trade Policy

Development and international relations theorists have offered various explanations for the exclusion of a gender perspective from dominant trade policy debates. Most significant of these explanations is the assumed neutrality of orthodox neo-liberal trade theories based on the notion of comparative advantage:

> The system of rules and agreements that currently governs international trade is based on the widely accepted view that expanding global trade is beneficial to all countries and their citizens … Despite the recognition that trade liberalisation creates both winners and losers within each country, it is held that there are net gains overall, allowing losers to be compensated through trade adjustment assistance or changes in taxation policies.[22]

Thus it is argued that orthodox economic policies, and the rules and agreements adopted to give effect to them, are gender blind, and that neo-liberal macro-economic discourses have such dominance that other perspectives are routinely excluded. Williams, for example, argues that acceptance of the neo-liberal orthodoxy meant that southern governments found themselves 'boxed-in' at the Doha Ministerial Meeting: 'in the end, in the WTO, they could only argue in terms of "imbalances", "technical assistance" and an already outmoded and increasingly irrelevant "special and differential treatment".'[23] Marchand and Runyan have similarly argued that the language of globalisation has acted to privilege particular sectors over others—finance capital over manufacturing; finance ministries over

---

[19] N Cagatay, above n 14, at 15, and references cited therein.

[20] UN, *Human Development Report: Millenium Development Goals: A Compact Among Nations to End Human Poverty* 2003; World Bank, *Gender Inequality and the MDGs* 2003; UN Task Force, *Trade and Gender*, above n 16.

[21] Cagatay argues that these impacts are complex and variable and need to be addressed in country and sector-specific contexts. Cagatay, above n 14, at 19.

[22] *Ibid*, 11.

[23] M Williams, above n 13, at 4.

social welfare ministries; market over state.[24] It is argued that this construction of the relationship between economic affairs and social issues is founded on a dichotomy between the 'economic' and the 'social' which is itself deeply gendered.[25]

This dichotomous thinking permeates policy-making:

> Although there is now widespread recognition of the need to integrate macro-economic management and 'social policies,' there is still a strong tendency to think this means continuing to design what are termed 'sound' macroeconomic policies with a focus on market-based criteria, an overriding emphasis on stabilizing the price level and reducing the role of the state, and then *adding* social policies in order to achieve socially desirable outcomes such as poverty reduction.[26]

As Nelson argues, this also means that policies in the 'social' sphere are considered secondary, 'often postponed and the first to be eliminated or scaled back in any time of budget tightening'.[27]

Elson and Cagatay have criticised the World Bank's *Comprehensive Development Framework* (CDF),[28] adopted in 1999 as a development framework for countries and regions, which posits the macro-economic on the one hand, and the 'social and human' on the other hand, as two sides of a single balance sheet: '[t]he distinct impression is left that macroeconomic policy is the responsibility of the International Monetary Fund (IMF) and is a separate domain, which sets the parameters to which the CDF has to accommodate.'[29]

Feminist commentators have sought to challenge this dichotomous approach to economic and social management, arguing that policies which do not take proper account of gendered social relations may fail, or prove an ineffective allocation of resources: '[v]arious sorts of bad policies can result from excluding social questions from economics.'[30] This in turn has led to various attempts to reconceptualise economics or redraw the subject boundaries.[31]

---

[24] M Marchand and AS Runyan, 'Introduction: Feminist Sightings of Global Restructuring: Conceptualizations and Reconceptualizations' in M Marchand and AS Runyan (eds), *Gender and Global Restructuring* (London, Routledge, 2000), 1–22.

[25] See further F Beveridge, 'Further Feminist Readings on International Economic Law' in A Qureshi (ed), *Perspectives in International Economic Law* (The Hague, Kluwer, 2002) at 177.

[26] D Elson and N Cagatay, 'The Social Content of Macroeconomic Policies' (2000) 28 *World Development* 1347, at 1347.

[27] JA Nelson 'Labour, Gender and the Economics/Social Divide' in MF Loutfi (ed), *Women, Gender and Work: What is Equality and How Do We Get There?* (Geneva, International Labour Office, 2001) 369, at 370.

[28] Available at <http://web.worldbank.org/WBSITE/EXTERNAL/PROJECTS/STRATEGIES/CDF> (last accessed 28 September 2004).

[29] Elson and Cagatay, above n 26, at 1351.

[30] JA Nelson, above n 27, at 371.

[31] N Folbre and H Hartmann, 'The Rhetoric of Self-interest: Ideology and Gender in Economic Theory' in A Klamer, DN McCloskey and R Solow (eds), *The Consequences of Economic Rhetoric* (Cambridge, Cambridge University Press, 1988); JA Nelson, *Feminism, Objectivity and Economics* (London, Routledge, 1996); JA Nelson, above n 27; VA Zelizer, 'The Creation of Domestic Currencies'(1994) 84 *American Economic Review* 138. More generally see J Peterson and M Lewis (eds), *The Elgar Companion to Feminist Economics* (Cheltenham, Edward Elgar Publishing Ltd, 1999).

These insights underpin feminist critiques of international trade. Cagatay, for instance, argues that the gains made in understandings of poverty must be reflected in trade policy: 'the assessment of trade liberalization, trade policies and trade performance from a human development perspective needs to go beyond traditional social impact analyses, which still view development in terms of growth and markets, to incorporate power and power relations within and across nations.'[32]

Yet the dichotomous thinking that characterises economic policy-making as separate and distinct from social policy-making may be embedded in government structures and disciplinary attitudes, making change difficult. Gita Sen, examining gender mainstreaming in finance ministries, points to the typical high status of finance ministries within government, holding the purse strings and setting long-term economic strategy, leaving other ministries to fight over budget shares. She also points to the apparent distance between the finance ministry and the impacts of policies on the ground; and the general air of technical specialism and mystery which surrounds macro-economic issues.[33] In addition, she suggests, the capacity of women's organisations to engage in macro-economic debate is limited.[34] Writing in 2000, Sen concluded that '[i]n gender terms, Ministries of Finance have tended to remain singularly untouched by the winds of gender change that are beginning to blow through other ministries.'[35] Since many aspects of trade policy are in fact within the remit of finance rather than trade ministries, or at least subject to tight parameters laid down by finance ministries, these points are clearly salient to an analysis of gender and trade policy.

Sen argues that macro-economics needs to be reconceptualised, to acknowledge properly the impact of macro-economic policies. The current focus on short-term economic stabilisation through budgetary controls 'seems to insulate the Finance Ministry from a need to weigh the implications of its actions for human resources development over the medium and longer terms.'[36] And to perform this weighing exercise effectively, full account will need to be taken of gender.[37] A practical development which may prove useful in this respect is the growing practice of producing a 'women's budget', or of subjecting the national budget of a state to gender analysis.[38] Budlender highlights, in particular, the move away from the production

---

[32] Cagatay, above n 14, at 12.
[33] G Sen, 'Gender Mainstreaming in Finance Ministries' (2000) 28 *World Development* 1379, at 1380.
[34] *Ibid.*
[35] *Ibid,* at 1379.
[36] *Ibid,* at 1385.
[37] *Ibid.*
[38] D Budlender, 'The Political Economy of Women's Budgets in the South' (2000) 28 *World Development* 1365; Commonwealth Secretariat, *Gender Budget Initiative* (London, Commonwealth Secretariat, 1999). One report prepared in 2001 suggests that 41 states (mostly developing) had taken steps to give greater attention to gender perspectives in national budgeting processes: Interagency Meeting on Women and Gender Equality Taskforce on Financing for Development, 'Mainstreaming Gender Perspectives in Issues Addressed in the Preparations for the ICFfD (IAMWGE Taskforce): An

of separate 'women's budget' publications, towards the incorporation of gender analysis into budget preparation, which she says, fits well with current concerns with performance:

> In monetary terms, when officials start thinking of policy goals at the same time as budgets, they recognize that gender analysis can result in expenditures that are both more efficient in targeting the truly needy, and more equitable.[39]

However, both Sen and Budlender suggest that only limited progress has been made in most states on incorporating gender into macro-economic planning.

The privileging of macro-economic considerations within national policy-making may also make the case for change more difficult to advance. Elson and Cagatay point to the disempowering effect of the economic/social dichotomy in relation to macro-economic policy: '[t]he claim that there is no alternative to the "sound" and "prudent" macroeconomic policy being implemented is at root a claim that there is no possibility of forging a different social consensus, different set of social norms, a different set of regulations; or that making such a difference is undesirable from the point of view of the policymaker.'[40] Elson and Cagatay seek to inject into such conceptualisations of macro-economic policy a yardstick of social justice and a more participatory approach to macro-economic policy-making, through a refurbished social dialogue. From this perspective another aspect of women's budgeting initiatives may be important:

> Gender budget initiatives also hold other benefits for civil society and for good governance more generally. One of the most important is the increased transparency and accountability which ensues when governments engage seriously in these exercises. Transparency and accountability are not simply of theoretical value. In order to engage in effective agitation and oversight, both parliamentarians and civil society need decent information. A good, ongoing gender budget exercise provides the basis for greater involvement of people in influencing policy and budget allocations and in monitoring their implementation, even if opportunities for drafting of budgets remain minimal.[41]

However it is clear that, whatever the potential of gendered budget analysis, the basic economic/social dichotomy identified by Cagatay, Elson, Sen and others remains in place in economic management.

Initial Analysis', available at <htpp:/www.wedoi.org/ffd/kitmain1> (last accessed 28 September 2004), para 1.2. For a review of practise among EU Member States see European Commission, Advisory Committee on Equal Opportunities for Women and Men, Opinion on Gender Budgeting, May 2003.

[39] D Budlender, above n 38, at 1376.
[40] Above, n 26, at 1360.
[41] *Ibid*, at 1377.

Gender and International Trade Law[42]

International trade law, like international trade policy, is presented as a gender-neutral set of rules, regulations and processes, an image which it shares with many other fields of international law.[43] Moreover, international trade law is a branch of international law and rests on a division between the *international* and the *national/domestic* arenas, a division identified by Charlesworth et al as international law's version of the public/private distinction.[44] An orthodox (or formal) analysis of international trade law would suggest that the absence of references to 'women' or other gendered categories lies in this distinction—that rules and regulations dealing with 'women's issues' or the particular situation of women would tend to be promulgated at national or sub-national levels and would be tolerated under international trade law provided that they did not breach any trade rules.

The system for regulating international trade established by the GATT 1947 and extended and institutionalised in the 1995 Uruguay Round Agreements is firmly rooted in the dualism between international and domestic laws. The Uruguay Round Agreements are obligations between states which, like other treaties, contain binding legal commitments requiring, where necessary, adjustment of state laws and policies. Domestic law or policy, whether national, sub-national or local, cannot serve as an excuse for breach of these international obligations. Compliance with and enforcement of WTO obligations lies entirely in the hands of states (the WTO Members), with individuals and other 'private' bodies such as firms playing no formal part. The core provisions of WTO agreements, though far from uniform, generally reflect the economic objectives of the WTO, including non-discrimination and market liberalisation. 'Social' objectives usually fall to be justified as exceptions or exclusions.

Thus quantitative restrictions to trade which are contrary to GATT Article XI might be justified under GATT Article XX as 'necessary to protect human life or health' or 'public policy'. This is the presumed justification for national laws prohibiting trafficking in women and children, regulating inter-country adoption trade, regulating the importation and distribution of pornographic materials, contraceptive drugs and, potentially, even health promotional literature deemed unsuitable for public distribution.

---

[42] 'Trade law' is used here to refer to WTO law; that is, the legal rules and processes governing international trade as currently represented by the Uruguay Round Agreements, and by the law and policy-making activities of the WTO. It does not include the activities of international financial institutions such as the World Bank, which is examined in the next section, below.

[43] See H Charlesworth and C Chinkin, *The Boundaries of International Law: a Feminist Analysis* (Manchester, MUP, 2000) at 48.

[44] H Charlesworth et al, 'Feminist Approaches to International Law' (1991) 85 *American Journal of International Law* 613, at 625; H Charlesworth, 'The Public/Private Distinction and the Right to Development in International Law' (1992) 12 *Australian Yearbook of International Law* 190; D Buss, 'Going Global: Feminist Theory, International Law, and the Public/Private Divide' in SB Boyd (ed), *Challenging the Public/Private Divide* (Toronto, University of Toronto Press, 1997) at 360.

Such measures, if challenged before a WTO panel, would be deemed acceptable provided that they satisfied the 'necessity' test and were not simply an arbitrary discrimination or a disguised restriction on trade.[45] In coming to a decision on such an issue a WTO panel would take as a starting point that each WTO Member remains free to set its own level of protection in the areas covered by Article XX; moreover, a decision to choose a high level of protection will not prejudice the position of a Member—in the Beef Hormones Case the Appellate Body confirmed that the choice of a high standard (in that case by the EC) was a valid choice for a WTO Member to make, and that it would not result in the reversal of the burden of proof, away from the party alleging a violation of GATT (in that case, the US).[46]

Similarly service providers, such as insurance companies, banks, or tour companies exercising rights of establishment or providing services by cross-border means under GATS Article XVI, could be subjected to local wage regulations, employment rights policies and other measures concerning the welfare, training and treatment of their workforce, provided that the treatment was no less favourable than that enjoyed by other foreign or domestic service providers.[47] Thus, it could be argued, there is ample scope for states to maintain existing laws and to introduce new laws addressing social issues of concern to them without jeopardising compliance with their WTO obligations. Under this analysis, the rules of international trade themselves can be argued to be gender neutral. Any undesirable gender impacts from increased international trade can be said to arise from failure on the part of the state itself to avail itself of the opportunities afforded within the agreements to pursue social objectives.

However, while it is true that social programmes or measures designed to tackle the gender impacts of trade could be justified as exceptions under WTO rules, the orthodox analysis outlined above does not address the fundamental issue of whether the construction of these legal provisions, particularly the '*(international) rule–(domestic) exception*', is justifiable. Does the practice of stating the general trade rule, and leaving it to states to argue the case for protecting social interests on the basis of national policy preferences, prejudice the pursuit of national policy

[45] National restrictions, as well as satisfying the provisions of one of the sub-paragraphs of Article XX, must satisfy the requirements of the *chapeau* that they are not 'applied in a manner which would constitute a means of arbitrary or unjustifiable discrimination between countries where the same conditions prevail, or a disguised restriction on international trade: GATT Art XX. For a discussion of the relationship between the individual paragraphs and the *chapeau*, see Report of the Appellate Body in United States—Standards for Reformulated and Conventional Gasoline, WT/DS2/AB/R, 22; Report of the Appellate Body in United States—Import Prohibition of Certain Shrimp or Shrimp Products, above n 7, 46–48.

[46] See Report of the Appellate Body in EC—Measures Concerning Meat and Meat Products (Hormones), WT/DS26&48/AB/R, 38–42.

[47] This 'national treatment' standard is provided for under GATS Art XVII. It applies only to the service areas where Members have made commitments in their Schedules and may be subject to conditions and qualifications (also detailed in the Schedules). The Agreement on Trade-related Intellectual Property Rights similarly incorporates exceptions, referred to within the basic national treatment and most-favoured nation obligations in Arts III and IV thereof.

preferences in a way which is gendered? In other words, can it be maintained that the construction of the WTO legal provisions replicates and strengthens the *inter-national/domestic* distinction of international law, and that in so doing it disguises the gendered nature of international economic law? Does WTO law, like the World Bank's *Comprehensive Development Framework*, see trade regulation and the protection of social interests as separate sides of the balance sheet, with trade law setting the parameters within which social laws and policies must operate?

This argument has been made about the law of the European Union and its treatment of economic and social issues. Shaw observes that many aspects of social policy are treated as 'protected domains' for the Member States, whereas economic or market issues are given 'canonical' status under EU law.[48] The issue is not the choice of location of competence or policy-making power at the national or supra-state level per se, but the 'ascription of priorities' which it reveals:

> [T]he choice between a more or less limited concept of 'what is the European Union' is important in terms of gender. Moreover, because of the canonical status of 'market' law within the EU, it must carry some message about priorities, embedded values and the allocation of resources. Above all, it restates a fundamental tenet of modern welfare capitalism, namely the consistent undervaluing of the unpaid work done primarily within the home and the family by women.[49]

Observations such as this have underpinned criticisms that EU equality laws stop short of tackling the very market forces that create and reproduce inequality. Ward, for example, argues that an attack on inequality in EC law 'must be directed against the entire metanarrative of the Community and its ideology'.[50]

Can a similar argument be made in relation to the WTO? Does the construction of the WTO agreements similarly establish trade liberalisation as the central 'canon' to which measures of social protection must always be subjected; and if so, does this convey a gendered set of values or 'ascription of priorities'? This question can be approached in a number of different ways, and via a range of methodologies. It is not possible to embark here on a comprehensive examination of all areas and all aspects of international economic law: what follows is selective in terms both of subject matter and methodologies.

Orthodox legal analysis, with its emphasis on the meaning and interpretation of legal provisions, offers one answer. WTO jurisprudence from the Dispute

---

[48] J Shaw, 'Law, Gender and the Internal Market' in T Hervey and D O'Keeffe, *Sex Equality Law in the European Union* (Chichester, Wiley, 1996) 283, at 289–94.

[49] *Ibid*, at 294.

[50] I Ward, 'Beyond Sex Equality: The Limits of Sex Equality in the New Europe' in T Hervey and D O'Keeffe, above n 48, at 369. See also S Fredman, 'European Community Discrimination Law: A Critique' (1992) 18 *Industrial Law Journal* 119; H Fenwick and T Hervey, 'Sex Equality in the Single Market: New Directions for the European Court of Justice' (1995) 32 *Common Market Law Review* 443.

Settlement Body (hereafter DSB) suggests that gender, like environmental considerations, is increasingly recognised as a valid policy objective justifying accommodation. In the Shrimp-Turtle dispute,[51] the DSB was called upon to rule on whether measures adopted by the US under environmental legislation to restrict imports into the US of shrimps caught in countries where certain 'turtle-friendly' harvesting methods were not required, were compatible with the GATT. Under GATT Article XI, quantitative restrictions, including bans such as this, are generally prohibited, but can be permitted where they can be justified under Article XX, the general exceptions article. Exceptions might include, inter alia, the protection of the life or health of humans or animals, the preservation of non-renewable resources or the protection of artistic treasures. Appealing against the ruling of the Panel to the Appellate Body, the US, the EC and others had argued that the approach of the Panel to the application of Article XX GATT effectively placed too much weight on trade concerns at the expense of other policy concerns of states.[52] The Appellate Body ruled that the Article XX *chapeau* required the balancing of the right of a Member to resort to Article XX exceptions against the trade rights of other Members under other GATT Articles (non-discrimination, market access, etc). Article XX made available certain exceptions, the Appellate Body stated, 'in recognition of the legitimate nature of the policies and interests there embodied'.[53] An interpretive approach must therefore be adopted, according to the Appellate Body, which does not render these exceptions illusory.[54] Thus the very existence of the Article XX exceptions, according to the Appellate Body, speaks to the legitimacy and recognition of the particular values and policies of State Members that might have a restrictive effect on trade. This argument is further supported by the Appellate Body's acceptance in the EC—Asbestos case[55] that each WTO Member has the right to determine its own level of protection under Article XX(b), in that case in the health field: 'France has determined, and the Panel accepted, that the chosen level of health protection by France is a "halt" to the spread of asbestos-related health risks.'[56]

Taken at face value, this line of decisions suggests two possible arguments. The first is that the mere omission of references to gender-based concerns in the WTO agreements is not of great significance, because it remains open to states to raise and protect such concerns within the scope of, say, Article XX GATT, which affirms their right to do so. The second, related argument is that it is the function of the DSB to protect the rights of states in this regard, in particular by ensuring that a balance is struck between a Member's rights under Article XX and its

---

[51] Report of the Appellate Body in United States—Import Prohibition of Certain Shrimp and Shrimp Products, above n 7.

[52] *Ibid*, at 8–9 (US), 25–26 (EC).

[53] *Ibid*, at 65.

[54] *Ibid.*

[55] EC—Measures Affecting Asbestos and Asbestos-Containing Products, WT/DS135/AB/R, p 61.

[56] *Ibid*, footnote omitted.

obligations to respect the rights of other Members under the GATT. The *chapeau* of Article XX, correctly interpreted and applied, will serve this purpose.

Feminist legal scholars have faced such claims before and will be sceptical for a variety of reasons. First, the inherent uncertainty of a process which depends on a judicial balancing of claims—the extensive room for dispute, for instance, over what is 'arbitrary' within the meaning of the *chapeau* of GATT Article XX—may be thought unsatisfactory. Such an approach falls far short of an explicit endorsement of equality laws and policies, and possibly risks a 'chilling' effect on government action (this point is taken up below). Secondly, it may seem to leave too much power in the hands of the judges who, as trade specialists, may be ill-equipped to make judgements about social policy. Thirdly, the DSB's ability to promote gender-based claims is circumscribed by the scope of the WTO agreements themselves. In the Shrimp-Turtle case, the Appellate Body was arguably emboldened in its interpretation of Article XX(g) to include exhaustible natural resources, by the inclusion of a reference to 'sustainable development' in the preamble to the WTO Agreement.[57] There is no similar reference to gender equality or the advancement of women which could inform a Panel's interpretive perspectives in a case involving gender policies. Indeed, the WTO agreements as a whole are silent on the subject and entirely gender neutral in their language.[58] Reliance on interpretation to address gender issues would seem to be a precarious course indeed.

In any case, there seems to be a broader need to examine the activities of the WTO as a whole, and in particular to explore proposals for the adoption of new rules, the WTO's activities in monitoring and overseeing the implementation of WTO rules, and the conduct of future rounds of trade negotiations. However satisfactory or unsatisfactory the DSB's custodianship of GATT Article XX and similar 'exceptions' provisions in other agreements, no answer will be found in existing WTO jurisprudence to the question of whether the further liberalisation of agricultural trade, an extension of rules on procurement, or the addition of subsidies disciplines in the services field, will be better or worse for women in different situations in different Member States.[59]

Thus it is necessary to look beyond orthodox legal analysis to assess the possible implications of the absence of any gender dimension from the WTO agreements.

---

[57] Report of the Appellate Body in United States—Import Prohibition of Certain Shrimp and Shrimp Products, above n 7, at 54.

[58] Note, however, the suggestion of the UN Task Force that gender equality could be seen as a dimension of sustainable development, which *is* mentioned in the Preamble to the Marrakesh Agreement Establishing the World Trade Organisation: *Trade and Gender*, above n 16, at 303–305.

[59] See eg N Cagatay, D Elson and C Grown (eds), 'Gender, Adjustment and Macro-Economic Models' Special Issue (1995) 23(11) *World Development*. NGO contributions include EWL, 'Engendering International Trade: Gender Equality in a Global World', available at http://www.womenlobby.org (last accessed 28 September 2004); WS Madonsela, 'The Impact of Trade Liberalisation in the Agricultural Sector on African Women: Links with Food Security and Sustainable Livelihoods', WIDE, available at http://www.eurosur.org/wide (last accessed 28 September 2004).

Gender-based Claims in the Processes of the WTO

Another approach is to examine the impact of the absence of any explicit gender concerns from international trade law on the *processes* of international economic law, that is, on the behaviour of governments, WTO officials, non-governmental bodies and others concerned with the implementation, enforcement and renegotiation of trade laws and policies. This builds on the observation that law as a discourse has the effect of privileging certain claims and voices over others, and of vesting certain claims with legitimacy which others by contrast appear to lack. It also raises the argument that law, through its conservatism and its legitimising force, institutionalises existing inequalities and disadvantages, so that greater effort is required to change the status quo than is required to maintain it. Such an argument is based on the proposition that the current absence of gender concerns from international trade law serves to perpetuate, deepen or aggravate gender inequality and gender-based disadvantage, or at least to thwart efforts to address such inequality and disadvantage. Thus it could be argued, in an echo of Elson and Cagatay,[60] that the exclusion of gender concerns from legal discourses can serve to disempower the advocates of social intervention.

In the context of WTO rules, for example, such exclusion could be said to occur by always casting advocates of social intervention, including of gender equality, in a defensive role, battling under, for example, Article XX GATT to justify exceptions to the 'canons' of market liberalisation. Such an approach would seem to echo similar claims made in relation to a range of 'trade-and' issues. Vázquez, examining the possibility of arriving at certain pro human rights readings of Article XX, concludes that the task 'strikes … as an attempt to fit a square peg into a round hole' and that the defence of human rights measures based on a Product–Production distinction would be 'an uphill battle'.[61] The comprehensive review by Charnovitz of the difficulties surrounding the interpretation of Article XX serves to highlight the essentially unsatisfactory nature of this clause as a basis for social protection.[62] Yet while a number of 'trade-and' issues may have been creeping up the WTO's agenda for reform, none has yet led to substantive change in the rules of the game.

Political scientists have offered some explanations of where and why particular gender-based claims will succeed within organisations. Hafner-Burton and

---

[60] See text, above, at n 40.

[61] C M Vázquez, 'Trade Sanctions and Human Rights—Past, Present, and Future' (2003) 6 *Journal of International Economic Law* 797, at 819, 820.

[62] S Charnovitz, 'The Moral Exception in Trade Policy' (1998) 38 *Virginia Journal of International Law* 689. In *Trade and Gender* the UN Task Force examines the possibility of addressing gender issues as human rights claims. While on the one hand an argument is made that the reference in the Preamble to the Marrakesh Agreement to 'standards of living' and to 'sustainable development' might act as a 'textual bridge' between gender equality and the trade norms of the WTO, they also point out that 'the link with human rights norms has never been tested in WTO dispute settlement proceedings': *Trade and Gender,* above n 16, 303–305.

Pollock, comparing the implementation of gender-based mainstreaming in the World Bank, the United Nations Development Program, the Organisation for Security and Cooperation in Europe and the European Union, identify significant diversity even between institutions where there is rhetorical acceptance of the legitimacy of the mainstreaming norm.[63] Their study suggests that factors other than the normative commitment to gender issues are greatly significant in determining the fate of gender claims, with the implication that the initial recognition or absence of gender norms is relatively unimportant.[64] Similarly, Liebert's study of the diffusion of gender mainstreaming in the EU from the supranational level to national and local levels identifies a range of domestic factors within Member States which foster or constrain the implementation of mainstreaming.[65] There is good evidence that, even where there is a strong normative framework of equality laws, implementation and compliance rates vary significantly. Moreover, these differences cannot be explained merely by reference to litigation and enforcement activity.[66] These studies suggest that other factors besides the mere existence or prominence of gender equality norms play an important part in determining the level of influence which gender advocates will have within institutions. The adoption of even strong gender equality norms is at best only one factor determining the response of institutions to gender-based claims.

A second, related argument is that the confinement of gender-based claims to the realm of 'national' exceptions to global rules may have a chilling effect on national governments in respect of economic and social regulation, making them reluctant to adopt policies which need to be 'defended' within the terms of international economic law. The argument about 'chilling' appears at heart to be an argument about legal certainty: that since the requirements of international trade law are set in the form of standards (most-favoured nation, national treatment and proportionality, for example), there is an inherent uncertainty about which exceptions will be deemed acceptable and which unacceptable. This uncertainty can be regarded as a disincentive to governments to embark on regulatory paths which seem to raise a 'risk' of being declared unlawful by such standards.

A third strand of process-related argument centres on the under-representation of women in international economic and financial institutions, and what this might imply. Here the evidence is ample that economic and financial institutions perform no better than other international bodies in securing appropriate representation of women amongst their senior staff.[67] This suggests that the low levels

---

[63] E Hafner-Burton and MA Pollack, 'Gender Mainstreaming and Global Governance' (2002) 10 *Feminist Legal Studies* 285.

[64] The factors examined by Hafner-Burton and Pollack are: political opportunity; mobilising structures; and strategic framing.

[65] U Liebert, 'Europeanising Gender Mainstreaming: Constraints and Opportunities in the Multilevel Euro-polity' (2002) 10 *Feminist Legal Studies* 241.

[66] *Ibid*, at 246.

[67] See, eg, Women's Environment and Development Organisation, 'Women and Economic Decision-Making: The Numbers Speak for Themselves', WEDO Fact Sheet No 1, available at <http://www.wedo.org> (last accessed 28 September 2004).

of participation by women in the activities of the WTO, particularly at higher levels and in bodies such as the DSB, limits the ability of the WTO to address gender-based concerns adequately and/or renders it unlikely that such concerns will even be raised. While space does not permit consideration of this issue here,[68] it can be noted that the Beijing Platform for Action, without prescribing any detailed action, links the participation of women in economic decision-making to their economic welfare: 'In order to eradicate poverty and achieve sustainable development, women and men must participate fully and equally in the formulation of macroeconomic and social policies and strategies for the eradication of poverty.'[69]

Thus the absence of gender concerns from the WTO's constitutive documents and its trade rules raises a number of specific process-related concerns which deserve further attention.

Gender and the WTO's Normative Framework

Turning to the normative content of international trade law, the starting point for any analysis would seem to be the absence of any gender dimension from the WTO agreements. This raises the question to what extent trade law reflects or fails to reflect the interests of women. This question can be addressed at both a specific and a general level. Specifically, are the interests of women reflected in the rules of international trade law? Generally, do the norms of international trade address women's needs and interests?

Looking at the specific issue first, it is clear that gender perspectives hardly feature at all in the operations of the WTO. Yet according to the Women's Environment and Development Organisation (hereafter WEDO), the rules of the international trade system serve to worsen the economic position of women: 'in the name of trade, governments, through the WTO, are undermining the gains women have made—gains endorsed by those same governments—in governance, economic equity, health and the environment.'[70] WEDO's central argument is that trade law, under the auspices of the WTO, is moving in the opposite direction to other international norms: 'It has been the trend in international environmental and social agreements to introduce new moral ethics and concerns as global norms.'[71] These can be found, according to WEDO, in the declarations and agreements adopted at the United Nations Conference on Environment and Development 1992, the World Conference on Human Rights 1993, the International Conference on Population and Development 1994, the World

---

[68] See A Rochette, this volume, for consideration of the limited effects of increased participation for women in the context of international environmental law.

[69] Above n 18, para 47.

[70] WEDO, 'WEDO Primer: Women and Trade', WEDO November 1999, available at <http://www.wedo.org> (last accessed 28 September 2004).

[71] *Ibid.*

Summit on Social Development 1995, the Fourth World Conference on Women 1995 and the World Food Summit 1996.[72] Juxtaposed against this trend, according to WEDO, are the expansion of WTO rules to cover trade-related investment measures, trade-related intellectual property and safety standards for traded goods, moves to extend the coverage of the WTO Government Procurement Agreement, and a general claim that whenever WTO rules and regulations have come into conflict with local and national agreements and intergovernmental agreements, the DSB of the WTO has ruled that WTO law must prevail. Thus, WEDO argues, the WTO is out of tune with developments in other fields of international organisation in pursuing a narrow, technocratic and economic-centred approach.

Some of the claims on which WEDO's analysis rests are difficult to sustain. It is not clear, as claimed, that the WTO 'may override' international environmental agreements such as the Basel Convention and the Montreal Protocol.[73] Nor is it clear that the ruling of the WTO DSB in the Shrimp/Turtle Case is as one-sided as is claimed. Rather, it could be argued that while US environmentalists may have lost out in the short term, the decision was an important victory for developing states in the longer term.[74]

However the larger claim, that the WTO as an institution has singularly failed to incorporate a gender perspective into its work, is sustainable. The WTO has shown no commitment to gender mainstreaming, and no systematic effort is made to consider the differential impact of the WTO trade rules on men and women. The WTO has failed to respond to a growing international trend. The World Bank, European Union, Asia-Pacific Economic Co-operation, ECOSOC and others at the international level, along with national aid agencies, have all signed up to gender mainstreaming and adopted some steps to implement gender perspectives in their work.

The more general issue of whether the norms of the international trade system address women's needs and interests is complex. The core values of international trade law—non-discrimination between goods and services on grounds of nationality, transparency in trade regulation, reciprocity in trade negotiations and equality before the law—are based on a dichotomy between market and state which has been problematised by feminists elsewhere[75] as a concept which

---

[72] A number of international agreements are also associated by WEDO with this trend: the UN Convention on Biological Diversity, the Basel Convention, and the Montreal Protocol.

[73] See, eg, TJ Schoenbaum, 'International Trade and Protection of the Environment: The Continuing Search for Reconciliation' (1997) 91 *American Journal of International Law* 268, at 281; D Vogel, 'The WTO, International Trade and Environmental Protection: European and American Perspectives' EUI Working Papers, RSC 2002/34.

[74] The ruling by the Appellate Body that states seeking to invoke GATT Art XX exceptions in situations like this are compelled to make serious efforts to seek multilateral solutions before imposing unilateral 'green' product bans, is an important milestone in the development of an inclusive approach to international rule-making.

[75] C Baachi, *Women, Policy And Politics: the Construction of Policy Problems* (London, Sage, 1999); F Olsen, 'The Family and the Market: A Study of Ideology and Legal Reform' (1983) 96 *Harvard Law Review* 1497: see further F Beveridge and S Nott, 'Mainstreaming: A Case for Optimism and Cynicism' (2002) 10 *Feminist Legal Studies* 299, at 308.

delegitimises state intervention and which positions social interests as somehow opposed to market interests.[76]

Thus, echoing points made earlier in this chapter, international trade law may on the one hand offer formal accommodation of gender-based claims but simultaneously, through signalling of its core values, bolster a dichotomous view of international economic relations which serves to devalue such claims.

On the other hand, it is difficult to generalise about the impact of trade law reforms based on WTO norms on the lives of women, since such impacts are as many and myriad as the interests of women themselves. There can be no doubt that international trade has expanded consumer choice for some, produced job opportunities for some, improved the standard of living of some and enhanced food security for some, while in other cases the opposite is true. As an institution the WTO avoids consideration of this issue: there is no official balance sheet on which to record such varying gender impacts.

Engendering the WTO: Identifying the Issues

> The impact of trade liberalisation policies on women depends upon women's position within her local, regional and national economy as well as her role in the social reproduction of family welfare and care services. Thus a gender analysis in relation to trade liberalisation should encompass an understanding of the social and cultural construction of the roles and relationships between men and women, which result in differential access to political power and economic resources ... [W]omen's experience of the processes of globalisation generally and of trade liberalisation in particular are significantly different from those of her male fellow citizens.[77]

As noted above, the 1995 Beijing Platform for Action exhorts states to mainstream gender concerns into all policy areas, including macro-economic policies.[78] It also urges states to '[p]ursue and implement sound and stable macroeconomic and sectoral policies that are designed and monitored with the full and equal participation of women' and to '[u]se gender impact analyses in the development of macro-economic and micro-economic and social policies in order to monitor

---

[76] Thomas challenges the distinction drawn between trade-related intellectual property standards (addressed by the WTO) and labour and environment standards (often cast as outside the jurisdiction or competence of the WTO), arguing that their exclusion from GATT disciplines is a matter of political will and orientation rather than any fundamental or real difference between the issues concerned: C Thomas, 'Trade-related Labor and Environment Agreements?' (2002) 5 *Journal of International Economic Law* 791. For contributions examining the possible contribution of regional economic integration agreements to the promotion of women's rights, see E Gottfried, 'Mercosur: A Tool to Further Women's Rights in the Member Nations' (1998) 25 *Fordham Urban Law Journal* 923; HL Meils, 'A Lesson from NAFTA: Can the FTAA Function as a Tool for Improvement in the Lives of Working Women?' (2003) 78 *Indiana Law Journal* 877.

[77] European Women's Lobby, 'Engendering International Trade: Gender Equality in a Global World', available at <http://www.womenlobby.org> (last accessed 28 September 2004).

[78] Platform for Action 1995, above, n 18.

such impact and restructure policies in cases where harmful impact occurs.'[79] More specifically, the Platform for Action calls on governments to pursue gender equality through public expenditure (para 58(d)), to try to introduce some gender analysis into budgets (para 346) and to increase the transparency of the budget processes (para 165(1)). More specific economic issues addressed include: the access of disadvantaged women to financial resources, including credit schemes;[80] the support of women's entrepreneurship;[81] and equality in social protection schemes and tax systems.[82]

In relation to trade policies, the Beijing Platform for Action exhorts national governments to '[s]eek to ensure that national policies related to international and regional trade agreements do not have an adverse impact on women's new and traditional economic activities' (para 165(k)), to '[e]nsure that all corporations, including transnational corporations, comply with national laws and codes, social security regulations, applicable international agreements, instruments and conventions, including those related to the environment, and other relevant laws' (para 165(l)), and '[t]o create non-discriminatory support services, including investment funds for women's businesses, and target women, particularly low-income women, in trade-promotion programmes' (para 173(d)).

These provisions make clear the potential role of laws and legal institutions in promoting economic equality and advancement for women. On their face these provisions are directed solely at national governments, rather than at international institutions such as the WTO. Similarly, the follow-up process has engaged largely with states.[83] However, the role and potential contribution of international institutions is recognised from time to time. For instance, in 2000, the UN General Assembly considered gender equality, development and peace at its 23rd Special Session, and took stock of progress made between 1995 and 2000 under each of the 12 critical areas for priority action identified in the Platform for Action.[84] Noted developments at the international level included: the increased attention given by multilateral, international and regional financial institutions to the incorporation of a gender perspective into their policies (para 4); the appointment by the UN Population Fund of a Special Ambassador for the Elimination of Female Genital Mutilation (para 10); the inclusion of a gender perspective, and specifically of gendered crimes, in the definitions of War Crimes and Crimes Against Humanity in the

[79] *Ibid*, paras 58(c) and (p).
[80] *Ibid*, paras 166, 167.
[81] *Ibid*, para 166.
[82] *Ibid*, paras 58, 165, 179.
[83] See, eg, Economic Commission for Europe, Report of the Regional Preparatory Meeting on the 2000 Review of Implementation of the Beijing Platform for Action, UN Doc E/ECE/RW.2/2000/7, 4 February 2000. In the 'areas for action' identified, the vast majority of exhortations are directed at ECE state governments, the private sector and social partners, with only a view identifying international financial or aid agencies as relevant actors.
[84] See, eg, 'Further actions and initiatives to implement the Beijing Declaration and the Platform for Action', UNGA Res A/55/71, adopted 4 December 2001, adopting the conclusions of the Twenty-Third Special Session of the General Assembly on 'Women 2000: Gender Equality, Development and Peace for the Twenty-First Century', 10 June 2000.

Rome Statute of the International Criminal Court (paras 12, 20); increased recognition by the United Nations and others that women and men experience humanitarian emergencies differently (para 12); progress made within the UN in gender mainstreaming, including, inter alia, the development of tools and the creation of gender focal points (para 18); and the adoption in the General Assembly of the Optional Protocol to CEDAW (para 20). The role of international institutions and international law is thus acknowledged over a range of issues and subject areas.

Obstacles to progress were also noted in this document and, given the acknowledged role of international institutions in contributing towards progress, there are implicit criticisms of international institutions in many areas. It is thus hard to argue that the WTO escapes responsibility (though the document does not 'name and shame' any institutions). Globalisation is recognised as presenting many challenges, sometimes adversely affecting the position of women, particularly in developing countries and countries in transition (paras 29, 30 *quinter*). 'Benefits of the growing global economy have been unevenly distributed leading to wider economic disparities, the feminization of poverty, increased gender inequality, including through often deteriorating work conditions and unsafe working environments especially in the informal economy and rural areas' (para 29) The failure to recognise 'the importance of a gender perspective in the development of macro-economic policy' is seen as an obstacle to improving the economic situation of women. In decision-making, the failure to increase the participation of women at the highest levels of national and international decision-making, and the gross under-representation of women in all areas of decision-making (including the economy), 'hinders the inclusion of a gender perspective in these critical spheres of influence' (para 17).

The wide-ranging conclusions of the 23rd session of the UN General Assembly included an endorsement of gender mainstreaming (para 109) and a call to international organisations, including the WTO, to 'support government efforts' and, where appropriate, to 'develop complementary programmes of their own' to achieve the implementation of the Programme of Action.

Support for the 'engendering' of international trade law also comes, in a rather muted form, from the European Commission:

> The neutrality of international trade law on gender issues—and neutrality must govern obligations between states—does not exclude discussion of the overall purpose of negotiations, whether on trade or other matters. For the European Union the purpose of global governance is to make possible development that is socially, economically and environmentally sustainable. Seen in this perspective, it is policies that provide suitable responses to gender-based issues, whether they be countries' domestic policies backed, where need be, by appropriate international aid, common policies such as those forming the building blocks of the European Union, or international commitments.[85]

---

[85] 'Trade liberalisation and globalisation—What are the impacts on Women's lives?', Contribution of Mr Pascal Lamy, European Trade Commissioner, to EWL Seminar, June 2001, text available at <http://www.womenlobby.org> (last accessed 28 September 2004). The wider context was the EU's

Finally, in 2004 a UN Inter-Agency Task Force on Gender and Trade acknowledged the need to assess the impact of trade on gender equality and to assist countries to design appropriate strategies and policies to advance gender equality in the face of globalisation.[86]

All of these sources suggest increased attention to 'gender and trade' questions in some international organisations, within the international community and amongst some NGOs, and a growing acknowledgement that the implementation of trade rules may have serious consequences in terms of gender. This increased level of activity has yet to be reflected within the WTO itself. This is despite the fact that at the 23rd Session of the UN General Assembly it was made clear that the WTO should be contributing more to efforts to tackle gender inequalities.

Gender and the World Bank

By contrast to the WTO, the World Bank has been far from silent on the subject of gender. The Bank has responded to the Women in Development/Gender and Development movements since the 1970s through a series of initiatives which have now evolved into a well-publicised commitment to gender equality and a fairly substantial institutional capacity to address gender issues. Particularly since renewing its commitment to poverty reduction in the early 1990s, the Bank has stepped up its efforts to address gender issues in development.

While the Bank's approach to gender issues has not always been lauded, there can be no doubt that its institutional 'take' on the relationship between gender and development has become more sophisticated over the decades. From seeing the situation of women in recipient countries as a 'social' issue to be addressed through 'flanking' measures to its main reconstruction work, the Bank came to see the understanding of gender relations as a key to economic efficiency in its spending and, finally, to accept the need to mainstream gender through all areas of the Bank's operation.[87] Thus by 1995, the year of the Beijing Conference, the World Bank already had a considerable institutional commitment to gender mainstreaming, and this remains at the centre of its gender agenda. Accordingly, the following analysis will focus on the implementation of gender in the work of the World Bank, looking first at the Bank's processes, then at its normative framework.

preparations for the Fourth WTO Ministerial Meeting in Doha later that year, which the EU sought to make a 'Development Round'.

[86] *Trade and Gender*, above n 16, ch 2.

[87] See, eg, N Kardam *Bringing Women In: Women's Issues in International Development* (Boulder Colorado, Lynne Rienner, 1991); S Ravazi and C Miller (eds), *Missionaries and Mandarins: feminist engagement with development institutions* (London, Intermediate Technology in association with the United Nation Research Institute for Social Development, 1998); E Hafner-Burton and MA Pollack, 'Mainstreaming Gender in Global Governance', EUI Working Paper RSC No 2001/46.

Gender-based Claims in the Processes of the World Bank

Given the wealth of opinion about the need to take gender into account fully in the design and implementation of development strategies, it is unsurprising that the World Bank has undertaken extensive studies and reports on this issue, justifying its attention to this issue perhaps for donors as much as borrowers. In 2000 the Bank published a report entitled *Engendering Development—Through Gender Equality in Rights, Resources and Voice*,[88] which examined the conceptual and empirical links between gender, public policy and development. This report argued that gender inequality was bad not only for women, but for the well-being of society as a whole, for economic productivity and growth, and for governance, thus presenting the 'banking' as well as the 'development' case for pursuing gender equality in its country programs.[89] Internally, the Bank's commitment to gender seems to be institutionalised and, to an extent, part of the routine of the Bank. Criticism, where it has come, has been more on the question of whose views have dominated the process of determining the gender policies of the Bank, and the extent to which NGOs and civil society, including women's groups, can influence those policies.

Historically, the image of the Bank has been one of a highly centralised organisation dominated by economists pursuing sound 'banking' policies, in which macro-economic effects have taken precedence over micro-economic impacts.[90] Thus the Bank has been characterised as a fairly closed organisation with limited links with NGOs.[91] However, in recent years, the Bank has been subject to sustained lobbying pressure from the NGO community to reform its behaviour to comply with a feminist agenda. At Beijing, a global campaign, 'Women's Eyes on the World Bank', was launched by women's NGOs to focus attention on particular areas of concern. The four aims of the campaign were:

1. Increased participation of grassroots women in the Bank's economic policy-making;
2. Institutionalisation of a gender perspective in its policies and programmes;

---

[88] (Washington, World Bank, 2000).

[89] See further independent research papers produced for the Bank, such as D Dollar and R Gatti, 'Gender Inequality, Income and Growth: Are Good Times Good for Women?' and S Klasen, 'Does Gender Inequality Reduce Growth and Development? Evidence from Cross-Country Regressions', available at <www.worldbank.org/gender/prr/wp.htm.> See also M McGillivray and JR Pillasisetti, 'International Inequality in Human Development, Real Income and Gender-Related Development', Centre for Research in Economic Development and International Trade, University of Nottingham Research Paper 02/02, available at <http://www.nottingham.ac.uk/economics/credit/research/index.htm> (last accessed 28 September 2004).

[90] For an analysis of the factors influencing the pursuit of policy-goals *within* the Bank, see W Ascher, 'New Development Approaches and the Adaptability of International Agencies: The Case of the World Bank' (1983) 37 *International Organisation* 415; see also AM Goetz, 'Introduction' in AM Goetz (ed), *Getting Institutions Right for Women in Development* (London, Zed Books, 1997).

[91] E Hafner-Burton and MA Pollack, above n 63, at 290.

3. Increased Bank investment in women's health services, education, agriculture, land ownership, employment, and financial services such as credits, savings and insurance; and

4. Implementation of the recommendations of the Stern Report (to increase the number and racial diversity of women in senior management positions within the World Bank).[92]

On the NGO side, the campaign also sought to enhance the capabilities and advocacy skills of NGOs seeking to engage with the World Bank on gender issues, to monitor the effects of Bank projects and policies on women, and to propose 'alternatives for sustainable, equitable development that challenge the inherent gender bias in the Bank's free market policies'.[93] This campaign identified a range of issues, in effect setting a feminist agenda for reform at the Bank.

The Bank undertook to address these issues and in 2000 reported back, as part of the Beijing +5 process, on the progress made. In its report *Advancing Gender Equality: World Bank Action Since Beijing*,[94] examples are given of gender-based reforms in the Bank's internal processes, in country assistance projects and, to a limited extent, in adjustment lending programs. In an assessment of the World Bank's progress in implementing its commitment to mainstreaming, Hafner-Burton and Pollack concluded that it 'largely delivered' on its promises, though there remained room for improvement in relation to its projects and programs, where mainstreaming was still patchy. Contrasting the World Bank's performance with that of other international institutions, Hafner-Burton and Pollack concluded that its centralised nature contributed to its ability to secure effective implementation of its mainstreaming polices in borrower countries.[95]

Overall it seems clear that, for a variety of reasons, gender has found a place in the processes of the World Bank. Despite the 'closed' nature of the Bank, it also seems to have engaged with its critics in the NGO community, though it is possible that this has happened only because to some extent the NGO message chimed with the thinking of the Bank's own staff.[96]

Engendering the World Bank's Normative Framework

Gender has featured in criticisms of the Bank's normative framework for several decades and is deeply-rooted in the WID/GAD debates of development studies of

---

[92] 'Women's Eyes on the World Bank', viewed at <http://www.laneta.apc.org/bmmm/bcomun2.htm> (last accessed 28 September 2004).

[93] *Ibid.*

[94] (World Bank, 2000); see more recently the annual reports on gender mainstreaming, eg, World Bank *Implementing the Bank's Gender Mainstreaming Strategy: Second Annual Monitoring Report*, FY03, 29 January 2004.

[95] E Hafner-Burton and MA Pollack, above n 63, at 292.

[96] W Ascher, above n 90, has noted that where Bank staff disagree with new approaches they have considerable ability to resist them, either by explicitly attacking them or their underlying premises, or by simply resisting their introduction at the technical level: *ibid,* 422–26.

the 1970s and 1980s. The contemporary manifestation of this debate can be traced through to the criticisms levied at the *Comprehensive Development Framework*[97] that it is based on an economic/social dichotomy which is false and which is deeply gendered. The charge laid at the door of the World Bank is that its overriding demand for sound financial management forces borrower states to implement economic policies which adversely affect women and which are themselves contrary to the stated aims of the World Bank in relation to gender equality:

> Under the trusteeship of the international financial institutions, the 'empowerment of women' is to be achieved through the usual macro-economic recipes: devaluation, budget austerity, the application of user fees in health and education, the phasing out of State-supported credit, trade liberalisation, the deregulation of grain markets, the elimination of minimum wage legislation, and so on. In other words, donor support to Women's programmes ... is conditional upon the prior derogation of women's rights through 'satisfactory compliance' with IMF–World Bank conditionalities.[98]

The adverse effects are only partly compensated for, in the eyes of critics, by gender-specific measures addressing the needs of women. In education, for example, the argument has been made that the Bank's overall economic policies do far greater harm than can be ameliorated by gender-specific measures:

> [An] area of [World Bank] intervention has been the implementation of scholarships and/or subsidies to girls ('Letting Girls Learn') to finance the costs of primary and secondary school tuition including books and school materials. [World Bank] support in this area however is conditional upon the prior laying off of teachers, a major curtailment of the educational budget and the adoption of double-shift and multigrade teaching ... The [World Bank] focus is to implement cost-effective 'targeted programmes' for girls while at the same time prescribing the withdrawal of the State from the financing of primary education.[99]

The World Bank's gender critics can be divided into two broad groupings: reformists and radicals. For reformists, the World Bank needs to take more seriously the gender agenda, 'understand how women shoulder the burden of the social impact of adjustment, how they are affected when health spending is cut',[100] and follow through its commitment to mainstreaming into all its policies and practices.[101] For more radical critics, however, the problem lies with the dominant

---

[97] Above, n 28.

[98] M Chossudovsky, 'The World Bank Derogates Women's Rights', at <http://www.twnside.org.. sgg/title/derog-cn.htm> (last accessed 28 September 2004).

[99] *Ibid.* See also G Mutume, 'Gender Discrimination Not Good for Growth', <http://www.twnside.org.sg/title/gender.htm> (last accessed 28 September 2004); Z Randriamero, 'Gender and Economic Reforms in Africa: The Hidden Political and Ideological Agenda', <http://www.twnside.org.sg/title/twrl122i.htm> (last accessed 28 September 2004).

[100] Angela Wood of the Bretton Woods Project, quoted in G Mutume, above n 99.

[101] This might summarise the project of 'Women's Eyes on the World Bank', as described above.

neo-liberal economic policies of the Bank,[102] and hence these criticisms can be associated with the broader 'anti-globalisation' movements evident since the late-1990s in trade policy arenas. For these critics, efforts to mainstream gender into the Bank's activities are neutralised by the Bank itself: 'Gender analysis is increasingly reduced to technical and sectoral matters and is not used as a political tool for women's emancipation and empowerment. Similarly, some of the central concepts of feminist analyses have been hijacked and "neutralised" to maintain the status quo of economic power relations.'[103] These radical critics deny any potential of the World Bank to deliver meaningful change and raise now-familiar anxieties about, on the one hand, the transformative potential of gender mainstreaming[104] and, on the other, the international legal response to globalisation, however it is defined and portrayed.[105]

Conclusions

This paper has attempted to sketch out potential foundations of a feminist critique of international economic law. Orthodox legal analysis suggests that trade law, in particular, need not concern itself with questions of gender equality and the situation of women because these can be dealt with by states, where appropriate, relying on areas of national autonomy and exceptions under WTO law. Feminist scholarship, on the other hand, suggests that the very construction 'international (public)/national (private)' de-legitimises the pursuit of gender-based claims in international forums and renders less likely meaningful international action on gender issues. Drawing on feminist critiques in economic and development studies, it can be argued that international institutions concerned with trade and development should be held to account for their records on gender issues.

Moreover, as this paper has shown, initiatives in other fields of international law support the need for such activity. Some success has been achieved by the World Bank in securing attention to gender issues, though criticisms remain both of the general normative framework (eg, *Comprehensive Development Framework*), through which social issues are seen as subordinate to macro-economic issues), and of

---

[102] See, eg, Z Randriamero, above n 99.

[103] *Ibid.*

[104] See, eg, F Beveridge and J Shaw (eds), 'Gender Mainstreaming in European Public Policy', Special Issue (2002) 10 *Feminist Legal Studies* 209.

[105] For a wide-ranging discussion see, eg, R Falk, 'Re-framing the Legal Agenda of World Order in the Course of a Turbulent Century' in M Likosky (ed), *Transnational Legal Processes: Globalisation and Power Disparities* (London, Butterworths, 2002) 355–77; A Orford, 'Contesting Globalization: A Feminist Perspective on the Future of Human Rights' (1998) 8 *Transnational Law and Contemporary Problems* 171.

the record of the Bank in ensuring effective implementation on the ground. This attention to gender issues in the Bank seems to be grounded in a widely accepted consensus that there are strong links between gender inequality and poverty. Indeed other international institutions with a poverty-focus share this concern with gender issues: both the Commonwealth Secretariat and the United Nations Development Programme, for example, appear to share the World Bank's commitment to address gender inequality through their work programmes.[106] On the other hand, gender advocates paid little attention, until relatively recently, to the WTO and its trade rules. In turn, little or no effort has been made by the WTO to address gender concerns in any areas of trade law or policy. Despite clear evidence of the differential impact of trade policies on men and women, and the links drawn in documents such as the Platform for Action between macro-economic policies and the advancement of women, the economic/social dichotomy in international trade law remains intact. This dichotomy may be bolstered by the systematic structuring of international trade law, whereby economic (or trade) issues are the subject of binding international norms whereas social concerns are largely to be pursued at the domestic level, within the parameters established by the WTO agreements.

In particular, the WTO seems singularly to lag behind other international institutions and states in its failure to adopt any commitment to pursue gender mainstreaming, or even to promote the participation of women in its institutions and processes. While evidence from other institutions suggests that a mere commitment to mainstreaming will not ensure its success, such a move would at least legitimise the raising of concerns about the impact of trade policies on the advancement of women, and signal to NGOs and others that the WTO was ready to accept responsibilities in this regard.

This leaves open the question of what specific issues might be included in a gender agenda for the WTO. In 1999, WEDO suggested that items to be addressed were: mandating the inclusion of women and gender in economic decision-making and governance; strengthening women's capacity to attain economic equity; protecting women's control over their health and safety; and preventing transnational corporations' exploitation of women's indigenous knowledge and plant genetic resources.[107] The European Women's Lobby similarly makes a number of recommendations regarding international trade, including the promotion of legislative and administrative reforms to give women equal rights with men to economic resources; action to eliminate pay discrimination and to re-evaluate wages in sectors dominated by women; the introduction of a social clause targeted at companies covering freedom of association, minimum wages, discrimination, maternity leave and worker consultation; childcare and access to sexual and reproductive health

---

[106] Commonwealth Secretariat, *Handbook on Gender Mainstreaming in Poverty Eradication and the Millenium Development Goals* (London, Commonwealth Secretariat, 2003); UNDP, *Transforming the Mainstream: Gender in UNDP* (New York, UNDP, 2003).

[107] WEDO Primer, above n 70; see also the recommendations made by the European Women's Lobby.

education.[108] More recently the UN Task Force has identified specific issues relating to the Agreement for Agriculture, the Agreement on TRIMs, the Agreement on Subsidies, the GATS and the Agreement on TRIPs, where some 'adaptation' of the rules may be appropriate.[109] These contributions, taken together, demonstrate what is clear from the range of materials already cited in this chapter: that there are many possible candidate 'topics' for inclusion in such an agenda. Some of these items call into question the content or operation of specific WTO agreements such as the GATS,[110] the SPS Agreement[111] or the Agreement on TRIPs;[112] others suggest the need for more systematic attention to gender concerns throughout the WTO's activities.[113] This broader policy agenda intersects both with other WTO-specific policy agendas, such as the on-going debate about the inclusion of 'trade-and' issues under the WTO's auspices[114] and the question of WTO–NGO relations,[115] and with gender perspectives developed in other institutional contexts which carry resonance within the WTO, such as the need to systematise the collection and analysis of gendered statistics,[116] and the need to promote balanced participation in decision-making.[117] Thus it is also clear that the 'field' of gender and trade is open-ended.[118]

---

[108] European Women's Lobby, 'Engendering International Trade: Gender Equality in a Global World', available at <www.womenlobby.org>. This is a wide-ranging document and the scope of its recommendations is often unclear, in particular to whom they are addressed.

[109] *Trade and Gender*, above n 16, at 306–18.

[110] The GATS has been portrayed as posing a threat to education and health provision, particularly in developing countries: see, eg, J Hilary, *The Wrong Model: GATS, Trade Liberalisation and Children's Right to Health* (London, Save the Children, 2001); for an alternative view see MG Bloche, 'WTO Deference to National Health Policy: Towards an Interpretive Principle' (2002) 5 *Journal of International Economic Law* 825.

[111] Eg, in relation to the balancing of national policy concerns against the principle of non-discrimination in international trade.

[112] Eg, in ensuring due recognition of indigenous knowledge in the patenting process.

[113] See also M Williams, above, at n 13.

[114] Above nn 61–62 and related text.

[115] See further DC Esty, 'Non-Governmental Organisations at the World Trade Organisation: Co-operation, Competition or Exclusion' (1998) 1 *Journal of International Economic Law* 123; JL Dunoff, 'The Misguided Debate over NGO Participation at the WTO' (1998) 1 *Journal of International Economic Law* 433; G Marceau and PN Pedersen, 'Is the WTO Open and Transparent? A Discussion of the Relationship of the WTO with Non-Governmental Organisations and Civil Society's Claims for More Transparency and Public Participation' (1999) 33(1) *Journal of World Trade* 5.

[116] See eg the UNESCO Report, *Follow-up to, and Progress in the Implementation of, the Beijing Declaration and Platform for Action and the Outcome of the Twenty-Third Special Session of the General Assembly*, UN ECOSOC E/2003/; UNDP, *Transforming the Mainstream*, above n 106, at 19. Discussing the Millennium Development Goals, this report concludes that gender is not specifically mainstreamed in the targets and indicators established to monitor progress towards the Goals.

[117] For European Community materials on gender balance in decision-making, see <http://europa.eu.int/comm/employment_social/equ_opp/decision_en.html> (last accessed 28 September 2004); on the Council of Europe, see J Lovecy, 'Gender Mainstreaming and the Framing of Women's Rights in Europe: The Contribution of the Council of Europe' (2002) 10 *Feminist Legal Studies* 271. On the UNDP, see *Transforming the Mainstream*, above n 106, ch 2; UNDP, *Women's Political Participation and Good Governance: 21st Century Challenges* (New York, UNDP, 2000).

[118] Academic contributions include UU Ewelukwa, 'Women and International Economic Law: An Annotated Bibliography' (2002) 8 *Law and Business Review of the Americas* 603; E McGill, 'Poverty and Social Analysis of Trade Agreements: A More Coherent Approach?' (2004) 27 *Boston College International and Comparative Law Review* 371.

But however constituted, any feminist agenda for the WTO will be founded on anxieties about the possibility of meaningful intervention and on doubts about the utility of any such endeavours.[119] This contribution has sought to cast light on the paucity of feminist interventions in international economic law to date, and to explore potential foundations for feminist critiques of international economic law. Some structural features of trade law have been identified which make feminist interventions at the WTO difficult, and the viability of feminist claims may be challenged for this reason. By contrast, gender concerns have achieved greater attention in the World Bank and other 'poverty-centred' institutions, where economists and development activists have done much to document the link between poverty and gender. However, there is no consensus on the success of those interventions.

The institutions and practices of international economic institutions are coming under increased scrutiny, and there is significant overlap between the concerns raised by feminist scholars in political science, international relations, development studies and international law. Non-legal and interdisciplinary approaches have much to offer to scholars of international economic law seeking to grapple with these issues.

---

[119] A Orford, above n 105; A Orford, 'Feminism, Imperialism and the Mission of International Law' (2002) 71 *Nordic Journal of International Law* 275; R Buchanan and S Pahuja, above n 11; S Rai, 'Engendered Development in a Global Age?' (Centre for the Study of Globalisation and Regionalisation, University of Warwick, Working Paper No 20/98, 1998).

10

Transcending the Conquest of Nature and Women: A Feminist Perspective on International Environmental Law

ANNIE ROCHETTE[*]

Introduction

Since the early 1900s, the international community has negotiated hundreds of bilateral and multilateral agreements to deal with different aspects of environmental protection.[1] Three major world conferences, Stockholm in 1972,[2] Rio in 1992[3] and Johannesburg in 2002,[4] have also brought international attention to global environmental issues, such as the loss of biodiversity, global climate change, the thinning of the ozone layer, the depletion of soils and freshwater supplies, and the pollution of the oceans. Despite the adoption of hundreds of environmental instruments, the health of the planet is rapidly declining, and with it the health of all species inhabiting it, including humans.[5] A number of global challenges continue to face humankind at the start of the twenty-first century. Widespread poverty,

[*] Assistant Professor at the Faculty of Law, University of British Columbia. The author wishes to express her greatest thanks to the editors Doris Buss and Ambreena Manji for their patience and insightful suggestions in the many revisions of this chapter.

[1] See generally E Brown-Weiss, 'International Environmental Law: Contemporary Issues and the Emergence of a New World Order' (1993) 81 *Georgetown Law Journal* 675, at 679.

[2] 'Report of the United Nations Conference on the Human Environment' (Stockholm, 5–16 June 1972), <http://www.unep.org/Documents/Default.asp?DocumentID=97> (25 May 2004).

[3] 'Report of United Nations Conference on Environment and Development' (Rio de Janeiro, 3–14 June 1992), UN Doc A/CONF 151/26 (Vol. I), <http://www.un.org/documents/ga/conf151/aconf15126-1annex1.htm> (25 May 2004) (UNCED).

[4] 'Report of the World Summit on Sustainable Development' (Johannesburg, 26 August–4 September 2002), UN Doc A/CONF 199/20, <http://www.johannesburgsummit.org/html/documents/documents .html> (25 May 2004) (WSSD).

[5] For a summary of declining environmental and humanity conditions, see generally Commission on Sustainable Development acting as the preparatory committee for the World Summit on Sustainable Development, 'Implementing Agenda 21: Report of the Secretary-General' (19 December 2001), 2nd Session, UN Doc E/CN 17/2002/PC 2/7 (Implementing Agenda 21). For a statement of global environmental conditions, see UNEP, *Global Environmental Outlook 3: Past, Present and Future Perspectives* (London, Earthscan, 2002). See also the yearly WorldWatch Institute, *State of the World* reports (NY, WW Norton & Company).

epidemics of diseases such as cancer, malaria and HIV/AIDS, an increase in the number and intensity of natural disasters, and the continuing destruction of our environment attest to the fact that humanity is pushing the limits of the earth's capacity in unsustainable ways.[6] The impacts of this decline are not evenly distributed, however. Other species, as well as women and the very poor, are feeling most of the consequences of over-production, over-consumption, pollution and the loss of biological diversity.[7]

In this chapter, I argue that international environmental law, the body of international law developed to address environmental problems,[8] is not equipped to deal with these challenges. In fact, the structures and assumptions of international environmental law enable the continuing decline of the planet and the continued marginalisation of women, the poor and all 'others'. I also show that feminist engagement with this body of international law can help to expose and challenge some of its underlying assumptions, and can suggest alternative frameworks for global environmental action.

This chapter is divided into three main parts. I begin by outlining the history of feminist engagement with environmental protection at the global level. In the second section, I trace what I see as the impacts of women's activism on the agreements and documents adopted at the 1992 Rio Conference on Environment and Development (UNCED) and subsequent global meetings. International environmental instruments adopted since the early 1990s have recognised both the gendered impacts of environmental degradation and the importance of including a gender politics in environmental protection. Despite this formal recognition, I will argue in the third and main part of this chapter that international environmental law remains problematic for women and for the protection of the global environment.

Reading international environmental law through a gendered lens reveals a number of difficulties with this area of law and its ability to address persistent environmental problems. First, I maintain that international agreements tend to be consensual documents, whose formal legal status is devalued within a (gendered) state system that distinguishes between hard and soft law. The result is that provisions designed to address some of the root causes of environmental problems are off-set by the much 'harder' legal recognition of a state's sovereign right to exploit its resources.

---

[6] See generally G Gardner, 'The Challenge for Johannesburg: Creating a More Secure World' in WorldWatch Institute, *State of the World 2002* (NY, WW Norton & Company, 2002) 3.

[7] See generally C Flavin, 'Rich Planet, Poor Planet' in WorldWatch Institutute, *State of the World 2001* (NY, WW Norton & Company, 2001) 3. For a statement of economic and environmental impacts on developing countries, see UNGA, Cocoyoc Declaration adopted by the participants in the UNEP/UNCTAD Symposium on 'Patterns of Resource Use, Environment and Development Strategies' (1 November 1974), 29th Session, 2nd Committee, UN Doc A/C 2/292.

[8] According to Birnie and Boyle, international environmental law is nothing more, nothing less than the application of international law to environmental problems. However, as environmental protection is increasingly intertwined with sustainable development, I also include in this body of law those instruments related to sustainable development: see PW Birnie and AE Boyle, *International Law and the Environment* (Oxford, Oxford University Press, 2002) at 2.

Second, I argue that because these provisions rely on a liberal equality paradigm, they do not address the structural barriers to women's participation in environmental decision-making. Finally, despite the inclusion of gender concerns, international environmental instruments leave intact the masculinist institutions that exploit the environment and marginalise women and all 'others'; in fact, international environmental law privileges the role of these institutions in achieving environmental protection. In conclusion, I will try to show that despite the limited success of women's lobbying efforts during the negotiation of environmentally related instruments in challenging the dominant masculinist institutions, and despite the dangers that essentialism presents in any concerted effort at the global level, the value of feminist critiques of these institutions is crucial and must continue.

Feminist Engagement with Global Environmental Protection

Surprisingly, international environmental law has not, to date, been the subject of sustained feminist analysis. At the grassroots level, however, women have been involved locally in environmental movements in order to protect the survival base of their families and communities.[9] While often important vehicles for women's political mobilisation, these grassroots movements do not necessarily reflect a 'feminist' commitment to environmental protection.[10]

Women are also attracted by and involved in the environmental movement, but they act mostly as volunteers or work in lower-level administrative positions; women comprise only a small portion of top-level management of large environmental organisations such as Greenpeace, Sierra Club or the National Wildlife Federation.[11] These large organisations have experienced increased 'professionalisation', characterised by corporate structures, slick communication strategies, professional management and lobbying.[12] As Joni Seager explains, professionalisation 'shifts the balance of power to men, it entrenches male prerogative, and

---

[9] Famous examples include the Chipko movement in India and the Green Belt movement in Kenya: for details on these and others, see R Braidotti et al, *Women, the Environment and Sustainable Development: Towards a Theoretical Synthesis* (London, Zed Books, 1994) at 77, 97–98 ; M Mellor, *Feminism and Ecology* (Cambridge, Polity Press, 1997), ch 2; P Philipose, 'Women Act: Women and Environmental Protection in India' in J Plant (ed), *Healing the Wounds: The Promise of Ecofeminism* (London, Green Press, 1994) 67 ; C Campbell, 'Out on the Front Lines but Still Struggling for Voice: Women in the Rubber Tappers' Defense of the Forest in Xapuri Acre, Brazil' in D Rocheleau, B Thomas-Slayter and E Wangari (eds), *Feminist Political Ecology: Global Issues and Local Experiences* (London, Routledge, 1996) 27.

[10] M Mellor, above n 9, at 29, citing B Agarwal, 'The Gender and Environment Debate: Lessons from India' (1992) 18 *Feminist Studies* 119 and C Jackson, 'Radical Environmental Myths: A Gender Perspective' (1995) 210 *New Left Review* 124.

[11] J Seager, *Earth Follies: Coming to Feminist Terms with the Global Environmental Crisis* (New York, Routledge, 1993).

[12] *Ibid*, at 185–94.

privileges masculine values and priorities at the top of the hierarchy'.[13] Professionalisation has thus widened the gap within the environmental move-ment between the 'mostly *male*-led professional elite and a mostly *female*-led grassroots movement'.[14] As Mary Mellor explains in the following passage, the result is that environmental movements do not often consider, let alone represent, women's interests:

> Women may be present in large numbers in the green movement, but sex/gender issues are not central to the (malestream) green political agenda. In a patriarchal soci-ety, failure to recognize the interests, experience and needs of women must mean that the values and experiences of men will determine the direction of green politics by default ... Evidence that women's contribution to green politics is being marginalized can be found in the male domination of green literature. Women's input into green thinking is becoming ghettoized into ecofeminism, rather than being at the core.[15]

Feminists have also been wary of the mainstream environmental position that population growth is a major threat to the global environment.[16] In the 1970s, publications such as the *The Population Bomb*[17] or *Limits to Growth*[18] pointed the finger at population growth in the South as one of the main causes of global environmental problems. Most American development programs were then tied closely with population control measures.[19] Even today, the link between population and environmental degradation continues to be part of mainstream environmen-talism,[20] although the approach to reduce population growth has shifted to

---

[13] *Ibid*, at 186. See also M Mellor, above n 9, ch 6; R Teverson, *Survival of the Fairest: Can Women Make it to the Top in the Conservation Movement?* (Newbury, British Association of Nature Conservationists, 1991).

[14] M Mellor, above n 9.

[15] *Ibid*, at 128–29.

[16] Braidotti et al note this fierce disagreement between feminists and environmentalists in the con-text of the United Nations Conference on Environment and Development (UNCED): see R Braidotti et al, above n 9, at 89; see also G Sen, 'Women, Poverty and Population: Issues for the Concerned Environmentalist' in W Harcourt (ed), *Feminist Perspectives on Sustainable Development* (London, Zed Books, 1994) 215.

[17] PR Ehrlich, *The Population Bomb* (NY, Ballantine Books, 1971).

[18] DH Meadows et al, *The Limits to Growth: A Report for the Club of Rome's Project on the Predicament of Mankind* (NY, Universe Books, 1972).

[19] M Mellor, above n 9, at 31. The 1987 Brundtland Report establishes a causal relationship between population growth, environment and economic development: high population growth rates stall eco-nomic development, and contribute to environmental degradation and reduced land mass; economic development, on the other hand, is necessary in order to decrease fertility: see World Commission on Environment and Development, *Our Common Future* (Oxford, Oxford University Press, 1987), com-monly referred to as the Brundtland Report, named after the Chair of the Commission, Gro Harlem Brundtland.

[20] A recent example is a publication by a major environmental watch dog, the WorldWatch Institute. See LR Brown, *Eco-Economy: Building an Economy for the Earth* (NY, WW Norton & Company, 2001), which devotes an entire chapter to 'stabilizing population by reducing fertility'. See also the environ-ment and security literature, including JT Matthews, 'Redefining Security' (1989) 68 *Foreign Affairs* 163, TF Homer-Dixon, 'The Project on Environment, Population and Security: Key Findings of Research' in Wilson Center, *Environmental Change and Security Project Report* (1996).

empowering women by giving them access to education and resources.[21] Feminists have criticised this causal equation, pointing instead to over-consumption in the North, colonial and post-colonial histories of developing countries, agribusiness and other large-scale commercial exploitation of resources as causes of environmental degradation.[22] Betsy Hartmann argues that the link between population growth and environmental degradation continues to be part of environmental discourse because it serves the current neoliberal interests:

> Neo-Malthusianism—the belief that rapid population growth is a major cause of poverty, environmental degradation, and political instability—dovetails nicely with the ideology of social and natural scarcity and has proved very compatible with neoliberalism's emphasis on the free market and dismantling of the social welfare functions of the state. It is not surprising that occupies such an important place in the environment and security framework.[23]

As a policy area, the environment is additionally uncomfortable for feminists because of its apparent privileging of 'nature', which, for some feminists, is too suggestive of an innate biological destiny for men and women. As Seager explains, the woman/nature issue is a 'thorny one for feminists',[24] who have been cautious about being identified too closely with 'nature' in advocating for environmental protection.[25] In their role as environmental advocates, feminists may be seen as reinforcing, rather than challenging, women's presumed roles as 'keepers' of nature. Additionally, environmental advocacy may feel dangerously close to the 'biological determinism' precipice that feminist theory has struggled so hard to keep at a distance.[26] The main concern related to a woman/nature connection is thus its implicit essentialism. Early feminists argued that the woman/nature connection, a male culturally constructed concept, was used to justify the continued oppression of women and exploitation of nature.[27]

On the other hand, ecofeminists have celebrated the woman/nature connection. Whether based on biology, culture, spirituality or from their twin oppression by patriarchal institutions such as capitalism, the connection between women and nature is an important framework for mobilising an environmental politics. On the surface, then, there appears to be a rift within feminism, with ecofeminists standing apart from other streams in feminist theory in its reliance on the presumed

---

[21] M Mellor, above n 9, at 31.

[22] See, eg, B Hartmann, 'Population, Environment and Security: A New Trinity' in J Silliman and Y King (eds), *Feminist Perspectives on Population, Environment and Development* (Cambridge MA, South End Press, 1999); G Sen, above n 16; H Moss, 'Consumption and Fertility' in W Harcourt, above n 16, at 238.

[23] B Hartmann, above n 22 at 3.

[24] J Seager, above n 11, at 176–81.

[25] *Ibid*, at 242–43. See also R Braidotti et al, above n 9, ch 4, which discusses different feminist views on the woman/nature connection.

[26] See J Seager, above n 11, at 10–12; R Braidotti et al, above n 9 at 98.

[27] J Seager, *ibid*; R Braidotti, *ibid*. See, eg, S De Beauvoir, *Le Deuxième Sexe* (Paris, Gallimard, 1949); J Biehl, *Finding Our Way: Rethinking Ecofeminist Politics* (Montreal, Black Rose Books, 1991).

nexus between the feminine and the natural. In my opinion, this rift is based on misconceptions of ecofeminist theories, which have not been given credit for moving beyond the cultural ecofeminist view that women and nature are biologically connected[28] to a position that reveals, among other things, the 'connections between how one treats women, people of color, and the underclass on one hand and how one treats the nonhuman natural environment on the other'.[29] This connection offers important insights into the limitations of an international environmental law that endeavours to define itself in distinction from the broad social, economic and political conditions through which we come to understand environmental 'problems'.

While reluctant to engage directly in environmental politics, feminist activists[30] and academics[31] have been extensively involved in challenging the mainstream development model that predominated in international policy circles from the 1970s and throughout the 1980s and 1990s. It is mostly through their critique of a development model based on scientific knowledge, industrial technology and the capitalist market economy that feminist attention was drawn to global environmental issues.[32] According to M Patricia Connelly et al, feminist scholarship and engagement with development has taken one of three conceptual forms: the 'Women in Development' (WID) model which dominated in the 1970s, the 'Women and Development' (WAD) or radical feminist approach, and the Gender and Development approach(GAD), which emerged as an alternative to the other two approaches in the late 1980s.[33] The Women, Environment and Development, and later the Women, Environment and Sustainable Development themes developed within those conceptual frameworks.

In the 1970s, Women in Development (WID) researchers such as Esther Boserup[34] showed that women in developing countries were not benefiting from development programmes; in fact, these programmes contributed to the deterioration of women's lives and status vis-à-vis men.[35] These feminists also pointed

---

[28] Examples of cultural ecofeminists include the work of Mary Daly and the early work of Susan Griffin: see M Daly, *Gyn/Ecology: The Metaethics of Radical Feminism* (London, The Women's Press, 1991); S Griffin, *Women and Nature: The Roaring Inside Her* (New York, Harper & Row, 1978).

[29] KJ Warren, 'Introduction' in K Warren (ed), *Ecofeminism: Women, Culture, Nature* (Bloomington, Indiana University Press, 1997) xi, at xi.

[30] See, eg, G Sen and C Grown, *Development, Crises and Alternative Visions: Third World Women's Perspectives* (NY, Monthly Review Press,1987), a report by DAWN (Development Alternatives with Women for a New Era); V Shiva, *Staying Alive: Women, Ecology and Development* (London, Zed Books, 1989); W Maathai, *The Green Belt Movement* (Nairobi, The Movement, 1988); women's groups in this category include Women's Environmental Network, DAWN.

[31] See, eg, E Boserup, *Woman's Role in Economic Development* (NY, St-Martin's Press, 1970); I Dankelman and J Davidson, *Women and Environment in the Third World-Alliance for the Future* (London, Earthscan, 1988).

[32] M Mellor, above n 9, at 26.

[33] MP Connelly, T Murray Li, M MacDonald and JL Parpart, 'Feminism and Development: Theoretical Perspectives' in JL Parpart, MP Connelly and VE Barriteau (eds), *Theoretical Perspectives in Gender and Development* (Ottawa, International Development Research Centre, 2000) 51.

[34] E Boserup, above n 31.

[35] R Braidotti et al, above n 9, at 78–79.

out that women's contribution to the productive sector (mostly agriculture) was largely ignored by development discourse and projects.[36] Within development agencies and programmes, WID was translated into giving women access to training and resources in order to ensure their full integration into economic development.[37] However, the WID approach did not question the mainstream development model, or address the fundamental causes of women's subordination.[38] As a result, a radical feminist approach to WID developed, which called for women's development projects to be completely separate from men's. This perspective, also referred to as the 'Women AND Development' (WAD) approach according to Connelly et al, argued for a recognition of the distinctiveness of women's work, knowledge, goals and responsibilities, and of the special role that women could play in the development process.[39] As these authors explain, the theorising of this approach was not well documented as its proponents were mostly occupied with activism.[40]

Starting in the late 1980s, the Gender and Development (GAD)perspective began to emerge as an alternative to both WID and WAD. This shifted the focus from women's participation as a way to make development more efficient and effective to one where development initiatives could transform unequal social and gender relations and empower women.[41] This approach emerged both from the grassroots experiences of Third World feminists[42] and from the analysis of Western socialist feminists interested in development. As Connelly et al explain, GAD examines the 'interconnection of gender, class and race and the social construction of their defining characteristics',[43] recognises the different impacts of development on men and women, and thus challenges both gender relations and the development process itself.[44] It is within these conceptual frameworks that the Women, Environment and Development (WED) (and later the Women, Environment and Sustainable Development) theme emerged.

The WED debate started from within environment-related development fields, such as agriculture and forestry, where environmental degradation most impacted

---

[36] *Ibid*; see also K Saunders, 'Introduction: Towards a Deconstructive Post-Development Criticism' in K Saunders (ed), *Feminist Post-Development Thought: Rethinking Modernity, Post-Colonialism and Representation* (NY, Zed Books, 2002) at 5–6.

[37] K Saunders, *ibid*.

[38] MP Connelly et al, above n 33, at 58–59.

[39] *Ibid*, at 60.

[40] *Ibid*.

[41] R Braidotti et al, above n 9, at 82–83.

[42] MP Connelly et al, above n 33, include feminists such as those involved in Development Alternatives with Women for a New Era (DAWN) within the GAD perspective. But see R Braidotti et al, who qualify these Third World Feminists as separate and critical of both the WID and GAD approaches for failing to challenge the dominant development paradigm: see R Braidotti et al, above n 9, at 82–83.

[43] MP Connelly et al, above n 33, at 63.

[44] *Ibid*. But see R Braidotti et al, above n 9, at 82–83, who describe GAD an an approach mainly used in development agencies, and critique Leach and GAD generally for neglecting to consider international economic processes in the ecological crisis and for failing to question the development model.

women.[45] At the same time, the stories of women's grassroots environmental actions such as the Chipko movement were circulating in international environmental circles, starting with the 1972 Stockholm Conference on the Human Environment.[46] According to Braidotti et al, the WED theme thus includes 'all women's interrelations with the environment in the context of economic development as well as all the effects that environmental degradation has had upon women's lives.'[47]

In the early 1980s, the WED literature portrayed women as victims of environmental degradation, with images of women struggling to find fuel and food in barren landscapes.[48] Gradually, this image shifted to one of women in developing countries as the main users and managers of environmental resources. Their daily experiences involving them closely with their environment, women were recognised as having extensive knowledge of environmental resources.[49] According to WED literature in the late 1980s and beyond, women's interests were thus intertwined with those of environmental protection programmes.[50] As in the WID context, the WED theme was mainstreamed in the development and environmental contexts into guiding principles where women were to be incorporated into environmental programmes and policies. As Green, Joekes and Leach explain, the inclusion of women was 'to ensure both that women benefit directly from environmental projects, and that projects are not undermined by the exclusion of women, who are the primary environmental resource management agents'.[51]

The publication of the 1987 Brundtland Report[52] crystallised the shift in discourse in international policy from environmental protection to sustainable development.[53] Although the Brundtland Report makes no mention of gender, its impact was felt in feminist development circles, with the theme of WED giving way to Women, Environment and Sustainable Development. This shift in discourse was additionally manifested at the institutional level, with the United Nations Environment Program (UNEP) creating the Senior Women's Advisory

---

[45] R Braidotti et al, above n 9, at 78.

[46] In 1988, Irene Dankelman and Joan Davidson published their book, above n 31, in which they presented cases of women's environmental activities in developing countries.

[47] R Braidotti et al, above n 9, at 78. Braidotti et al include in this debate both WED and GED (Gender and Environment). On the other hand, Green et al distinguish between these, as WID and GAD are distinguished: see C Green, S Joekes and M Leach, "Questionable Links: Approaches to Gender in Environmental Research and Policy' in C Jackson and R Pearson (eds), *Feminist Visions of Development: Gender Analysis and Policy* (London, Routledge, 1998) at 272–76.

[48] C Green et al, above n 47 at 272.

[49] *Ibid*, at 271–72.

[50] *Ibid*.

[51] *Ibid*.

[52] Brundtland Report, above n 19.

[53] Sustainable Development was first codified in the 1980 *World Conservation Strategy*, commissioned by the UNEP and prepared by the IUCN (International Union for the Conservation of Nature): IUCN, UNEP and WWF, *World Conservation Strategy: Living Resources Conservation for Sustainable Development* (Gland, Switzerland, IUCN, 1980). The concept was further developed and defined in the Brundtland Report, above n 19.

Group on Sustainable Development in 1984, which was instrumental in the inclusion of provisions dealing with women and environment in the context of development into the 1985 Nairobi Forward-looking Strategies.[54] In UN agencies such as UNEP, FAO,[55] UNIFEM[56] and INSTRAW,[57] women working on environmental issues related to women focused on their participation in programmes aimed at sustainable development.

During the 1980s, there was also considerable growth of women's movements in the South that were critical of the dominant development model.[58] Development Alternatives with Women for a New Era (DAWN),[59] a group of women researchers from the South, held its first meeting in 1984. With the publication of its report *Development, Crises and Alternative Visions*,[60] DAWN helped to change the image that predominated in development discourse of the poor Third World woman with too many children using too much fuel and thus destroying her environment, to one where women from developing countries were portrayed as privileged knowers of environmental processes and environmental managers. Critical of the WID approach, which aimed to include women into development, DAWN challenged the mainstream development model based on industrial technology and economic growth in a capitalist global market.[61] In 1989, Vandana Shiva published her landmark book *Staying Alive,* in which she argued for an alternative development model based on subsistence agriculture. [62] However, it was not until the preparatory process for UNCED that DAWN activists fully incorporated a 'women and environment' perspective.[63]

DAWN argued the poor have the greatest stake in environmental protection for their immediate survival. This viewpoint framed the ecological problem as arising from practices of global economic growth accompanied by state collusion with capital in export-oriented production, and over-consumption of resources and

[54] UNGA, The Nairobi Forward-looking Strategies for the Advancement of Women Adopted by the World Conference to review and appraise the achievements of the United Nations Decade for Women: Equality, Development and Peace (Nairobi, 15–25 July 1985), <http://www.un.org/womenwatch/confer/nfls/> (25 May 2004).

[55] Food and Agriculture Organisation, Women and Sustainable Development programmes at <http://www.fao.org/sd/pe1_en.htm> (25 May 2004).

[56] United Nations Development Fund for Women: <http://www.unifem.org> (25 May 2004) .

[57] United Nations International Training and Research Institute for the Advancement of Women has a project entitled 'Gender Aspects of Resource Management and Sustainable Development', <http://www.un-instraw.org/en/research/gaemsd/index.html> (25 May 2004).

[58] R Braidotti et al, above n 9, at 81. But see Green et al, who describe DAWN and the writings of these Third World feminists as part of the GAD perspective described above: see above n 47.

[59] DAWN is a group of women researchers from the South, who were critical of the dominant development model and proposed alternative development models. DAWN is still an important voice in the sustainable development debate. See DAWN website for more information on this organisation, access to their newsletter and publications: <http://www.dawn.org.fj/> (25 May 2004).

[60] G Sen and C Grown, above n 30.

[61] M Mellor, above n 9, at 32–33.

[62] V Shiva, above n 30.

[63] M Mellor, above n 9, at 33, citing R Wiltshire, *Environment and Development: Grassroots Women's Perspective* (Barbados, DAWN, 1992).

goods by élites from the North and South. There was a demand for a sustainable development that is locally controlled, affirmative of civil rights and of material, spiritual and socio-cultural well-being. DAWN enunciated a claim that the poor and women in the South have the best knowledge of their local environments, problems, needs and solutions. This is the basis of a demand for the inclusion of women in environmental decision-making and management.[64]

With the joining together of development critics, feminists, women environmentalists and ecofeminists, representing both North and South, the Women, Environment and Sustainable Development debate gained momentum at the international level during the preparatory process for the 1992 United Nations Conference on Environment and Development (UNCED).[65] The presence of women's organisations at UNCED in 1992 was unprecedented in the environmental context.[66] Despite the diversity of women involved in the women's movements, the networks of women activists involved worldwide in the UNCED process adopted at *Planeta Femea* (the forum of women's NGOs held parallel to UNCED) the Women's Action Agenda 21,[67] a common vision for sustainable, people-centered and peaceful development process.[68] In this document, women's groups challenged the Western development model and blamed the 'global economic military and industrial system based on economic growth and a free market ideology as the root cause of the problem'.[69]

Women's organisations were also involved in the preparatory process for the 2002 World Summit on Sustainable Development (WSSD)[70] and again presented a unified position contained in the Women's Agenda for a Healthy and Peaceful Planet 2015.[71] Ten years after UNCED, this document contains the same principles as the Women's Action Agenda 21, but reflects the reality of the late 1990s of economic globalisation, neoliberal politics and global insecurity.[72]

---

[64] K Saunders, above n 36, at 17. See also R Wiltshire, above n 63.

[65] R Braidotti et al, above n 9 at 77; J Seager, above n 11, at 10–11; K Saunders, above n 36, at 16.

[66] K Saunders, above n 36, at 16–18. Also important to note is that until the UNCED preparatory process, women had not been an explicit concern within the governmental preparations, although they were active in the NGO preparatory process: R Braidotti et al, above n 9, at 90–91.

[67] Women's Action Agenda 21, adopted at the NGO parallel conference to UNCED (June 1992), <http://www.iisd.org/women/action21.htm> (25 May 2004).

[68] Women organised two major events leading up to and during the UNCED Process: World Congress for a Healthy Planet, Miami, 1991 and *Planeta Femea*, taking place during the parallel NGO forum at UNCED in 1992. See R Braidotti et al, above n 9, at 102–104, for a description of these events.

[69] R Braidotti et al, above n 9, at 5.

[70] The World Summit on Sustainable Development was the 10-year follow-up conference to UNCED. It was held in Johannesburg, South Africa, in September of 2002. The instruments adopted at this UN conference include the non-binding Political Declaration and Plan of Implementation for Sustainable Development: see WSSD Report, above n 4.

[71] WEDO (Women, Environment and Development Organisation), Women's Action Agenda for Healthy and Peaceful Planet 2015: A Decade of Women's Advocacy for Sustainable Development, <http://www.wedo.org/sus_dev/waa1.htm> (25 May 2004).

[72] The five pillars of this action plan are: peace and human rights, globalisation and sustainability, access and control of resources for women, environmental security and health, and governance for sustainable development.

The strong lobbying by women's organisations resulted in the inclusion of gender concerns into international environmental law, starting with some of the instruments adopted at UNCED,[73] as well as other environmental instruments adopted in the 1990s,[74] leading up to WSSD in 2002. Provisions relating to women and environment or sustainable development are also found in agreements reached at related world conferences on population (Cairo, 1994),[75] social development (Copenhagen, 1995),[76] habitat (Istanbul, 1996),[77] food (Rome, 1996)[78] and women (Beijing 1995),[79] as well as their follow-up conferences.[80]

[73] The binding agreements adopted at UNCED include: the Convention on Biological Diversity (adopted 5 June 1992, entered in force 29 December 1993), 1760 UNTS 79, (1992) 31 *International Legal Materials* 818 (Biodiversity Convention), the United Nations Framework Convention on Climate Change (adopted 9 May 1992, entered in force 21 March 1994), 1771 UNTS 107, (1992) 31 *International Legal Materials* 849 (UNFCC), although the latter makes no mention of gender. The non-binding instruments include the non-legally binding Authoritative Statement of Principles for a Global Consensus on the Management, Conservation and Sustainable Development of All Types of Forests (signed 13 June 1992), UN Doc A/CONF 48/14, (1992) 31 *International Legal Materials* 882 (Forest Principles), the Rio Declaration on Environment and Development (signed 13 June 1992), UN Doc A/CONF 151/5/Rev 1, (1992) 31 *International Legal Materials* 876 (Rio Declaration), and Agenda 21: Programme for Action for Sustainable Development (signed 14 June 1992), UN Doc A/CONF 151/26/Rev 1 (Vol I and III) (Agenda 21).

[74] Conventions adopted since UNCED that include provisions related to gender are: the United Nations Convention to Combat Desertification in Countries Experiencing Serious Drought and/or Desertification, Particularly in Africa (adopted 17 June 1994, entered in force 26 December 1996), 1954 UNTS 3, < http://www.unccd.int/convention/text/convention.php> (25 May 2004), (UNCCD), the Stockholm Convention on Persistent Organic Pollutants (signed 22 May 2001, entered in force 17 May 2004), UN Doc UNEP/POPS/CONF/4, (2001) 40 *International Legal Materials* 532,<http://www.pops.int>(25 May 2004) preamble, Arts 7(2), 10(1)(c) (POPs Convention). On the other hand, the following treaties do not include any provisions dealing with gender: the Cartagena Protocol on Biosafety (adopted 29 January 2000, entered in force 11 September 2003), (2000) 39 *International Legal Materials* 1027, <http://www.biodiv.org/ biosafety/protocol.asp> (25 May 2004)(Cartagena Protocol), the Kyoto Protocol to the United Nations Convention on Climate Change, (adopted 11 December 1997, not yet in force), (1998) 37 *International Legal Materials* 22, <http://unfccc.int/> (25 May 2004) (Kyoto Protocol) and the Rotterdam Convention on the Prior Informed Consent Procedure for Certain Hazardous Chemicals and Pesticides in International Trade (adopted 10 September 1998, entered in force 24 February 2004), (1999) 38 *International Legal Materials* 1, <http://www.pic.int/en/ViewPage.asp?id=104> (25 May 2004) (PIC Convention).

[75] Report of the International Conference on Population and Development (Cairo, 5–13 September 1994) (18 October 1994), UN Doc A/CONF 171/13, < http://www.un.org/popin/icpd/conference/offeng/poa.html> (25 May 2004)(Cairo). For an account of the impact of feminist activists' interventions at the Cairo Conference on Population and Development, see D Buss, 'Racing Populations, Sexing Environments: The Challenges of a Feminist Politics in International Law' (2000) 20 *Legal Studies* 463.

[76] Report of the World Summit for Social Development (Copenhagen, 6–12 March 1995) (19 April 1995), UN Doc A/CONF 166/9, <http://www.un.org/esa/socdev/wssd/documents/index.html> (25 May 2004).

[77] Report of the United Nations Conference on Human Settlements (Istanbul, 3–14 June 1996) (7 August 1996), UN Doc A/CONF 165/14, <http://www.unhabitat.org/istanbul+5/agenda.htm> (25 May 2004).

[78] Report of the World Food Summit (Rome, 13–17 November 1996), UN Doc WFS 96/Rep, <http://www.fao.org/wfs/index_en.htm> (25 May 2004).

[79] Report of the Fourth World Conference on Women (Beijing, 4–15 September 1995)(17 October 1995), UN Doc A/CONF 177/20, <http://www.un.org/womenwatch/daw/beijing/platform/ index.html> (30 April 2004)(FCWC); for details on women's groups' influence in the context of the Beijing Conference on Women, see D Otto, 'Holding Up Half the Sky, But for Whose Benefit?: A Critical Analysis of the Fourth World Conference on Women' (1996) 6 *Australian Feminist LLNN Law Journal* 7.

[80] UNGA, 'Report of the Secretary-General on the Twenty-Fourth Special Session of the General Assembly entitled 'World Summit for Social Development and Beyond: Achieving Social Development

As I discuss in the next section, a number of provisions in international environmental instruments reflect some of the concerns related to the environment put forward by women's groups such as the Women, Environment and Development Organisation (WEDO)[81] and DAWN, and recognise the important role that women can play in environmental protection and the achievement of sustainable development.

Including Gender in International Environmental Law

Perhaps because of the lack of pressure from women's groups on the global environmental agenda up until UNCED, international environmental agreements did not pay much attention to the gender dimensions of environmental protection. The early environmental agreements dealt mostly with fisheries,[82] specific species that needed protection or conservation,[83] or identifiable threats to the use of natural

for All in a Globalizing World" (Geneva, 26 June–1 July 2000)(1 September 2000), UN Doc A/55/344, <http://www.un.org/esa/socdev/geneva2000/documents/index.html> (26 May 2004) (Social Summit +5); UNGA, Report of the Secretary-General on the Twenty-Fifth Special Session of the General Assembly for an Overall Review and Appraisal of the Implementation of the Outcome of the United Nations Conference on Human Settlements (Habitat II) (Istanbul, 6–8 June 2001)(16 October 2001), UN Doc A/56/477, < http://www.unhabitat.org/istanbul+5/outcome.htm> (26 May 2004); UNGA, Report of the Ad Hoc Committee of the Whole of the Twenty-Third Special Session of the General Assembly, UN GAOR 23rd Special Session Supp No 3 UN Doc A/S-23/10/Rev 1 (2000), <http://www.un.org/womenwatch/daw/followup/reports.htm> (25 May 2004)(Beijing+5); Report of the World Food Summit: 5 Years Later (Rome, 10–13 June 2002), <http://www.fao.org/worldfood-summit/english/documents.htm> (26 May 2004).

[81] The Women, Environment and Development Organisation (WEDO) was involved in organising *Planeta Femea* and has, since UNCED, acted as the convenor for the Women's Caucus participating, as a major group, in the activities of the Commission on Sustainable Development, an ECOSOC body created after UNCED. See the Women's Caucus website: <http://www.earthsummit2002.org/wcaucus/Introduction/introduc.htm> (26 May 2004).

[82] See, eg, Agreement Concerning Measures for the Protection of the Stocks of Deep-Sea Prawns, European Lobsters, Norway Lobsters and Crabs (adopted 7 March 1952); Agreement on the Protection of the Salmon in the Baltic Sea, Stockholm, 1952; Convention Concerning Fishing in the Black Sea (Varna, 7 July 1959); Convention for the Conservation of the Salmon in the North Atlantic Ocean (Reykjavik) (adopted on 2 March 1982, entered in force 10 october 1983) [1982] OJ L378/25; Convention on Fishing and Conservation of the Living Resources in the Baltic Sea and the Belts (Gdansk, 13 September 1973), all available: <http://sedac.ciesin.columbia.edu/entri/treatySearch.jsp> (26 May 2004).

[83] P Sands, *Greening International Law* (London, Earthscan Publications, 1993), ch 2. See, eg, Agreed Measures for the Conservation of Antarctic Fauna and Flora, 2 June 1964, Convention for the Protection of Antarctic Seals (1 June 1972), Agreement on Conservation of Polar Bears (Oslo)(adopted 15 November 1973, in force 26 May 1976) (1974) 13 *International Legal Materials* 13; Benelux Convention on the Hunting and Protection of Birds (10 June 1970), Convention for the Protection of Birds Useful to Agriculture, 1902, International Convention for the Protection of Birds (18 October 1959), all available: <http://sedac.ciesin.columbia.edu/entri/ treatySearch.jsp> (26 May 2004).

resources.[84] In the period between the 1972 Stockholm Conference on the Human Environment[85] and the 1992 UNCED,[86] environmental agreemesnts began to connect the conservation of species to the protection of their habitats, finally recognising the impacts of human activities on the natural environment.[87]

However, these agreements fell short of acknowledging the gendered nature of the human impacts on the environment, or the gendered impacts of environmental degradation. The exclusion of gender from environmental instruments is due in part to the the the lack of women's participation in the negotiation of these instruments, but also because the environmental agenda has been driven by the male eco-establishment, often hostile, or at least indifferent, to women's concerns and resistant to feminism.[88]

With the linking of environmental protection to development and the resulting increased feminist activism since at least 1992, environmental initiatives began to reflect some of the views and concerns outlined by WED activists and academics outlined above. As a result, many environmental instruments include provisions dealing with the gendered impacts of environmental degradation and the role that women can play in environmental protection.

For example, the preamble to the 2001 Stockholm Convention on Organic Persistent Pollutants acknowledges the health impacts that these substances specifically have on women:

> Aware of the health concerns, especially in developing countries, resulting from local exposure to persistent organic pollutants, in particular impacts upon women and, through them, upon future generations.[89]

---

[84] See, eg, Agreement concerning Cooperation in taking Measures against Pollution of the Sea by Oil, 16 September 1971 (Copenhagen), Convention on Civil Liability for Nuclear Damage (Vienna)(adopted in 1963, entered into force 12 November 1977), (1963) 2 *International Legal Materials* 727; Convention on the Prevention of Marine Pollution by Dumping of Wastes and Other Matter (London)(adopted on 29 December 1972, entered into force 30 August 1975), (1976) UKTS 43, (1972) 11 *International Legal Materials* 1294; Convention on the Prohibition of the Development Production and Stockpiling of Bacteriological (Biological) and Toxin Weapons and on their Destruction (Washington, 1972), Agreement for Cooperation in Dealing with Pollution of the North Sea by Oil and Other Harmful Substances (Bonn) (adopted on 13 September 1983, entered in force in 1989); Agreement on Regional Co-operation in Combatting Pollution of the South-East Pacific by Hydrocarbons or Other Harmful Substances in Cases of Emergency (Lima) (adopted 12 November 1981, entered in force 19 May 1986), all online: <http://sedac.ciesin.columbia.edu/entri/ treatySearch.jsp> (26 May 2004).

[85] Stockholm, above n 2. The non-binding Stockholm Declaration on the Human Environment (signed 16 June 1972) UN Doc A/CONF 48/14, (1972) 11 *International Legal Materials* 1416, was adopted at Stockholm.

[86] United Nations Conference on Environment and Development, above n 3.

[87] See, eg, Convention on the International Trade of Endangered Species (adopted on 3 March 1973, entered into force 1 July 1975), (1973) 12 *International Legal Materials* 1085; Convention on the Protection of Wetlands of International Importance Especially as Waterfowl Habitat (adopted on 2 February 1971, entered into force 21 December 1975), (1975) 11 *International Legal Materials* 903.

[88] J Seager, above n 11, at 10.

[89] POPs Convention, above n 74, preamble. See also Agenda 21, above n 73, ch 6 (Protecting and Promoting Human Health), para 6.11, which notes the greater impacts of HIV/AIDS on women and children.

However, women's and men's different susceptibilities to environmental hazards, or the fact that, because of their poverty, women are more likely to be
exposed to toxic substances and less likely to obtain adequate treatment, are not
mentioned. [90] Most references to women's health in environmental instruments
in fact relate to women's access to reproductive health services as a way to achieve
sustainable development. [91]

Agenda 21, the blueprint for sustainable development adopted at UNCED in
1992, also contains important language recognising the disproportionate effect of
environmental degradation on women living in rural areas in developing countries, who are likely to depend directly on their environment for the survival of
their families and communities. [92] Agenda 21 acknowledges that women have to
travel further distances to access clean water, food and fuel sources as a result of
environmental degradation, and encourages national governments to implement
programmes to reduce women's heavy workloads, by, among other measures, 'the
sharing of household tasks by men and women on an equal basis', and the 'provision of environmentally sound technologies which have been designed, developed
and improved in consultation with women, accessible and clean water, an efficient
fuel supply and adequate sanitation facilities'. [93] Agenda 21 also encourages states
to create gender-sensitive databases on the impacts of environmental degradation
on women and children. [94]

The legal recognition of the impacts of environmental degradation on women
is accompanied by the acknowledgement that women have a role to play in environmental management and in achieving sustainable development. For example,
the preamble to the Convention on Biological Diversity notes 'the vital role that
women play in the conservation and sustainable use of biological diversity'. [95]
Reflecting some of the WED literature, women in developing countries are recognised as having extensive knowledge of ecosystems, including 'the management of
pests, the conservation of soil and the development and use of plant and animal
genetic resources'. [96] Agenda 21 encourages states to create databases and collect

---

[90] See WEDO, 'Gender Analysis of the WSSD Plan of Implementation, World Summit on Sustainable
Development 2002', <http://www.wedo.org/sus_dev/analysis2.htm> (26 May 2004) (Gender
Analysis). See also Women's Action Agenda 21, above n 67.

[91] See, eg, Agenda 21, above n 73, paras 6.21, 6.25, 6.26, 24.3(e).

[92] *Ibid*, para 24.6. See also FCWC, above n 79, paras 248 and 250.

[93] Agenda 21, above n 73, para 24.3(d).

[94] *Ibid*, para 24.8(c); see also the FCWC Platform for Action, above n 79 above, para 258(b)(ii).

[95] Biodiversity Convention, above, n 73, preamble. See also Rio Declaration, above n 73, Principle 20;
UNCCD, above n 74, preamble, and ch 24 of Agenda 21, above n 73, which recognises and aims to
achieve the role of women in sustainable development.

[96] FAO, Women—Users, Preservers and Managers of Agrobiodiversity, SD Dimensions, December
2001, <http://www.fao.org/sd/2001/PE1201a_en.htm> (26 May 2004). See discussion above. See also
M Hemmati, 'Women and Sustainable Development: from 2000 to 2002' in F Dodds (ed), *Earth
Summit 2002: A New Deal* (London, Earthscan 2002), 65-83, at 66; V Shiva, above n 30, where the
author gives many examples of women as conservers and managers of biological diversity, in the forest and agricultural context; Commission on the Status of Women, 'Follow-up to the Fourth World
Conference on Women: Review of Mainstreaming in Organisations of the UN System', UN ESCOR,
42nd Session, U N Doc E/CN 6/1998/3 (1998), paras 248 and 250.

gender-disaggregated data on women's knowledge and experience in environmental management.[97] The Beijing Platform for Action and the Beijing +5 Programme for Further Implementation also specifically recognise the importance of integrating women's knowledge, as well as their priorities, in the management of environmental resources,[98] and of protecting women's knowledge, in areas relating to traditional medicine, for example.[99]

International environmental instruments have also stated that women's full participation is essential to achieve sustainable development, and that women's equality is a necessary condition to that end.[100] In many environmental instruments, states are thus encouraged to adopt measures to eliminate all 'obstacles to women's full participation in sustainable development and in public life'.[101] The Cairo Programme of Action also recognises that women's autonomy and the improvement of their political, social and economic situation is essential to the attainment of sustainable development, and encourages states to sign, ratify and implement their obligations under the Convention for the Elimination of All Forms of Discrimination Against Women and other women's rights instruments.[102]

Encouraging women's full participation in sustainable development also means giving them specific rights, such as the right to have control over land and resources,[103] to access education and training,[104] and to participate in decision-making.[105] As to the last, international environmental instruments stress the importance of encouraging women's participation in all decision-making related to environmental protection and sustainable development, both at the planning and the implementation levels. For example, in Chapter 24 of Agenda 21, states are encouraged to adopt and implement a series of measures in order to implement the Nairobi Forward-looking Strategies for the Advancement of Women,[106] particularly with regard to women's participation in national ecosystem management, and to increase the proportion of women in positions of decision-making,

---

[97] Agenda 21, above n 73, para 24(8)(a). See also Rome Declaration, above n 78, objectives 1.3(f) &(h).

[98] See FCWC Platform for Action, above n 79; Beijing +5, above n 80, at para 56.

[99] FCWC Platform for Action, above n 79, para 258(b)(i). The Biodiversity Convention, above n 73, requires the protection of indigenous knowledge but does not refer specifically to women.

[100] See, eg, Principle 20 of the Rio Declaration, above n 73.

[101] Agenda 21, above n 73, para 24.2(c).

[102] Cairo, above n 75, para 4.1.

[103] See, eg, the WSSD Plan of Implementation, above n 4, paras 6(h), 10 and 61(b) ; Agenda 21, above n 73, paras 3.8(f), 24.1, 24.3(f); Rome Declaration, above n 78, objectives 1.2(b), 1.3(b), 2.1(e).

[104] See, eg, Agenda 21, above n 73, paras 24.1, 24.2(f), 24.3(c); FCWC Platform for Action, above n 79, strategic objectives B1–B6; Cairo Programme of Action, above n 75, objective 4.3(c); Rome Declaration, above n 78, objective 1.3(d).

[105] See, eg, FCWC Platform, above n 79, strategic objectives G1 and G2; Cairo Programme of Action, above n 75, objective 4.3(b).

[106] UNGA, *Report of the World Conference to Review and Appraise the Achievements of the United Nations Decade for Women: Equality, Development and Peace*, Nairobi, 15–26 July 1985 (United Nations publication, Sales No E 85 IV 10), ch I, sect A.

planning, scientific and technical advising in all policies relating to sustainable development.[107] Linked to the obligation of states to ensure women's participation in decision-making is the additional obligation to gender mainstream policies[108] relating to environmental protection and sustainable development.[109]

In summary, since the 1992 UNCED preparatory process, women's groups have been included to some extent in the negotiations of environmental instruments,[110] as well as in the different United Nations bodies working on sustainable development issues such as the Commission on Sustainable Development.[111] As a result, many environmental instruments now consider gender dynamics to be important to global environmental action. Despite the ostensible gains in securing stronger language linking women's equality to environmental protection,[112] progress on the goals enunciated at UNCED and beyond has been slow, in terms both of women's participation[113] and environmental protection.[114] In fact, reports on national plans for the follow-up to UNCED and the implementation of Agenda 21 have indicated that plans for the advancement of women have been designed but not implemented at both the international and national levels.[115] Women still only make up just over 14% of the total number of government

---

[107] Agenda 21, above n 73, paras 24.2(a) and (b), 24.3(a) and 24.7; see also Cairo Programme of Action, above n 75, para 4.3(b); FCWC Platform, above n 79, strategic objective K1; WSSD Plan of Implementation, above n 4, paras 6(d), 38, 42(k), 44(b).

[108] The Economic and Social Council of the United Nations defines gender mainstreaming as 'the process of assessing the implications for women and men of any planned action, including legislation, policies or programmes, in all areas and at all levels. It is a strategy for making women's as well as men's concerns and experiences an integral dimension of the design, implementation, monitoring and evaluation of policies and programmes in all political, economic and societal spheres so that women and men benefit equally and inequality is not perpetuated. The ultimate goal is to achieve gender equality.' See ECOSOC, 'Report of the Economic and Social Council for 1997: Agreed Conclusions 1997/2', ECOSOC UN Doc /52/3(1997), <http://www.un.org/womenwatch/daw/followup/main.htm> (26 May 2004). For a discussion of gender mainstreaming, see S Kouvo (this volume).

[109] M Hemmati, above n 96 at 67. See also FCWC Platform for Action, above n 79, Strategic objective H2; Agenda 21, above n 73, para 24.8(f).

[110] It is important to note that women's participation is alongside other NGOs and non-governmental interests such as transnational corporations, youth and indigenous peoples. For example, ch 30 of Agenda 21 is dedicated to the role of business and industry in achieving sustainable development.

[111] The Women's Caucus, organised and facilitated by WEDO, is one of the major groups that is allowed to participate in CSD meetings, in the form of Major Groups dialogues: see WEDO, <http://www.wedo.org/programs/sustainable.htm>(30 April 2004).

[112] Women's Action Agenda, above n 67; see generally M Hemmati, above n 96, at 68 for areas of progress.

[113] Women still represent only a minuscule proportion of decision-makers and policy-planners in United Nations organisations and national governments. For example, in 2002, only 11 states had achieved the benchmark 30% of women in Parliament set by the Beijing Platform. See UNIFEM, Annual Report 2002/2003: Working for Women's Enpowerment and Gender Equality (UNIFEM, 2003), < http://www.unifem.org/index.php?f_page_pid=180> (5 April 2004).

[114] For example, one-third to one-half of the world's surface land area, and anywhere from 1 in 6 to 1 in 3 people are affected by the process of desertification; in less than 25 years, two-thirds of the world's people wil live in water-stressed countries (where water consumption is more than 10% of renewable freshwater); 1.1 billion people don't have access to safe drinking water, most in Africa and Asia: GEO3, above n 5, at 65 and 150–52.

[115] Commission on Sustainable Development, 'Report of the Secretary-General on the Overall Progress Achieved since the United Nations Conference on Environment and Development' UN CSD, 5th Session, UN Doc E/CN 17/1997/2/Add 22 (1997), para 9. See also M Hemmati, above n 96, at 67.

ministers.[116] Even when women have been included in sustainable development projects, they have not necessarily received any benefits. Green, Joekes and Leach point out that often women are simply used as cheap (or free!) labour for environmental projects, which more often than not do not reflect their needs.[117]

Moreover, women's situation worldwide, in terms of health, wealth and education, is still far from reaching the goals relating to women's access to education, health services, training, credit, land and control over resources enunciated in Agenda 21 and the Beijing Platform.[118] In 2000, for example, 1.3 million women died of AIDS and over 16.4 million are currently living with HIV/AIDS.[119] Women still have less access to credit than men. For example, in Latin America and the Caribbean only 7–11% of women are beneficiaries of credit programmes.[120] Of the 880 million people who are illiterate, two-thirds are women, and one out of every three adult women cannot read or write.[121]

Furthermore, despite the adoption of hundreds of global environmental instruments, the decline of the planet continues at a rapid pace. The Malmö Declaration, adopted by the world's Ministers of Environment at the turn of the new century, summarises the continuing environmental threats:

> Environmental threats resulting from the accelerating trends of urbanization and the development of megacities, the tremendous risk of climate change, the fresh-water crisis and its consequences for food security and the environment, the unsustainable exploitation and depletion of biological resources, drought and desertification, and uncontrolled deforestation, increasing environmental emergencies, the risk to human health and the environment from hazardous chemicals, and land-based sources of pollution, are all issues that need to be addressed.[122]

It would appear, then, that the inclusion of gender politics in international environmental law has not dramatically improved the situation of women or of the environment. While all of the language and formal commitments outlined above are important gains, and while it may be somewhat premature to conclude as to their long-term effectiveness, I remain sceptical about the vision of an environmental

---

[116] M Hemmati and R Gardiner, 'Gender and Sustainable Development' (Heinrich Böll Foundation), <http://www.boell.de/index.html?http://www.boell.de/en/04_thema/1313.html> (2 May 2004) at 10.

[117] C Green et al, n 47, at 264–75.

[118] See nn 103 and 104 above; for provisions relating to access to health services, see FCWC Platform, above n 79, strategic objectives C1 to C5; as to women's equal access to credit and markets, see *ibid*, strategic objectives A2, A3 and F1 to F6. Also, the gap between the rich and the poor, both between states and within states, continues to widen: 3.5 billion people in low-income countries earn less than 20% of the world's income, while 1 billion people living in developed countries earn 60%. More than 1 billion people living in urban areas live in slums or as squatters: GEO3, above n 5, at 35.

[119] M Hemmati and R Gardiner, above n 116, at 8.

[120] *Ibid*, at 9.

[121] *Ibid*.

[122] Global Ministerial Environment Forum, 'Malmö Ministerial Declaration', 6th Special Session of the Governing Council, 5th plenary meeting (31 May 2000), <http://www.unep.org/malmo/malmo_ministerial.htm> (26 May 2004). See also Implementing Agenda 21, above n 5, at paras 2 and 3, which mention the state of the world's environment and the limited progress towards reducing poverty.

and economic future that underpins these documents, even if such a vision includes women. Such a vision, I argue in the following section, promotes the status quo and the hegemony of sustained economic growth in a global capitalist market, and of science and technology in addressing the environmental problems we face.

In the following section, I consider some of the difficulties inherent in attempts to bring a gender politics to environmental issues. First, I will argue that the gendered nature of the state system itself makes it difficult to address women's issues in the context of global environmental protection. Second, I argue that to date most of the efforts to link gender and environmental protection have focused on the inclusion of women within existing frameworks for environmental protection and sustainable development. This approach does little to address the structural barriers to women's equal participation in decision-making, or the obstacles to environmental protection. In fact, I argue that this approach acts to protect the hegemony of the masculinist institutions that have worked to marginalise women and exploit the environment.

The Masculinisation of Environmental Protection: a Feminist Perspective on International Environmental Law

The Gendered International State System

The first obstacle to achieving gender equality within, and a strengthening of global environmental protection is the gendered structure of the international system of nation states, which distinguishes between binding and non-binding obligations. With the exception of the Convention on Desertification,[123] provisions that acknowledge women's role in environmental protection or that mandate women's equal participation in the achievement of sustainable development are found in either the preambles of binding treaties such as the Biodiversity Convention,[124] or in non-binding soft law instruments such as the Rio Declaration[125] or Agenda 21.[126]

---

[123] UNCDD, above n 74, Art 5, which mandates states to promote the participation of women, and Art 10, which mandates states to ensure the effective participation of women in the preparation of national action programmes. This Convention has been praised for its bottom-up approach to solving the problem of desertification in Africa, but unfortunately has been plagued with a lack of implementation due mostly to a lack of resources: See generally KW Danish, 'International Environmental Law and the "Bottoms-Up" Approach: a Review of the Desertification Convention' (1995) 3 *Indiana Journal of Global Legal Studies* 133.

[124] Biodiversity Convention, above n 73.

[125] Rio Declaration, above n 73.

[126] Agenda 21, above n 73. See also the FCWC Platform for Action, above n 79; the WSSD Plan of Implementation, above n 4; Cairo, above n 75; World Summit for Social Development, above n 76; Istanbul, above n 77. Women's rights are also found in special conventions such as the Convention on the Elimination of All Forms of Discrimination against Women (adopted 18 December 1979) 1249 UNTS 13, < http://www.un.org/womenwatch/daw/cedaw/econvention.htm#intro> (15 April 2004).

Hilary Charlesworth and Christine Chinkin explain the double-marginalisation effect of including women's concerns in soft law instruments:

> The subject matter of many 'soft' law instruments is significant. States use 'soft' law structures for matters that are not regarded as essential to their interests ('soft' issues in international law) or where they are reluctant to incur binding obligations. Many of the issues that concern women thus suffer a double marginalisation in terms of traditional international law-making: they are seen as the 'soft' issues of human rights and are developed through 'soft' modalities of law-making that allow states to appear to accept such principles while minimising their legal commitments.[127]

Like the area of human rights, environmental protection is considered a 'soft' issue by states; in fact, much of today's soft law has been developed in the environmental context, starting with the 1972 Stockholm Declaration on the Human Environment.[128] Many international environmental law scholars still argue that the significance of soft law instruments should not be overlooked simply because they are not binding. Hunter, Salzman and Zaelke, for example, argue that the value of soft law lies in its dynamic and democratic process because it involves a broad range of actors, including non-governmental actors.[129] The process of soft law-making also permits international consensus in contested areas. For example, because of economic interests, the international community has not been able to agree on a binding convention dealing specifically with the protection of forests but has adopted a number of soft law instruments in that regard.[130] Dupuy contends that soft law 'creates and delineates goals to be achieved in the future rather than actual duties'.[131] Soft law is thus significant because it has the potential to become 'hard law' in the future, either as it becomes codified into treaties or, if practised by states over a period of time, if it can be said to reflect customary law.[132]

As Charlesworth and Chinkin explain, '[i]nternational legal scholarship does not discount the value of "soft" law entirely, but "hard", binding law remains the preferred paradigm of international law, and all forms of international law-making

---

[127] H Charlesworth and C Chinkin, *The Boundaries of International Law: A Feminist Analysis* (Manchester, Manchester University Press, 2000) at 66.

[128] Stockholm Declaration, above n 85. See PM Dupuy, 'Soft Law and the International Law of the Environment' (1991) 12 *Michigan Journal of International Law* 420; PW Birnie and AE Boyle, above n 8, at 24–27.

[129] D Hunter, J Salzman and D Zaelke, *International Environmental Law and Policy* (New York, Foundation Press, 2002) at 349.

[130] See Forest Principles, above n 73; Commission on Sustainable Development acting as the preparatory committee for the World Summit on Sustainable Development, 'Ministerial Declaration and Message from the United Nations Forum on Forests to the World Summit on Sustainable Development' 3rd Session, UN Doc A/CONF 199/PC/8 (19 March 2002).

[131] PM Dupuy, above n 128, at 420–35.

[132] *Ibid.* See also PW Birnie and AE Boyle, above n 8, at 25; See generally D Shelton (ed), *Commitment and Compliance: The Role of Non-binding Norms in the International Legal System* (New York, Oxford University Press, 2000).

are assessed in relation to this form'.[133] In international environmental law, provisions that include gender considerations are weighed against binding provisions that do not reflect, and could possibly be at odds with, women's interests in environmental protection. For example, many international environmental instruments affirm states' sovereign right to exploit their own natural resources in accordance with their economic and development priorities, a principle that was first enunciated in the environmental context as Principle 21 of the Stockholm Declaration:

> States have, in accordance with the Charter of the United Nations and the principles of international law, the sovereign right to exploit their own natural resources *pursuant to their own environmental policies*, and the responsibility to ensure that activities within their jurisdiction or control do not cause damage to the environment of other States or of areas beyond the limits of national jurisdiction. [134]

On the insistence of developing countries concerned with what they see as 'green colonialism'—Western states robbing them of their natural resources in a post-colonial era[135]—this principle has been reiterated in many environmental treaties since the 1972 Stockholm Conference.[136] However, provisions privileging states' sovereign right to exploit their natural resources for economic development could potentially conflict with provisions mandating the conservation of those same resources, or with women's rights to land and resources; how this conflict is resolved for each state will depend on its definition of 'environmental and developmental priorities'.[137] Given that women tend to be unrepresented in state governments, this privileging of state interest may have the result of marginalising environmental protection or the role of women in achieving it.

The Equality Paradigm

The second difficulty with the inclusion of gender-friendly provisions in international environmental instruments is the reliance on a formal equality paradigm. While the recognition of gender issues in environmental and related instruments is an important development, it is done mostly through the addition of half-sentences, such as 'particularly women' or 'with a particular emphasis on vulnerable groups such as women, youth and the elderly'. As Minu Hemmati argues, this language may in fact be more formal than substantive, 'to fulfil an obligation

---

[133] H Charlesworth and C Chinkin, above n 127, at 70.

[134] Stockholm Declaration, above n 2, Principle 21 (emphasis added).

[135] See J Seager, above n 11, at 141–44.

[136] Since UNCED, however, the wording of Principle 21 has been changed to '... pursuant to their own developmental and environmental policies'. See, eg, Rio Declaration, above n 73, Principle 2; Biodiversity Convention, above n 73, Arts 3 and 15(1); UNFCC, above n 73, preamble; POPS Convention, above n 74, preamble.

[137] See eg, C Green et al, n 47 at 268–70, on the issue of land tenure and rights to land.

rather than to reflect competent analysis and creative problem-solving'. [138] Much like the WID approach in the context of development, as Green, Joekes and Leach explain, the approach reflected in the provisions recognising the role that women can play in sustainable development simply aims to include women in environmental projects.[139] The assumption appears to be that the gendered impacts of environmental degradation will be addressed simply by giving women the same rights as men, and that women's role in environmental protection will be realised by giving women access to environmental and developmental decision-making.

Even if these provisions represent gains for women who, up until UNCED, were invisible in international environmental law, the inclusion of gender concerns based on the equality paradigm is problematic for three reasons. First, an approach to equality defined in terms of access to decision-making,[140] 'forecloses questioning of the underlying structures and assumptions of existing decision-making structures, which have resolutely functioned to exclude women'.[141] In this way, as Dianne Otto argues, the masculinist foundations of liberal democracy that work to continue male privilege are left intact.[142] Green et al explain that at the local level, this approach also denies that community-level social institutions often reflect gender hierarchies; women are often excluded from community councils, or not invited to speak.[143] Further, environmental projects often use women's labour, often unremunerated, in activities that do not meet their needs. Women's inclusion in environmental protection has thus largely meant that new 'environment' chores have been added to women's already long list of chores.[144]

Second, under the formal equality paradigm, equality is defined in terms of a comparison between women and men; the recognition of intersections between gender and other systems of inequality such as race, class, culture, ability and sexuality is thus foreclosed.[145] In the context of international environmental law, the 'obligations' of states to give women access to land, resources, education and health, and to environmental and developmental decision-making thus fail to address the different barriers that exist for women who experience different intersections between these inequalities. All women are lumped together and portrayed as one Third World Woman, both a victim of environmental degradation and an environmental user and manager, who, if given equal access to decision-making, will empower herself and save the environment. This approach fails to

---

[138] M Hemmati, above n 96, at 70.

[139] C Green et al, above n 47 at 263–65. Green et al explain that many donors did in fact develop guidelines and checklists for integrating women into projects; they also list as an example UNDP's PROWWESS project (Promotion of the Role of Women in Water and Environmental Sanitation Services).

[140] D Otto, above n 79, at 14.

[141] *Ibid*, at 13. Otto's argument here is made in reference to the 'formal equality' model she finds in the 1995 Beijing Conference on Women agreement. Her insights are apt about the formal equality model also found in international environmental agreement.

[142] *Ibid*, at 13–14.

[143] C Green et al, above n 47, at 273–75.

[144] *Ibid*.

[145] D Otto, above n 79, at 15.

recognise the differences between women, but as Green et al argue, it can also lead to the disillusionment of policy-makers when women-inclusive projects fail.[146]

The third inherent flaw in the equality approach is that it leaves intact the masculinist institutions that have worked to exclude women and unsustainably exploit nature.[147] Women are invited to participate 'in a project the terms of which are already set'.[148] In the context of international environmental law, that project is sustainable development, but a sustainable development defined as sustained economic growth in a global capitalist trading system, aided by Western science and technology.

The Hegemony of Western Scientific Knowledge and Technology

As discussed above, international environmental law recognises, to some extent, women's unique knowledge of ecosystems and the role that women can play in environmental management. However, international environmental law institutionalises a preference for, and deference to, conventional science in predicting and reducing environmental threats, and as an essential component 'in the search for feasible pathways towards sustainable development',[149] as is demonstrated by the language of Principle 9 of the Rio Declaration:

> States should cooperate to strengthen endogenous capacity-building for sustainable development by improving scientific understanding through exchanges of scientific and technological knowledge, and by enhancing the development, adaptation, diffusion and transfer of technologies, including new and innovative technologies.[150]

Global environmental instruments also include many binding provisions encouraging research,[151] scientific cooperation[152] and the exchange of scientific information[153] between signatory states, and urging developed states to transfer

---

[146] C Green et al, above n 47, at 275.

[147] J Seager, above n 11, at 7–8.

[148] A Orford, 'Feminism, Imperialism and the Mission of International Law' (2002) 71 *Nordic Journal of International Law* 275, at 282.

[149] See Agenda 21, above n 73, para 35.2. Agenda 21 dedicates a whole chapter to the role of science in the achievement of sustainable development. See also UNFCC, above n 73, preamble. See generally J Marton-Lefèvre, 'The Role of the Scientific Community in the Preparation of and Follow-up to UNCED' in BI Spector, GI Sjöstedt, IW Zartman (eds), *Negotiating International Regimes: Lessons Learned from the United Nations Conference on Environment and Development* (London, Norwell, MA, Graham & Trotman/Martinus Nijhoff, 1994) 171, at 178; S Boehmer-Christiansen, 'Scientific Uncertainty and Power Politics: The Framework Convention on Climate Change and the Role of Scientific Advice' in BI Spector, GI Sjöstedt, IW Zartman, *ibid*, 199.

[150] Rio Declaration, above n 73.

[151] See, eg, see Biodiversity Convention, above n 73, Art 12(a) and (b).

[152] *Ibid*, Arts 12(c) and 18; UNFCC, above n 73, Art 4(g); POPs Convention, above n 74, Art 11.

[153] UNFCC, above n 73, Art 4(h); Forest Principles, above n 73, Principle 12(c); Biosafety Protocol, above n 74, Art 20; PIC Convention, above n 74, Art 14.

technology[154] to developing states as ways to achieve environmental protection. For example, the Biosafety Protocol mandates that decisions concerning the import of modified living organisms shall be made according to risk assessment procedures carried out 'in a scientifically sound manner' as set out in Appendix III of the Protocol.[155] Appendix III makes no mention of local knowledges, or even of the participation of local communities, in assessing these organisms. Similarly, the Rotterdam Convention on Prior Informed Consent Procedure for Certain Hazardous Chemicals and Pesticides in International Trade sets up a Chemical Review Committee to make decisions about listing banned or severely restricted chemicals in Annex III of the Convention, which would then have an impact on the ability of member states to trade these chemicals. The procedure for listing these chemicals refers to 'review of scientific data', 'scientifically recognized methods' and 'generally recognized scientific principles and procedures',[156] in this way perpetuating the hegemony of Western science and its scientific method.

Feminists have criticised mainstream science's claim to universality, neutrality and objectivity, and have shown that in fact, science and the production of knowledge are socially and culturally embedded, and rely on asymmetrical dichotomies (male/female; nature/culture; subject/object; mind/matter).[157] Vandana Shiva points out how Western 'reductionist' science, which she characterises as a 'patriarchal project', has excluded women as experts and rejected ecological and holistic ways of knowing, which respect nature's processes and interconnectedness.[158]

While in some places the formal language of international environmental agreements recognises local knowledges, including women's knowledges, these are devalued through the privileged status of 'objective' and hard science.[159] Because women's knowledge is not considered to be 'scientific', it is usually ignored and rarely integrated in the design of environmental and developmental policies, as Joni Seager explains:

> 'Science' takes environmental assessment further and further away from the realm of lived experience—which is, not coincidentally, the realm in which most women are expert. Reliance on 'scientific facts' (and on the experts who collect such facts)

---

[154] These provisions are often contained in provisions dealing with 'capacity-building' and usually comprise technology transfer, technical assistance and financial assistance. For specific provisions dealing with the transfer of technology, see, eg, Biosafety Protocol, above n 74, Art 22; POPs Convention, above n 74, Art 12(4).

[155] Biosafety Protocol, above n 74, Art 10.

[156] PIC Convention, above n 74, Annex II.

[157] R Braidotti et al, above n 9, at 30–31. See also V Shiva, above n 30, at 20–21. For feminist critiques of science, see S Harding, *The Science Question in Feminism* (Ithaca NY, Cornell University Press, 1986); D Haraway, *Simians, Cyborgs, and Women: the Reinvention of Nature* (NY, Routledge, 1991); EF Keller, *Reflections on Gender and Science* (New Haven, Yale University Press, 1985).

[158] V Shiva, above n 30, at 14–15.

[159] C Zabinski, 'Scientific Ecology and Ecological Feminism: The Potential for Dialogue' in KJ Warren, above n 29, 314–26, at 320. See also D Rocheleau, B Thomas-Slayter and E Wangari, 'Gender and Environment: A Feminist Political Ecology Perspective' in D Rocheleau, B Thomas-Slayter and E Wangari (eds), *Feminist Political Ecology: Global Issues and Local Experiences* (New York, Routledge, 1996) 3, at 9.

pushes amateurs to the fringes, and undercuts the valuable environmental knowledge that amateurs have accumulated over the years ... Since a higher proportion of
environmental 'amateurs' are women, and women are still very much a minority in
the ranks of scientists, an integral byproduct of the shift towards science-based
environmentalism is the increasing marginalization of women within the movement.[160]

The potential benefits that could be derived from women's knowledge for the
environment and for local communities are thus not often realised.[161]
International environmental instruments also privilege the transfer of sustainable
technologies[162] from North to South over traditional and small-scale technologies
in achieving sustainable development.[163] DAWN activists point out that the focus
of the transfer from North to South of these technologies ignores the longstanding sustainable practices, mostly used by women, of many communities in the
South. International environmental law, however, does little to value, let alone
protect or promote, those sustainable practices.[164]

International environmental law's preference for Western science also ignores
the role that science has played in environmental degradation. As both Vandana
Shiva and Carolyn Merchant explain, the scientific revolution of the sixteenth
century enabled the rise of Western patriarchal domination of nature. Merchant
explains that before the 'Enlightenment' period, people perceived nature both as a
living, nurturing mother and as wild, uncontrollable and capable of violence,
storms and droughts.[165] However, with the rise of Western science working at the
service of capitalism, nature was transformed into inert maleable matter, suited
for exploitation in order to fulfil the project of industrial modernisation, or
'progress'.[166] Shiva explains how the partnership between capitalism and reductionist science has led to the environmental crisis:

> In the reductionist paradigm, a forest is reduced to commercial wood, and wood is
> reduced to cellulose fibre for the pulp and paper industry. Forests, land and genetic
> resources are then manipulated to increase the production of pulpwood, and this
> distortion is legitimised scientifically as overall productivity increase, even though it

[160] J Seager, above n 11, at 195.

[161] See generally C Green et al, above n 47.

[162] According to Agenda 21, environmentally sound technologies '... protect the environment, are less
polluting, use all resources in a more sustainable manner, recycle more of their wastes and products,
and handle residual wastes in a more acceptable manner than the technologies for which they were
substitutes': see Agenda 21, above n 73, ch 34 entitled 'Transfer of Environmentally Sound Technology,
Cooperation and Capacity-building', para 34.1.

[163] See eg, Biodiversity Convention, above n 73, Art 16(1); UNFCC, above n 73, Arts 4(3) and 5.
International environmental instruments in fact do not contemplate the transfer of sustainable practices from South to North.

[164] E Charkiewicz, 'Agenda 21: A Viable Alternative to Hyper-liberalisation' in *DAWN informs:
Development Alternatives with Women for a New Era*, May 2002, p 1, <http://www.dawn.org.fj/publi-
cations/DAWNInforms/dawninformsindex.html> (26 May 2004).

[165] C Merchant, *Earthcare: Women and the Environment* (New York, Routledge, 1996), at 77.

[166] *Ibid*, at 86; see also R Braidotti et al, n 9, at 47.

might decrease the output of water from the forest, or reduce the diversity of life forms that constitute a forest community. The living and diverse ecosystem is thus violated and destroyed by 'scientific' forestry and forestry 'development'. In this way, reductionist science is at the root of the growing ecological crisis, because it entails a transformation of nature such that its organic processes and regularities and regenerative capacities are destroyed.[167]

The hegemony of Western science reductionism might also explain the tendency for mainstream approaches to environmental protection, as reflected in earlier environmental instruments, to address the symptoms rather the underlying causes of species extinction and environmental degradation.[168]

Shiva further explains that reductionist science was imposed through development on non-Western cultures and displaced the knowledges of indigenous and local cultures.[169] Further, feminist critics of development have also pointed to the role that Western science and technology have played in the displacement of women in the South. The green revolution in the 1960s, science's way of increasing food production, worked alongside structural adjustment programmes and macro-economic policies, and led to the displacement of many rural communities in order for developing states to convert lands to export-oriented monocrop agriculture, benefiting the large agri-business sector and the men who were subsequently employed, often leaving women without the means to sustain their communities.[170] Contrary to its claims of assisting humanity to feed an increasing population, the green revolution caused widespread soil erosion and crop susceptibility to pests, thus worsening the situation of many, most of them poor women.[171] Large-scale water management plans, such as dams and hydroelectric plants, have also contributed to environmental degradation and displaced large numbers of people, mostly small farmers who tend to be women.[172] More recently, the spread of genetically modified crops by global biotechnology/chemical corporations, such as 'terminator technology' seeds—seeds that are genetically modified to self-destruct after one harvest—endangers the world's biological diversity and the livelihood of most of the world's population, who cannot afford to buy the seeds every year and who depend on the richness of local biodiversity for food, energy, livelihood and medicine.[173]

What I am critiquing is not the fact that international environmental law relies on Western science and technology in order to address environmental problems and achieve sustainable development. Science and technology, more particularly the science of ecology and the development of sustainable technologies, certainly

---

[167] V Shiva, above n 30, at 24.
[168] J Seager, above n 11, at 2–4.
[169] V Shiva, above n 30, at 22. See also J Seager, above n 11, at 196.
[170] See V Shiva, above n 30.
[171] M Mellor, above n 9, at 119–20.
[172] *Ibid.*
[173] See V Shiva, *Tomorrow's Biodiversity* (New York, Thames & Hudson, 2000).

have a role to play in the fulfillment of these goals. The development of the precautionary principle in international environmental law, which mandates action on possible environmental threats despite scientific uncertainty, also demonstrates the international community's recognition that science does not always have all the answers to environmental questions.[174]

Instead, what I question is international environmental law's failure to question the hegemony of Western science and technology. This omission obscures the role that these masculinist institutions have played in the environmental crisis we are facing today, and devalues the role that other types of knowledge can play in achieving environmental protection. To replace this hegemony, Braidotti et al argue for a feminist post-modernist epistemology in the field of the environment, which would mean 'the systematic loosening up of scientific discourse, working towards displacing reason from its central position, so as to reduce its status to that of simply another kind of discourse among a plurality of possible discourses'.[175] As Subramaniam, Bever and Schultz suggest, then, science should be embraced as playing a part in sustainable development, but on equal footing with local knowledges.[176] I would add to this that if science is to play a role in achieving sustainable development then, at the very least, the historically close relationship between Western science, technology and capitalism, and its unequal impacts on women, nature and on non-Western cultures, must be recognised.

Sustainable Development as Sustained Economic Growth in a Capitalist Global Trading System

Despite the persuasive evidence that uncontrolled exploitation of the environment for economic growth has led to environmental degradation, international environmental law's dominant paradigm is still one where sustained economic growth, capital and economic development are essential to achieving sustainable development and environmental protection.[177]

---

[174] Principle 15 of the Rio Declaration, above n 73, articulates the precautionary principle: 'Where there are threats of serious or irreversible damage, lack of full scientific certainty shall not be used as a reason for postponing cost-effective measures to prevent environmental degradation.' This principle has been reiterated in many environmental instruments, including the UNFCC, above n 73, Art 3(3); the Convention on the Protection and Use of Transboundary Watercourses and International Lakes (adopted 17 March 1992, entered in force 6 October 1996) (1992) 31 *International Legal Materials* 1312, Art 2(5)(a); the Biodiversity Convention, above n 73, preamble; and the POPs Convention, above n 74, preamble and Art 1. See generally O McIntyre and T Mosedale, 'The Precautionary Principle as a Norm of Customary International Law' (1997) 2 *Journal of Environmental Law* 221; D Freestone and E Hey (eds), *The Precautionary Principle and International Law: The Challenge of Implementation* (The Hague, Kluwer Law International, 1996).

[175] R Braidotti et al, above n 9, at 47.

[176] B Subramaniam, J Bever and P Schultz, 'Global Circulations: Nature, Culture, and the Possibility of Sustainable Development' in K Saunders above n 36, 199. But see M Nanda, 'Do the Marginalized Valorize the Margins? Exploring the Dangers of Difference' in K Saunders, *ibid*, 212 at 216, who argues that local knowledges are potentially all different and incompatible.

[177] See, eg, Rio Declaration, above n 73 , Principle 4. The preamble to the UNFCC, above n 73, states that '... responses to climate change should be coordinated with social and economic development in an

The fundamental assumption that sustainable development depends on sustained economic growth ignores the role played by a capitalist market economy in causing the destruction of the environment through the exploitation of 'natural resources'. Ecofeminists have argued that a capitalist economic system attaches value to people and the environment solely based on their usefulness for human and economic ends.[178] The 'value of people and nonhuman nature lies in their utility in attaining a given end, such as economic supremacy or political power',[179] rather than in the survival of humanity and the planet. Marilyn Waring has also criticised the global economic system for not valuing the environment as such, or the unpaid work of women.[180]

International environmental instruments also create a symbiotic relationship between poverty eradication and sustainable development. The instruments adopted at UNCED and WSSD recognise the importance of alleviating poverty in the economic South in order to achieve sustainable development, and the role of sustainable development in eradicating poverty.[181] For example, the Johannesburg Declaration adopted at the WSSD states that poverty eradication is an 'overarching objective of and essential requirement for sustainable development'.[182] Similarly, the WSSD Plan of Implementation views poverty reduction as a way to enpower poor people and to achieve sustainable development.[183]

Environmental instruments also recognise more specifically that women's empowerment is a precondition to eradicating poverty. For example, Chapter 3 of Agenda 21, entitled 'Combating Poverty', refers to granting rights (participation, equality, education, rights to land) to women as a way to promote sustainable development.[184] This was reiterated at the Beijing Conference in 1995, where

---

integrated manner ...'. Article 3 of the same Convention reiterates that economic development is essential for adopting measures to address climate change. See also Forest Principles, above n 73, principle 13(d).

[178] See eg, V Shiva, above n 30; C Merchant, above n 165.

[179] J Biehl, above n 27, at 19–20; see also J Plant, 'Learning to Live with Differences: The Challenge of Ecofeminist Community' in KJ Warren, above n 29, 120 at 123; R Braidotti et al, above n 9, at 251–52.

[180] See M Waring, *Counting for Nothing: What Men Value and What Women are Worth*, 2nd edn (Toronto, University of Toronto Press, 1999). See also WorldWatch Institute, *State of the World 1998* (NY, London, WW Norton & Company, 1998) at 27. For example, forests are seen by capitalism as 'vast uninhabited spaces that are valuable only when converted to agriculture or mined for timber. Standing forest is seen as wasted and unproductive. The benefits derived from forests such as producing food, fodder, fish and medicines, purifying and regulating water supplies and climates, providing pollination, pest control, habitat and refuge, as well as educational, recreational, aesthetic and cultural benefits are ignored.'

[181] See, eg, Rio Declaration, above n 73, principle 5; Agenda 21, above n 73, ch 3 entitled 'Combating Poverty'.

[182] Johannesburg Declaration, above n 4, para 11. See also WSSD Plan of Implementation, above n 4, at para 7.

[183] WSSD Plan of Implementation, above n 4, at para 7(c).

[184] See Agenda 21, above n 73: para 3.4(d) states that to achieve sustainable livelihoods, policies should integrate development, sustainable resource management and poverty eradication. Para 3.5 encourages states to reduce the inequalities between various population groups, and assist the most disadvantaged groups such as women, youth, and indigenous peoples. Para 3.7(a) promotes the empowerment of women through full participation in decision-making. Para 3.8(f) asks states to

states recognised that women are affected differently from men by poverty, and that this poverty is inextricably linked to women's lack of rights. Therefore, to combat women's poverty, they must have access to education, property rights, and they must be free from violence.[185]

The recognition of the relationship between poverty eradication, women's empowerment and sustainable development has been cited by DAWN activists as an achievement of the UNCED process.[186] Indeed, to the extent that establishing such a relationship might make it more convincing for the North to do its part to eradicate poverty as a way to achieve sustainable development, this is a step forward.

However, what is problematic is that women's empowerment is implicitly imagined in ways that align with the dominant expectation of the market economy. Feminists have argued that in linking issues such as environment, poverty and women's empowerment, international law and policy has relied on troubling models of the 'good' woman. Doris Buss, for example, argues that in the context of population policy, the 'good' woman is environmentally friendly, economically productive, and reproductively restrained.[187] Dianne Otto points out that the 'good' woman is one who participates equally in the free market economy.[188] If the Woman of international legal discourse is market friendly, 'poverty' emerges as a 'problem' for the market economy. Subsistence economies, largely sustained by women in developing countries, are depicted in environment and related agreements as 'poor' and problematic, even though they might satisfy the basic needs of those communities involved in them.[189] The role of sustainable development, then, is to transform those 'poor' people, mostly women, into full participants of the market economy by giving them access to resources and decision-making.

The provisions making the link between empowerment of women, poverty eradication and sustainable development thus do not address the root causes of poverty in the South, and of women in particular. In this fashion, the impacts on the environment and the lives of women and the poor in developing countries of structural adjustment programmes, massive development projects such as dams and cash-crop

---

consider developing legal frameworks for land management, access to land resources and land ownership, in particular for women. Para 3.8(i) encourages states to develop mechanism for popular participation, especially of women.

[185] FWCW, above n 79, at para 48, which states the following: 'In the past decade the number of women living in poverty has increased disproportionately to the number of men, particularly in the developing countries. The feminization of poverty has also recently become a significant problem in the countries with economies in transition as a short-term consequence of the process of political, economic and social transformation. In addition to economic factors, the rigidity of socially ascribed gender roles and women's limited access to power, education, training and productive resources as well as other emerging factors that may lead to insecurity for families are also responsible. The failure to adequately mainstream a gender perspective in all economic analysis and planning and to address the structural causes of poverty is also a contributing factor.' See also, WSSD Plan of Implementation, above n 4, para 7(d)(h).

[186] E Charkiewicz, above n 164, at 3.

[187] D Buss, above n 75, at 464.

[188] D Otto, above n 79, at 23.

[189] See V Shiva, above n 30.

agriculture, or the unequal distribution of the world's resources are completely glossed over.[190] The role that the capitalist market economy and northern consumption and production patterns play in environmental destruction and widespread poverty is downplayed. For example, Principle 8 of the Rio Declaration asserts in the same breath that states should reduce and eliminate unsustainable patterns of production and consumption, and promote 'appropriate demographic policies'.[191]

Not surprisingly, then, international environmental law has increasingly advocated that necessary economic growth to achieve sustainable development should be based on multilateral trade. The assumption is that trade in a global capitalist system will lead to economic growth, which will lead to the eradication of poverty, which will then allow for environmental protection. Agenda 21 devotes an entire chapter to the importance of economic instruments in achieving sustainable development and recommends the following:

> Environment and trade policies should be mutually supportive. An open, multilateral trading system makes possible a more efficient allocation and use of resources and thereby contributes to an increase in production and incomes and to lessening demands on the environment. It thus provides additional resources needed for economic growth and development and improved environmental protection. A sound environment, on the other hand, provides the ecological and other resources needed to sustain growth and underpin a continuing expansion of trade. An open multilateral trading system, supported by the adoption of sound environmental policies, would have a positive impact on the environment and contribute to sustainable development. [192]

Agenda 21 thus reflects in part the neoliberal agenda that was enshrined in the establishment of the World Trade Organisation in 1995. The WSSD Plan of Implementation, 10 years later, develops this link between trade, economic growth and environmental protection even further. The WSSD Plan of Implementation stresses the role of 'trade liberalisation', 'foreign direct investment' and 'public-private partnerships' in achieving sustainable development, moving further away from the cooperative approach that had been fostered up to and during the UNCED process based on increased state-to-state financial assistance.[193]

---

[190] The only mention of the impacts of structural adjustment programmes on women is found in Agenda 21, above n 73, para 24.8, which encourages states to develop gender-sensitive databases, information systems and participatory action-oriented research and policy analyses on the impact of structural adjustment programmes on women, with special attention given to the differential impact of those programmes on women, especially in terms of cut-backs in social services, education and health, and in the removal of subsidies on food and fuel.

[191] Rio Declaration, above n 73. See also Agenda 21, above n 73, ch 4 entitled 'Changing Consumption Patterns', which states that it should be read in conjunction with ch 5, entitled 'Demographic Dynamics and Sustainability'.

[192] Agenda 21, above n 73, para 2.19.

[193] See, eg, WSSD Plan of Implementation, above n 4 para 90: 'Recognizing the major role that trade can play in achieving sustainable development and in eradicating poverty, we encourage members of the World Trade Organization (WTO) to pursue the work programme agreed at their Fourth Ministerial Conference. In order for developing countries, especially the least developed among them, to secure their share in the growth of world trade commensurate with the needs of their economic

International environmental law's push for trade liberalisation is surprising considering the role that economic globalisation has played in widening the gap between rich and poor nations, as well as within nations.[194] For too many people, especially women who represent 70% of the world's poor,[195] the promises of economic globalisation have not been realised.[196] The positive relationship between economic globalisation, trade liberalisation, poverty eradication and sustainable development established in environmental instruments thus obscures the fact that the first two have in fact contributed to the increasing gap between North and South and the growing feminisation of poverty.[197] As Anne Orford argues, 'the narrative of economic globalization, in which we move together into a future of greater freedom, prosperity and integration, itself erases the conditions of its possibility'.[198] These conditions are the exploitation of the environment and of women, as reflected in the international gendered division of labour.[199]

Despite the gains reached in environmental instruments since the 1992 United Nations Conference on Environment and Development (UNCED) in recognising that women should have equal rights to participate through increased access to resources, land and decision-making, the continued hegemony of Western science,

---

development, we urge WTO members to take the following actions.' See also *ibid* para 84. Pledges for 'new and additional financial assistance' were an integral part of all international environmental instruments adopted since UNCED. Since 1992, however, ODA has decreased in all developed states except for the Netherlands, Sweden and Norway: see Implementing Agenda 21, above n 5, at paras 4–7. On the other hand, foreign direct investment has increased through the 1990s to reach $120 billion in 2000: *ibid*, para 183.

[194] World Bank, *World Bank Report 2000/2001: Attacking Poverty* (London, Oxford University Press, 2001) at 50; see also AK Duraiappah, 'Poverty and the Environment: A Role for UNEP' (IISD Concept paper written for UNEP, October 2001), <http://www.iisd.org/pdf/2001/economics_unep_poverty_guidelines.pdf> (2 February 2003).

[195] United Nations Development Programme, *Human Development Report 1995* (New York, Oxford University Press, 1995), cited in M Hemmati and R Gardiner, above n 116.

[196] GEO-3 cites the Human Development Report, 1999, where UNDP states that one-fifth of the world's people living in the highest income countries have 86% of the world GDP, 82% of world export markets, 68% of foreign direct investment and 74% of telephone lines. The bottom one-fifth have about 1% in each category. In the 1990s, more than 80% of foreign direct investment in developing countries went to 20 countries only, notably China: see *GEO3*, above n 5, at 24. See generally A Orford, above n 148.

[197] See D Buss, above n 75, at 482; N Kanji and K Menon-Sen, 'What does the Feminisation of Labour Mean for Sustainable Livelihoods?' (International Institute for Environment and Development, August 2001), < http://www.poptel.org.uk/iied/wssd/pubs.html#brief> (26 May 2004). See also K Menon-Sen, *Gender, Governance and the 'Feminisation of Poverty': the Indian Experience* (India, UNDP, 2001). World Bank reports and reports from the United Nations Secretary-General, have admitted the devastating impacts of these economic trends on certain developing countries and on a large portion of the world's population, but in the same breath offer the same mechanisms for eradication of poverty and environmental protection: see Implementing Agenda 21, above n 5, at paras 190, 191 and 197; *World Development Report 2000/2001*, above n 194. See also R Braidotti et al, above n 9, at 80, who talk about the international debt crisis of the 1980s leading to the feminisation of poverty.

[198] A Orford, above n 148, at 290.

[199] On this last point, see D Buss, above n 75; D Otto, above n 79; and S Sassen, 'Counter-geographies of Globalization: Feminization of Survival' in K Saunders, above n 36, at 89.

technology and capitalism in the project of sustainable development leaves the status quo intact. If global environmental protection is to be achieved, and if women are to take part in it, feminists must continue to challenge these institutions.

Conclusion: What Can Feminists Bring to International Environmental Law?

In this chapter, I have outlined the gains made in the inclusion of gender considerations in international environmental law, largely achieved because of women's participation in the negotiation of international environmental instruments since the United Nations Conference on Environment and Development in 1992. The international community has acknowledged to a certain extent the gendered impacts of environmental degradation, and the role that women can play in environmental management and the achievement of sustainable development. Accordingly, international environmental instruments have encouraged states to grant women certain rights related to control over land and resources, access to education and woman-centered reproductive health care, and participation in decision-making related to environmental management and development.

Despite these considerable gains, I have shown that international environmental law remains problematic, both from a feminist and an environmentalist perspective. First, the formal gains achieved in the inclusion of gender language have not translated into concrete improvements relating to women's situation and participation in decision-making. The lack of progress has been in part due to the nature of the gendered state system, which distinguishes between 'hard' or binding and 'soft' or non-binding obligations, and which relies on individual states to implement the commitments reached.

Most importantly, however, the inclusion of women in international environmental law has not translated into a questioning of the basic assumptions underlying it. International environmental law continues to rely on scientific evidence, and has strengthened its commitment to a worldview in which environmental protection is secured through a particular model of economic growth. The result is that the gender-friendly policy objectives of international environmental law do not meaningfully address the structural and institutional barriers to women's equal participation in environmental decision-making, the same barriers that prevent effective environmental protection. On the contrary, international environmental law actually works to preserve the hegemony of masculinist institutions such as the global capitalist system and Western science and technology.

To the extent that any meaningful recognition of gender in international environmental law has occurred, it is due in large part to the concerted lobbying of women's organisations at the 1992 UNCED and 2002 WSSD world conferences. As opposed to the gender-friendly provisions that ended up in the final documents, the documents produced by women's organisations at *Planeta Femea*[200] and in preparation for the WSSD summit posed a direct challenge to the masculinist institutions of global trade and the military state. These documents advocated instead for peace, a gender-sensitive and environmentally sound development, environmental health and security, and the replacement of 'the neo-liberal paradigm with a sustainable, gender-sensitive and environmentally sound development framework that puts people and the planet before profits'.[201] Through their global networks and local movements, women demonstrated that they can transcend issues of essentialism and embrace their differences in order to offer a new approach to environmental protection, one that is based on sustainable livelihoods, peace and a more sustainable relationship between humans and nature.[202] Although the compromises found in the resulting environmental instruments, both at UNCED and WSSD, do not come close to the alternative vision of sustainable development presented by these women's united position, their voices were heard.

Therefore, despite the meagreness of accomplishments arrived at in the final documents of environmentally-related conferences and negotiations, feminist engagement with international environmental law must continue. Feminists have brought to light the impacts suffered by women because of environmental degradation and the important role that women play in environmental protection because of their daily interactions with their environment. Feminists also challenge the masculinist institutions that are at the root of the environmental crisis and of the oppression of women and all 'others'.[203] As we saw above, feminists have challenged capitalism for ignoring women's unpaid labour, for contributing to the feminisation of poverty, for the increasing gap between the rich and the poor, for the marginalisation of developing countries and for the plundering of the earth. Moreover, despite the criticisms directed at ecofeminists for the implicit essentialism related to a woman/nature connection, ecofeminists also offer a critique of the androcentric assumptions underlying these institutions, and an alternative view of the relationship between humans and nature that is crucial to saving the planet from an environmental disaster.[204]

Further, these critiques are increasingly significant in international environmental law's current context of economic globalisation and increasing privatisation. Chandra Mohanty points to the role that a feminist anti-capitalist critique can play in challenging this context, and points us to the future:

[200] Women's Action Agenda 21, above n 67.

[201] Women's Action Agenda for a Healthy Planet 2015, above n 71.

[202] See the two Women's Action Agendas, above n 67 and n 71 , for what this new approach could look like.

[203] J Seager, above n 11, at 3. Seager points to a handful of large institutional structures: militaries, multinationals and governments.

[204] See, eg, C Merchant, above n 165; V Plumwood, *Feminism and the Mastery of Nature* (New York, Routledge, 1993); V Shiva, above n 30.

[A] critique of the operation, discourse, and values of capitalism and of their naturalization through neoliberal ideology and corporate culture. This means demystifying discourses of consumerism, ownership, profit, and privatization—of the collapse of notions of public and private good, and the refashioning of social into consumer identities within corporate culture.[205]

Strategically, then, a feminist engagement with international environmental agreements must continue both from the outside, in a critique of its fundamental assumptions, and from within, in the process of negotiation of future agreements, as long as it does so from a position informed by the political economy of environmental protection.

---

[205] C Talpade Mohanty, *Feminism Without Borders: Decolonizing Theory, Practicing Solidarity* (Durham, Duke University Press, 2003).

11

The United Nations and Gender Mainstreaming: Limits and Possibilities

SARI KOUVO*

Better never means better for everyone, he says. It always means worse, for some.[1]

Simply naming and identifying a problem does not solve it; naming is only one stage in the process of transformation. It is the courage to live our lives consciously and to act that will enable us to implement new strategies and goals.[2]

Introduction

During the 1990s the feminist analytical category 'gender', together with the strategy of mainstreaming, travelled well.[3] The Beijing Declaration and Platform for Action (Beijing Platform), adopted at the Fourth World Conference on Women (Beijing, 1995), established gender mainstreaming as 'the global strategy for promoting gender equality'.[4] At the United Nations a broad-based and system-wide

* Department of Law, School of Economics and Commercial Law, University of Göteborg (Sweden). Versions of this paper have been presented over the last few years, and it has benefited from comments by many people. I want to thank Fanny Tabak and the participants at the Workshop on the Role of Communitarian Law in Implementing Equal Rights (Oñati International Institute for the Sociology of Law, June 2000) and Hilary Charlesworth for comments on early drafts of this paper, and Eva-Maria Svensson and Per Cramér for comments on later versions. Doris Buss and Ambreena Manji have provided excellent comments on the later versions of the paper. The Swedish Cultural Foundation (Svenska kulturfonden) in Finland provided funding for this research.

[1] M Atwood, *The Handmaid's Tale* (New York, Random House, 1998).

[2] B Hooks, *Talking Back: Thinking Feminist—Thinking Black* (Boston, South End Press, 1989).

[3] S Mazey, *Gender Mainstreaming in the EU: Principles and Practice* (UK, Kogan Page Limited, 2001). Mazey identifies the gender mainstreaming strategy as a Nordic strategy, developed mainly in Sweden and Norway, and which thereafter has been adopted by Nordic development agencies and the European Union. For example, the European Commission adopted a gender mainstreaming approach through the Commission Communication on Incorporating Equal Opportunities for Women and Men into All Community Policies and Activities (COM(96) 97 final), and the decision was operationalised through the Community Framework Strategy on Gender Equality (2001–2005) (COM(2000) 335 final). A decision to integrate a gender perspective into all Community activities is also included in the Treaty of Amsterdam, Art 2. For further reading, see (2002) 10 *Feminist Legal Studies* (Special Issue: Gender Mainstreaming) and (2000) 7 *Journal of European Social Policy* (Special Issue: Gender Mainstreaming).

[4] *Gender Mainstreaming: An Overview* (DAW/OSAGI, New York, 2001) and *Gender Mainstreaming: Strategy for Gender Equality* (New York, OSAGI, 2001).

gender mainstreaming mandate was created through the adoption of the Economic and Social Council's (ECOSOC) Agreed Conclusions, on gender main-streaming in 1997 and through the Secretary-General's communication to man-agement the same year.[5] The ECOSOC Agreed Conclusions, which will be addressed below, gave the UN woman-centred institutions—the inter-govern-mental Commission on the Status of Women and the Secretariat institutions, the Division for the Advancement of Women and the Office of the Special Adviser on Women's Advancement and Gender Issues—the mandate to develop, initiate and promote UN gender mainstreaming. The ECOSOC Agreed Conclusions also stressed that gender mainstreaming is a system-wide and broad-based strategy. That is, equality between the sexes should no longer be addressed as a separate 'women's issue', but the promotion of equality should be part of all UN activities. Gender mainstreaming has been promoted through, for example, inter-agency cooperation coordinated through the Inter-Agency Network for Women and Gender Equality (Inter-Agency Network), as well as by different institutions and specialised agency-specific initiatives.

Carol Bacchi, in her analysis of national equality policies in the United States and in the Nordic countries, notes that feminists need to be careful not to pre-sume that '… achieving social problem status for one's cause is in itself a sign of success [and] a commitment to important change.'[6] According to Bacchi, '[i]t is impossible to talk about any social condition without putting an interpretation to it.'[7] Hence, public equality policies, well-meaning as they may be, are developed in order to address a certain interpretation of a social problem, and they seldom cap-ture or address the real-life complexities of those social problems, Bacchi has developed what she calls the 'What is the problem?' approach as a methodology for shifting the focus from viewing policies as solutions to social problems to analysing the interaction between the policies and the dominant interpretation of a social problem.[8] Elsewhere, I have found Bacchi's approach useful for analysing the interaction between strategies for equality and dominant explanations for per-sisting inequalities between the sexes.[9] Here I want to refer to Bacchi's methodol-ogy as a way to question the development over time of different strategies for equality between the sexes within the UN. The dominant explanation for persist-ing inequalities tends to be the inadequacy of previous strategies.[10] Hence, for example, the 'gender mainstreaming turn' in UN equality politics was developed in order to overcome the limitations of having only specialised, woman-centred equality initiatives.[11] However, while the adoption of strategies for mainstreaming

[5] ECOSOC Agreed Conclusions 1997/2.

[6] CL Bacchi, *Women, Policy and Politics: The Construction of Policy Problems* (London, Sage Publications, 1999) at 7.

[7] *Ibid*, at 9.

[8] *Ibid*, at 4.

[9] S Kouvo, *Making Just Rights? Mainstreaming Women's Human Rights and a Gender Perspective* (Uppsala, Iustus Publications, 2004).

[10] *Ibid*, at 45.

[11] *Ibid*; for further reading see, also J Connors, 'Mainstreaming Gender within the International Framework' in H Barnett (ed), *Sourcebook on Feminist Jurisprudence* (Sydney, Cavendish Publishing

a gender perspective has resulted in an increased focus on what in the UN tends to be called 'women's advancement and gender equality' issues, it is not as evident that gender mainstreaming efforts have resulted in long-term changes in the UN's approach. Fiona Beveridge and Sue Nott have noted that gender mainstreaming strategies are 'strategies that everybody can understand, although no-one is sure what they require in practice'.[12] It is not always evident what gender mainstreaming is, how it should be done, nor what are its expected outcomes.[13] Gender mainstreaming strategies can promote equality, but they can also distort equality and social justice politics. I argue in this paper that it is necessary, when analysing the development and content of UN gender mainstreaming strategies, to be aware that what seems to be UN bureaucrats' sudden and passionate concern for 'women's advancement and gender equality' can have very little to do with a feminist or radical social justice agenda. I argue that we should be alert to the depoliticising effects of gender and the dispersing effects of mainstreaming.

The aim of this chapter is to provide an introduction to, and context for, the UN gender mainstreaming strategy. I will analyse some of the persistent constraints that have been identified in the process of mainstreaming a gender perspective within the UN system.

The 'Gender Turn' in United Nations Equality Politics

The so-called 'woman question' has been part of the UN agenda since the San Francisco Conference in February 1945.[14] The principle of equality between women and men is enshrined in the UN Charter (1946) through a reaffirmation in the Charter preamble of '... faith in fundamental human rights, in the dignity and worth of the human person, in the equal rights of men and women and of nations large and small.' The wording of the preamble is said to have been formulated by Field Marshal Smuts of South Africa, who wanted it to be 'a statement of ideals and aspirations which would rally world opinion in support of the Charter.'[15] At the first UN General Assembly session in 1946, the 'woman question' was highlighted by Eleanor Roosevelt, who presented an Open Letter to the World's Women. According to the letter:

Ltd, 1995); A Gallagher, 'Ending the Marginalization—Strategies for Incorporating Women into the United Nations Human Rights System' (1997) 19 *Human Rights Quarterly* 283; and L Reanda, 'The Commission on the Status of Women' in P Alston (ed), *The United Nations and Human Rights. A Critical Appraisal* (Oxford, Clarendon Paperbacks, 1996).

[12] F Beveridge and S Nott, 'Mainstreaming, A Case for Optimism and Cynicism' (2002) 10 *Feminist Legal Studies* 299, at 308.

[13] *Ibid.*

[14] For a discussion, see D Otto, this volume.

[15] D Stienestra, *Women's Movements and International Organizations* (New York, The MacMillan Press Ltd, 1994).

[T]he United Nations marks the second attempt of the peoples of the world to live peacefully in a democratic world community. This new chance for peace was won through the joint efforts of men and women working together for common ideals of human freedom at a time when the need for united efforts broke down barriers of race, creed and sex.[16]

While many of the state representatives who spoke following Roosevelt's presentation articulated a strong belief in the goodwill of the UN and in women's abilities, not all in attendance were convinced the ostensible political commitment to equality between women and men was sincere. Mrs Vervey from the Netherlands sardonically expressed her gratitude to the General Assembly's male members who had so warmly supported women's quest for recognition within the UN, noting that perhaps there were no opposing voices because no one in the General Assembly expected that '... a recommendation like this [for women's equality] would result in a future Assembly with as many women as there are men.'[17] Her words suggested that supporting formal equality for women takes less effort than ensuring such equality in practice.

The UN has, nevertheless, over the years and through various initiatives, promoted what it calls 'women's advancement and gender equality'. Before the 1990s 'gender turn', when the UN began explicitly to use the language of gender, the organisation had attempted to promote equality either by adding equality and non-discrimination principles to general initiatives, or by creating specific woman-centred institutions, programmes and policies. Both approaches have been criticised as insufficient methods of promoting equality.[18] Choosing to add equality and non-discrimination principles to general initiatives, as was the case in the International Covenants on Civil and Political and Economic, Social and Cultural Rights (1966), has been criticised for failing to address the historical exclusion of women from international law and politics.[19] Women-centred initiatives, such as the Convention on the Elimination of All Forms of Discrimination against Women (1979), have been criticised for marginalising

---

[16] UN Doc A/Pv.29.

[17] *The United Nations and the Advancement of Women 1945–1995* (The Blue Book Series Vol VI), (New York, Dept of Public Information, United Nations, 1995), at 105.

[18] Above n 9.

[19] For an analysis of UN woman-centred initiatives, especially in the human rights sector, see M Bustelo, 'The Committee on the Elimination of Discrimination against Women at the Crossroads' in P Alston (ed), *The Future of the UN Human Rights Treaty Monitoring* (Cambridge, Cambridge University Press, 2000); A Byrnes, J Connors and L Bik (eds), *Advancing the Human Rights of Women: Using International Human Rights Standards in Domestic Litigation* (London, Commonwealth Secretariat, 1997); A Byrnes, 'Using International Human Rights Law and the Procedures to Advance Women's Human Rights' in K Askin and D Koenig (eds), *Women and International Human Rights Law, Volume II* (New York, Transnational Publishers Inc, 2000); S Cartwright, 'The Committee on the Elimination of All Forms of Discrimination against Women' in K Askin and D Koenig (eds), *Women and International Human Rights Law, Voume II* (New York, Transnational Publishers Inc, 2000) and H Charlesworth, 'Transforming the United Men's Club: Feminist Futures for the United Nations' (1994) 4 *Transnational Law and Contemporary Problems* 420.

women and for creating a ghetto of women's issues within the UN.[20] Laura Reanda refers to this tension between promoting equality through general initiatives and doing so through woman-centred initiatives as feminism's 'familiar dilemma':

> The historical development [of the UN's women's advancement and human rights framework] reflects a familiar dilemma in efforts to achieve equality for women. The creation of separate institutional mechanisms and the adoption of specialised measures for women are often necessary in order to rectify existing situations of discrimination. The danger of creating a 'women's ghetto' endowed with less power and resources, attracting less interest and commanding lower priority than other ... goals is latent in this approach.[21]

Even in contexts where women's issues appear to have been included within the UN as the central theme of political discussion, there is still the tendency to distinguish between 'women's issues' and 'real politics'. For example, Arvonne Fraser, in her analysis of the Second World Conference on Women held in Copenhagen in 1980, described the physical change in the conference room when discussion moved from 'women's issues' to 'important political issues' such as the situation in the Middle East. While women had been the heads of country delegations throughout most of the conference, when some political issues were discussed, there was '... a flurry of activity as women delegates were moved aside and the men in virtually every delegation began to move into the chairs behind the microphones'.[22]

Malin Björk provides a similar insight from the Commission on the Status of Women session in March 2003, held 'in the caves of the UN', while three floors above in the Security Council '... the men were deciding on different degrees of militarism or war'.[23] Björk notes that women activists did not have access to the floor where the Security Council held its meetings. She describes the Commission on the Status of Women session as a 'cave world' and as a 'surrealist place', where '... we [the women] through little adjustments in an official document try to remain sane, try to make sense'.[24]

The continuing marginalisation of women's issues within the UN system has, since the Third World Conference on Women held in Nairobi in 1985, led to the growing conviction that equality between the sexes cannot be achieved solely through the inclusion of equality language in UN documents, or through woman-centred initiatives. 'Women's issues', it was felt, needed to be integrated into and to

---

[20] Above n 9.

[21] L Reanda, 'The Commission on the Status of Women' in P Alston (ed), *The United Nations and Human Rights. A Critical Appraisal* (Oxford, Clarendon Paperbacks, 1996), at 267.

[22] A Fraser, *The UN Decade for Women. Documents and Dialogue* (Boulder and London, Westview Press, 1987), at 81.

[23] M Björk, 'Trying to Make Sense ... in the Caves of the UN Building in New York' (2001) 3 *Scum Grrrls* 14.

[24] *Ibid.*

become part of the general UN agenda. The idea that the promotion of equality between the sexes should be the shared responsibility of the UN woman-centred institutions and the overall UN system was further recognised during the World Conference on Human Rights (Vienna, 1993), the World Conference on Population and Development (Cairo, 1994) and the Fourth World Conference on Women (Beijing, 1995).[25] The final reports arising from these conferences emphasise both the continuing importance of targeted intervention for women, and the importance of different 'integrative' or 'mainstreaming' initiatives, aimed at moving equality issues from the margins into the core of UN activities.

The dual strategy promoted by the Fourth World Conference on Women (Beijing, 1995), for example, emphasises both targeted interventions for women's advancement, including for women's human rights, and the importance of mainstreaming a gender perspective. The negotiated Beijing Platform for Action is thus structured around 12 critical areas of concern. In each of these areas '[g]overnments and other actors should promote an active and visible policy of mainstreaming a gender perspective into all policies and programmes, so that, before decisions are taken, an analysis is made of the effects on women and men, respectively'.[26] The dual strategy, emphasising both the strengthening of woman-centred institutions, programmes and policies, and the mainstreaming of a gender perspective, was also reflected in the final report of the Beijing five-year review organised as a special session of the UN General Assembly in June 2000.

Introducing the UN Gender Mainstreaming Strategy

The ECOSOC Agreed Conclusions on Gender Mainstreaming

In 1995, ECOSOC, which is the UN's main inter-governmental institution responsible for economic and social matters, devoted the coordination segment of its annual session to the follow-up to UN conferences. The 1996 coordination segment, stemming from the Beijing Conference, included a focus on the cross-cutting theme of poverty eradication and gender mainstreaming.[27] According to the Secretary-General's report prepared for the ECOSOC session, mainstreaming a gender perspective in poverty eradication requires 'a conscious effort to ensure

---

[25] Above n 8. For analysis of the advances made in integrating women's human rights and a gender perspective at the Vienna and Cairo Conferences, see eg, S Abeyesekere, 'Consolidating Our Gains at the World Conference on Human Rights: A Personal Reflection' (1995) 4 *Canadian Women's Studies/Cahiers de la femme* 6, and C Bunch and N Reilly, 'Demanding Accountability: The Global Campaign and Vienna Tribunal for Women's Human Rights' (New York, Center for Women's Global Leadership, Rutgers University, 1994).

[26] Beijing Platform, Art 79; see also the Beijing Platform, Arts 105, 123, 141, 164, 189, 202, 229, 238, 252 and 273.

[27] UN Doc E/1996/61, part II.

that gender is taken into consideration in activities on poverty eradication on a routine basis to avoid either marginalisation or invisibility of women.'[28] The gender mainstreaming theme was further developed during the ECOSOC session in 1997, where the crosscutting theme was Mainstreaming the Gender Perspective into All Policies and Programmes in the United Nations System.[29] The discussion led to the adoption of the ECOSOC Agreed Conclusions on gender mainstreaming, which include what has become the authoritative definition of gender mainstreaming within the UN system, and which began the process of establishing principles and general recommendations for UN gender mainstreaming efforts.[30] 'Mainstreaming a gender perspective' is, according to the Agreed Conclusions:

> ... the process of assessing the implications for women and men of any planned action, including legislation, policies and programmes, in all areas and at all levels. It is a strategy for making women's as well as men's concerns and experiences an integral dimension of the design, implementation, monitoring and evaluation of policies and programmes in all political, economic and societal spheres so that women and men benefit equally and inequality is not perpetuated. The ultimate goal is to achieve gender equality.[31]

According to this definition, gender mainstreaming is a process-oriented strategy. It demands continuing analysis and evaluation, and entails a shift from approaching equality issues from a 'woman only' frame to one that views equality as the concern of women and men. It asks that gender mainstreaming efforts should focus on both women and men, and especially on how inequalities are reproduced. However, the Agreed Conclusions do not focus in any detail on the conceptual content of gender, or on how gender analyses should be carried out. Instead the ECOSOC Agreed Conclusions simply outline principles and recommendations for gender mainstreaming.

Six gender mainstreaming principles are contained in the ECOSOC Agreed Conclusions to ensure the UN-wide institutional implementation. These gender mainstreaming principles highlight the importance of defining issues so that gender-neutrality is not presumed and gender differences can be detected. They also stipulate high-level responsibility for the action and set out concrete steps to be taken. Finally, the Agreed Conclusions can be read as pledging clear political will and sufficient human and financial resources for implementing gender mainstreaming, whilst also supporting the work of woman-centred institutions.

---

[28] *Ibid*, ch II, para 83.

[29] ECOSOC 1997 Report, ch IV, para 1. See also UN Doc E/CN 6/Res/41/6 and UN Doc E/1997/NGO/1.

[30] As a follow-up measure to the Fourth World Conference on Women, the Secretary-General submits yearly reviews to the Commission on the Status of Women and ECOSOC detailing progress made in mainstreaming a gender perspective into the UN system. See UN Doc A/Res/50/203 and UN Doc A/Res/51/69.

[31] ECOSOC Agreed Conclusions 1997/2, ch 1, para A.

The heart of the recommendations is their emphasis on broad-based and system-wide initiatives and action for mainstreaming a gender perspective, together with an emphasis on the role of UN woman-centred institutions as knowledge banks and initiators in the mainstreaming process. It is made clear that while all UN structures and institutions are under an obligation to mainstream a gender perspective, it is the woman-centred institutions, namely the Commission on the Status of Women, the Division for the Advancement of Women and the Office of the Special Adviser, together with inter-agency networks and gender focal points, that should enable the mainstreaming efforts within the UN system.

The UN Woman-centred Institutions and the UN Gender Mainstreaming Strategy

The UN gender mainstreaming strategy was designed as a response to the perceived failure of woman-centred strategies. A key aspect of the UN's gender mainstreaming strategy has been to work towards equality by combining woman-centred initiatives with gender mainstreaming. This dual strategy is offered as a way to overcome the shortcomings of 'advancing women' solely through woman-centred equality measures. The Office of the Special Adviser has said that targeted interventions should complement gender mainstreaming: [32]

> These interventions could include special research on the differential impact of trade patterns on women, support for a network of women's NGOs looking at women in the media, training to sensitize the judiciary on domestic violence and rape, or training for male politicians on discriminatory practices against women in politics. These types of targeted interventions do not in any way contradict the gender mainstreaming strategy.[33]

Hence, the UN woman-centred institutions, and especially the Secretariat institutions (the Division for the Advancement of Women and the Office of the UN Special Adviser on Gender Issues and Advancement of Women), have been given a dual role. They are now responsible for the targeted interventions for women's advancement and at the same time must work to add content to the ECOSOC Agreed Conclusions on gender mainstreaming.[34]

---

[32] *Gender Mainstreaming: An Overview* (New York, DAW/OSAGI, 2001), at 2.

[33] *Ibid.*

[34] Actions for gender mainstreaming have been taken by UN programmes and funds—see eg, <http://www.un.org/womenwatch/ianwge/gmfacts> (13 May 2004); <http://www.un.org/women-watch/osagi/gendermainstreaming.htm> (13 May 2004); <http://www.un.org.pk/undp/gender/> (14 September 2003); <http://www.unfpa.org/gender> (13 May 2004); <http://www.unicef.org/pro-gramme/ gpp/policy/genmain#gen> (13 May 2004)—and by UN specialised agencies, see eg <http://www.ilo.org/public/english/bureau/gender> (13 May 2004) and <http://www.unesco.org/women> (date accessed 13 May 2004).

The continuing relevance of woman-centred equality initiatives is important. They can be described as providing a 'reality check' on the dual strategy by having women's advancement as their main priority. Targeted intervention is also a reminder that equality strategies, including gender mainstreaming strategies, are necessary because of the structural disadvantages faced by women in many areas of UN activities. This reminder is necessary because there has been a tendency to promote gender mainstreaming strategies without attention to the reality of power relationships between men and women.[35]

The UN woman-centred institutions have fulfilled their mandate as knowledge banks for gender mainstreaming through developing the definitions and guidelines crucial for gender mainstreaming. The Division for the Advancement of Women has, for example, provided a definition of the term 'gender', a definition that is based on the presumption that 'gender' is the social dimension of what can be perceived as biological 'sex'. The Division for the Advancement of Women has in its clarification of the gender mainstreaming strategy defined gender as 'the socially constructed roles of women and men that are ascribed to them on the basis of their sex, in public and in private life'.[36] Similarly, 'gender equality', which is the goal of the UN gender mainstreaming strategy, was not defined in the ECOSOC Agreed Conclusions, but the Office of the Special Adviser has provided a definition of this goal.[37] It sees 'gender equality' as referring to the '… the equal rights, responsibilities and opportunities of women and men and girls and boys.'

> Gender equality implies that the interests, needs and priorities of both women and men are taken into consideration—recognizing the diversity of different groups of women and men. Gender equality is not a 'women's issue' but should concern and fully engage men as well as women.[38]

The Division for the Advancement of Women and the Office of the Special Adviser have developed the content of the UN's gender mainstreaming programme. While gender analysis borrows much of its terminology as well as its conceptual tools from social sciences, it has had to adapt to particular policy contexts when employing these for the purposes of mainstreaming. Moreover, as these strategies aim to make gender concerns an integral dimension of everyone's work, the language of gender analysis must also be accessible.[39] The Office of the Special Adviser therefore published a report entitled *Gender Mainstreaming: An Overview* (2001), which aims to provide an adaptable and accessible framework

---

[35] R Braidotti, *Nomadic Subjects: Embodiment and Sexual Difference in Contemporary Feminist Theory* (New York, Columbia University Press, 1995), at 151.

[36] UN Doc HRI/MC/1998/6, para 16.

[37] See eg the ECOSOC Agreed Conclusions 1997/2 on gender mainstreaming; C Chinkin, *Gender Mainstreaming in Legal and Constitutional Affairs: A Reference Manual for Governments and Other Stakeholders* (UK, Commonwealth Secretariat, 2001).

[38] OSAGI, Fact Sheet 1, August 2001.

[39] Above n 31, at 27.

which highlights concrete and practical steps for carrying out gender analyses in a range of different sectors.

The Office of the Special Adviser acknowledges that gender mainstreaming is a difficult strategy and that efforts to implement it need to be alert to context, as gender differences and inequalities 'manifest themselves in different ways in specific countries or sectors'.[40] However, the Office of the Special Adviser recommends that certain issues should always receive attention.[41] These include: inequalities in political power (such access to decision-making and representation); inequalities within households; differences in legal status and entitlements; gender division of labour within the economy; inequalities in the domestic/unpaid sector; violence against women; and discriminatory attitudes.[42]

The adoption of the ECOSOC Agreed Conclusions on gender mainstreaming and the subsequent work explored above has not, however, ensured that a gender perspective is now mainstreamed within the UN system. On the contrary, the process itself has revealed that there are persistent constraints, which continue to hamper the implementation of the strategy.

Persistent Constraints in UN Gender Mainstreaming Efforts

Conceptual and Analytical Constraints

The gender mainstreaming component of the dual strategy discussed above was designed to ensure that 'women's issues' were re-conceptualised as 'gender issues'. It was hoped that 'equality' would no longer be considered the sole responsibility of woman-centred institutions but would be perceived as the responsibility of all UN institutions. In response to the limited achievements of gender mainstreaming strategies, however, the Office of the Special Adviser has been compelled to attempt to specify the persistent constraints which are hampering successful implementation. These persistent constraints include '... conceptual confusion, inadequate understanding of the linkages between gender perspectives in different areas of the work of the United Nations and gaps in capacity to address gender perspectives once identified.'[43] While gender mainstreaming strategies have been successful at a rhetorical level, and while policy decisions to gender mainstream have been adopted by many different UN institutions, much more work needs to

---

[40] Above n 32, at 5 and 6.
[41] *Ibid*, at 5.
[42] *Ibid*, at 5 and 6.
[43] *Ibid*. For evaluation of the gender mainstreaming strategy see, eg, the Inter-Agency Network's best practice database on gender mainstreaming, at <http://www.un.org/womenwatch/ianwge/ gm_facts/> (13 May 2004).

be done to turn rhetoric into practice. The challenge is educational: different sectors of the UN must understand what 'gender' means, how this perspective can be employed and how mainstreaming can be implemented in different contexts. As will be shown below, a failure to develop an adequate conceptualisation of what is meant by gender can contribute to a neutralisation and re-marginalisation of equality politics.

The UN woman-centred institutions appear to have been inspired by feminist scholarship in adopting a social constructivist interpretation of gender. This is reflected in the UN guidelines on mainstreaming.[44] The definition relies on the distinction between gender and sex, according to which gender is socially constructed and is the social and cultural consequence of biological sex. The motivation behind the feminist adoption of the distinction between gender and sex in the 1970s was to some extent strategic.[45] Feminists needed to be able to challenge the hitherto hegemonic construction of the sexes as naturally different.[46] I would argue that the reason for the UN's adoption of a social constructionist approach to gender is similar. The notion of 'gender' provides a means to argue that the relative positions of men and women can be challenged and changed. Promoting the use of 'gender perspectives' in UN equality politics allows innovative thinking regarding both women's and men's roles. However, we should not lose sight of the fact that introducing the sex/gender distinction into feminist argumentation in the 1970s did, as Donna Haraway notes, 'cost blood in struggle in many social arenas'.[47] Rosi Braidotti has argued that the feminist scholars have, in order to promote the notion of gender and in order to make the 'struggle' easier, undermined the power-impregnated and hierarchical content of the concept, and that the development of 'gender studies' has contributed to the depolitisation of feminism. This suggests that feminism's ongoing critiques of the analytical categories it chooses to use may, as well as leading to the development of vibrant theoretical debates, have watered down analyses of hierarchy and power.[48] Braidotti argues that

[o]n a more theoretical level I think that the main assumption behind 'gender studies' is a new symmetry between the sexes, which practically results in a renewal of

---

[44] Above, n 32, at 5.

[45] For an analysis of the history of the concept of gender, see, eg, Å Carlson, *Kön, kropp och konstruktion. En undersökning av den filosofiska grunden för distinktionen mellan kön och genus* (Stockholm, Brutus Östlings Bokförlag Symposium, 2001); D Glover and C Kaplan, *Genders* (New York, Routledge, 1999); S Kouvo, *Making Just Rights. Mainstreaming Women's Human Rights and a Gender Perspective* (Uppsala, Iustus Publications, 2004); T Moi, '*Vad är en kvinna? Kön och Genus i feministisk teori*' (1997) 1-2 *Res Publica* 71; and J Scott, 'Gender: A Useful Category of Historical Analysis' in A Rao (ed), *Women's Studies International—Nairobi and Beyond* (New York, The Feminist Press at the City University of New York, 1991); J Butler, *Gender Trouble: Feminism and the Subversion of Identity* (New York, Routledge, 1990) 3–4.

[46] D Haraway, *Simians, Cyborgs, and Women. The Reinvention of Nature* (New York, Routledge, 1991), at 134.

[47] *Ibid*, at 127.

[48] Above n 35, at 150 and 151.

interest for men and men's studies. Faced with this, I would like to state my disagreement with this illusion of symmetry...[49]

Similarly, within the UN context, there have been strong reactions against a social constructionist approach to gender, and attempts have been made to reassert the importance of sex as an analytic category. The introduction of the language of gender into the Beijing Platform was, for example, controversial. During the preparations for the Beijing Conference the Commission on the Status of Women established an informal working group to discuss the meaning of the term. The working group could not agree on a substantial definition, but concluded that:[50]

> The word 'gender' had been commonly used and understood in its ordinary, generally accepted usage in numerous other United Nations forums and conferences; there was no indication that any new meaning or connotation of the term, different from accepted prior usage, was intended in the Platform for Action.[51]

The word 'gender' remained in brackets in the draft Beijing Platform for Action and was subject to further discussion throughout the Beijing Conference drafting process. While the term 'gender' was eventually adopted into the final version of the Beijing Platform, it remains subject to interpretive statements and reservations. The Beijing debates focused on two competing understandings of gender. The first was as the socially construed dimension of 'biological' sex and the second was as alternative term for 'sex'. The European Platform for Action at Beijing promoted an understanding of gender as the social dimension of sex, noting, for example, the close interrelatedness of human sexuality and gender relations, and emphasising that gender analyses should be used '... systematically to identify the gender-specific impact and implications of economic, political and social reforms and policies.'[52] The Holy See, on the other hand, reacted against the idea that gender was socially construed and against the questioning of women and men's different roles. The Holy See submitted an interpretive statement regarding the concept of gender, accepting its usage in the Beijing Platform, but noting that:

> The term 'gender' is understood by the Holy See as grounded in biological sexual identity, male or female. Furthermore, the Platform for Action itself clearly uses the term 'both genders'. The Holy See thus excludes dubious interpretations based on

---

[49] *Ibid*, at 151.

[50] UN Doc E/1995/26 – E/CN6/1995/14, ch I, decision 39/3 and ch VIII, para 17. See also D Otto, 'Holding up Half the Sky, but for Whose Benefit? A Critical Analysis of the Fourth World Conference on Women' (1996) 7 *Australian Feminist Law Journal*, 11. Statements made by the Chairperson, by the representatives of Australia, Pakistan, the Sudan, Chile, Namibia, and the Philippines, and by the observers for Benin, Egypt, the USA, Canada, Guatemala, Morocco and Norway, UN Doc E/1995/26–E/CN6/1995/14, ch VIII, para 17.

[51] UN Doc A/Conf 177/L2, annex, para 2.

[52] European Platform for Action, paras 9 and 94.

world views which assert that sexual identity can be adapted indefinitely to suit new and different purposes.[53]

The definitions of gender included in the International Criminal Court Statute, and in the final report of the World Conference against Racism, Racial Discrimination, Xenophobia and Related Intolerance held in Durban in 2000, seem to rely on the a definition of gender similar to that in the Holy See interpretive comment. They favour an interpretation of gender as synonymous with sex. Article 7(3) of the International Criminal Court Statute defines gender as referring '… to the two sexes, male and female, within the context of society. The term "gender" does not indicate any meaning different from the above.' The final document from the Durban Conference, the Durban Declaration and Programme for Action, reproduces the definition from the International Criminal Court Statute.[54] Its inclusion in a statute means that it carries considerable interpretive power.

As this discussion has shown, while the UN woman-centred institutions promote a social constructionist approach to gender, this definition remains controversial and cannot be said to be widely supported or accepted within the UN system. The preference for equating gender with sex, especially in key documents such as the final report from the Durban Conference and the International Criminal Court Statute, weakens the notion of gender and consequently its potential as an analytical tool at the heart of UN equality politics.

Persistent Constraints

These conceptual and analytical constraints are only one part of the persistent constraints hampering the implementation of the gender mainstreaming strategy. The mainstreaming strategy itself poses difficulties. Mainstreaming strategies consist of moving an issue into a framework from which it has previously been excluded, and allowing it to be integrated into or to transform that framework.[55] That is, gender mainstreaming strategies have *at their best* a two-fold aim: moving issues from the margins to the mainstream, and allowing the issue to have an impact on and ideally to transform the mainstream. The 'mainstream' includes, for example, high-level decision-making bodies within an institution.[56] However,

---

[53] UN Doc A/Conf 177/20.

[54] Durban Declaration and Programme for Action, footnote 1. Note that there are only two footnotes in the whole Durban Declaration and Programme for Action.

[55] Beveridge and Nott, above n 12, at 308, note that mainstreaming has been defind as a '"deceptively simple concept that is likely to be extremely difficult to operationalize" and as "an extraordinarily demanding concept, which requires the adoption of a gender perspective by all the central actors in the policy process"'.

[56] ECOSOC Agreed Conclusions 1997/2.

these two aims are not always recognised to be intricately connected. Within the literature on mainstreaming, a distinction is made between *integrative* and *agenda-setting* or *transformative* mainstreaming approaches.[57] Integrative mainstreaming includes moving a certain issue, such as gender or human rights, into a pre-existing framework, while agenda-setting or transformative mainstreaming includes reorientation and transformation of a whole agenda.[58]

According to Fiona Beveridge and Sue Nott, who have analysed gender mainstreaming efforts within the European Union, the strategy is 'fuzzy' as it does not give adequate attention to the question of how to mainstream, or what the expected results of mainstreaming should be.[59] This has led to a preference for integrative mainstreaming approaches within many public institutions. Feminist scholars have argued, however, that gender mainstreaming strategies cannot be successful without a transformative agenda.[60] The Commission on Human Rights has defined mainstreaming as involving '… the placing of an issue within the pre-existing institutional, academic and discursive framework. It is the opposite of marginalization.'[61] This definition suggests a preference for integrative mainstreaming. The Office of the Special Adviser, in its gender mainstreaming document *Gender Mainstreaming: An Overview* (2001), provides some conceptual clarification in the hope of encouraging a transformative approach:

> Mainstreaming is not about adding a 'women's component', or even a 'gender equality component', to an existing activity. It involves more than increasing women's participation. Mainstreaming situates gender equality issues at the centre of policy decisions, medium-term plans, programme budgets, and institutional structures and processes. Mainstreaming entails bringing the perceptions, experience, knowledge and interests of women as well as men to bear on policy-making, planning and decision-making. Mainstreaming can reveal a need for changes in goals, strategies and actions … It can require change in organizations … to create organizational environments which are conducive to the promotion of gender equality.[62]

Despite formal commitments to mainstreaming at the policy and institutional level, questions regarding the advancement of women and gender equality remain marginalised within the UN system. There is little to suggest that the introduction of gender mainstreaming has altered the structural discrimination and oppression

---

[57] Above n 12.

[58] R Jahan, *The Elusive Agenda. Mainstreaming Women in Development* (Dhaka and London, University Press Limited/Zed Books, 1995).

[59] Above n 12.

[60] Above n 12.

[61] UN Doc CN4/1998/49, para 8.

[62] Above n 32. In *Gender Mainstreaming: An Overview*, it is noted that although there is 'no set formula [for gender mainstreaming] that can be applied in every context. … [W]hat is common to mainstreaming in all sectors or development issues is that a concern for gender equality is brought into the "mainstream" of activities rather than being dealt with as an add-on'.

of women.[63] And for UN bureaucrats who are not interested in women's issues (or who might be convinced that women and men are equal, that feminism is *passé* or that feminists have gone too far) the very process of understanding why a gender perspective is important and how it might affect their area of expertise is a difficult one. For these reasons, integrative mainstreaming strategies may in reality be easier to achieve than transformative ones.

Some of the difficulties of implementing gender mainstreaming are exemplified in Hilary Charlesworth and Mary Wood's analysis of the UN Transitional Administration in East Timor (hereafter, UNTEAT).[64] According to the authors, UNTEAT was at first sight 'an example of women's rights sensitive nation-building'.[65] Their analysis goes on to show the ambivalent role played by UNTEAT's Gender Advisory Unit. The main criticisms cited by Charlesworth and Wood against the Gender Advisory Unit echo the persistent constraints to mainstreaming which have been identified by the Office of the Special Adviser. East Timorese women criticised UNTEAT and the Gender Advisory Unit for '... the failure to produce a clear definition of gender mainstreaming and its subjects.'[66] It was not clear whether the efforts to gender mainstream were aimed at the UNTEAT's international personnel or at the East Timorese people, or how the Gender Advisory Unit was in fact supposed to support East Timorese women.[67] Charlesworth and Wood conclude that a number of difficulties converged to hamper UNTEAT's ability to fully mainstream gender into the East Timor peace and reconstruction processes.

Within the UN system there seems to have been a tendency to promote integrative mainstreaming strategies, which only implies moving issues from the margins. Thus, integrative mainstreaming may well give the appearance of successful mainstreaming—and of a system that takes gender issues seriously—but this is achieved without insisting on transformation or on thorough changes within the system.

Conclusions

The aim of this chapter has been to present an overview of the development of UN gender mainstreaming strategies, and to analyse the potential and limitations of these strategies. In particular, I argued that, as with other policy prescriptions, there is a danger that gender mainstreaming is offered as 'the solution', rather than as one part of a broader political response to a complex of social problems. Hence, I argued here for a more challenging interrogation of gender mainstreaming, one

---

[63] Above n 7.
[64] H Charlesworth and M Wood, 'Women and Human Rights in the Rebuilding of East Timor' (2002) 71 *Nordic Journal of International Law* 325, at 326 and 328.
[65] *Ibid*, at 329.
[66] *Ibid*, at 344.
[67] *Ibid*, at 344.

that focuses on gender mainstreaming as one strategy among other efforts to address inequality.

Recently, feminist scholars such as Anne Orford have began to question what lies behind the claim that gender mainstreaming is, as the Office of the Special Adviser puts it, 'a global strategy for equality'. How does gender mainstreaming really work within the UN and in the field? In Orford's words:

> Does gender work as a category in such situations [in attempts to support the role of women in peace processes and in reconstructive projects in Bougainville, the Solomon Islands and East Timor], and if so, whose work does it do? How does this officially sanctioned desire to 'include' women as participants relate to the current enthusiasm for exporting institutions of the free market in the name of democracy? Such issues are much more complicated than the picture painted by these UN documents of a world in which, to paraphrase Spivak, white women save brown women from brown men. Failing to ask such questions of the role played by 'gender mainstreaming' in the new world order may mean that feminism ends up simply facilitating the existing projects and priorities of militarised economic globalisation in the name of protecting and promoting the interests of women.[68]

While there is a danger that gender mainstreaming may be offered as an easy solution, it is also clear that this strategy is far from easy to understand or implement. While the core components of the UN gender mainstreaming strategies can be explained in relation to the shortcomings of the earlier woman-centred strategies, they are less easy to keep in focus when they are being implemented in different institutional contexts within the UN. This is also highlighted by the Office of the Special Adviser, which has identified persistent constraints in the process, according to which uncertainties remain about what gender mainstreaming means, what it is supposed to do and how it is supposed to be done.

The fact that persistent constraints have been identified may be said to demonstrate that the UN has taken its gender mainstreaming mandate seriously, and that different parts of the UN system are struggling with how to implement the strategy. While this may be true, Charlesworth and Wood's case study of the efforts to gender mainstream in the process of rebuilding East Timor shows that gender issues remain institutionally and politically sidelined. Under-funded and marginalised, gender mainstreaming strategies may prove to be politically ineffective as a means to achieve equality between men and women.[69]

---

[68] A Orford, 'Feminism, Imperialism and the Mission of International Law' (2002) 71 *Nordic Journal of International Law* 275, at 283.

[69] ECOSOC has, after a request from the Commission on the Status of Women, decided to review the efforts made to implement the ECOSOC Agreed Conclusions on gender mainstreaming from 1997 at one of its sessions before 2005. The ECOSOC review will probably contribute to determining the future of the UN gender mainstreaming efforts, ie determining whether the UN gender mainstreaming strategies will become yet another paper tiger for equality, or whether institutional and political substance can be inserted into the strategies.

12

Women's Rights and the Organization of African Unity and African Union: The Protocol on the Rights of Women in Africa

RACHEL MURRAY*

Introduction

While the Organization of African Unity's (OAU) Charter of 1963 made no mention of women, and the 1981 African Charter on Human and Peoples' Rights (ACHPR) only a passing reference, recent developments have illustrated a greater awareness of the position of women's rights in the African regional mechanism. The inclusion of an additional Protocol to the ACHPR on Women's Rights is one of the most significant developments. This increased attention is further reflected in the provisions of the Constitutive Act of the new African Union (AU).[1]

The reasoning and philosophy behind the recent increased attention to women's rights has, however, not been clear. This chapter will examine the background and reasons behind the adoption of an additional Protocol on the Rights of Women in Africa to the ACHPR. It will consider the use of existing international standards by those drafting the Protocol, and why they felt it necessary to adopt a protocol, rather than use existing mechanisms available under the ACHPR. As will be seen, the decision to adopt an additional Protocol on the Rights of Women in Africa was not driven, as might have been expected, by a clear vision of the rights already protected by existing international instruments such as CEDAW and the ACHPR, and those not so protected. Instead, the decision to adopt the Protocol was seen as a way to compel the African Commission on Human and Peoples' Rights to be attentive to women's rights and, additionally, to give women

* Reader in Law, University of Bristol. This paper is a version of that given to the SPTL International Law Section Conference on 'Gender Perspectives and International Law', 25 March 2002. I would like to thank Fareda Banda, Amanda Lloyd, Betty Mould-Iddrisu, Elize Delport and the editors of this collection for their tremendous help and ideas in writing this article.

[1] The OAU has recently been transformed into the African Union, see Constitutive Act of the African Union, adopted Lomé, Togo, 11 July 2000; entered into force July 2002.

a sense of ownership over rights at this level. The problem with this approach, however, was that in the process of adopting the Protocol there was no clear philosophy behind why some rights were included and others were not. While existing enforcement mechanisms in the ACHPR in particular could have been used more fully, the preference was to create an additional protocol. Thus, the opportunity to take a comprehensive look at what was available and build upon them has never been fully grasped. The result is a Protocol that is not consistent in its approach to UN standards or the ACHPR and is weak on enforcement.

Use of International Law by African Institutions

It has been argued that Africa has 'generally been a recipient of, rather than a contributor to, the development of international law',[2] yet the importance of the OAU/AU and its organs in advancing international human rights law should not be overlooked.[3] The adoption of the African Charter on Human and Peoples' Rights in 1981, with its provisions, more importantly, on individual duties and peoples' rights, was said to reflect the continent's own view of human rights standards. This led many to question whether there was an 'African' concept of human rights.[4] The relationship between international human rights standards and instruments adopted at the regional level is an interesting and complex one. It is clear that African institutions at the level of the OAU/AU and the African Commission on Human and Peoples' Rights have used and relied on principles and standards developed by the UN and regional bodies.

The African Charter provides expressly for the African Commission, the body established under the African Charter on Human and Peoples' Rights, to draw inspiration from international law on human and peoples' rights, particularly from the provisions of various African instruments on human and peoples' rights, the Charter of the United Nations, the Charter of the Organization of African Unity, the Universal Declaration of Human Rights, other instruments adopted by the United Nations and by African countries in the field of human and peoples' rights as well as from the provisions of various instruments adopted within the Specialised Agencies of the United Nations of which the parties to the present Charter are members.[5] The Commission is also required to 'take into consideration,

---

[2] AP Mutharika, 'The Role of International Law in the Twenty-First Century: An African Perspective' (1995) *Fordham International Law Journal* 1706; T Maluwa, 'International Law Making in the Organization of African Unity: An Overview' (2000) *Revue Africaine des Droits Internationales et Comparatif* 201, 201.

[3] TO Elias, *Africa and the Development of International Law* (The Hague, Martinus Nijhoff, 1988) ch 1.

[4] See, eg, I Shivji, *The Concept of Human Rights in Africa* (London, Codesria Book Series, 1989); A An-Na'im and F Deng, *Human Rights in Africa: Cross Cultural Perspectives* (Washington DC, Brookings Institute, 1990).

[5] Art 60, ACHPR.

as subsidiary measures to determine the principles of law, other general or special international conventions ... African practices consistent with international norms of human and peoples' rights, customs generally accepted as law, general principles of law recognised by African states as well as legal precedents and doctrine'.[6]

The African Commission and other OAU/AU institutions have sometimes argued that they are *African* bodies developing *African* standards which somehow differ from those available elsewhere. Yet it would seem that the African Commission has often relied more in its decisions on European or UN documents and jurisprudence. For example, in some of its decisions on cases it has used non-African jurisprudence to support its findings on various provisions in the African Charter, and in some instances has relied on them almost to the point of applying the UN body or European Court on Human Rights' decision in that particular case.[7] The Commission has rarely referred to decisions from African national courts or other African institutions in the same way.[8] This may have been due in the past to the number of Western interns based at the Secretariat and involved in drafting decisions, and, more recently, to the relatively easy availability of UN and European case law and documentation.

Where the Commission thinks the rights it is interpreting are contentious, or the jurisprudence it seeks to develop goes beyond what has been easily accepted in the international field, it has, paradoxically, looked to the international arena rather than to Africa itself to support its position. So, for example, in a recent communication relating to the exploration of oil in Ogoniland in Nigeria which impacted on the lives, health and environment of the population of the area,[9] the Commission found a series of violations of economic and social rights in the Charter, as well as the right of a people to a safe and satisfactory environment. In doing so, the African Commission referred to Articles 60 and 61 of its Charter to justify paying considerable attention to the interpretations as developed by the UN Committee on Economic, Social and Cultural Rights, and its General Comments. Using the Committee's jurisprudence, as well as writers mostly from the West, and case law from the Inter-American system and the ECHR,[10] the

---

[6] Art 61, ACHPR.

[7] For example, see Communication 224/98, *Media Rights Agenda v Nigeria*, 14th Annual Activity Report of the African Commission on Human and Peoples' Rights, 2000–2001, Annex V; Communication 225/98, *Huri-Laws v Nigeria*, 14th Annual Activity Report of the African Commission on Human and Peoples' Rights, 2000–2001, Annex V. See also Communication 211/98, *Legal Resources Foundation v Zambia*, 14th Annual Activity Report of the African Commission on Human and Peoples' Rights, 2000–2001, Annex V.

[8] Where it has drawn upon national court decisions, these have been largely because they are the same case before the national courts, see, eg, Communication 97/93 *John K Modise v Botswana*, 14th Annual Activity Report of the African Commission on Human and Peoples' Rights, 2000–2001, Annex V.

[9] Communication 155/96, *The Social and Economic Rights Action Centre and the Centre for Economic and Social Rights v Nigeria*, 15th Annual Activity Report of the African Commission on Human and Peoples' Rights, 2001–2002, Annex V.

[10] For example, it referred to A Eide, 'Economic, Social and Cultural Rights As Human Rights', in A Eide, C Krause and A Rasas (eds), *Economic, Social, and Cultural Rights: A Textbook* (The Hague, Brill, 1995); General Comment No14 (2000) of the Committee on Economic, Social and Cultural

African Commission found violations of the rights to housing and food which are not expressly mentioned in the African Charter. Although this case used a variety of sources, it did not draw upon any African source, domestic or regional, of which there are many useful examples.[11] The OAU/AU organs have also used the fact that states have signed and ratified UN treaties on particular issues as an encouragement to ratify similar African documents,[12] and have constantly stressed that regional arrangements often 'should be complementary to, rather than in competition with, the universal processes undertaken within the wider UN system'.[13]

It would seem that the African Commission and the OAU/AU seem wary of validating their own findings through African jurisprudence, or believe that their findings will not be accepted unless they display some reference to international law, rather than African sources. The Commission and AU organs should have the courage to rely on their own standards and African initiatives, rather than solely on European or UN ones. Not to do so will exacerbate the perception that the UN or European systems are in some way preferable.

This is reflected in the decision to create a separate instrument on the rights of women rather than to use existing mechanisms and procedures that were already available under the OAU/AU and ACHPR. The following section outlines what these are.

The Organization of African Unity and African Union

The majority of work done on human rights within the context of the OAU/AU has taken place under the African Charter on Human and Peoples' Rights, adopted under the auspices of the OAU in 1981 and coming into force in 1986. However, in more recent years the OAU, now the AU, as the political organisation for Africa, has considered human rights issues increasingly to be part of its mandate.[14]

Rights; Inter-American Court of Human Rights, *Velàsquez Rodrígeuz* Case, Judgment of 19 July 1988, Series C, No 4; *X and Y v The Netherlands*, 91 ECHR (1985) (Ser A) at 32.

[11] The *Grootboom* decision in the South African Constitutional Court is one such example, Case No CCT 11/2000, *Government of the Republic of South Africa v Grootboom and others*. See also a similar approach adopted by the African Commission in Communication 218/98, *Civil Liberties Organisation, Legal Defence Centre, Legal Defence and Assistance Project v Nigeria*, 14th Annual Activity Report of the African Commission on Human and Peoples' Rights, 2000–2001, Annex V.

[12] For example, in respect of the African Charter on the Rights and Welfare of the Child which came into force in 1999, despite the fact that practically all African states have ratified the UN Convention on the Rights of the Child.

[13] T, Maluwa, 'International Law Making in the Organization of African Unity: An Overview' (2000) *Revue Africaine des Droits Internationales et Comparatif* 201, 202.

[14] The reasons for increased attention to human rights are complex but include a change in leadership of states and increasing desire for democratisation; see R Murray, *Human Rights in Africa: From Organization of African Unity to African Union* (Cambridge, Cambridge University Press, 2002).

In relation to women's rights, the OAU/AU has paid increasing attention to women's participation and the role of women in decision-making. The creation of a Women's Unit in the Secretariat and the adoption by the various OAU organs of declarations and decisions relating to the position of women are a product of this increased interest.[15] Particular attention has been paid to women in situations of conflict[16] and development.[17] The OAU/AU organs have requested the UN to include more women in their election observation teams. They have also suggested the appointment of more female special envoys who are sent to deal with settlement of disputes and select quotas for women. For example, that five out of the 10 members of the Secretariat of the new African Union should be women[18] and that women should 'form at least half of all peace negotiations panels'. This latter suggestion, it is believed, would help 'in the resolution of differences between warring factions, in the African way'.[19] The OAU/AU has also noted the particular position of women as refugees.[20] The establishment of a Women's Committee on Peace and Development in 1997[21] consolidated this further.[22] Treaties adopted under the auspices of the OAU/AU also take gender into account.[23]

The OAU's recent transformation into the African Union has been modelled in part on the European Union. It involved a new foundation treaty, the Constitutive Act. This provided an opportunity to give more attention to women, with the

[15] See Report of the 73rd Ordinary Session of the Council of Ministers, February 2001, CM/Rpt (LXXIII), paras 74–75; Decision on Women and Gender, CM/Dec 579 (LXXIII). See also Addis Ababa Declaration on Violence Against Women, OAU AHSG, 31st Session, June 1998; Draft Resolution on the African Conference on the Empowerment of Women Through Functional Literacy and the Education of the Girl Child, DM/Draft/Res 19 (LXIII) Rev 1; and the African Declaration on Violence Against Women by Harmful Traditional Practices, 34th Ordinary Session of the Assembly of Heads of State and Government, 1998.

[16] For example, see Lessons from a Decade of Conflicts: Prospects of Peace and Security by the Year 2000. A Presentation by His Excellency Salim Ahmed Salim Secretary General, Conference of African Ministers of Planning and UNDP Resident Representatives, 31 January–2 February Ouagadougou, Burkina Faso, p 24 (on file with the author): 'the major victims of conflicts in Africa are women and children'.

[17] *Ibid*, at 24.

[18] This had been lobbied by NGOs and other organs under the Consultation on Gender Mainstreaming and Effective Participation of Women in the African Union that took place prior to the African Union Summit in Durban, South Africa, 28–30 June 2002.

[19] Report of the Secretary-General on the Twenty-Second Ordinary OAU Session of the Labour and Social Affairs Commission, CM/2112 (LXX), considering the Report of the Secretary-General on the Role and Contribution of Women to Peace-Making, Peace-Building and Socio-Economic Development in Africa (Doc LSC/8 (XXII)).

[20] 'As refugees and internally displaced persons, women can play a very important role in conflict resolution, rehabilitation and peace-building': Report of the Secretary-General on the Twenty-Second Ordinary Session of the OAU Labour and Social Affairs Commission, CM/2112 (LXX), considering the Report of the Secretary-General on the Role and Contribution of Women to Peace-Making, Peace-Building and Socio-Economic Development in Africa (Doc LSC/8 (XXII)).

[21] Report of the Secretary-General on the Implementation of the African Platform of Action: Women, Peace and Development, CM/Dec.337 (LXVI).

[22] See Terms of Reference and Rules of Procedure, OAU/ECA/AF/WM/PD/6(1). Report of the Secretary-General on the Implementation of the African Platform of Action: Women, Peace and Development, CM/Dec.337 (LXVI).

[23] For example, the African Charter on the Rights and Welfare of the Child.

'promotion of gender equality' being one of the principles of the Union[24] and the functions of the Executive Council including 'social security, including the formulation of mother and child care policies, as well as policies relating to the disabled and the handicapped'.[25] Similarly, the recent instruments relating to the New Partnership for Africa's Development (NEPAD) refer to women's rights several times.[26] Yet neither appeared to have involved wider society and women in general in their formation. The mention made of women is rather general, and in respect of NEPAD, 'mainly linked to [its] limited plans for women'.[27] As a result this has led some to conclude that 'the structure and language ... is a reflection of the patriarchal nature of African society that encourages little or no female participation in its evolution'.[28] Merely declaring that women should have rights and be involved is too easy a way to appear to be doing something about their position without really challenging political power.[29]

The African Charter on Human and Peoples' Rights

It is through the work of the African Commission on Human and Peoples' Rights and the ACHPR that most attention to women's rights has been paid. The Charter itself gave little express attention to the position of women, with Article 2 providing only a general non-discrimination clause and Article 18(3) requiring states to eliminate 'every discrimination against women and also ensure the protection of the rights of women'. There were concerns that reference to traditional values in the Charter[30] would take precedence over women's concerns.[31] Two important recent developments have dominated the Commission's work on the rights of women, namely the appointment of the Special Rapporteur on Women's Rights and moves towards the adoption of a Protocol on the Rights of Women in Africa. There has been little use of existing provisions or mechanisms that are available under the Charter. These will be examined briefly.

---

[24] Art 4(l), Constitutive Act.

[25] Art 13, Constitutive Act.

[26] See <http://www.uneca.org/nepad,> (last accessed 12 December 2003), at paras 49, 67, 68, 118 and 119.

[27] T Ige, 'NEPAD and African Women: Mechanism for Engagement Input and Ownership', produced at: <http://www.unesco.org/women/NEPAD/tokunbo.htm> (last accessed 12 December 2003).

[28] *Ibid.*

[29] See F Banda, 'Going it Alone: SADC and the Gender Debate', paper presented to SPTL Public International Law Group, 12th Conference on Theory and International Law, Gender Perspectives and International Law, 25 March 2002.

[30] S Wright, 'Economic Rights and Social Justice: A Feminist Analysis of Some International Human Rights Conventions' (1992) *Australian Yearbook of International Law* 242, at 258.

[31] Comments from Elize Delport, Commissioner, Commission on Gender Equality, South Africa.

Using Existing Mechanisms of the ACHPR

On a positive note, there have been considerable efforts made both to increase the number of women members on the Commission[32] and to ensure gender representation among the judges of the proposed African Court of Human and Peoples' Rights.[33] This appears to have been part of the attempts to increase attention to women under the ACHPR. There is a great deal of potential to employ the existing enforcement mechanisms of the African Charter to promote and protect the rights of women, even though the substantive provisions pay limited express attention to women.[34]

The Commission has a broad remit under Articles 45 and 46 of the African Charter to promote and protect the rights contained in the Charter. It also has a potentially large variety of mechanisms at its disposal, yet few have been used to advance the rights of women. For example, although the Commission has adopted a number of resolutions, none has focused on interpreting the Charter from the perspective of women.[35] Further, the ability of individuals or groups to submit cases before the African Commission under its communication procedure[36] is automatic on ratification of the Charter and does not require the applicant to be a victim of a violation. Most cases before the Commission, despite the wide provisions in its Charter (covering not only civil and political rights, but also economic, social and cultural rights, peoples' rights and individual duties), have related to rights to be free from arbitrary detention, fair trial and torture.[37] Despite the available procedure for bringing cases, something which was not possible under CEDAW for many years, there have been no cases specifically relating to women's rights and only very few in which the violation of the rights of women has been even a secondary or indirect issue.[38] Consequently, little jurisprudence on the rights of women has emerged from the Commission. Further, the ability of

---

[32] Five of the 11 Commissioners are women: Dr Angela Melo, Mrs Jainaba Johm, Mrs Sawadogo Tapsoba, Dr Vera Chirwa and Ms Sanji Monageng.

[33] Art 12(2) of the Protocol.

[34] See further, R Murray, 'A Feminist Perspective on Reform of the African Human Rights System' (2001) *African Human Rights Law Journal* 205.

[35] The only resolutions that specifically relate to women are those on the Special Rapporteur and Draft Protocol. Women, where they are mentioned, are merely referred to in passing; see, eg, in the Resolution on HIV/AIDS Pandemi—Threat Against Human Rights and Humanity, 14th Activity Report of the African Commission on Human and Peoples' Rights, 2000–2001, AHG/229 (XXXVII), Annex IV.

[36] Arts 55–59.

[37] See R Murray and M Evans, *Documents of the African Commission on Human and Peoples' Rights* (Oxford, Hart Publishing, 2001).

[38] See, eg, Report of the Mission to Mauritania of the African Commission on Human and Peoples' Rights, Nouakchott 19–27 June 1996, 10th Annual Activity Report of the African Commission on Human and Peoples' Rights, 1996–1997, ACHPR/RPT/10th, Annex IX. Communications 54/91, 61/91, 98/93, 164/97 to 196/97, 210/98, *Malawi African Association, Amnesty International, Ms. Sarr Diop, Union Interafricaine des Droits de l'Homme and RADDHO, Collectif des Veuves et Ayants-droit, Association Mauritanienne des Droits de l'Homme v Mauritania*, 13th Activity Report, 1999–2000, AHG/222/36th, Annex V. See R Murray and M Evans, n 37 above.

complainants to request provisional measures from the African Commission to prevent irreparable damage,[39] a mechanism which has been used on various occasions, has never been employed in respect of the rights of women.[40]

Under Article 62 of the Charter, states are required to submit a report every two years on the measures taken to implement the Charter.[41] The report is then orally examined by the Commission at one of its sessions. States are specifically requested to report on the situation of women's rights in their countries, with the Commission's original guidelines making express reference to CEDAW in this regard,[42] and states are frequently asked questions by Commissioners about the rights of women during the examination process.[43] Even where they are not being examined, states in their general statements to the Commission have referred to the position of women in their countries.[44]

Special Rapporteur on the Rights of Women

In 1998, the Commission appointed one of its female Commissioners, Julienne Ondziel-Gnelenga, to the position of Special Rapporteur on the Rights of Women.[45] She was the third Special Rapporteur to be appointed by the Commission.[46] This event had the potential to ensure that women's rights were integral to all of the Commission's work. The Special Rapporteur's mandate was very broad and she was required to

> carry out a study on the situation of the human rights of women in Africa; draw up guidelines on drafting and examination of state parties reports on the rights of women in Africa; ensure or make a follow up on implementation of the Charter by

[39] Rule 111, Rules of Procedure of the African Commission on Human and Peoples' Rights.

[40] In respect of the Nigerian woman, Amina Lawal, who was sentenced to death by stoning by a Shari'a court for having a child out of wedlock, the Commission did contact the Nigerian government in this regard. This may, however, have been more to do with the international attention that this case generated than with the issue of a violation of the rights of a woman.

[41] Most states are behind in their obligations.

[42] Guidelines for National Periodic Reports, Second Annual Activity Report of the African Commission on Human and Peoples' Rights 1988–1989, ACHPR/RTP/2nd, Annex XII, para VII; see also Amendment of the General Guidelines for the Preparation of Periodic Reports by States Parties, DOC/OS/27 (XXIII), para 5.

[43] See R Murray, 'Report on the 1999 sessions of the African Commission on Human and Peoples' Rights' (2001) *Human Rights Law Journal* 172.

[44] *Ibid.*

[45] After lobbying from NGOs such as WILDAF (Women and Law in Development in Africa), the International Commission of Jurists (ICJ) and African Centre for Democracy and Human Rights Studies. This post has now been occupied by a newly-appointed Commissioner, Dr Melo, from Mozambique.

[46] The Commission has also created a Special Rapporteur on Summary, Arbitrary and Extrajudicial Executions, and a Special Rapporteur on Prisons and Other Conditions of Detention; see M Evans and R Murray, 'The Special Rapporteurs in the African System' in M Evans and R Murray, *The African Charter on Human and Peoples' Rights: The System in Practice, 1986–2000* (Cambridge, Cambridge University Press, 2002) 280–304.

states parties ... ; assist African governments in the development and implementation of their policies of promotion and protection of women's rights; ... encourage and work with NGOs ... ; serve as a link between the Commission and inter-governmental and nongovernmental organisations at regional and international levels in order to harmonise the initiatives on the rights of women; ... collaborate with Special Rapporteurs from the UN and other regional systems.[47]

Although Commissioner Ondziel-Gnelenga did undertake a number of activities as Special Rapporteur,[48] and this work was continued by her successor, Dr Melo,[49] her remit was extremely broad. The majority of the Special Rapporteur's work has focused on developing the Protocol on the Rights of Women in Africa.

Protocol on the Rights of Women in Africa

The mechanisms such as the state reporting system and the ability to submit cases before the African Commission have not been fully explored in promoting and protecting the rights of women. Why did the NGOs, such as Women in Law and Development in Africa (WILDAF), and the International Commission of Jurists (ICJ), proposing this Protocol not consider using these existing provisions more creatively, at least in parallel to forming a Protocol? Why did they take the considerable time and trouble of proposing a Protocol which even then would require additional ratification by states?

The idea to have a Protocol was raised in a seminar organised by the Commission with WILDAF in 1995 in Lomé, Togo.[50] NGOs recognised the inadequacy of the African Charter on Human and Peoples' Rights for women and started to drive the process for greater recognition. However, rather than use existing Charter mechanisms, or CEDAW, they argued for the need to have a separate Protocol. The Lomé seminar thus considered a number of options, but concluded that 'since an amendment to the Charter would be too difficult to realise, and the optional protocol would lack strength because it would not require states to adopt it, ... an additional protocol requiring state ratification was preferable'.[51] It is not clear why this route was chosen, but there is a sense that there was a concern that women's rights would be accorded less attention by the African Commission on Human and Peoples' Rights if anything other than a legally binding document was considered. Having a Protocol would at least make the Commission take note.

---

[47] Draft Terms of Reference for the Special Rapporteur on the Rights of Women in Africa (no reference), on file with author.

[48] See 14th Activity Report of the African Commission on Human and Peoples' Rights, 2000–2001, AHG/229 (XXXVII), para 24.

[49] See R Murray, 'Report of the 31st session of the African Commission, 2–16 May 2002, Pretoria, South Africa', on file with author.

[50] See <http://www.wildaf.org.za> (last accessed 12 December 2003).

[51] <http://www.wildaf.org.zw/news4.html> (last accessed 12 December 2003).

There was also a perception that women, and African women, needed to create a sense of ownership over these rights.

Yet there was no vision among those lobbying for the Protocol of what its ideal content should be, or how, if at all, it should build upon existing international and regional instruments. One might expect, if the original aim of the Protocol had been to ensure that women's rights were more central to the African Charter, that a clear analysis of the latter's provisions and omissions would be provided. Secondly, if the intention was to create an 'African' CEDAW, then there should have been more discussion about a possible 'African' approach, and how CEDAW contradicted or supported this. This does not appear to have taken place, yet the underlying presumption never fully spelt out was that this was an *African* instrument.

The OAU Assembly of Heads of State and Government agreed to the suggestion to consider adopting a protocol in July 1995,[52] and experts were appointed to draft it. The first experts' meeting in April 1997 brought together both Commissioners and NGOs, and a draft protocol was prepared and submitted to the Commission for comments. A further workshop in November 1997 adopted a resolution on women's rights, calling for completion of the Protocol.[53] A working group was appointed by the Commission, and held a series of meetings[54] between January 1998 and November 1998 to consider the content of the proposed Protocol. At its Kigali session in 1998 the African Commission adopted a Draft Protocol[55] and sent it to the OAU for further consideration and adoption. The OAU later passed the document back to the Commission, asking it to take into account a parallel development by the Inter-African Committee on Harmful Traditional Practices Affecting Women's and Children's Health[56] which had been in the process of drafting an Inter-African Convention on Harmful and Traditional Practices. The Women's Unit and Legal Division of OAU also made suggestions for amendments to the Commission's Draft Protocol, and a final document was produced by the Commission in September 2000. The Protocol was finally adopted by the Second African Union Summit in July 2003.[57]

It is interesting to explore why women's rights started to receive increasing attention at this stage in the Charter's history. It would seem to be as the result of lobbying and activities of NGOs such as WILDAF, the African Centre for Democracy and Human Rights Studies (ACDHRS) and the ICJ. Like many of the Commission's initiatives, this development was prompted not by Commissioners

---

[52] AHG/Res240 (XXXI).

[53] As well as the appointment of a Special Rapporteur on the Rights of Women.

[54] Composed of Commissioners and NGOs.

[55] Draft Protocol to the African Charter on Human and Peoples' Rights on the Rights of Women in Africa, [Final Version], 13 September 2000, CAB/LEG/66.6.

[56] Founded in 1984 following a seminar in Dakar on the subject. It brings together national committees from a number of African countries and links with some organisations from Europe. It is based in Switzerland.

[57] This is the version referred to in this chapter.

themselves, but by outside pressure from NGOs. Attention to women's rights in respect of the Charter has since focused on adopting the Protocol. These proposals did receive support by the Commission and by the OAU/AU organs. The reasons for this are not entirely clear, but it would appear that in an era of increased attention to human rights in the OAU/AU as a whole, this was a concrete measure that was not seen as being particularly controversial. The African Commission on Human and Peoples' Rights had paid little attention to women in its work so far and this Protocol provided it with a good opportunity to be seen to be doing something, and the Protocol complemented the various declarations and decisions relating to women that had been adopted at various stages of the OAU/AU's history.

During the drafting process there was a lack of wide consultation among relevant African organisations, with the document being largely in the domain of the working group at the Commission. Consequently, the Protocol is little known among NGOs, governments or the population in Africa.[58] During the Special Rapporteur's visit to West Africa she met with local NGOs and talked about the Protocol to them. There is, therefore, evidence that, for example, NGOs in Ghana were aware of its existence and had seen and commented on earlier drafts. Yet at the experts' meeting in Addis Ababa in November 2001 it was believed this was the first time many of the participants had even seen a copy of the Draft Protocol,[59] arguably limiting the scope for meaningful discussion.

There seem to have been four aims identified for the Protocol, which, although not mutually exclusive, did pull the Protocol in a number of different directions and increased the risk of there being a lack of overall vision. The first was to improve the protection accorded to women under the African Charter, with the Commission noting that 'the African Charter [as the] sole juridical instrument at the regional level in charge of promotion and protection of human rights does not offer enough neither specific guarantees as regards women's rights in Africa'.[60] A second aim was to elaborate an African document on the rights of women:

> [T]o date no African instrument relating to human rights proclaimed or stated in a precise way what are the fundamental rights of women in Africa. There is thus a vacuum in the African Charter as regards real taking care of women's current preoccupations in Africa.[61]

The Commission, under its mandate outlined in Articles 45 and 66, 'felt the necessity of filling the gap'.[62] Thirdly, a Protocol was seen as a way of consolidating existing international standards for African states and 'to allow African governments

---

[58] Comments from Elize Delport, Commissioner, Commission on Gender Equality, South Africa, on file with author.

[59] *Ibid.*

[60] Drafting Process of the Draft Protocol on the Rights of Women in Africa, 27th Session, April–May 2000, DOC/OS(XXVII)/159b, at 1.

[61] *Ibid*, at 1.

[62] *Ibid.*

to fulfil the international commitments [to which] they have subscribed'.[63] Lastly, the Protocol offered an enforcement mechanism for the existing obligations for the protection of women in Africa.

The following section provides an examination of the main influences on the provisions of the Protocol, the use of CEDAW and other international documents as well as African instruments.

Use of International and African Documents

At various stages of the drafting process of the Protocol, reference was made to a number of what were described as 'key' documents. These included CEDAW, the Universal Declaration of Human Rights, the International Covenant on Civil and Political Rights, the International Covenant on Economic, Social and Cultural Rights, ILO Conventions,[64] the UN 1993 Plans of Action on Environment and Development and Declaration on Human Rights, as well as the 1994 Declarations on Population and Development and Social Development and in 1995, the Beijing Platform of Action. African documents that were seen as important included the ACHPR, the Dakar Plan of Action from November 1994, the African Charter on Rights and Welfare of the Child, the SADC Declaration by Heads of State or Government on Gender and Development,[65] recommendations from the Pan-African Women's Conference on a Culture of Peace and Non-Violence in Zanzibar in May 1999, and the Addis Ababa Declaration on Violence Against Women. [66]

It is not clear from the drafting process whether CEDAW was taken as the benchmark, or whether it was felt that certain of its provisions were not relevant or appropriate in an African context. In its present state, the Protocol wavers between being an interpretation of the ACHPR for women on the one hand, and a collection (not a comprehensive one) of some existing international standards on the other.[67] It ends up falling short of both these objectives.

Initially the Draft Protocol was structured around the ACHPR and its rights, thus reflecting closely the content of the African Charter and interpreting each

---

[63] *Ibid.*

[64] See, eg, comments from the Women's Unit at the OAU on the Article on the right to work: 'this Article must recognise the standards set in the ILO Conventions with which the OAU has been collaborating so closely, particularly within the framework of the Labour and Social Affairs Commission', Suggestions of the Women's Unit to Improve the Existing Text of the Draft Protocol as Presented to the OAU, 15 March 2000.

[65] Adopted in Malawi, 8 September 1997.

[66] The preamble of the Protocol; see also Suggestions of the Women's Unit to Improve the Existing Text of the Draft Protocol as Presented to the OAU, 15 March 2000.

[67] E Delport, Commissioner in Commission for Gender Equality, South Africa, paper on gender and development, on file with author, at 15. This is also noted by WILDAF, www.wildaf.org.zw/news4.html (last accessed 12 December 2003).

Article in respect of women. However, later versions moved away from this framework, in part because the Commission had to take on board parallel developments by the Inter-African Committee on Harmful and Traditional Practices. As a result, various rights that are included in the ACHPR are omitted from the final Protocol. This appears to have been more by chance than deliberate.

It is worth highlighting various examples in the Protocol which illustrate a lack of consistency as to the choice made in incorporating or rejecting provisions from international and African documents. Various provisions of the Protocol evidence influences from some African documents but not others. It was clear, for example, that the African Charter on the Rights and Welfare of the Child had an influence, with some provisions of the Charter being harmonised in the Protocol to fall in line with it.[68] The inclusion of a right to peace in Article 10 of the Protocol would initially appear to have come from such a right being in the ACHPR itself, there being no such provision in CEDAW, for example. Yet further recommendations on these issues by the Women's Unit of the OAU were not fully incorporated.[69] The Protocol appears to use the ACHPR to determine the lists of rights that should be included. Yet this approach would have prevented the omission of, for example, right to property.[70] However, earlier versions of the Protocol did not give explicit protection in respect of contractual rights or rights to administration of property of which many women are deprived.[71] Whilst the African Commission itself has interpreted the cultural provisions of the Charter as covering arts, communications, science and technology,[72] Article 17 of the Protocol and the right to a positive cultural context does not mention such issues, or the right to participate in cultural life itself.[73] Furthermore, whereas the Commission has been spending some time considering indigenous populations or communities,[74] the Protocol fails to consider in detail their position.[75]

---

[68] For example, the provision on economic and social rights in the Protocol, see Report of the Meeting of Experts on the Draft Protocol to the African Charter on Human and Peoples' Rights of Women in Africa, 12–16 November 2001, Addis Ababa, Ethiopia, Expt/ProtWomen/Rpt(I), para 110.

[69] Commenting on the first draft, that it be amended in light of the establishment of the African Committee on Peace and Development, the Pan-African Women's Conference on a Culture of Peace and Non-Violence in Zanzibar in May 1999 and the Regional Conference on Women in Addis Ababa in November 1999, Suggestions of the Women's Unit to Improve the Existing Text of the Draft Protocol as Presented to the OAU, 15 March 2000.

[70] Article 14 ACHPR.

[71] This has now been amended and is reflected in the provisions of the final Protocol.

[72] Guidelines on National Periodic Reporting.

[73] See CEDAW Art 13(c). Article 17 of the Protocol reads: '(1) Women shall have the right to live in a positive cultural context and to participate at all levels in the determination of cultural policies. (2) States Parties shall take all appropriate measures to enhance the participation of women in the formulation of cultural policies at all levels'.

[74] Resolution on the Rights of Indigenous People/Communities in Africa, 28th session. See also reports on various sessions, R Murray, 'Report on the 1999 Sessions of the African Commission on Human and Peoples' Rights' (2001) 22 *Human Rights Law Journal* 172–98.

[75] There is only brief mention in Art 18(2)(c) of the need for states to 'protect and enable the development of women's indigenous knowledge systems'; and in Art 24(a) for them to protect 'poor women and women heads of families including women from marginalized population groups'.

The Protocol clearly adds, in other instances, to existing international standards. For example, its provisions on protection for women in armed conflict in Article 11[76] and for refugee women[77] are to be commended. The definition of violence is also broader, with its reference to 'economic harm' and threats of harm,[78] than that provided for in the Inter-American Convention on Violence against Women[79] as well as in the UN Declaration on the Elimination of Violence Against Women[80] and CEDAW. It may owe its inspiration to the Addendum on the Prevention and Eradication of Violence Against Women and Children, and to the SADC Declaration on Gender and Development.[81]

Similarly, the right to health in Article 14 of the Protocol is largely focused on reproductive rights.[82] Whilst the provision appears to go further than other international documents in its requirement that states provide 'adequate, affordable and accessible health services', pre- and post-natal health and authorisation of 'medical abortion in cases of sexual assault, rape, incest or where the continued pregnancy endangers the mental and physical health of the mother or the life of the mother or the foetus', the rather limited protection with respect to HIV/AIDS was added at the last minute. So, although the African Commission had recently

[76] Art 11 reads: '(1) States Parties undertake to respect and ensure respect for the rules of international humanitarian law applicable in armed conflict situations which affect the population, particularly women. (2) States Parties shall, in accordance with the obligations incumbent upon them under the international humanitarian law, protect civilians including women, irrespective of the population to which they belong, in the event of armed conflict. (3) States Parties undertake to protect asylum seeking women, refugees, returnees and internally displaced persons, against all forms of violence, rape and other forms of sexual exploitation, and to ensure that such acts are considered war crimes, genocide and/or crimes against humanity and that their perpetrators are brought to justice before a competent criminal jurisdiction. (4) States Parties shall take all necessary measures to ensure that no child, especially girls under 18 years of age, take a direct part in hostilities and that no child is recruited as a soldier'.

[77] For example, Art 4(2)(k) provides that states should take appropriate and effective measures to 'ensure that women and men enjoy equal rights in terms of access to refugee status, determination procedures and that women refugees are accorded the full protection and benefits guaranteed under international refugee law, including their own identity and other documents'. Art 10(2)(c) and (d) provide that states should take measures to ensure the increased participation of women 'in the local, national, regional, continental and international decision making structures to ensure physical, psychological, social and legal protection of asylum seekers, refugees, returnees and displaced persons, in particular women (d) in all levels of the structures established for the management of camps and settlements for asylum seekers, refugees, returnees and displaced persons, in particular, women'. See also Art 11, *ibid*.

[78] Art 1(j) defines violence against women as 'all acts perpetrated against women which cause or could cause them physical, sexual, psychological, and economic harm, including the threat to take such acts; or to undertake the imposition of arbitrary restrictions on or deprivation of fundamental freedoms in private or public life in peace time and during situations of armed conflicts or of war'.

[79] 1994, Art 1.

[80] GA Res A/RES/48/104, 23 February 1994.

[81] Declaration on Gender and Development, SADC Heads of State or Government, Grand Baie Mauritius, 14 September 1998.

[82] CEDAW's Art 12 is broader. The CEDAW Committee looked at women and the right to health. General Recommendation No 24 mentions the need to give specific attention to those women who are particularly vulnerable, such as migrant women, refugees, internally displaced persons, girls and older women, prostitutes, indigenous people and those with disabilities (para 6), General Recommendation No 24, Women and Health (Article 12), 2 February 1999, CEDAW Committee.

adopted a Resolution on HIV/AIDS Pandemic—Threat Against Human Rights and Humanity, where it declared HIV/AIDS to be a human rights issue,[83] and despite this being a central issue in Africa as a whole, the Protocol simply states that women should have the 'right to self protection and to be protected against sexually transmitted infections, including HIV/AIDS' and the 'right to be informed on your own and partner's health status in this context'.[84]

On other occasions the Protocol appeared to reopen controversial arguments that had been settled in previous OAU documents. For example, the discussion during the drafting of the Protocol over the issue of polygamy resulted in not one, but three options at one stage in the drafting process,[85] and it could be questioned whether the final provision[86] comes close to the standard suggested by the CEDAW Committee.[87] Similarly, during the government experts' meeting in November 2001, although 'there was a general consensus that there was a need for harmonisation of national laws to recognise 18 years as the age of majority, with particular reference to the African Charter on the Rights and Welfare of the Child and the UN Convention on the Rights of the Child to which the majority of the OAU Member States are signatories',[88] there was still discussion over its inclusion.[89]

---

[83] There was no specific mention of the plight of women in particular, only calling on 'African Governments, State Parties to the Charter to allocate national resources that reflect a determination to fight the spread of HIV/AIDS, ensure human rights protection of those living with HIV/AIDS against discrimination, provide support to families for the care of those dying of AIDS, devise public health care programmes of education and carry out public awareness especially in view of free and voluntary HIV testing, as well as appropriate medical interventions'. See A Byrnes, 'Women, Feminism and International Human Rights Law—Methodological Myopia, Fundamental Flaws or Meaningful Marginalisation? Some Current Issues' (1992) 12 *Australian Yearbook of International Law* 205–41. See also General Recommendation No 15 on HIV/AIDS of the CEDAW Committee; Avoidance of Discrimination against Women in National Strategies for the Prevention and Control of Acquired Immunodeficiency Syndrome (AIDS), A/45/38, 3 February 1990.

[84] Art 14(1)(d) and (e) of the Protocol.

[85] Art 6(c) of the November 2001 draft read: 'Option 1: polygamy shall be prohibited. Option 2: they adopt the appropriate measures in order to recognise monogamy as the sole legal form of marriage. However, in existing polygamous situations, State Parties shall commit themselves to guarantee and protect the rights and welfare of women. Option 3: polygamy shall be the subject of mutual consent between the parties. The State parties shall commit themselves to guarantee and protect the rights and welfare of the women. However, the State parties shall ensure to encourage monogamy as the preferred form of marriage'.

[86] Art 6(c) of the Protocol reads: 'monogamy is encouraged as the preferred form of marriage and that the rights of women in marriage and family, including in polygamous marital relationships are promoted and protected'.

[87] General Recommendation No 21, Polygamy, para 14.

[88] Report of the Meeting of Experts on the Draft Protocol to the African Charter on Human and Peoples' Rights of Women in Africa, 12–16 November 2001, Addis Ababa, Ethiopia, Expt/ProtWomen/Rpt(I), para 49.

[89] The November 2001 Draft Protocol, Arts 2 and 21(2) read that: 'Child marriage and the betrothal of girls and boys shall be prohibited and effective action, including legislation, shall be taken to specify the minimum age of marriage to be 18 years and make registration of all marriages in an official registry compulsory'. CEDAW, Art 16(2) notes that 'the betrothal and the marriage of a child shall have no legal effect, and all necessary action, including legislation, shall be taken to specify a minimum age for marriage' The final Protocol provision, Art 6(b), states clearly that 'the minimum age of marriage for women shall be 18 years'.

Elsewhere the Protocol falls clearly below existing international standards, for example by its failure to include express reference to the right of women to vote or to participate in private life as well as at the international level,[90] despite the latter being in CEDAW[91] and the OAU itself having referred to it on several occasions. Similarly, although the Protocol covers economic, social and cultural rights,[92] and takes a broader interpretation in some respects,[93] it is narrower in others.[94]

The Protocol clearly did not automatically adopt existing African documents and standards into its provisions. For example, the articles on female genital mutilation were not fully incorporated from the OAU's proposed Convention on the Elimination of All Forms of Harmful Practices Affecting the Fundamental Human Rights of Women and Girls.[95] The Protocol does not go further than existing standards and offer greater protection for all women in Africa. Thus, whilst the drafting meetings of the Protocol led to the inclusion of references to the position of refugee women and women during times of conflict, women living rurally,[96] migrant women and prostitutes are given little mention.[97]

---

[90] Art 9 of the Protocol states '(1) States Parties shall take specific positive action to promote participative governance and the equal participation of women in the political life of their countries through affirmative action, enabling national legislation and other measures to ensure that: (a) women participate without any discrimination in all elections; (b) women are represented equally at all levels with men in all electoral processes; (c) women are equal partners with men at all levels of development and implementation of State policies and development programmes. (2) States Parties shall ensure increased and effective representation and participation of women at all levels of decision-making'.

[91] CEDAW Committee, General Recommendation No 23, Political and Public Life, 13 January 1997.

[92] See S Wright, 'Economic Rights and Social Justice: A Feminist Analysis of Some International Human Rights Conventions', (1992) 12 *Australian Yearbook of International Law* 242, 247.

[93] For example, in respect of Art 12 of the Protocol and the 'right to education and training', CEDAW only refers to 'education'. References to recognition of work in the home being of equal value and the responsibility for children, however, can also be found in CEDAW, General Recommendation No 17 and Art 5(b) of CEDAW respectively. See, eg, CEDAW General Recommendation No 16, Unpaid Women Workers in Rural and Family Enterprises, A/46/38, 2 January 1991. General Recommendation No 17 on Measurement and Quantification of the Unremunerated Domestic Activities of Women and Their Recognition in the Gross National Product, A/46/38, 3 January 1991.

[94] For example, the reference in Art 12(b) of the Protocol for states to 'eliminate all stereotypes in textbooks, syllabuses and the media, that perpetuate such discrimination', is narrower than CEDAW's 'at all levels'. Similarly, Art 13 on provision of economic and social welfare rights does not appear to give as much protection as CEDAW Art 11 with respect to discrimination on grounds of marriage in terms of employment.

[95] See C Campaore, 'Experience of the Inter-African Committee on Harmful Traditional Practices Affecting Women's and Children's Health (CI-AF) in the Battle Against Harmful Traditional Practices, notably Female Genital Mutilation' (2000) *Awaken l'Eveil* 8, at 8. CEDAW General Recommendation No 14, A/45/38, 2 February 1990.

[96] There is some mention of rural women: for example, Art 14(2)(b), in respect of health and reproductive rights, notes that states should take measures to provide health services 'to women especially those in rural areas'.

[97] Art 4(2)(g) requires states to 'prevent and condemn trafficking in women, prosecute the perpetrators of such trafficking and protect those women most at risk'.

Poor Drafting and Inconsistencies

A further criticism must be that the manner in which the provisions are termed varies. The Protocol adopts a variety of approaches, in contrast to some degree of consistency displayed by instruments such as CEDAW.[98] Some provisions are listed as 'states shall combat/ensure ...' that women have equal rights with men,[99] others as providing for rights for women per se,[100] still others as providing rights for 'women and men' then 'men and women'. This makes it confusing as to the exact obligations of the states parties. There is also no express provision on reservations in the Protocol, presumably leaving it to the principles of international law to define what is acceptable. Although this is commendable if it is implying that no reservations are permissible,[101] reservations are likely to be an issue, particularly when at the experts' meeting states were already inserting objections to some provisions.[102]

In sum, it can hardly be said that the Protocol is a comprehensive restatement of existing obligations,[103] neither is it structured to be an interpretation of the ACHPR for women. The omission of some international standards but the inclusion of others does not give a clear vision of what it intends to reflect, and the Protocol is not consistent about its use of African instruments or jurisprudence.

Problems of Enforcement

Leaving aside the issue of the Protocol requiring additional ratification by states before it can come into force,[104] the Protocol places itself firmly under the umbrella of the ACHPR and the mandate of its Commission and the proposed Court. Thus, it is the Commission, and eventually the Court,[105] which must enforce the Protocol. The Protocol does not add additional mechanisms, but

---

[98] The rights in CEDAW are usually termed: 'states parties shall ...' and 'states parties ... shall ensure to women, on equal terms with men, the right ...'.

[99] For example, Art 6 of the Protocol, on marriage.

[100] For example, 'every woman shall be entitled to respect for her life', Art 4(1) of the Protocol.

[101] See CEDAW Committee, General Recommendation No 4, Reservations to the Convention, A/42/38, 12 April 1987. The following African states are party to CEDAW: Algeria, Angola, Benin, Botswana, Burkina Faso, Burundi, Cameroon, Cape Verde, CAR, Chad, Comoros, Congo, Côte d'Ivoire, DRC, Djibouti, Egypt, Equatorial Guinea, Eritrea, Ethiopia, Gabon, Gambia, Ghana, Guinea, Guinea-Bissau, Kenya, Lesotho, Liberia, Libya, Madagascar, Malawi, Mali, Mauritania, Mauritius, Morocco, Mozambique, Namibia, Niger, Nigeria, Rwanda, Sao Tome and Principe, Senegal, Seychelles, Sierra Leone, South Africa, Togo, Tunisia, Uganda, Tanzania, Zambia, Zimbabwe. Of those states, only three have ratified the Optional Protocol, Mali, Namibia and Senegal.

[102] See Report of the Meeting of Experts on the Draft Protocol to the African Charter on Human and Peoples' Rights on the Rights of Women in Africa, 12–16 November 2001, Addis Ababa, Ethiopia, Expt/ProtWomen/Rpt(I).

[103] '... so weak that one is not that optimistic of their value if retained in their present form', Personal Communication, Betty Mould-Iddrisu, Chief State Attorney, Ghana, 15 March 2002.

[104] The Protocol requires 15 ratifications to come into force, Art 29(1).

[105] In 1998 the Assembly of Heads of State and Government of the OAU adopted a Protocol Establishing an African Court on Human and Peoples' Rights to the African Charter on Human and

rather stresses some of those which are already available under the Commission's existing mandate.

There are a number of difficulties with this approach. First, all OAU/AU states are party to the ACHPR, and this an instrument which clearly could and should be interpreted for the benefit of women as well as men. Why is it necessary, therefore, to have an additional Protocol to the Charter, requiring further ratification to come into force? For those states who refuse to ratify the Protocol, it may leave the Commission and the Court in a difficult position regarding how to interpret the Charter in respect of women. Secondly, the Protocol provides for monitoring in Article 26, and basically uses the provisions of the ACHPR in this respect. As noted above, while the Commission has wide powers to adopt resolutions and consider cases and reports, few of these have been used in respect of women. States are already required to, and indeed do already, provide details on the rights of women when reporting under Article 62 of the Charter.[106] Further, although the communication mechanism has not been used fully to protect women's rights, the potential for it to do so exists. Yet it is not mentioned in the Protocol as a possible means of enforcement. The Protocol does also not mention mechanisms available at the level of the OAU/AU, sub-regionally or in national courts,[107] or constitutions,[108] despite reference to the importance of national enforcement in the Beijing and Dakar Plans of Action and cases that have been successfully argued before the national African courts.[109] The only addition to the enforcement mechanisms which are already provided by the African Charter, is the express mention in Article 25 of the Protocol, which requires states to provide an appropriate remedy for violations of the Protocol.[110] However, this is arguably already

---

Peoples' Rights, OAU/LEG/MIN/AFCHPR/PROT (I) Rev2. This requires 15 ratifications to come into force and this was achieved in January 2004.

[106] See above.

[107] Although some aspects are included throughout the Protocol provisions in respect of some rights, for example, Art 8(d), access to justice and equal protection before the law, requires that states ensure 'that law enforcement organs at all levels are equipped to effectively interpret and enforce gender equality rights'.

[108] Unfortunately, there does not appear to have been that much consideration of national protection or examples of good practice from the national level incorporated in this respect. In fact, some of the provisions in the Protocol are less than are to be found in national legislations, eg, those on widow's rights in Article 20 are less protective than to be found in the Ghanaian Constitution: email from Betty Mould-Iddrisu, 15 March 2002, on file with author.

[109] For example, in *Ephrahim v Pastory*, the High Court of Tanzania used a number of international instruments including the African Charter and held equality in the Tanzanian Bill of Rights had primacy over customary laws preventing women, but not men, from selling land, (1990) 87 *International Law Reports* 106; [1990] *Law Reports of the Commonwealth (Const)* 757, High Court of Tanzania. In addition, in *Attorney-General of Botswana v Unity Dow*, the courts held against a law which prevented a Botswanan woman married to a non-Botswanan to pass on citizenship to children of the marriage, [1991] *Law Reports of the Commonwealth (Const)* 574, High Court of Botswana; [1992] *Law Reports of the Commonwealth (Const)* 623, Court of Appeal of Botswana.

[110] Art 25 reads: 'State parties shall undertake to: (a) provide for appropriate remedies to any woman whose rights or freedoms, as herein recognised, have been violated; (b) ensure that such remedies are determined by competent judicial, administrative or legislative authorities, or by any other competent authority provided for by law'.

implied from the Commission's jurisprudence. Whilst national NGOs may be able to use the Protocol's provisions to lobby their own governments for changes in the national legislation, beyond this it is difficult to see what the Protocol adds to existing methods of enforcement.

Conclusion

While the rights of women could not have been said to have been ignored by the African organs, the various mechanisms and rights available outside of the Protocol have not been exploited to their full potential. It is clear that there is a rather ad hoc approach to the Protocol in particular and women's rights in general within the OAU/AU. The idea of the Protocol and the provisions of the Constitutive Act, for example, could have acted as important catalysts, ensuring better coordination of existing efforts and providing an opportunity to consolidate achievements and identify gaps. Instead they risk, at the most, adding another level to a confusing number of instruments and organs.

One of the reasons for these difficulties is that with all of these developments, and particularly the Protocol, there is an underlying sense that the African organs and NGOs are trying to achieve an 'African' approach to women's rights; yet what this 'African' vision is, has not been clearly developed. Prompted and pushed by African-based NGOs, it would seem one of the underlying aims was to develop a document which would be a promotional tool, and a document over which there was a sense of ownership. Beyond this, there does not appear to have been an overall vision of what the Protocol was, or how, if it all, it would differ from existing international and regional standards or what it intended to add to them.

Thus, rather than consolidating existing standards, interpreting the African Charter for women or ensuring a mechanism for enforcement, what the drafters did (and indeed this may be a feature of the African human rights system more generally) was to try to create a document over which they would have a sense of ownership. Whilst the outcome may be labelled as 'African', the resulting provisions may be less a reflection of strategic choices about what is 'African' and more of the need to put a stamp on the Protocol and be part of a process of creating it. Thus, just as both Africans and women were largely neglected from the drafting process of the UN human rights mechanisms, so African women felt neglected in the drafting of the ACHPR and other developments at the OAU/AU. Unfortunately, efforts to create their own instrument do not appear to have been accompanied by a clear analysis or consensus on the acceptance and applicability of existing international and African statements on the rights of women. The result may well be, therefore, that the Protocol will be a reworking of many of these issues, offering some protection in some quarters, but less in others. Where the Protocol sits in the new AU structures and how it will be used by the African Commission on Human and Peoples' Rights in its future work has yet to be seen. Although calling on states to ratify the Protocol can be used as a vehicle for providing continued attention to women's rights if the Protocol comes into force, it is not clear how it will be enforced, and whether it will contribute to the integration of women's rights into the ACHPR and African Union structures or sit uneasily on the sidelines.

13

Sexual Violence, International Law and Restorative Justice

VESNA NIKOLIC-RISTANOVIC

Introduction

The majority of victims of sexual violence in war are women.[1] A large number of women are raped in war with extreme cruelty and as a means for men to confront each other through women's bodies. However, in spite of that knowledge, as well as in spite of serious and long-term consequences for victims, rape in war has for a very long time been 'the crime that is by reputation "the easiest to charge and the hardest to prove", but which "has traditionally been the easiest to disprove as well".[2] Despite notable gains in the Yugoslav and Rwandan war crimes tribunals in prosecuting defendants for wartime rape and sexual violence, perpetrators of wartime violence are only rarely punished, and women raped in war often suffer in silence, their experiences unrecorded and out of both legal and historical memory of their nations/countries.

War rape was publicly addressed in an international context during the First World War in relation to rapes committed by German soldiers against Belgian women. After the Second World War, rape was again the subject of some public discussion. Despite this public exposure, rapes in both wars did not result in punishment.[3] After the Second World War, the international community's commitment to prosecute war criminals did not extend to prosecuting them for rape. War rapes once again received international publicity starting in 1992, in relation to

---

[1] It should not be ignored that, especially in recent civil wars, the number of male victims of sexual violence increased. Men and boys were raped in Bosnia, albeit much less often than women and girls. See E Hague, 'Rape, Power and Masculinity: The Construction of Gender and National Identities in the War in Bosnia-Herzegovina' in R Lentin (ed), *Gender and Catastrophe* (London, Zed Books, 1997). However, these kinds of sexual violence are even more hidden than sexual violence against women since they do not fit social constructions of 'victim' of sexual violence, which are based on traditional gender stereotypes: (D Zarkov, 'The Body of the Other Man' in C Moser and F Clark (eds), *Victims, Perpetrators or Actors* (London and New York, Zed Books, 2001). Thus, male victims are even less likely than women to make their victimisation visible and become the subject of criminal prosecution.

[2] S Brownmiller, *Against Our Will* (New York, Penguin Books, 1975) at 47.

[3] *Ibid.*

rapes committed in the Bosnian war.[4] This time, however, the end of media attention did not mean the end of international action. Once awakened, public and professional attention led to a concerted campaign to secure more precise and comprehensive legal prohibition of rape, as well as a political commitment to prosecuting rape at the ad hoc tribunals, first for Yugoslavia and then for Rwanda.[5] Over time, that campaign extended to lobbying for strengthened international recognition of sexual violence against women in the Statute of the International Criminal Court,[6] as well as developing more effective victim protection within the tribunals for Yugoslavia and Rwanda. These developments related not only to rape but also to sexual slavery, forced prostitution and forced pregnancies. At the same time, interest in restorative justice and the emergence of alternative ways of dealing with war atrocities led to more appropriate care for victims of war rapes and inclusion of their narratives in the collective memories of post-conflict societies.

This paper explores sexual violence in war in the context of recent trends in both international law and restorative justice initiatives. The paper seeks to examine some of the limitations of the punishment model of justice, as evidenced by the International War Crimes Tribunal for the Former Yugoslavia (ICTY), for women who have suffered sexual violence in war, and in particular the Yugoslav war. I argue here, however, that neither punitive nor restorative justice models on their own are satisfactory. The answer may be to borrow aspects from both.

The Role of Punitive and Restorative Justice in Post-Conflict Societies

The establishment of the Yugoslav and Rwanda Tribunals, together with the new International Criminal Court, is part of a recent trend of addressing past atrocities in post-conflict societies through legal means, primarily punitive justice. International law and international tribunals have been established as key players in bringing to justice individual perpetrators of gross violations of international humanitarian law. This emphasis on individual accountability is due in part to the prevailing view that prosecuting human rights violations can substantially enhance the chances for establishing the rule of law in post-conflict society by signalling that no individuals are outside the reach of law.[7] The statutes and Rules of

---

[4] V Nikolic-Ristanovic, *Women, Violence and War* (Budapest and New York, CEU Press, 2000).

[5] HJ Steiner and P Alston, *International Human Rights in Context* (Oxford, Oxford University Press, 2000).

[6] B Bedont and H Martinez, 'Ending Impunity for Gender Crimes under the International Criminal Court' (2004) 1 *The Brown Journal of World Affairs* 65.

[7] S Landsman, quoted by M Minow, *Between Vengeance and Forgiveness* (Boston, Beacon Press Books, 1998).

evidence and procedure of the Rwandan and Yugoslav Tribunals and the new International Criminal Court, suggest that international criminal courts should contribute to the following goals: punishment of perpetrators, protection of victims, and prevention of future atrocities.[8] In addition, through the establishment of legal truth about crimes, both international and national criminal courts are supposed to contribute to the creation of collective memories and, consequently, historical truth about the past of post-conflict societies.[9]

These goals—punishment of perpetrators, protection of victims and prevention of future atrocities—are also the most controversial aspects of punitive justice, and the subject of debate within sociology, criminology, law and conflict studies, and particularly among scholars dealing with human rights, restorative and transitional justice. These academic debates tend to adopt three main approaches toward the role of punitive and restorative justice in post-conflict societies: exclusive or primary use of punitive justice, exclusive or primary use of restorative justice, or a combination of both.[10]

Human rights lawyers,[11] for example, have advocated criminal trials—international, national or hybrid—as offering the best opportunity to achieve the essential tasks of social repair. While some international legal scholars recognise the limitation of tribunals in achieving the broad policy goals of post-conflict reconciliation, they tend to advocate alternative—restorative justice—models *alongside* tribunals.[12]

On the other hand, those scholars who advocate the use of reconciliation and victim–offender mediation instead of a criminal trial process, together with critical criminologists, also known as abolitionists, tend to be strongly critical of the criminal justice system. Criminologists and victimologists, such as Van Ness and Strong,[13] Coates[14] and Lea,[15] argue for the use of restorative justice because of the failures they see in the criminal justice system.

---

[8] <http://www.Icls.de/dokumente.icty_statut.pdf,> (last accessed 9 June 2004); <http://www.wilson-centre.org/subsites/ccpdc/pubs/addm/rwan.htm,> (last accessed 9 June 2004); <http://www.un.org/law/icc/statute/romefra.htm,> (last accessed 9 June 2004).

[9] R Teitel, *Transitional Justice* (Oxford, Oxford University Press, 2000).

[10] C Vanspauwen, S Parmentier and E Weitekamp, 'Collective Victimization in Post-Conflict Situations: in Search of a Restorative Justice Approach for Countries in Transition', paper presented at XI International Symposium on Victimology, Stellenbosch, South Africa, 2003.

[11] Eg Diane Orentlicher, Naomi Roht-Arriaya, Jose Alvarey, Tom Farer, Theodor Meron and many others. For an overview of the human rights literature on the role of punitive justice in post-conflict society, see L Fletcher and H Weinstein, 'Violence and Social Repair: Rethinking the Contribution of Justice to Reconciliation' (2002) 3 *Human Rights Quarterly* 573.

[12] For a discussion, see D Buss, 'Of Trials and Tribulations: Human Rights and War Crimes in a Global Order', paper delivered at 'New Wars, Global Governance and Law' Workshop held at the International Institute for the Sociology of Law, 13–14 May 2004, Onati, Spain.

[13] DW Van Ness and KH Strong, *Restoring Justice* (Cincinnati, Anderson Publishing, 1997).

[14] R Coates, 'Victim-offender Reconciliation Programs in North America An Assessment' in J Hudson and B Galaway (eds), *Criminal Justice, Restitution and Reconciliation* (Criminal Justice Press, Monsey, 1990).

[15] J Lea, 'Criminology and Post Modernity' in P Walton and J Young (eds), *The New Criminology Revisited* (London, Macmillan, 1998).

Lastly, leading scholars in the field of transitional justice see punitive justice as a necessary element in the overall process toward reconciliation, at the same time recognising that other ways of dealing with past atrocities, such as truth and reconciliation commissions, are also important.[16] A similar, eclectic, model is suggested by Fletcher and Weinstein.[17]

Fletcher and Weinstein propose an ecological model of response to social breakdown, which locates justice in 'the web of possible interventions that must be addressed in order to promote social reconstruction'.[18] In that regard, they suggest several interventions as critical components of a carefully planned attempt at social repair: state-level intervention, criminal trials (national and international), truth commissions, individual and/or family psycho-social support, externally-driven community interventions and community-based responses. According to Fletcher and Weinstein, each type of intervention contributes uniquely to the reversal of one or more of the features of social breakdown.[19] An approach that draws on a wide spectrum of intervention possibilities, as advocated by Fletcher and Weinstein, seems promising in terms of reaching a more holistic approach and prospect for 'positive peace'[20] in post-conflict societies. Due to the fact that action is needed from the state and community, as well as from the family and the individual, in dealing with prosecution and also in acknowledging individual and collective trauma, I too advocate this model in relation to war sexual violence.

My interest in searching for different approaches to post-conflict resolution, such as the model discussed above, stems from concerns about the efficacy of the criminal trial and punishment process in securing lasting peace and justice. As some transitional justice authors suggest, punishment can be understood as vengeance 'curbed by the intervention of someone other than the victim and by principles of proportionality and individual rights'.[21] As such, punishment may also contribute to feeding rather than ending the cycle of violence. This may happen especially if retribution is the only response to crimes of the past, or if the post-conflict societies remain divided, as in the cases of South Africa, Northern

---

[16] L Huyse, 'Justice' in D Bloomfield, T Barnes and L Huyse (eds), *Reconciliation After Violent Conflicts: A Handbook* (Stockolm, International IDEA, 2003); M Minow, *Between Vengeance and Forgiveness* (Boston, Beacon Press Books, 1998); NJ Kritz, *Transitional justice: how emerging democracies reckon with former regions*, quoted in C Vanspauwen et al, n 10 above at 13.

[17] L Fletcher and H Weinstein, n 11 above.

[18] *Ibid*, at 636.

[19] *Ibid*, at 623.

[20] This term is originally conceptualised by Quinney, as the part of his critique of criminal justice systems where he views peacemaking criminology as part of the movement toward 'positive peace': R Quinney, 'Socialist Humanism and Critical/Peacemaking Criminology: the Continuing Project', in B Maclean and D Milovannovic, *Thinking Critically about Crime* (Vancouver, Collective Press, 1997). Also, some authors see critical criminology in general as useful theoretical departure for building on arguments for the use of restorative justice in post-conflict societies (C Vanspauwen et al, n 10 above).

[21] M Minow, *Between Vengeance and Forgiveness* (Boston, Beacon Press Books, 1998) at 12.

Ireland and Serbia,[22] for example. Moreover, relying exclusively on retribution, without building a more comprehensive and accurate picture about the past, and without assisting victims and acknowledging their sufferings, may generate feelings of vengeance in victims who are normally ready to forgive rather than to retaliate.[23]

In addition, neither international tribunals[24] nor national criminal courts have the capacity to prosecute all offenders, hear all victims and offer adequate protection to all witnesses. The administration of justice in general, and international criminal trials in particular, focuses on a limited category of crimes called gross human rights violations[25] and on a limited number of high-level perpetrators. The concern is always that focusing on a narrow range of offenders and violations may send a dangerous message that other offenders are innocent, since 'selective prosecution inevitably risks what happened in Argentina—sending the signal that whoever is not charged is innocent and that there can be impunity for collective and institutional aspects of responsibility that do not throw up soft individual targets'.[26]

The fragmented nature of a trial process that focuses on select defendants is compounded by an equally selective use of witnesses. Not all victims can be brought before the courts. This may send the message that other victims are non-existent or less worthy as victims, or that victims are once again manipulated and misused for political purposes. As Rombouts stresses, victims all want a piece of the '*gateau de la souffrance*', so gaining recognition, through testifying, is crucially important to them.[27] Unfortunately, there is an enormous gap between the numbers of people victimised and the numbers of victims who obtain redress,[28] so that only a small number of victims have had the chance to be heard.

Martha Minow identifies justice and truth as the two main purposes animating societal responses to collective violence. Justice, she argues 'may call for truth but also demands accountability'.[29] Accountability through the trial process, however,

---

[22] For more details about that, see V Nikolic-Ristanovic, 'Possibilities for Restorative Justice in Serbia' in L Wolgrave (ed), *Positioning Restorative Justice* (Devon, Willan Publishers, 2003) and V Nikolic-Ristanovic, 'Truth and Reconciliation in Serbia: The Process So Far', paper presented at XI International Symposium on Victimology, Stellenbosch, South Africa, 2003.

[23] V Kesic, 'A Response to Catharine MacKinnon's Article "Turning Rape Into Pornography: Postmodern Genocide"' (1994) 2 *Hasting Women's Law Journal* 267.

[24] The 1997 decision of the International Tribunal for the Former Yugoslavia to pursue the strategy to indict only high-level offenders significantly reduces the number of perpetrators who may be brought to justice before the Tribunal: S Murphy, 'Progress and Jurisprudence of the International Criminal Tribunal for the Former Yugoslavia' (1999) 1 *The American Journal of International Law* 57. It also poses significant problems. Will victims who have testified at the tribunal also be required to testify in a domestic proceeding? Will a selective criminal tribunal process establish comprehensive legal truth/memory if it is reached in such largely fragmented way?

[25] C Vanspauwen et al, n 10 above.

[26] J Braithwaite, '*Restorativna i reaktivna regulativa u cilju uspostavljanja mira u svetu*' (Restorative and Responsive Regulation of World Peace) (2001) 2 *Temida* 3, at 24.

[27] H Rombouts, 'Importance and Difficulties of Victim-Based Research in Post-Conflict Societies' (2002) 2–3 *European Journal of Crime, Criminal Law and Criminal Justice* 216.

[28] J Balint, 'Conflict, Conflict Victimisation, and Legal Redress, 1945–1996' (1996) 4 *Law and Contemporary Problems* 231.

[29] M Minow, n 21 above, at 9.

does not necessarily equate with truth. The trial process may impede or ignore 'truth', and there is no guarantee that legal proceedings generate impartial and comprehensive knowledge about past atrocities. The objective of the criminal trial is a determination of the criminality of the accused for the charges laid. In this context, justice and truth rarely go together in the criminal trial, even where the trial process respects human rights and democratic guarantees:

> Democratic guarantees protecting the rights of defendants place those rights at least in part ahead of truth-seeking; undemocratic trials may proceed to judgment and punishment with disregard for particular truths or their complex implications beyond particular defendants.[30]

Many authors stress the limited nature of legal truth and its inadequacy for recovering relationships between people from opposing sides of a conflict.[31] Cohen, for example, is perfectly right when he stresses that 'only cultural dummies would think of reading a legal verdict as a historical record of the event, let alone its context and why it happened'.[32] 'Even a complete mosaic of legal truths', says Cohen, 'cannot create a full or shared knowledge of "what really happened", let alone *why* it happened.'[33] Similarly, Akhavan warns that 'legalization' of war crimes risks trivialising the immense suffering that occurs, especially if the broader context of the human experience is ignored.[34]

Since the main aim of a war crimes trial is bringing offenders to justice for violating the domestic or international legal order, the trial's focus is on the offender rather than on the victim. This poses two particular difficulties for the victim and witness. The rights of victims are to be kept in balance with the rights of the defendant, and even the best-developed victim protection frameworks are implemented with difficulty. Second, the model of witness evidence—examination followed by cross-examination—does not afford the witness the opportunity to tell of their experience:

> The chance to tell one's story and be heard without interruption or scepticism is crucial to so many people, and nowhere more vital than for survivors of trauma.If the goals are to gain public acknowledgement for the harms and accounts, as full as possible, of what happened, the trial process is at best an imperfect means.[35]

---

[30] *Ibid.*

[31] H Arendt, *Eichmann in Jerusalem: A Report on the Banality of Evil* (New York, Penguin, 1994); M Osiel, *Mass Atrocity, Collective Memory and the Law* (New Brunswick NJ, Transaction Publishers, 1997); S Cohen, 'Introduction: Unspeakable Memories and Commensurable Laws', paper presented at the International Conference 'Legal Institutions and Collective Memories', at The IISL, Onati, Spain, 1999; S Cohen, *States of Denial* (Cambridge, Polity, 2001).

[32] S Cohen, 'Introduction: Unspeakable Memories and Commensurable Laws', n 31 above.

[33] *Ibid.*

[34] P Akhavan, 'Accountability for Human Rights Atrocities in International Law: Beyond the Nuremberg Legacy' (1999) 1 *The American Journal of International Law* 235.

[35] M Minow, n 21 above, at 58.

The failure of legal responses to address past atrocities in an appropriate way is connected to the fact that the power gap between the US and other, less powerful countries is reflected in the way international law and international criminal tribunals function. Martha Minow, for example, identifies the enormous gap in time between the Nuremberg trials (starting in 1945) and the establishment of tribunals for the Former Yugoslavia (1993) and Rwanda (1994). She stresses the lack of interest by the US in establishing tribunals during the period when it was responsible for war crimes, which, together with the recent US rejection of the jurisdiction of International Criminal Court, is largely understood in some countries, such as the Former Yugoslavia, as sending the message that war crimes are not universally punishable. That is, international justice is not as impartial and apolitical as it pretends to be.[36]

Thus, countries such as the Former Yugoslavia and Rwanda were put under pressure by the international community, under the threat of international sanctions, to hand over war criminals to the ad hoc tribunals. At the same time, the US not only refused to agree to the new International Criminal Court, but also launched an internationally controversial 'war on terror'. In the Former Yugoslavia, this contributed to an increased lack of confidence in international justice, which is widely perceived as imposed from abroad and as being partial.[37] Moreover, the apparent international double standard has severe negative consequences for the process of facing the past, weakening already vague support for prosecuting war criminals, and even encouraging aggression and the political ambitions of its opponents.[38] As observed by Fletcher and Weinstein, the historical record produced by the ICTY is not engendering a sense of contrition or shame among members of national groups whose forces committed atrocities. On the contrary, it is a useful 'foil in the hands of political propagandists to solidify a sense that their national group is misunderstood or an unacknowledged victim of the conflict.'[39] For Fletcher and Weinstein,[40] this raises the question of 'what justice means to a particular society or even whether there is a single answer to that question'.

---

[36] *Ibid.*

[37] This is shown by recent survey in Serbia: DJ Pavicevic, '*Zlocini i odgovornost*' (Crimes and Responsibility) in Z Golubovic, I Spasic and DJ Pavicevic, *Politika i svakodnevni zivot, Srbija 1999–2002* (Politics and Everyday Life, Serbia 1999–2002) (Beograd, Institut za filozofiju i drustvenu teoriju, 2003), as well as by the findings from a 1999 survey based on interviews of judges and prosecutors from Bosnia and Herzegovina, discussed in L Fletcher and H Weinstein, n 11 above.

[38] The March 2003 assassination of Serbian Prime Minister Zoran Djindjic demonstrated how risky it can be to support cooperation with, in this case, the International Tribunal for the Former Yugoslavia. The assassination was part of an attempted *coup d'état* and was seen as a serious challenge to the new government. The Prime Minister was the symbol of a new Serbia and was very committed to cooperation with the ICTY and meeting the requirements of international communities. The man accused of the assassination stated that he killed Djindjic in order to stop sending people from Serbia to The Hague, since he thinks that these people should be tried in Serbia, not abroad.

[39] L Fletcher and H Weinstein, n 11 above, at 600. A very good example of this is the trial against Slobodon Milosevic at the ICTY. The broadcasting of the trial on Serbian TV, up until April 2004, helped to portray Milosevic as a national hero. See MP Scharf, 'The Legacy of the Milosevic Trial' (2003) 37 *New England Law Review* 915.

[40] L Fletcher and H Weinstein, n 11 above, at 636.

Given the limitations of war crimes trials as outlined above, it is not surprising that in the 1980s and 1990s alternative models for truth and reconciliation began to emerge, and which contained elements of both restorative and transitional justice. The key principles of restorative and transitional justice are: bringing victims and offenders together, focusing on the harm caused by the crimes, holding perpetrators responsible for their acts, meeting the needs of victims for redress, promoting the reintegration of both victims and perpetrators, and prevention of future harm by building on the strengths of the community and government.[41] It is important here to draw attention to the goal-oriented definition of restorative justice given by Bazemore and Walgrave, which is also reflected in the transitional justice literature, that 'restorative justice is every action that is primarily oriented towards doing justice by repairing the harm that has been caused by the crime.'[42] Restorative justice, understood in this way, opens the door for new (community-based) innovative approaches in dealing with past atrocities in non-legal ways.

The alternative models of reconciliation to which I refer, which include story-telling workshops, days of reflection, permanent living memorial museums,[43] as well as truth and reconciliation commissions, contain elements of restorative justice. The result is that their focus is on victims, including forgotten victims in forgotten places, as well as on reconciliation and healing. Echoing the assumptions of psychotherapy, religious confession and journalistic exposure, truth commissions, for example, presume that telling and hearing the truth is healing and so has restorative power.[44] Thus, truth and reconciliation commissions, as well as different community-based initiatives, fill an important gap in dealing with the legacy of war violence in post-conflict society.

Sexual Violence in War—the Potential and Limits of Punitive Justice

The establishment of the ad hoc tribunal to prosecute war crimes committed in the Former Yugoslavia was marked, at the outset, by a concerted feminist effort to ensure that wartime rape would not be allowed to fade into obscurity.[45] Feminists,

---

[41] C Vanspauwen et al, n 10 above, at 3.

[42] G Bazemore and L Walgrave, 'Restorative Juvenile Justice: In Search for Fundamentals and an Outline for Systematic Reform' in G Bazemore and L Walgrave (eds), *Restorative Juvenile Justice: Repairing the Harm of Youth Crime* (Monsey, New York, Criminal Justice Press, 1999).

[43] *'Healing Through Remembering'* The Report of the Healing Through Remembering Project (Belfast, Healing Through Remembering, 2002).

[44] M Minow, n 21 above, at 9.

[45] Feminists were active within academia (eg, Brownmiller, Copelan, Askin, MacKinnon), as amicus curiae (eg, Chinkin, Askin), as advocates (The Women's Caucus for Gender Justice at the ICC), or as journalists (eg, Styglemayer) and researchers who collected women's accounts about war victimisation (eg, Nikolic-Ristanovic). However, some aspects of the global campaign on wartime sexual violence have been criticised for offering only a partial advocacy, contributing to a marginalisation of local activism and a possible distortion of the record on sexual violence during war (see V Kesic, n 23 above, at 627).

noting that existing legal prohibitions against wartime rape and violence against women were deficient, demanded substantial legal change. As a consequence, the provisions of the Statutes of the ad hoc tribunals for Yugoslavia and Rwanda, and the International Criminal Court, have strengthened language, allowing war rape to be prosecuted as a crime against humanity and a war crime. Greater protections were also secured for victims as witnesses at these courts, with some particular attention to the needs of victims of sexual violence.

Prosecution of Perpetrators

Although the Statute of International Tribunal for the Former Yugoslavia failed to include rape explicitly as a grave breach of the Geneva Convention,[46] various decisions of the Yugoslav and Rwandan Tribunals classified rape as falling within other categories of grave breaches of the 1949 Geneva Convention as 'wilfully causing great suffering or serious injury to body or health', as well as constituting 'torture or inhuman treatment'. Rape has also been held to be a violation of the laws and customs of war (Article 3 of the ICTY Statute).

Key decisions by the ICTY suggest a willingness to recognise and prosecute war rape and sexual violence against women. The Tribunal's decision in *Tadic*,[47] for example, marks the first time sexual crimes received concerted judicial testament in international law. In the 1998 *Celebici* case,[48] Hazim Delic was sentenced to 20 years by the Yugoslav Tribunal in a decision that recognised rape as an instrument of torture. The same year, Ante Furundzija[49] was sentenced to 10 years for rape as a war crime (violation of laws and customs of war), and the case is additionally notable as confirming that 'sexual violence committed against a single victim is a serious violation of international law deserving of prosecution in an international criminal court'.[50] In *The Foca* case (Kunarac, Jankovic, Gagovic and others),[51] sexual crimes were, for the first time, the sole focus of the prosecution. In this case,

[46] Because war rape was not mentioned explicitly as a war crime, there was initial uncertainty about the ICTY's ability to prosecute rape other than where it was a crime against humanity, which has particular evidentiary requirements. For some feminists, the ICTY Statute suggested a reluctance to treat sexual violence as a gender specific crime and to connect its punishment to the consequences which it has for the victim. As stressed by Buss, 'explicitly defining rape only as a crime against humanity suggests that wartime rape is still equated with a crime against a people, rather than a crime against women': D Buss, 'Women at the Borders: Rape and Nationalism in International Law' (1998) 2 *Feminist Legal Studies*, 171.

[47] *Prosecutor v Dusko Tadic, Sentencing Judgement*, <http://www.un.org/icty/tadic/trial2/judgement/tad-tsj970714e.htm,> (19 August 2003), para 4(a).

[48] Case IT–96–21 *Prosecutor v Zdravko Mucic, Hazim Delic and Esad Landzo*, <http://www.un.org/icty/celebici/appeal/judgement2/index.htm,> (9 June 2004).

[49] Case IT–95–17/1–T (1998), *Prosecutor v Furundzija, Trial Chamber 2 Judgment*, <http://www.un.org/icty/furundzija/appeal/judgement/index.htm,> (9 June 2004).

[50] KD Askin, 'Prosecuting Wartime Rape and Other Gender-Related Crimes under International Law: Extraordinary Advances, Enduring Obstacles' (2003) 21 *Berkeley Journal of International Law* 288, at 299.

[51] *Prosecutor v Kunarac*, Case IT–96–23–T and IT–96–23/1–T, *Foca Judgement 22 February Transcript*, <www.un.org/icty/cases/indictindex-e.htm,> (9 June 2004).

rape was treated both as a crime against humanity and as a war crime (grave breach of the 1949 Geneva Convention and violation of the laws and customs of war). The Tribunal additionally considered the issue of enslavement as a crime against humanity and found that the defendants were also guilty of enslaving some Muslim women.[52] In the *Kvocka* judgment,[53] rape was found to constitute persecution in the context of a joint criminal enterprise.[54]

The Statute of the International Criminal Court (the ICC Statute) contains all the advances regarding international regulation of sexual violence achieved over the last few years, and in this way makes concrete most feminist demands in this area:

> It includes rape, sexual slavery and other forms of sexual violence in the enumeration of serious violations of the laws and customs of war and separates them from outrages on personal dignity, humiliating and degrading treatment. The ICC Statute also specifically includes the same offences as crimes against humanity as well as defines forms of sexual violence as war crimes in armed conflict not of an international character.[55]

One of the main achievements in comparison to the International Tribunals for the Former Yugoslavia and Rwanda is that in the Statute of the ICC sexual slavery is explicitly included as a war crime, and both sexual slavery and forced prostitution are defined as crimes against humanity. Forced pregnancy is, for the first time, recognised as both a crime against humanity and as a war crime. Finally, the ICC Statute recognises that forced sterilisation, as well as other forms of serious sexual violence, can be crimes against humanity.[56] Notably, the ICC Statute develops some aspects of restorative effects of criminal justice. While the only restorative provision of ad hoc tribunals related to claims of compensation through national courts, the ICC Statute provides that the Court shall establish principles for reparations for victims, 'including restitution, compensation and rehabilitation.'[57]

Victim and Witness Protection

Within the Statutes and Rules of the International Tribunals for the Former Yugoslavia and Rwanda, as well as International Criminal Court, significant

---

[52] KD Askin, 'Women and International Humanitarian Law' in KD Askin and DM Koenig (eds), *Women and International Humanitarian Law* (New York, Transnational, 1997); D Buss, 'Prosecuting Mass Rape: Prosecutor v Dragoljub Kunarac, Radomir Kovac and Zoran Vukovic' (2002) 10 *Feminist Legal Studies* 91.

[53] Case IT–98–30–T *Prosecutor v Kvocka Judgement* (2001).

[54] K Askin, n 50 above, at 299.

[55] H Charlesworth and C Chinkin, *The Boundaries of International Law: a Feminist Analysis* (Manchester, Manchester University Press, 2000), at 321.

[56] The above-mentioned achievements of the Statute of the International Criminal Court are largely the result of the advocacy of the Women's Caucus for Gender Justice in the ICC (<www.iccwomen.org/index.htm,> Aug 4, 2003).

[57] Rome Statute for the ICC, Art 75.

efforts were made to enable the protection of victims and witnesses.[58] Article 20 of the Statute of the Yugoslav Tribunal, for example, provides in paragraph 1 that the Trial Chamber 'shall ensure that a trial is fair and expeditious, in accordance with procedure and evidentiary rules, with full respect for the rights of the accused and due regard for the protection of victims and witnesses.' This general obligation for the protection of victims is of significant importance for the interpretation of other provisions of both the Statute and Rules of the ICTY.

The Rules of Procedure and Evidence of the ICTY also contain provisions on the measures intended to protect the privacy of victims and witnesses, as well as to guarantee witness anonymity in relation to the accused. These measures are of major importance for alleviating victims' and witnesses' fear of revenge and, consequently, for increasing their readiness to testify. It is especially worth emphasising the importance of being able to enforce these measures in the period before the trial. This possibility is especially significant for victims and witnesses who still live in the territory where the war was waged (or have relatives who live there), since they are more vulnerable to revenge for their decision to testify before the Tribunal.

The protection of the victim from meeting the accused during the trial is also important, since any new confrontation with the rapist is a potential source of retraumatisation for the victim. Also, the Rules provide that the Chamber shall, whenever necessary, control the manner of questioning to avoid any harassment or intimidation of the witness. This provision is of special importance for victims of rape and other sexual offences, since they are, as before national courts, vulnerable to secondary victimisation as a consequence of inappropriate questioning by defence counsel. Rule 96, intended specifically to protect women victims of sexual offences from inappropriate questioning by the representatives of the defence,[59] provides that corroboration of the victim's testimony is not required and consent is not allowed as a defence if the victim has been subject to physical or psychological constraints. Also, the victim's prior sexual conduct is inadmissible.

Finally, both the ICTY and the ICTR have a Victims and Witnesses Unit with responsibility for recommending protection measures for victims and witnesses, and providing counselling and support to victims and witnesses. For victims of sexual violence, this Unit can provide the counselling and support necessary in the cases of rape and sexual assaults, a feature that may be strengthened by the provision that the Unit is to give consideration to the appointment of qualified women counsellors. However, as will be shown below, because of many practical problems, these formal gains are still problematic in practice.

The Statute and Rules of Procedure and Evidence of the International Criminal Court follow the trend set by the ICTY and ICTR Statutes and Rules, further strengthening the role of the victim and putting special emphasis on protection of

---

[58] V Nikolic-Ristanovic, *Women, Violence and War* (Budapest and New York, CEU Press, 2000).
[59] See *Decision on the Prosecutor's Motion Requesting Protective Measures for Victims and Witnesses in Tadic case*, at 10.

victims of sexual violence, gender violence and violence against children. Moreover, according to Article 68, paragraph 5 of the ICC Statute, 'where the disclosure of evidence or information pursuant to this Statute may lead to grave endangerment of the security of a witness or his or her family, the Prosecutor may, for the purpose of any proceedings conducted prior to the commencement of the trial, withhold such evidence or information and instead submit a summary thereof'.

The Limits of Punitive Justice and Victims of Sexual Violence

In spite of these legal provisions, the decisions of the ICTY and ICTR, and the promise of the ICC, there are still many problems in practice with the criminal prosecution model as a means to address wartime sexual violence. At the most fundamental level, the court-based model requires selective prosecutions, and it is not realistic to expect that all perpetrators of sexual violence will be prosecuted, and all victims protected and heard. Thus, international law alone is not sufficient for making visible and acknowledging all suffering of women victims of sexual violence in war. This is partly because of the partial nature of international prosecutions, but partly also because of the limits of the law, and particularly criminal law itself, and its focus on perpetrators rather than on victims' experience.

The number of trials for sexual crimes is still very low, so that only a small number of perpetrators are heard and sentenced.[60] Also, in spite of special emphasis on victims' protection and relatively good provisions protecting witnesses *during* trial, as outlined above, in practice there are many problems with the protection of victims. First the tribunals are faced with the problem of getting victim witnesses to testify at all,[61] a difficulty exacerbated in sexual crime trials.

Second, protection for victims and witnesses *before and after* the trial is not ideal, possibly discouraging potential witnesses from testifying. For example, there is not adequate protection for witnesses for the period covering questioning by the prosecutor's investigators and the trial itself. Further, individuals who testify are in a difficult situation, especially if, after leaving the tribunal, they return to communities where they risk meeting the family and acquaintances of the accused. This is intensified by the inevitable weakness of the concept of protection of victims in the face of the necessity to protect the rights of the accused. The result is that even if the strongest protective measures are adopted, the identity of the witness will be known to the defendant.[62] One of the most extreme examples

---

[60] In the following trials before the ICTY the judgments for sexual violence are reached: *Tadic, Celebici, Furundzija, Omarska Keraterm (Kvocka, Radic, Kos), Foca, Todorovic* and *Sikirica and others.* Before the ICTR, the *Akayesu* judgment is the only one.

[61] P Wald, 'The International Criminal Tribunal for the Former Yugoslavia Comes of Age: Some Observations on Day-to-Day Dilemmas of an International Court' (2001) 5 *Washington University Journal of Law and Policy* 87.

[62] CN Niarchos, 'Women, War and Rape: Challenges Facing the Suffering or International Tribunals for the Former Yugoslavia' (1995) 4 *Human Rights Quarterly* 649.

of the tragic consequences of the low level of actual protection of victims and witnesses is found in Rwanda, where many potential and actual witnesses (including women victims of sexual violence) are intimidated, attacked and killed.[63]

In spite of the protection provided by 'law on the books', protection measures are rarely used in practice, and when they are used, there are not enough guarantees that the confidential information will not be disclosed to the public.[64] The Rules of Procedure and Evidence do not guarantee the confidentiality of the information obtained by the Victim and Witnesses Unit. Additionally, the Unit's staff does not establish contact with victims before they come to the Tribunal, so that they meet the victims and witnesses for the first time at the Tribunal. This limits the staff's ability to assist the witnesses, or to establish trusting relationships. Witnesses giving testimony may have to wait at the Tribunal for a period of time which may last for hours, but which could be as long as two days. This puts an immense psychological burden on the witnesses, since 'the present fears mix uncontrollably with the fear from the past'.[65]

Like national courts, international criminal tribunals are not the best place for victims traumatised by crime to appear, in general, and for the woman victim of sexual violence, in particular. Whatever the law, victims are met with hostility rather than with empathy and solidarity. This is especially emphasised when, as in the case of ad hoc tribunals, common law is used, according to which victim is marginalised even more than in the continental law.[66] One of the most striking examples is the negative effect of the possibility of cross-examination of the victim by the defendant.[67] As noted by Arendt and quoted by Drumble, 'a trial resembles a play in that both begin and end with the doer, not with the victim.'[68] Very telling in that regard are the words of Patricia Wald, a former judge at the ICTY:

> As an American judge, I frankly find many ICTY defence cross-examinations painfully unhelpful to my own judgment. I have noticed how often the witnesses seem to resent the cross-examination and pull back into a litany of 'don't remember.' They see the defence counsel allied with their nemeses in the docks. Several witnesses have at the end of their testimony addressed concluding remarks to the defence counsel rather than to the accused: 'How can you stand there and defend these men who have taken everything away from us, our families, our health, our homeland?[69]

[63] L Walleyn, '*Victimes et temoins de crimes internationaux: du droit au protection vers le droit a la parole*', paper presented in Leuven (Belgium) on Expert Seminar Reparation for Victims of Gross and Systematic Human Rights Violations in the Context of Political Transitions, 2002.

[64] See S Murphy, 'Progress and Jurisprudence of the International Criminal Tribunal for the Former Yugoslavia' (1999) 1 *The American Journal of International Law* 57 for a discussion of unsanctioned public disclosure of information about prosecution, including protected witnesses appearing before the ICTY.

[65] M Zepter, 'Suada R, Witness for the Prosecution' in E Richter-Lyonete (ed), *In the Aftermath of Rape: Women's Rights, War Crimes and Genocide* (Givrius, The Coordination of Women's Advocacy, 1997) at 139.

[66] Interestingly, this is not the system victims who appear before ICTY are most familiar with.

[67] This became especially extreme in the case of Milosevic trial.

[68] H Arendt, *Eichmann in Jerusalem: A Report on the Banality of Evil* (New York, Penguin, 1994), at 23, quoted in M Drumble, 'Punishment Goes Global: International Criminal Laws, Conflict Zones, and Gender (In)equality' (2000) 4 *Canadian Woman Studies* 23.

[69] P Wald, n 61 above. For the more detailed example in the *Celebici* case, see V Nikolic-Ristanovic, 'Victimization by War Rape: The International Criminal Tribunal for the Former Yugoslavia' (2004) 4 *Canadian Woman Studies* 28.

The position of the witness before an international criminal court is delicate also, since the witness is usually afraid of not being able to tell all the important details or that she/he will not speak clearly and in a systematic way.[70] This feeling is intensified by the fact that the testimony is given through an interpreter, with the additional fear of being wrongly interpreted. Moreover, the victim of war rape is faced with some additional fears and frustrations: fear of being rejected by persons close to her, shame and anxiety at how people who know her will react when they learn about her having being raped, and the trauma of seeing the rapist again and reliving again all the horrifying details of the rape.[71] For Rhonda Copelon, a leading advocate of international gender justice, 'the designers of the tribunal have done nothing to mitigate these fears'.[72]

While my discussion so far has focused on the particular difficulties the *war crimes* trial poses for victims and witnesses of sexual violence, this is also a mechanism modelled on the domestic criminal trial process, in itself a problematic arena for women who have been raped. As Buss has observed,[73] by finding evidence of rape camps and yet finding that the individual women are not to be believed in their accounts of rape and violence at those same camps, the Yugoslav Tribunal reproduces many of the same problematic aspects of the rape trial found in Western domestic legal systems.

As in any other rape trial, women are at risk of being victimised by the legal system itself, with its focus on the perpetrator and public interest rather than on the victim.[74] As Herman alleges, the legal system of the state is 'designed to protect men from the superior power of the state but not to protect women or children from the superior power of men. It therefore provides strong guarantees for the rights of the accused but essentially no guarantees for the rights of the victims'.[75]

Some of the difficulties identified by feminists in the domestic criminal trial have become problems at the ICTY, particularly 'the myth of the inherently uncreditworthy complainant whose memory cannot be trusted'.[76] In the *Furundzija* trial,[77] for example, the credibility of a rape victim as witness was challenged by the defence because of the therapy she was exposed to as a consequence

---

[70] For more details see V Nikolic-Ristanovic, n 69 above.

[71] *Ibid.*

[72] R Copelon, 'Surfacing Gender: Reconceptualizing Crimes against Women in Times of War' in LA Lorentzen and J Turpin (eds), *The Women and War Reader* (New York and London, New York University Press, 1998), at 73.

[73] D Buss, n 52 above.

[74] H Barnett, *Introduction to Feminist Jurisprudence* (London and Sydney, Cavendish Publishing Limited, 1998); R Copelon, n 72 above.

[75] J Herman, *Trauma and Recovery* (New York, Basic Books, 1992), at 72.

[76] K Campbell, 'Legal Memories: Sexual Assault, Memory, and International Humanitarian Law' (2002) 1 *Signs: Journal of Women in Culture and Society* 149, at 175.

[77] Case IT–95–17/I–T, *Prosecutor v Ante Furundzija* (1998).

of the trauma caused by the rape, leading to reopening of the trial.[78] The defence presented two different arguments concerning the implications of the diagnosis of post traumatic stress disorder (PTSD) for the reliability of witness evidence. The first argument was that, because of PTSD, the witness's memory was unreliable. The other argument was that this unreliability was the result of both the inadequacy of treatment and the type of treatment of the trauma offered by the Medica Women's Therapy Centre. In addition, the expert witness clamed that the so-called mixed mission of Medica, of both providing treatment for trauma patients and of campaigning for the prosecution of war criminals, 'may be incompatible with the recovery and treatment of trauma patients'.[79]

As stated by Campbell, 'the paradoxical position of the complainant derives from the fact that she must demonstrate the breach to her bodily integrity, while also demonstrating that her "self" and hence her memory remain "intact".[80] The inability of international law properly to address women's experience of sexual violence in war is best shown in the *Furundzija* case, where the victim went through the ordeal of testifying in both the original and re-opened trial, had to endure negative procedural consequences for having failed to disclose previously the certificate from Medica Women's Centre as well as her statement given to the Centre,[81] and her credibility as a witness was put in question. This is a remarkable story given that the witness was called to give evidence that the accused, who was charged for aiding and abetting rape, was present while she was cruelly raped by another man, whose crime was not the subject of that particular trial.

Ironically, the *Furundzija* case, which was devastating for the victim,[82] was argued by some commentators to 'represent an enormous moral and legal victory both for the Yugoslavian Tribunal and for women worldwide.'[83] But what sort of 'victory' is it, and at what cost? An alternative assessment of the *Furundzija* case might call attention to the possible gap between the interests of Western feminist efforts to secure formal legal recognition of violence against women and the experience of those women who are actually present before the tribunal.

A further concern about the emphasis of this 'new' international criminal law is that it remains focused on women's sexual and reproductive identities,[84] while numerous other forms of harm to women in armed conflict, such as the killings

---

[78] For more detailed analyses of this case see K Campbell, n 76 above, and K Askin, 'The International War Crimes Trial of Anto Furundzija: Major Progress Toward Ending the Cycle of Impunity for Rape Crimes' (1999) 12 *Leiden Journal of International Law* 935.

[79] K Campbell, n 76 above, at 163.

[80] *Ibid.*

[81] K Askin, n 78 above.

[82] For details see K Askin, n 78 above and K Campbell, n 76 above.

[83] See K Askin, n 78 above, at 936. Also, for an argument about the necessity for the law to recognise its ethical responsibility to the complainant in its judgment, see K Campbell, n 76 above, at 175.

[84] H Charlesworth and C Chinkin, n 55 above.

and wounding of their children and other persons close to them, the loss of property, their expulsion from homes etc, do not receive the same level of attention.

As outlined above, the criminal trial is not ideally suited for acknowledging victims' sufferings, let alone for their healing and empowerment through enabling them to tell their truth. Punitive systems of justice, and adversarial systems in particular, do not give victims chances to tell the 'whole' truth, as they may define it, nor to convey the complexity of the crime and the lives of both the victim and perpetrator. Thus the victimisation that the woman endured, which may be the most important truth for some women, is not heard and acknowledged before the tribunal. For female victims of sexual violence, the high level of traumatisation combined with fear and gender prejudices around sexual violence (both in their 'home' communities and at the Tribunal), may lead to them being silenced rather than encouraged. The original trauma may be increased by insufficient or partial protection and support, as well as by the lack of appropriate acknowledgement of the victim's suffering.

In addition, the fact that witnesses are often frightened, and refuse to testify, contributes to the fragmentation of legal truth. Added to this are the enormous court files, which run to thousands of pages, and which often contain vague and misleading language, especially regarding gender-based violence.[85] It is not surprising that, as happened in the *Tadic* case, even when some sexual crimes are included in the judgment, they are largely invisible for the wider public.[86] This brings us once again to the point that legal records may offer a limited framework for the creation of collective memories and, thus, for the prevention of future sexual violence.

The lack of proper acknowledgement of women's suffering becomes even more evident in cases where plea-bargaining is arranged. Where plea-bargaining is used, and an accused receives a reduced sentence in exchange for a guilty plea, rape and other victims will not have a chance to tell their stories. For example, despite the Rwanda Tribunal's notable success in convicting Jean-Paul Akayesu[87] of rape and sexual violence, similar charges against other detainees have been dropped as part of the plea-bargaining process.[88] Certainly, a guilty plea may spare victims from testifying. This is exactly what happened at the ICTY in the *Todorovic* case.[89] However, a guilty plea may mean that any perception of rape is dismissed, also possibly undermining the hard-won status of rape as a crime.[90] While plea-bargaining may offer many procedural advantages for an overburdened

---

[85] S Murphy, n 64 above.

[86] KD Askin, 'Sexual Violence in Decisions and Indictments of the Yugoslav and Rwandan Tribunals: Current Status' (1999) 1 *The American Journal of International Law* 97.

[87] Case ICTR– 96–4–T, *The Prosecutor of the Tribunal against Jean-Paul Akayesu*.

[88] M Drumble, n 68 above.

[89] Case IT–95–9/1–S, ICTY.

[90] M Veljanovska, *Silovanje u rata: Continuity Across War and Peace Regarding Sexual Assault* (Honours Thesis, University of New South Wales, Australia, 2003).

tribunal, it has serious implications for the tribunal's function in establishing collective memory: 'anyone can grasp that a plea-bargaining truth (the fate of most criminal cases) is neither the truth nor whole truth; by definition, it is anything but the truth.'[91]

The lack of appropriate acknowledgement of women's suffering is found even in cases where women are believed and the rapes and other forms of sexual violence are established. The *Stakic* decision, for example, established that persecution, as a crime against humanity, was committed through various acts, including rape and sexual assault. Yet, in the disposition of the sentence, the acts of persecution are cited only as murder and deportation.[92] Thus, although Stakic was sentenced to life imprisonment and one can assume that punitive justice is achieved, the suffering of women who took the burden of testifying remained invisible and unacknowledged.

Even the very idea of a truth established through the ICTY as a mechanism for creating collective memory is difficult to reconcile with the location and functioning of this tribunal. Located in The Hague, the Tribunal is not physically proximate to the communities it purports to address through its judgments, nor is it necessarily supportive of, or conducive to, grassroots efforts to reconcile past wrongs.[93] Although some authors argue that the legal affirmation of a social wrong that is offered by an international court is enough to establish collective memory,[94] it is difficult to believe that the creation of collective memory, at least in a post-conflict society and by the use of the law, is so simple. At least in the *Furundzija* case, it seems that the message received in the Former Yugoslavia does not contribute very much to 'collective' memory. The focus of Serbian media, when reporting about this case, was on the fact that the credibility of victim was put in question rather than on the decision's importance as a legal precedent.[95] The testimonies of some rape victims who dared to go through the traumatic experience of testifying before the ICTY ended without acknowledgement of their suffering, either because the rape they testified about was not included in the judgment, since it was not the trial of the direct perpetrator (eg, Furundzija was sentenced for aiding and abetting), or because most of the charges were dropped (eg, the *Tadic* case).[96]

---

[91] S Cohen, 'Introduction: Unspeakable Memories and Commensurable Laws', paper presented at the International Conference 'Legal Institutions and Collective Memories' at The IISL, Onati, Spain, 1999.

[92] See Judgment of 31 July 2003 in *Prosecutor v Milomir Stakic*, IT–97–24–T.

[93] N Kritz, 'Progress and Humanity: The Ongoing Search for Post-Conflict Justice' in MC Bassiouni (ed), *Post-Conflict Justice* (Ardsley NY, Transnational Publishing, 2002).

[94] K Campbell, n 76 above.

[95] '*Odbrana ne veruje zrtvi*' (The defence do not believe victim), *Danas*, 15 July 1998.

[96] For more details about that, as well as about the devastating impact of the violation of rules of procedure on victims see KD Askin, n 78 above.

In *Tadic*, the defendant was acquitted of most of the charges of sexual violence in the Omarska camp because of lack of evidence, and in spite of the fact that Suada Ramic, a victim of war rape, testified using her full name and in an open session. The testimony, as described by Zepter, was a stressful experience for Suada and the fact that she gave her statement publicly added to her the trauma of the testimony itself .[97]

Drumble noticed similar experiences of victims in Rwanda:

> 'Conversations I have had with Tutsi women who have survived sexual torture, gen-
> dered violence, and ethnic hatred in the Rwandan genocide also evidence victim
> frustration at the lack of resolution arising out of criminal trial, the silencing effects
> of adjudication, and the absence of victim control over the process'[98]

Given the difficulties with the 'rape trial' in the international criminal setting, as outlined above, the critique of the retributive and punitive criminal justice paradigm as the outcome of feminist advocacy (national and international) may be worth considering. In that regard Drumble[99] may be right when he argues that the International Criminal Court represents a similar pattern of dominance of the punitive paradigm, this time at the global level, as well as that some authors' exhortation to avoid 'retributive trap' in the international promotion of women's rights should be taken seriously.[100]

Conclusion

The above analysis demonstrates that progress achieved within international law regarding both prosecution of offenders and protection of victims of sexual violence in war is significant, yet not sufficient for acknowledging the suffering of victims and addressing the consequences of sexual violence in a comprehensive and holistic way. Equally, the experience of feminist activism around wartime sexual violence also demonstrates that notwithstanding formal legal recognition of women's rights, it is only through the vigilant efforts of feminist lawyers and advocates that international humanitarian law has recognised the seriousness of wartime violence against women.

Notwithstanding important legal gains, and the impressive efforts of feminist activists, the criminal trial remains a difficult forum in which to acknowledge women's sufferings, let alone facilitate their healing and empowerment through truth telling. Any attempt to include restorative or healing dimensions in the legal

---

[97] M Zepter, n 65 above at 139.
[98] M Drumble, n 88 above.
[99] *Ibid.*
[100] Martin, quoted in M Drumble, n 88 above at 22.

process should be assessed in the context of the critique of law itself and its limits, in particular criminal law's focus on the offender rather than the victim. In this context, it seems that mixing up principles of criminal and restorative justice may have unexpected damaging effects on a victim. For example, Murphy and Whitty argue that 'the telling of wider, more personal stories within the courtroom runs the risk of introducing more "relevant" evidence into the trial process, and opening the door to cross-examination on the type of records and information [that] should not be subject to forced disclosure (such as past sexual history and therapy records.' [101] The better solution may be to combine both criminal and restorative justice models, yet keep them within separate procedures and agencies.

Various alternative mechanisms, containing elements of restorative and transitional justice may be useful supplements to the war crimes trial in addressing wartime sexual violence. The use of a truth and reconciliation commission as well as different community based initiatives[102] may significantly encourage both victims and perpetrators to speak out. A TRC process, in this context, may encourage more discussion not only about individual acts of sexual violence, but also about the reasons why sexual violence occurred, the broader patterns of victimisation, and the social, political and economic context leading to war. This may help both individual women and the nation as a whole in reaching healing and empowerment, and may help create conditions for ending cycles of violence breaching reconciliation.

The work of Truth and Reconciliation Commission in South Africa, for example, is based on the assumption that the telling of, and listening to, the truth has healing effects on both individuals and society as a whole.[103] Therefore, one of the important goals of truth commissions is to produce a 'coherent, if complex, narrative about the entire nation's trauma, and the multiple sources and expressions of its violence'.[104] Thus, truth commissions help victims who testify as well as those who do not, to locate their own experience in the broader context of political violence. Those who are too scared to testify, or those who found testifying too painful, can benefit from listening to the testimonies of others with similar experiences.[105] This is especially important for victims of sexual violence who are able to place their own victimisation in a broader socio-political context. This can be

---

[101] For example, Murphy and Whitty suggest that South African attempt 'to look for more participatory and empowering ways of hearing victims "voices" via the Truth and Reconciliation Commission, has obvious resonance with some of most powerful recent writing about revisioning the rape trial'. They argue that 'this writing highlights the need to allow rape victims "both the status of personhood and the chance to approach the court as an audience capable of acknowledging their trauma—a process which is arguably crucial to surviving the trauma and among the most important things which a public rape trial should achieve": T Murphy and N Whitty, 'What is the Fair Trial? Rape Prosecution, Disclosure, and the Human Rights Act', (2000) 8 *Feminist Legal Studies* 143, at 160.

[102] L Fletcher and H Weinstein, n 11 above.

[103] See also J Herman, n. 75 above at 72 for a discussion of the therapeutic effects of truth-telling, and M Minow, n 21 above at 58.

[104] Minow, n 44, p. 58

[105] M Minow, 21 above.

important in helping to shift latent convictions about self-blame and the consequent feelings of shame, and to educate the public in general about widespread victimisation. The idea is that women stop blaming themselves when they understand that what happened to them is not unique and that it is the part of broader social context.

Judith Herman, who developed a theory on trauma and recovery that connects the experiences of Holocaust victims, US soldiers in Vietnam, battered women, child abuse victims and incest survivors, argues that 'through the process of truth telling, mourning, taking action and fighting back, and by reconnecting with others, even individuals severely traumatized by totalitarian control over a prolonged period can recover'[106] Not speaking of what happened exacerbates trauma. In contrast, speaking before sympathetic listeners and in a setting where the experience is acknowledged, documented and located in the larger political context can be restorative.[107] This narrative, which is detailed and precise, contributes to the establishment of historical truth. As Teitel puts it:

> The victims of prior oppression are the historical inquiry's primary source of evidence, the stewards of the nation's newfound history. Truth commissions depend on victim's testimonies and it is fulsome, as unlike a trial, lacking in challenging confrontation or cross-examination. When the victims' testimony is narrated by the commissioners' quasi/state authors, it becomes a sharable truth, a national story, and the basis of transitional consensus.[108]

It is essential that women's voices be continually heard in relation to alternative forms of truth telling and reconciliation. However, as the experience of the South African Truth and Reconciliation Commission shows, using alternative ways of truth telling does not automatically guarantee gender sensitivity and better treatment of victims of sexual violence. Thus, continuing feminist critique, advocacy, and vigilance are necessary to ensure that women's issues in general, and wartime sexual violence in particular, are appropriately dealt with through both criminal (international and domestic) law and alternative mechanisms such as truth and reconciliation.[109]

The experience of the Truth and Reconciliation Commission in South Africa shows that among those who came to testify, women were disproportionately represented. However, women tended to speak about the victimisation of persons close to them, usually men—sons, husbands, and fathers—rather than about their own victimisation.[110] Similarly, research on violence against women in war in the former Yugoslavia shows that they experience more difficulties with the victimisation

---

[106] J Herman, n 75 above at 157.

[107] M Minow, n 21 above.

[108] R Teitel, *Transitional Justice* (Oxford University Press, Oxford, 2000), at 83.

[109] M Minow, n 21 above.

[110] B Goldblatt, and S Meintjes, 'South African Women Demand the Truth' in M Turshen and C Twagiramariya (eds), *What Women do in Wartime* (London and New York, Zed books, 1998).

of persons close to them than with their own victimisation, including rape.[111] It was therefore very important that the South African TRC accepted a broad definition of victim, including relatives and dependents.[112] With the right approach and with the help of women's groups, women may be ready to speak about their own experiences as well.[113]

Women's speaking out is essential for their healing since 'exposing the wounds and having them acknowledged creates the possibility for the healing process to start.'[114] Women's private suffering needs to be made 'visible as social suffering, enabling them to stake their historical claims and thereby restore their dignity'.[115] However, it also requires careful planning of hearings as well as securing safe space, assistance, empathy and support. During the war in the former Yugoslavia, the role of feminist activism was essential in assuring help and support for women victims of war, as well as for advocating changes in the law. It is thus realistic to expect that their role also will be important in monitoring trials and truth and reconciliation processes. Moreover, the contribution of feminists may be precious in supporting and empowering victims and survivors as well as in collecting the pieces of truth about women's experience of war and integrating those experiences into the 'shared narrative for the future.'[116]

[111] V Nikolic-Ristanovic, *Women, Violence and War* (Budapest and New York, CEU Press, 2000).

[112] L Graybill, 'The Contribution of the Truth and Reconciliation Commission toward the Promotion of Women's Rights in South Africa' (2001) 1 *Women's Studies International Forum* 1.

[113] The example of South African can be helpful in the former Yugoslavia and in other countries as well. In South Africa ad hoc group was formed to advocate and lobby the TRC to ensure that gender-specific concerns were given space in the process of the hearings. After the problem with women's testimonies was noticed, and as a result of women's groups advocacy, the Commission created hearings specifically focused on women's own experience (Minow, n 21 above). As a result, three women-only hearings were held by the TRC. In addition, the mechanisms, such as *in camera* hearings, training of commissioners, possibility for women to give a testimony as a collective and on behalf of other women, are proposed to the TRC to incorporate gender in the truth and reconciliation process: B Goldblatt and S Meintjes, n 110;above Graybill, n 112 above.

[114] M Ramphela, 1996, quoted by L Graybill, n 112 above at 6.

[115] M Ramphela, 1996, quoted by L Graybill, *ibid*.

[116] R Tietel, n 108 , above at 229.

Index

Africa
  African feminism 12–13
  land reform in 170
  Organisation of African Unity see
      Organisation of African Unity
  African Charter on Human and People's
      Rights 253–272
  interpretation 271
  African Commission on Human and
      Peoples' Rights 254–6, 258–264
  African Commission 254–6
  Protocol on the Rights of Women in
      Africa, 261–4 see also
      Protocol on the Rights of
      Women in Africa
  remit 259
  Special Rapporteur on the Rights of
      Women 260–1
African institutions
  use of international law by 254–6
AIDS
  HIV/ AIDS statistics 219
Akitsiraq Law School 36–43
  achievements of students 41–2
  aims of training indigenous lawyers
      43
  family responsibilities of students 41
  feminist account of international law,
      and 43
  indigenous self-determination in
      circumpolar region, and 42
  influences on instructors and staff
      42–3
  Inuit students 36
  movement of Inuit into coastal
      settlements 40–1
  need for 36–7
  nomadic nature of Inuit 40
  origin of name 37
  predominance of women 38
  sex discrimination, and 37–8
  sovereignty, and 39–40
  traditional role of Inuit men, and 39
  traditional role of Inuit women,
      and 38–9
Amnesty International 96–100
  argument for concept of 'due diligence'
      97
  Broken Bodies, Shattered Minds: Torture
      and Ill-Treatment of Women
      96–100

challenging architecture of
    international law 99–100
  limitations of approach 98–9
  political mandate 99
  spatial politics, and 97–8
Antwerp citadel 90
Architecture
  European
    violence of 90–1
Armah, Ayi Kwei 159–171
Austerlitz 87–104
  Antwerp citadel 90
  architecture of space 89–93
  international law, and 87–104
  paradox of size 91–2
  political nature of spatial form 92
  spaces of international law, and 91
  violence of the citadel 92–3
  violence of European architecture 90–1

Bacchi, Carol
  gender mainstreaming, on 238
Beveridge, Fiona
  international economic law, on 9
Bjork, Malin
  'gender turn' in UN equality politics,
      on 241
Braidotti, Rose
  persistent constraints in gender
      mainstreaming efforts,
      on 247–8
Brundtland Report 1987, 210–211
Buchanan, Ruth
  frontiers of law, on 13
  law at the boundaries, on 102
Budlended, D
  gender and international trade law, on
      180–1
Buss, Doris
  boundaries of international law, on 14

Cairo Programme of Action 217
Catagay, Nilufer
  gender and the economy, on 177–8
CEDAW 18, 117–120
  comprehensive definition of
      discrimination against women
      117–18
  continued marginalisation of women,
      and 120

marginalised subjectives, and   118–19
promotion of women's equality   117
Protocol on the Rights of Women in
      Africa, and   261–4
removal of universal masculine
      comparator   119–120
substantive approach to women's
      equality   118
'victim' subject of discourse of
      neo-colonialism   119
Charlesworth, Hilary
    feminist question, on   55
    historical context, on   7–8
    successes of feminist activism, on   7–8
Chinkin, Christine
    historical context, on   7–8
    successes of feminist activism, on   7–8
Choice   67–86
    allure of the international, and   75–6
    'Anglo-American' terminology   70
    borrowed theory   77–82
    boundaries between international and
          domestic orientation   68–9
    cosmopolitanism, and   75
    'critical theory'   83
    critique of international legal
          scholarship   74
    domestic feminism   70–1
    dynamic of 'here' and 'there' in
          academic legal feminism   69
    evangelical discipline of international
          law   73
    feminist engagements   67
    feminist internationalist, and   77–82
        'borrowing'   78
        concept of gender, use of   81–2
        domestic innovation, and   79
        effect of 'call to theory'   79
        matters being borrowed   81
        overviews, preponderance of   80
        'turn to ethics'   79
    feminist theorising in India   85–6
    jurisdiction   77
    Kapur, Ratna on   84–5
    Koskenniemi, Marti on   73–4
    metanarrative of feminist legal
          internationalism   76
    Mohanty, Chandra Talpade on   84
    New Approaches to International Law,
          and   72–3
    Probyn, Elspeth on   68
    'seeing the big picture'   72
    themes of international law, and   71–2
    victim subject   82–6
    'what counts as feminist theory'   83
Cohen, S
    role of punitive and restorative justice
          in post-conflict societies, on
          274–280

Cosmopolitanism   75
Criminal trials
    alternative mechanisms to   291
    domestic
        limits of punitive justice, and
              286–7

Declaration on the Elimination of
      Violence Against Women
      (DEVAW)   121–2
Development
    law, and   14
Development Alternatives with Women for
      a New Era (DAWN)   211–12
Developments since   1991, 17–45
Discrimination
    intersectional forms of   114
Doha Ministerial Declaration
    Williams, Mariana on   176
Due diligence
    argument for concept of   97

Economic law
    International *see* International
          economic law
Economic liberalisation
    globalisation, and   31
Economic reconstruction
    globalisation, and   30
ECOSOC Agreed Conclusions   238
    gender mainstreaming, on   242–4
Environmental law
    International see International
          environmental law
    Rochette, Annie on   9–10
European Commission   193–4
European Women's Lobby
    World Trade Organisation, and
          199–200

Facio, Alda
    globalisation, on   32
Films see 'Unforgiven' sources of
      international law
Fletcher, L
    role of punitive and restorative justice
          in post-conflict societies, on
          276
Fourth World Conference on Women
    dual strategy promoted by   242
Fraser, Arvonne
    'gender turn' in UN equality politics,
          on   241

Gender
    meaning   248–9
Gender discrimination
    war on terror, and   35

Gender hybridities 126
Gender mainstreaming
definition 243
ECOSOC Agreed Conclusions on
242–4
Kouvo, Sari on 9
United Nations, and *see* United Nations
Women's International War Crimes
Tribunal, and 27–8
Gender relations
effect of globalisation on 29
Gendered subjects of international human
rights law 105–129
General Comment 28, 123–4
Globalisation 28–32
benefits 31
economic liberalisation, and 31
economic reconstruction, and 30
effect on gender relations 29
Facio, Alda on 32
'from above' 29–30
human rights, and 28–9
migration, and 30–1
non-liberal ideology, and 31–2
Good governance 163–8
formalisation of land relations 165–6
historical perspective 164
non-governmental organisations, and
164
oppressive role of family, and 167
racism, and 164
World Bank, and 166

Hartmann, Betsy
international environmental law, on
207
Health
right to 266–7
HIV / AIDS
statistics 219
Human rights
globalisation, and 28–9
international *see* International human
rights
law female subjects *see* Human rights
law's female subjects
Otto, Dianne on 10–11
war on terror, and 32–6
women's *see* Women's human rights
Human rights law's female subjects
105–129
British imperialism, and 110
colonised women 110
common humanity of women and men
109–110
compulsory military service, and 125
embryonic equality principle 109–110
endemic problem of gendered violence
122

gender hybridities 126
gender-specific forms of rights
violations 121–2
genealogy 108–111
improvement in conditions of
marginalisation 124
League of Nations, and 108–9
marginalisation of women 110–111
protective approach 108–9
rescripting of gender hierarchies 125
rethinking strategy of universalising
women's specificities 124–8
strategy of specialised women's human
rights instrument 116–120
three recurring female subjectivities
106
UN Charter, adoption of 111
women's equality 109
women's lost histories of grass roots
resistance 127–8
women's-rights-are-human-rights
strategy 120–4
promotion of 'mainstreaming' of
women's human rights
122–3

India
feminist theorising in 85–6
Inequality of women
failure of international law to
address 2
International courts
judicial positions in, statistics 20–1
International Covenant on Civil and
Political Rights (ICCPR) 115–16
International Covenant on Economic,
Social and Cultural Rights
(ICESCR) 115–116
International Criminal Court
sexual violence in war, and 279
International economic law 173–201
background 173–7
Beveridge, Fiona on 9
feminist legal critiques 176
feminist perspectives 173–201
gender and the economy 177–8
1995 Platform of Action 177
Catagay, Nilufer on 177–8
gender and international trade law
182–4
Budlenden, D on 180–1
globalisation, language of 178–9
gender and trade policy 178–181
dichotomous approach 179
gender budget initiatives 181
impact of macro-economic policies
180
macroeconomic policy 179
Sen, Gita on 180

social and human policy   179
need for feminist critique   198–9
potential foundations of feminist
    critique   173–201
role of law in development   173–4
World Trade Organisation   173–6
International environmental law   203–235
    Agenda   21, 216, 217, 218
    Brundtland Report   1987, 210–11
    Cairo Programme of Action   217
    challenges to mainstream development
        model   208
    Convention on Biological Diversity
        216
    Development Alternatives with Women
        for a New Era (DAWN)
        211–12
    environmental degradation   206–7
    exclusion of gender, reasons for   215
    feminist anti-capitalist critique, role of
        234–5
    feminist engagement with global
        environment protection
        205–214
    feminist perspective   203–235
    gains made by inclusion of gender
        considerations   233–5
    Gender and Development perspective
        209
    gendered international state system
        220–4
        access to decision-making   223
        addition of half-sentences   222–3
        comparison between women and
            men   223–4
        equality paradigm   222–4
        hard law, and   221–2
        masculinist institutions   224
        soft law instruments   220–1
        Stockholm Declaration, Principle
            21, 222
    Hartmann, Betsy on   207
    hegemony of Western scientific
        knowledge and technology
        224–8
        asymmetrical dichotomies   225
        potential benefits from women's
            knowledge   226
        reductionist science   227
        Rio Declaration, Principle   9, 224
        science, and   225–6
        science and technology   227–8
        Shiva, Vandara on   226–7
    HIV/AIDS statistics 219
    including gender in   214–220
    inclusion of gender concerns   213
    international agreements   203–4
    lobbying of women's organisations
        233

Malmo Declaration   219
masculinisation of environmental
    protection   220–233
Mellor, Mary on   206
'nature', privileging of   207
neo-Malthusianism   207
population growth   206–7
reading through gendered lens   204
reliance on scientific evidence   233
Stockholm Convention on Organic
    Persistent Pollutants   2001,
    215
sustainable development   228–233
    Agenda   21, 231
    economic growth, and   228–233
    international instruments, and
        229–230
    multilateral trade, and   231
    poverty eradication   230–1
    trade liberalisation, and   232
UNCED   1992, 212
UNCED preparatory process   1992,
    218
woman/nature connection   207–8
Women in Development research, and
    208–9, 210
women, role of   205–6
women as victims of environmental
    degradation   210
Women's Agenda for a Healthy and
    Peaceful Planet   2015, 212
International human rights   47–66
    criticism of public/private distinction
        53–4
    culture question   57–8
    development of feminist critiques   48
    dichotomies in public international
        law, and   53
    'exotic other female'   57–8
    feminist question   54–7
        Charlesworth, Hilary on   55
        Knop, Karen   56
        Orford, Anne   56
        structural bias instrumentalism
            55–6
    inclusion of sexual violence in
        international criminal law   50
    liberal inclusion:1985–1990   51–2
    literature   47–66
    structural bias critique:1987–1995
        52–4
    structural bias feminism, and   50–1
    third world feminist critiques   59–66
        critiques of international law
            59–60
        critiques of structural bias feminism
            60–6
        critiques of Western representations
            of women   61–2

culturally sensitive universalism 63–5
culture, class or colonialism 65–6
culture, focus on 62
liberal inclusion form 60–1
Nesiah, Vasuki on 65
Obiora, L A on 65
representation of women as victims 62
structural bias form 61
time periods 49
International law 13–15
Austerlitz, and 87–104
boundaries of 14, 88–9
challenging architecture of 99–100
critiques of 59–60
dichotomies in 53
evangelical discipline of 73
feminist analysis
disciplinary boundaries 5
human rights, and 4
literature on 4
piecemeal nature of 5
publications and research during 1990s 1–2
responses to 3
feminist approaches to
war on terror, and 34–5
feminist campaigns, and 3–4
functioning as conservative force 133
implication of spatial construction 87–8
Koskenniemi, Martti on 44
law at the boundaries 101–3
Buchanan, Ruth on 102
feminist theory 101–2
Sylvester, Christine on 102–3
Walker, Rob on 101
public and private spheres 94–100
Amnesty International 96–100
construction of state as analytically equivalent to the individual 95–6
normative dimension to gendered division 94–5
problems inherent in feminist analyses 95
socio-spatial critique 96
sexual violence in war, and *see* Sexual violence in war
spaces of 91
spatial location 87–8
'*Unforgiven*' sources of *see* Unforgiven sources of international law
International trade law 182–194
gender, and 182–194
gender-neutrality, and 182
quantitative restrictions to trade 182–3

construction justifiable, whether 183
EU law 184
implications of absence of gender dimension 186
judicial balancing of claims 186
'necessity' test 183
service providers, and 183
Shrimp-Turtle dispute 185
trade liberalisation, and 184–5
Uruguay Round Agreements 182
International War Crimes Tribunal for the Former Yugoslavia 274, 279
Inuits *see* Akitsiraq Law School

Johnson, Rebecca
frontiers of law, on 13
Judicial positions in international courts and tribunals
statistics 20–1

Kapur, Ratna
choice, on 84–5
Knop, Karen 56
Koskenniemi, Martti
choice, on 73–4
international law, on 44
Kouvo, Sari
gender mainstreaming, on 9

Land relations
formalisation of 165–6
Law and development 168–171
African land reform, and 170
market-oriented development model 169
neo-liberal triumphalism, and 170
revival of 169–170
role of law 168–9
Law, theory and choice, 67–86 *see* also Choice
Lazarus, N
The Beautyful Ones Are Not Yet Born, on 160–1

Manji, Ambreena
law and development, on 14
Marginalised female representations 111–16
persistence in new era of universality 111–16
Mellor, Mary
international environmental law, on 206
Migration
globalisation, and 30–1
Military conscription
gender injury, as 125–6

Minow, Martha
  role of punitive and restorative justice
      in post-conflict
      societies, on   276
Modernism   15–16
Mohanty, Chandra Talpade
  choice, on   84
Murphy, Therese
  feminism, on   11–12
Murray, Rachel
  African feminism, on   12–13

Necessity test   183
Neo-colonialism
  'victim' subject of discourse of   119
Neo-Malthusianism   207
NEPAD   258
Nesiah, Vasuki
  third world feminist critiques, on   65
Nikolic-Ristanovic, Vesna
  sexual violence, on   8
Non-governmental organisations
  good governance, and   164

Obiora, L A
  third world feminist critiques, on   65
Orford, Anne   56
  persistent constraints in gender
      mainstreaming efforts, on
      252
Organisation of African Unity
  NEPAD   258
  transformation into African Union
      257–8
  women's rights, and   257
Organization of African Unity   253,
      256–8
Otto, Dianne
  human rights, on   10–11

Polygamy
  Protocol on the Rights of Women in
      Africa, and   261–4
Poverty
  eradication of   230–1
Probyn, Elspeth
  choice, on   68
Protocol on the Rights of Women in Africa
      261–4
  ACHPR, and   264–5
  adding to existing international
      standards   266
  adoption   262
  'African' outcome   271
  age of majority   267
  aims   263
  CEDAW, and   264–6, 268
  enforcement, problems of   269–271

health, right to   266–7
  inconsistencies   269
  influences   264–272
  'key' documents, and   264
  lack of consistency in choosing
      provisions from
      documents   265
  no automatic adoption of existing
      African documents   268
  origin   261–2
  polygamy   267
  poor drafting   269

Racism
  good governance, and   164
Rape *see* Sexual violence
Reanda, Laura
  'gender turn' in UN equality politics,
      on   241
Representing women   19–21
  judicial positions in international
      courts and tribunals   20–1
Restorative justice
  sexual violence in war, and see Sexual
      violence in war
Rochette, Annie
  environmental law, on   9–10

Saul, John
  neo-liberal 'reforms', and   171
Science
  international environmental law, and
      see International
      environmental law
Sen, Gita
  gender and trade policy, on   180
September 11th
  political effect   19
Service providers
  quantitative restrictions to trade, and
      183
Sex discrimination   37–8
Sexual violence see also Sexual violence in
      war
  alternative mechanisms to criminal
      trials   291
  inclusion in international criminal law
      50
  limits of punitive justice   284–290
      attitude to victims   285
      collective memory, and   289
      discouragement of witnesses
          284–5
      domestic criminal trials, and
          286–7
      dominance of punitive paradigm
          290
      fragmentation of legal truth   288

lack of appropriate
    acknowledgement of
    suffering 289
low number of trials 284
paradoxical position of complainant
    287
plea-bargaining 288–9
sexual and reproductive identities of
    women 287–8
Wald, Patricia on 285
witnesses, position of 284–6
narratives contributing to establish-
    ment of historical truth 292
Nikolic-Ristanovic, Vesna on 8
potential and limits of punitive justice
    280–290
    ICC Statute 282
    key decisions by ICTY 281–2
    prosecution of perpetrators 281–2
    victim protection 282–4
    witness protection 282–4
South African Truth and Reconciliation
    Commission 291–2
war, in *see* Sexual violence in war
Sexual violence in war 273–293
    international law, and 273–293
    restorative justice, and 273–293
    role of punitive and restorative justice
        in post-conflict
societies 274–280
    abolitionists, and 275
    aim of war crimes trial, and 278
    alternative models 280
    Cohen, S on 278
    failure of legal responses to address
        past atrocities 279
    Fletcher, L on 276
    fragmented nature of trial, and
        277
    gross human rights violations
        277
    human rights lawyers, and 275
    individual accountability, emphasis
        on 274–5
    International Criminal Court 279
    International War Crimes Tribunal
        for the Former Yugoslavia
        274, 279
    Minow, Martha on 277–8
    vengeance, and 276
    Weinstein, H on 276
    war rape 273–4
    women as victims 273
Shiva, Vandara
    international environmental law, on
        226–7
Soft law
    international environmental law, and
        220–1

South African Truth and Reconciliation
    Commission 291–2
Sovereignty 39–40
    'Unforgiven' sources of international
        law, and 132
Spatial form
    political nature of 92
Structural bias feminism 50–1
    critiques of 60–6
Sustainable development *see* International
    environmental law
Sylvester, Christine
    law at the boundaries, on 102–3

Terrorists *see* War on terror
The Beautyful Ones Are Not Yet Born
    159–171
    birth and rebirth 162–3
    imagery 161
    Lazarus, N on 160–1
    regenerative vision 168
Tribunals
    judicial positions in, statistics 20–1

UN Commission on the Status of Women
    (CSW) 106–7, 111–116
    equal rights of men and women 113
    goal 112
    intersectional forms of discrimination,
        and 114
    masculine descriptors 112–13
UN Convention on the Elimination of All
    Forms of Discrimination Against
    Women *see* CEDAW
Unforgiven sources of international law
    131–158
    'apocryphal jurisprudence' 132,
        133–4
    effect of films 156–7
    films as jurisprudential texts 134
    frontier myth, and 134–5
    gendered and racialised narratives
        157–8
    humanitarian intervention 155
    international law functioning as
        conservative force 133
    law and violence on the frontier
        140–2
    spatialisation 140–1
    legal traditions as part of 'nomos' 131
    locating women in the Western
        142–5
    marriage, and 144–5
    rejection of feminine 143–4
    maintenance of boundaries, and 133
    Orford, Anne, and 156
    origin myths 135–7
    paradox of law's self-founding 136–7

reading the international   154–7
reading nation, violence and gender
          through Unforgiven   145–154
  authorising heroic intervention
          149–152
  flawed call for justice   148–9
  injury   146–8
  outlaw hero, role of   153–4
  portrayal of wives   149–152
  showdown   152–4
  sovereignty, and   132
  stories of legal origins   135–7
  Unforgiven   134–5
  Western films as founding myth
          137–140
    American cultural frame of
            reference, and   139–140
    operation of genre   137–8
    series of 'classic' oppositions
            138–9
United Nations   237–252
  ECOSOC Agreed Conclusions on gen-
          der mainstreaming   238,
          242–4
    definition of gender mainstreaming
            243
    six principles   243
  gender mainstreaming, and   237–252
    Bacchi, Carol on   238
    'gender turn' in UN equality politics
            239–242
      Bjork, Malin on   241
      dual strategy promoted by Fourth
              World Conference on
              Women   242
      Fraser, Arvonne on   241
      promotion of equality, and   240–1
      Reanda, Laura on   241
      UN Charter preamble   239–240
    introducing gender mainstreaming
            strategy   242–4
  persistent constraints in gender main-
          streaming efforts   246–251
    aim of gender mainstreaming
            strategies   249–250
    analytical constraints   246–9
    Braidotti, Rose on   247–8
    conceptual constraints   246–9
    'fuzzy' strategy   250
    gender, meaning   248–9
    Office of the Special Advisor   250
    Orford, Anne on   252
    social constructivist interpretation,
            and   247
    UNTEAT   251
  woman-centred institutions   244–6
    development of definitions and
            guidelines   245
    equality initiatives   245
    Office of the Special Adviser
            245–6
    targeted interventions   244
Universal Declaration of Human Rights
        111–116
  formal non-discrimination, and
          113–14
  privileging of European experience,
          and   114–15
  translation into legally binding
          instruments   115
Unlawful combatants   34
Uruguay Round Agreements   182

Victimhood
  women's human rights, and   28
Violence
  Sexual see Sexual violence
  women, against
    war on terror, and   35

Wald, Patricia
  limits of punitive justice, on   285
Walker, Rob
  law at the boundaries, on   101
War
  sexual violence in see Sexual violence in
          war
War on Terror   32–6
  effect   32–6
  feminist approaches to international
          law, and   34–5
  gender discrimination, and   35
  human rights, and   32–6
  perspectives of women, and   35–6
  ramifications for women, international
          law and gender   33
  suspected terrorists   34
  unlawful combatants   34
  violence against women, and   35
Weinstein, H
  role of punitive and restorative justice in
          post-conflict societies, on   276
Williams, Mariana
  Doha Ministerial Declaration, on   176
Witnesses
  discouragement of
          sexual violence, and   284–5
  protection   282–4
Women
  inequality of see Inequality of women
Women's Agenda for a Healthy and
        Peaceful Planet   2015, 212
Women's human rights   21–6
  advances during   1990s 21–2
  distinction between liberal and
          non-liberal states   24–5
  Eastern Europe   24

guarantee of 25–6
Ignatieff, Michael 24
liberal model 25
rhetorical progress 23
victimhood, and 28
Women's International Tribunal on
     Japanese Military Sexual Slavery
     44–5
Women's International War Crime
     Tribunal 26–8
  basis of 26–2
  comfort women 27
  gender mainstreaming 27–8
  origin 26
World Bank 194–8
  Advancing Gender Equality: World
       Bank Action since Beijing 196
  engendering normative framework
       196–8
     Comprehensive Development
          Framework 197
     groupings of gender critics
          197–18
  gender, and 194–8
  gender-based claims in processes of
       195–6
  good governance, and 166
  image of 195–6
  institutional 'take' on gender issues
       194
  Women's Eyes on the World Bank'
       195–6

World Trade Organisation
  engendering 191–4
     European Commission, and
          193–4
     identifying issues 191–4
     obstacles to progress 193
     Platform for Action 1995, 191–2
     potential role 192–3
  European Women's Lobby, and
       199–200
  gender agenda for 199–201
  gender and WTO's normative
       framework 189–191
     failure to incorporate gender
          perspective 190–1
     WEDO, and 189–190
  gender-based claims in processes
       187–9
     'canons' of market liberalisation,
          and 187
     legitimacy of mainstreaming norm
          187–8
     'national' exceptions to global rules,
          and 188
     under-representation of women in
          international economic and
          financial institutions 188–9
  international economic law, and
       173–6
Wright, Shelley
  historical context, on 7–8
  successes of feminist activities, on 7–8